D1090421

THE FIRST FIRANGIS

BOOKS BY JONATHAN GIL HARRIS

Foreign Bodies and the Body Politic: Discourses of Social Pathology in Early Modern England

Sick Economies: Drama, Mercantilism and Disease in Shakespeare's England

Untimely Matter in the Time of Shakespeare

Shakespeare & Literary Theory

Marvellous Repossessions: The Tempest, Globalization and the Waking Dream of Paradise

BOOKS EDITED BY JONATHAN GIL HARRIS

Staged Properties in Early Modern English Drama (with Natasha Korda)

The Shoemaker's Holiday by Thomas Dekkar

Indography: Writing the 'Indian' in Early Modern Literature and Culture

THE FIRST FIRANGIS

Remarkable Stories of Heroes, Healers, Charlatans, Courtesans
& other Foreigners who Became Indian

JONATHAN GIL HARRIS

ALEPH

Milind Kulshrestha
Nov '16

ALEPH BOOK COMPANY
An independent publishing firm
promoted by *Rupa Publications India*

Published in India in 2015 by
Aleph Book Company
7/16 Ansari Road, Daryaganj
New Delhi 110 002

Copyright © Jonathan Gil Harris 2015

All rights reserved.

While every effort has been made to trace copyright
holders and obtain permission, this has not been possible
in all cases; any omissions brought to our attention will
be remedied in future editions.

No part of this publication may be reproduced,
transmitted, or stored in a retrieval system, in any form
or by any means, without permission in writing from
Aleph Book Company.

ISBN: 978-93-82277-63-7

5 7 9 10 8 6 4

Printed and bound in India by
Parksons Graphics Pvt. Ltd. Mumbai

This book is sold subject to the condition that it shall
not, by way of trade or otherwise, be lent, resold, hired
out, or otherwise circulated without the publisher's prior
consent in any form of binding or cover other than
that in which it is published.

To Nikhil Armaan and Rohan Jannek,
who are also becoming Indian.

There is as much difference between us and ourselves as there is between us and others.

– Michel de Montaigne, *The Essays*

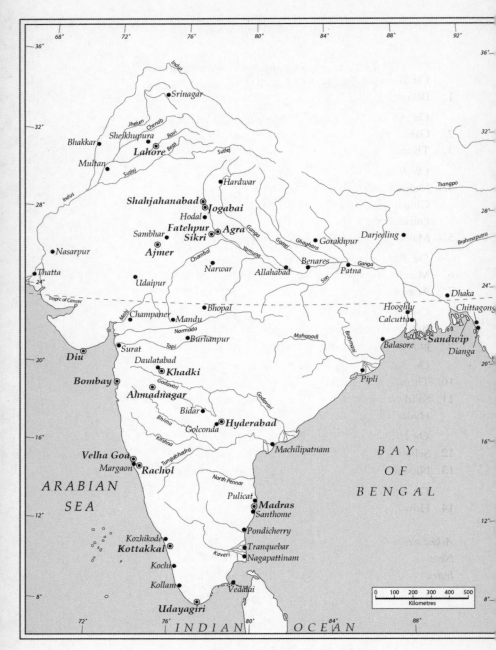

Indian subcontinent circa 1600-1700

CONTENTS

ON BECOMING ANOTHER

My body is not quite my body.

I like to think of it as mine. My dream of possession is really a dream of self-possession: our bodies, ourselves, as the old adage goes. But the fact is my body is never fully mine. It is constantly changing in ways I can't control. Not only does it age over time; it is also forever being modified by what it comes in contact with. Because I am writing this in a hot and humid room at the height of the Delhi summer, I am sweating and losing fluids. The namak nimbu paani I am drinking cools me and replenishes my depleted body salts; the light khadi cotton of my kurta lets in air that also keeps me from overheating. But in order to type these English and Hindi words, I have to rest my forearms on the surface of my hot laptop—baked both by the ambient air and Delhi's electrical power surges—as a result of which my sweaty wrists are ringed by an increasingly angry heat rash. Are these 'my' wrists anymore? Or are they the property of other entities: the hot laptop, the humid summer air, the cool fabrics of Indian clothes, the multilingual stew of north India?

My body is clearly not an unchanging unit. It isn't even a unit. That word suggests something self-contained and neatly divided from what is outside it. My body is, rather, an extension of the larger environment that I work in, against and with. As my environment changes, so does my body. And when my environment changes in extreme ways—geographically, climatically, gastronomically, culturally, linguistically, economically—my body's changes are most obvious to me. These changes never amount to full makeovers: wherever I go, my body carries with it the imprint of its past environments. But it is always becoming different in its new ones. It is always becoming another.

And here in India, I am becoming Indian. As have so many other migrants to the subcontinent before me. Our migrant bodies were not quite ours long before there was an independent or even a British India.

1 | BECOMING INDIAN; OR, THE TWO DAKAITS OF HODAL

28 June 1656. Two dakaits (Hindi for 'bandits') approach a teenaged European boy in the scorching summer heat of Haryana. The bandits have spied him at the Hodal Sarai, some 90 kilometres short of Delhi on the imperial highway from Agra. The boy wears a glum expression; he keeps casting anxious glances at his luggage, which is far bulkier than we might expect of someone travelling alone. A runaway from Venice, he has been in India for just a few months. His name is Niccolò Manucci. And he is in something of a pickle.

Manucci is the servant of an Englishman, Lord Bellomont, who had journeyed to India in the hope of meeting the Mughal emperor Shah Jahan. But three days into their journey from Agra to Delhi, without warning, Bellomont dropped dead. In the eight days since, young Manucci has had to fend for himself in unfamiliar and dangerous terrain. His wits have been expended on protecting his late master's belongings, which he cannot carry alone. In sum, Manucci is stranded at the sarai, unable to advance to Delhi or return to Agra.

The two dakaits smell Manucci's vulnerability. Dressed in Mughal clothes, they introduce themselves to him as captains in the army of Shah Jahan; one of them explains that they have instructions from the emperor to confiscate the property of the Englishman, which has now lapsed to the crown. Manucci asks to see official documentation authorizing the confiscation. None is forthcoming. He accuses the men of using Shah Jahan's name as a ruse with which to steal other people's property. At this, the dakaits start laughing like a pair of guffawing Bollywood villains. Predictably, they proceed to rob Manucci of all his late master's effects.

But here's the rub: the two Indian dakaits weren't exactly Indian. Writing about the incident fifty years later, Manucci explains that this Mughal-era Gabbar Singh and Sambha were, in fact, two Englishmen named Thomas Roch and Raben Simitt. Forget Bollywood villains: the bandits, it seems, were really seventeenth-century predecessors of Michael Caine's and Steve Martin's con-artist characters in *Dirty Rotten Scoundrels*—low-life expatriates in a foreign country, preying on unsuspecting travellers through their skills of deception. Manucci damns the pair as 'two English impostors'. But the imposture that exercises him is not their Indian disguise. Indeed, their dress doesn't strike him as being in any way abnormal, let alone deceitful. Manucci shrugs off what we might regard as the bandits' most unusual feature, because Roch and Simitt had been truthful about one thing: they were indeed servants of Shah Jahan, part of a ragtag group of foreigners whom the emperor retained as mercenaries and who were obliged to wear Mughal clothes. What irks him, rather, was their fraudulence in claiming to act with the authority of the emperor, a major misdemeanour—in Mughal eyes as much as Manucci's. Upon reaching Shah Jahan's court in Delhi, Manucci lodged an official complaint against the emperor's wayward employees, who were located and taken into custody.

Roch and Simitt's story has haunted me for some time now. It is altogether different from the standard narrative about the British presence in India—a narrative of angrezi cultural, linguistic and racial supremacy, and of Indian oppression. Instead, Manucci presents us with the unexpected spectacle of two, presumably poor, Englishmen who were servants, if rather badly behaved ones, of the Great Mughal. I am fascinated as much by what Manucci's story leaves out as by what it includes. How had Roch and Simitt come to be in Hindustan? What drove them to seek service with Shah Jahan? If they wore desi clothes, what other aspects of Mughal Hindustani culture had they assumed? Did they eat English food or Mughlai khana? When speaking with the Italian Manucci, did they resort to English, another European tongue, the local Hindavi dialect of the north, or Persian (the language of the Mughal court, in which Manucci was already partly fluent after spending some years in Iran)? And what happened after their punishment—did they remain in India and, if so, did they have Indian partners and even children? In short, to what extent did they become Indian?

Both Manucci and the historical records are silent on all these questions. Nothing Roch and Simitt may have written—letters, financial accounts, travel narratives, last wills and testaments—survives. For all we know, neither man was even literate. And there is nothing about them in either Indian or English seventeenth-century records, save for one passing mention of Thomas Roch's name in a 1655 East India Company court book record that lists him as an employee.

Yet Manucci's own life as documented in his *Storia Do Mogor*, the multilingual account of Mughal history that he wrote decades after the incident at the Hodal Sarai, holds up a mirror to what the two dakaits may have experienced in Hindustan. For Manucci was himself a foreigner from a very poor background who, after journeying to Delhi, spent the rest of his life—some sixty-four years—wearing Indian clothes, serving Indian masters, fighting in Indian armies, learning Indian languages, performing Indian rituals, acquiring Indian knowledge, eating Indian food, making Indian friends and enemies, and marrying an Indian-born woman. He also practiced Indian medicine, becoming a Tamil-style siddha vaidya in Parangi Malai (or 'Foreigner Mountain') near Madras. And the more I scoured the archives, the more I came to realize that Roch, Simitt and Manucci were just three of many people from diverse Christian lands—Portugal, England, Russia, Malacca, Holland, Ethiopia, France, Armenia, Italy—who migrated to India in the sixteenth and seventeenth centuries and, to lesser and greater extents, became Indian.

◆

Readers of William Dalrymple's magnificent *White Mughals* might regard Roch, Simitt and Manucci as instances of a familiar phenomenon. Dalrymple writes of British men in India who, during the late eighteenth and early nineteenth centuries, assumed local dress and customs, married Indian women and had mixed-race offspring. But there is a significant difference between the stories of Roch and Simitt and the lives of these later British men. As Dalrymple's title makes clear, *White Mughals* deals with powerful people. Many came from privileged backgrounds; like the Mughals they emulated, they easily re-assumed positions of privilege once in India—the East India Company Resident of Hyderabad, for instance, or high offices in the British military. Their embrace of Indian culture was implicated in the machinery of nineteenth-century British colonialism. For all its seeming subversiveness, their becoming Indian did little to challenge British power in the subcontinent.

By contrast, a large number of the foreign migrants to India in the centuries before the British white Mughals came not to conquer and command, but with much humbler ambitions: to escape poverty and persecution. Some were economic refugees; some were criminals; some were religious dissidents; some were even what we might call sexual dissidents. Many others had no choice at all in the matter of their migration, having arrived in India as slaves, indentured servants, or possessions of their lords, fathers or husbands. Nearly all of them served an Indian master, and in a way that necessitated submitting to local languages and customs. To become Indian in such circumstances entailed an altogether different calculus of power from that which shaped the lives of the white Mughals.

This difference is largely due to the enormous shift in the global balance of economic power that took place between the sixteenth and the eighteenth centuries. Dalrymple's white Mughals reached India via a sea route that had only recently become the blueway of European global domination. Vasco da Gama's 1498 'discovery' of the passage to India via the Cape of Good Hope offered European travellers to India an alternative to the more dangerous overland Silk Route through Turkey, Persia and Afghanistan. Over the next two centuries, this sea route became crucial to European strength in India. With heavily armed ships, European trading companies and their state sponsors—first Portuguese, then English, French, Dutch and Danish—could now sail directly to the subcontinent. By the eighteenth century, British migrants to India arriving via the sea route were absorbed into a well-established colonial system designed to empower them. At the time of the white Mughals, the British Raj was still more than half a century away: it would be formally instituted only in 1858, when the East India Company-administered territories were handed over to the Crown. Yet, in the century following the Battle of Plassey and the nawab of Bengal's surrender of his territories in 1757, the Company was to construct a formidable commercial and military machine throughout South Asia, morphing from a mere joint-stock trading company into a global imperial power.

This machine did not yet exist in the sixteenth and seventeenth centuries. Or rather, its incipient forms were eclipsed by other networks of globalization in which European nations were not yet at the centre. Global economic power at this point was still largely concentrated in Asian empires—Ottoman Turkey, Safavid Persia, Mughal Hindustan, Ming and then Qing China—who controlled the diverse trade networks linking them to the Spice Islands, Africa, Arabia and Europe. What was later to become the major artery sustaining European colonial supremacy in the subcontinent, the sea route via the Cape of Good Hope, dispatched sixteenth- and seventeenth-century migrants to a rather different India from that in which the white Mughals would live two centuries later. It was an India in which the chief powers were still Asian rather than European. Following Babur's invasion in 1526, and Akbar's radical expansion of the empire's territories after 1556, Mughal Hindustan came to cover much of what is now northern India: by the 1650s, it spanned the subcontinent from Gujarat to east Bengal, as well as most of what is now Pakistan and even parts of Afghanistan. The five Bahmani Deccan sultanates—Ahmadnagar, Berar, Bidar, Bijapur and Golconda—extended across the middle band of the subcontinent; immensely powerful in the sixteenth century, they underwent a steady decline at the hands of the Mughals in the 1600s, culminating in Aurangzeb's conquest of Golconda and Bijapur in 1687. And the Hindu-ruled kingdom of Vijayanagar, abutted by the Malabar kingdoms of Calicut, Cannanore and Quilon, was the principal power in the south until a military defeat by the Deccan sultanates in 1565 prompted its eventual demise in 1646.

The Portuguese militarized the East African coast and the Arabian Sea in the sixteenth century, wresting control of the old maritime trade routes from the Arabs, the Persians, and other local merchants. This allowed them to gain footholds in Goa and parts of the Malabar Coast, including Cochin; they also acquired Daman and Diu from the Gujarat sultan, as well as Hooghly in Bengal and the island of Bombay, though they ceded the latter to the British in 1668. But outside Goa and the tiny possessions of the Portuguese Estado da Índia, the subcontinent remained under the control of powerful Muslim and Hindu rulers. The glamour of such power is partly why Goa was not the final Indian destination for many Europeans who migrated there. Like Roch and Simitt, a number of less well-off Portuguese who made landfall in Goa proceeded to find reasonably remunerated positions as employees in the service of Indian masters elsewhere in the subcontinent.

To give just two examples: Sancho Pires, who came to Goa in the 1530s, fled to the sultanate of Ahmadnagar following a charge of murder. There he converted, though probably not with full conviction, to Islam. Pires proceeded to find service in the Ahmadnagar army, first as a bombardier and later as captain of the cavalry; he became a special favourite of Burhan Nizam Shah, the sultan, and eventually came to be known as Firangi Khan. Pires was not a lone figure. The Ahmadnagar Sultanate army, like those of the other Deccan sultanates and the Mughal Empire, welcomed hundreds of Portuguese recruits, many of whom—like Pires—became renegade converts to Islam. These soldiers, assigned in the Deccan armies to divisions called the firangiyan, were reputed for their prowess as artillerymen. But there were other non-military opportunities available to European migrants who chose to leave Goa. In the 1590s, Fernão Rodrigues Caldeira—like Pires a so-called New Christian, which is to say a member of a Portuguese Jewish family forced to convert to Christianity—quit Goa to serve as an advisor to Muhammad Quli Qutb Shah, the sultan of Golconda. Pires and Caldeira were just two of a number of migrants who probably came to Goa less as colonists than as covert religious refugees, escaping not only the Inquisition in the Iberian Peninsula but also persecution in northern Protestant countries. Habituated to underground lives in the countries they had escaped, and therefore comfortable at a safe distance from European religious and political authority, these refugees sometimes forged stronger ties with local peoples, languages and customs than they did with other Portuguese.

Early English migrants had similar experiences. In the seventeenth century, the fledgling English East India Company—formed in 1600—sent many men (and a handful of women) to the subcontinent via the same sea route as the Portuguese. Upon arrival, these migrants found themselves in far more precarious positions than did the white Mughals two centuries later. The first English factory at Surat, Gujarat—where Manucci disembarked with his master in January of 1656—was hardly an economic powerhouse. The Company employees, many of them poor, operated in miserable conditions. Drunkenness and disease prevailed. The temptation to move elsewhere, to richer and healthier zones outside the limited reach of Company authority, was immense. The two dakaits Manucci encountered en route to Agra had succumbed to this temptation. So had Joshua Blackwell, a Company official who converted to Islam and served in Shah Jahan's army in 1649, and twenty-three Company employees who deserted Surat en masse in 1654. Several others who arrived from England via the sea route did not linger in Surat or the Company factories, but moved to Mughal-ruled areas where they assumed local clothes, customs, tongues, and even faiths. But these men did not become white Mughals in Dalrymple's sense, as there wasn't yet a colonial English political or administrative system that could grant them high offices. Instead, their trajectories were altogether humbler.

Take the example of Gilbert Harrison. Harrison worked for some years at the tiny East India Company factory in Thatta, a river port city in what is now the Pakistani province of Sindh. The factory had been set up in 1635 as a meagrely staffed outpost of the Company's calico trade; only three other Englishmen were stationed there. On 16 August 1647, Harrison died of a fever. A surviving letter concerning his burial arrangements suggests that, prior to his death, he had become something rather different from what we might expect of a Company employee. The letter notes that he had requested a colleague to give his 'Hindustani clothes' and his 'dagger' to his Indian servant; he had also asked to be interred in the 'chief burial place' of Nasarpur, as the

'Nasarpur chief men' wanted him 'to lie there sepulized' (i.e. buried). These stray remarks hint that Harrison had become at least partly Indian. He had taken to wearing Indian clothes, an embrace of local culture not always followed by Englishmen in seventeenth-century India: Sir Thomas Roe, the English ambassador to the court of Jahangir from 1615-19, had insisted that his retinue remain clothed in English taffeta—a taxing assignment in the 45-degree heat of the north Indian summer. Harrison had also become intimate enough with his servant to make him the sole heir of his decidedly humble estate. Was theirs a simple domestic arrangement, or were they closer? And was this relationship one reason for his transformation?

Harrison's burial site suggests he had made other unconventional choices. First, he had relocated from Thatta to the small town of Nasarpur, more than 100 kilometres to the north. We don't know if the move was prompted by East India Company business; but the English didn't have a factory in Nasarpur. It was instead the base of the Rizvi Sayyids, an influential Sufi family. Harrison was obviously known to the family; that the town's 'chief men'—including, one assumes, members of the Rizvi Sayyids—wanted him 'sepulized' or buried in its chief burial ground indicates that he was no longer a Christian, at least not outwardly: a Christian could not find a resting place in what was almost certainly a Muslim cemetery. Had Harrison converted to Islam? We cannot recover all the details of Gilbert Harrison's last years. But it does seem as if his journey from Thatta to Nasarpur took him much further afield than just the geographical distance between the towns.

◆

This book asks: what did it mean to become Indian before the time of the white Mughals? I pose this question partly to trouble modern ideas of racial identity, including the 'white' of 'white Mughals'. Which isn't to say that pre-colonial India wasn't colour conscious. Long before Fair & Lovely became the skin product of choice among modern Indians, distinctions of class and caste were enmeshed in hierarchies of skin colour that, as in the West, favoured fairness over darkness. Obviously people have different complexions. But these skin-deep differences have been transmuted into core racial identities in a variety of pernicious ways. Even when we reject the canard of race, we still continue unselfconsciously to tether a person's identity to the colour of his or her skin. The false biologism of white racial supremacy has been discredited, but most westerners are quite happy to abide by what seems to be a value-neutral distinction between 'white people' and 'people of colour'. Consequently, we assume that any Englishman who becomes a 'Mughal' must be still, at his core, 'white', as if this is the one fundamental truth of his body that trumps its other attributes, including the unexpected changes it may have undergone in India.

Of course there are limits to bodily transformation: none of us can grow a third leg, or a second heart. But our obsession with epidermal colour as the basis of an irreducible identity, whether white or brown or black, can overlook how much our bodies are constantly changing as our environments—cultural as much as climatic—change. Moving from a cold to a hot place changes our bodies' diurnal rhythms, leading many of us to nap during the hottest afternoon hours and stay up late to savour the cooler hours of the night. Sweating more means we crave saltier food to replenish electrolytes lost through dehydration. Eating the cuisine of a different country changes not just our taste buds but also how our bodies smell. Absorbing a new terrain's distinctive germs alters our bodily functions and immune systems. Treating our bodies for local diseases means ingesting new plants, chemicals, or minerals that transform our chemical as well as mental composition. Speaking a new language necessitates using our tongues, lips, facial muscles and even hands in new ways. Performing the gestures or wearing the clothes appropriate to a foreign religious or cultural community demands that we use our bodies differently. Moving repeatedly through a new landscape or cityscape necessitates transforming our skills, training our bodies to acquire new proficiencies within the physical limitations imposed by the space.

Before the age of British rule, bodily transformation was rarely about adapting to a new environment so that it may be more effectively dominated or ruled. In the sixteenth and seventeenth centuries, the demand to transform one's body was both more pressing and more mundane: it was often a matter of survival. Travel to India in pre-colonial times meant adjusting to dangerous new environments where one's life was potentially at risk from extreme climates, deadly diseases, and human as well as animal predators. The challenge of survival necessitated comprehensive work on the body. Just as an actor or an athlete has to train her muscle memory to perform new tasks, so did the new migrants have to re-train and transform their bodies to cope with the demands of their new locations. It's no accident that the word 'travel' derives from the French travail, meaning work. We may associate travel now with rest and recreation, but in pre-colonial times, it was always work—work *on* the body as much as *with* the body.

Such work was necessary. Yet it was also potentially scary. And migrants alarmed by the changes their bodies experienced in India often found themselves longing for a core identity—an irreducible part of the self—immune to transformation. For many Christians, as we will see, this core identity was their soul. But for some pre-colonial European migrants to India, their inner essence was racial as much as it was religious. In this context, we might see the idea of a stable 'white' identity less as a fundamental truth of the body than as a consoling fantasy—what psychologists would call a reaction formation—that seeks to repudiate the traumatic experience of bodily transformation.

It is perhaps no coincidence that the first global system of racial classification was proposed by a European who lived in, and was transformed by, India. François Bernier was a French doctor who journeyed to Delhi in the 1660s and served a Mughal lord, Danishmand Khan, from whom he learned about Sufism even as he taught him about the ideas of Descartes and Gassendi. After his period of service with Danishmand Khan, Bernier subsequently became personal physician to the Mughal emperor Aurangzeb. In 1684, following his return to France, he published a treatise called *Nouvelle division de la terre par les différentes espèces ou races qui l'habitent* ('New division of the world through the different species or races which inhabit it'), in which he theorized the fundamental differences between the bodies of Europeans, Asians and Africans. Yet Bernier's theory of race was arguably occasioned by a frightening experience of bodily transformation in India: falling sick.

In 1664, Bernier travelled with the Mughal court to Kashmir. The journey was undertaken for medical reasons: Aurangzeb had suffered from a spell of illness and was convinced that relocation to the cooler climate of Kashmir would benefit his health 'by change of air' as well as help him 'avoid the approaching summer heat, from which a relapse might be apprehended'. Although the causes of Aurangzeb's illness are unclear, Bernier welcomed the change, not least to avoid sickness himself. In his view, Delhi's environment was not conducive to his health. 'I am…happy', he wrote in his diary, 'at the idea of not being any longer exposed to the danger of eating the bazaar bread of Delhi, which is often badly baked and full of sand and dust'. If eating the local food exposed him to the threat of Delhi Belly, drinking its water was an even more sickening prospect. He longed to taste 'better water than that of

JONATHAN GIL HARRIS

the capital, the impurities of which exceed my power of description; as it is accessible to all persons and animals, and the receptacle of every kind of filth'. Although he does not admit to any personal experience of illness, he remarks of Delhi's drinking water that 'fevers most difficult to cure are engendered by it, and worms are bred in the legs which produce violent inflammation, attended with much danger'.

The royal procession to Kashmir presented considerable challenges. According to Bernier, the entire population of Delhi—by his reckoning, 200,000 humans and 100,000 animals—accompanied Aurangzeb to ensure his protection as well as the victualling of his court and army. Even more intimidatingly, the huge travelling party also had to journey through the torrid heat of northern Punjab. Bernier was initially sanguine about undertaking the trip: as he boasts in his diary, he had previously survived the desert heat of Arabia. But he quickly lost confidence, for the heat of Punjab was fiercer than anything he had previously experienced. Bernier declared in his diary that 'I have been reduced by the intenseness of the heat to the last extremity; scarcely believing when I rose in the morning that I should outlive the day.' He proceeded to fall terribly sick. 'The whole of my face, my feet, and my hands are flayed', he complained; 'My body too is entirely covered with small red blisters, which prick like needles.' His awful rash was nothing compared to what one of the Indian soldiers in his contingent had to suffer. 'Yesterday', he wrote at the height of his sickness, 'one of our poor troopers, who was without a tent, was found dead…I feel as if I should myself expire before night'.

Despite the Indian trooper's and Bernier's common experience of heat exhaustion, the Frenchman chose to understand his own sickness as a sign of his irreducible bodily difference from Indians. In the process, he resorted to one of the first specifically racial usages of the term 'European'. He asked in his diary: 'What can induce a European to expose himself to such terrible heat, and to these harassing and perilous marches?' Here 'European' suggests a distinctive bodily type that can retain its integrity only within certain climates. Bernier's conviction that his illness had a racial cause was strengthened when he reached the cooler air of the Kashmir valley. Suddenly he found himself transported, in fantasy, back to Europe:

> …we breathed a pure, mild, and refreshing air. What surprised me still more was to find myself, as it were, transferred from the

Indies to Europe; the mountains we were traversing being covered with every one of our plants and shrubs, save the hyssop, thyme, marjoram, and rosemary. I almost imagined myself in the mountains of Auvergne, in a forest of fir, oak, elm, and plane trees, and could not avoid feeling strongly the contrast between this scene and the burning fields of Hindustan.

The French doctor's miraculous recovery in Kashmir led him to conclude that there are certain climates to which the European race is biologically predisposed—this despite the fact that Aurangzeb partook of exactly the same cure as he.

Bernier's account of his time in India, however, also reveals another story about bodies, one that undermines his insistence on a unique European racial identity. Often he observes Indians in order to learn from them how to manage the challenges of a local climate that negatively affects *all* bodies. Recoiling from the filth of Delhi's worm-infested river water, he notes how members of Aurangzeb's court imbibe healthy drinking water from the holy Ganges river. For Bernier, it is not the Ganges's sacredness but rather the ingenious local technologies of water purification that make it so healthy. The Indians, he notes, store water from the Ganges in tin flagons that are covered with moist cloths and fanned by servants. As Bernier explains, 'the moisture of the cloth, the agitation of the air, or exposure to the wind, is absolutely necessary to keep the water fresh, as if this moisture…arrested the little bodies, or fiery particles, existing in the air at the same time that it affords a passage to the nitrous or other particles which impede motion in the water and produce cold, in the same manner as glass arrests water, and allows light to pass through it'. Bernier adds that the water is cooled also by mixing it with saltpetre or gunpowder—a practice still observed in parts of India today. This gunpowder produces strange effects when drunk: 'The liquid thus becomes very cold and is by no means unwholesome, as I apprehended, though at first it sometimes affects the bowels.' Here Bernier acknowledges what his theory of global racial difference overlooks. To survive the torrid climate of Delhi, to avoid sickening there, one needs to transform one's body by becoming at least partially Indian—by keeping out certain noxious Indian 'particles', but also by letting in others that positively, if somewhat ambivalently, 'effect the bowels'. In other words, one needs to acquire a healthy rather than a sick Delhi Belly. And this necessity is as explosive to the idea of racial identity and difference as the gunpowder that Bernier took into his gut.

One might note that Bernier's gunpowder-assisted travail of becoming Indian did not amount to 'going native', a concept that dates to the high tide of the colonial age. The latter presumes a civilized identity replaced by an inferior one, a cultural degeneration from a European norm. For Bernier, by contrast, the work of becoming Indian did not assume any such degeneration. Nor did it entail a clean transition from one identity to another. Rather, as Bernier's ambivalence makes clear, it meant something altogether more open-ended and messy. Those who became Indian may have transformed their bodies, consciously or unconsciously, to adapt to their new environments. But they could not entirely shed the tendencies and habits of their previous lives. This often resulted in a volatile, global mix of bodily aptitudes. It also meant that the cultural loyalties of those who became Indian weren't always predictable. They may have served Indian masters, but their sense of 'home' was often complex and bifurcated.

◆

How do we recover the stories of these migrants and their bodies? Traditional archival research can only reveal so much. As the cases of Roch and Simitt demonstrate, the historical record is tantalizingly elusive. We can scan official records of the English East India Company, the Portuguese Estado da Índia, and the Mughal court for fleeting references to foreigners who became Indian; we can read the few autobiographical accounts, like Manucci's or Bernier's, of migrants' lives. But so many details have vanished, and most migrants have left only the faintest trace, if any, in the historical record. Often we have to deal with the archival equivalent of mere ripples and vapour trails. This is hardly surprising given that many of these migrants were illiterate. And even when they weren't, it was only very rarely that they or the people they met thought to document their experiences.

But there was another archive available to me as I tried to recover the experiences of Roch, Simitt, and their peers: my own body. For in many ways, I was interested less in the precise chronological details of the migrants' lives—when exactly they did what—than their biographies in that word's most literal sense. Biography, derived from the Greek 'bios' (body) and 'graphein' (to write or mark), means not just to write a life history but also to imprint on a body. And 'the body' is not an unchanging entity that can be known simply by its colour or its geographical origin. Indeed, we should speak not of the body but of bodies, plural. As we have seen, bodies are changeable nodes within larger ecologies. Which is to say, bodies interact with and are imprinted by a variety of elements: environmental conditions, including the climate; the landscape, whether geological or human-made; cultural imperatives that direct bodies to act in certain ways and not others; languages, which demand not only unique ways of thinking but also specific ways of using facial muscles and hands; and the large ensemble of transformative matter that we take into our bodies—food, drink, medicines, germs. (We are not just what we eat; we are also what we come into contagious contact with.) Beyond all these factors, perhaps more intangible but no less real for that, is what historians have traditionally called political economy: the larger systems of production, both local and global, that shape our actions and direct our movements, allowing our bodies more or less privileges, more or less possibilities, than others. As this might suggest, one does not just write bodies. Bodies are more accurately written *upon*, inasmuch as they are imprinted and transformed by all these external elements. The tales of foreign migrants who became Indian are biographies in this much more literal sense.

My body's experiences in India have helped me plot these elusive biographies. I first visited India in 2001; I have returned every year, and since 2011, I have been living in Delhi more or less permanently. Watching the ways in which my own body has adapted to the weather, landscapes, diseases and foodstuffs of India might not allow me to recover in precise detail the diverse experiences of my predecessors. After all, my body is different from theirs. And the particular India to which I have adapted—urban, middle-class, mostly Anglophone and largely air-conditioned, therefore westernized in its climatic as well as its linguistic preferences—is a world away from the Indias in which poor sixteenth- and seventeenth-century migrants settled. But my body's experiences in India have taught me something about the lives of these earlier migrants. It has repeatedly alerted me to the fact that the dislocations of migration aren't simply mental or emotional. Ever since my first visit to India, 'my' body has increasingly felt not like my own, at least not in the sense of being entirely within my control. It has been felled by food poisoning in Delhi, sunstroke in Chennai, and viral fever in Kolkata. It has tripped and broken its big toe on a stray root in the Deer Park of Hauz Khas. It has been pushed and shoved by pickpockets in the throng at Moinuddin Chishti's dargah in Ajmer. Yet these disabling experiences have also been matched by the acquisition of new competencies fitted to my body's new environments. My body has developed a tolerance, even a craving, for mirchi (chilli). It has perfected the art of the head waggle. It has adapted sufficiently well to the heat and humidity of the north that it can now run a half marathon in Delhi.

To understand what it means to become Indian demands attending to the agonies and the ecstasies of the migrant body's encounters with new environments. Indeed, 'ecstasy' is a useful word in this context: it derives from the Greek 'ek-stasis', meaning standing outside oneself. We might regard ecstasy as simply an emotional state. But in its Greek usage, it is also an embodied condition: standing outside oneself means having a body that is no longer one's body. Or rather, it means finding that one's body has become something very different after entering into a new mode of being. After all, standing outside oneself still implies legs on which to stand, no matter how much one's body has been transformed by the ecstatic experience. This condition has recognizably Indian counterparts. The Sufi concept of the mast qalandar, a person overcome with ecstatic love for Allah, refers not simply to a religious or spiritual ideal. It more precisely describes someone who has surrendered to, and been transformed by, an overpowering bodily intoxication. Likewise, Tantric forms of Hinduism recognize a state of ecstasy that is not just spiritual but also profoundly embodied: in this state, one transcends the singular bounded self and finds within one's body the traces of an infinite universe that has previously seemed exterior to it. Rather than a solipsistic exercise in navel-gazing, then, looking at my own body's diverse experiences in India has provided me with ecstatic points of entry into the larger environments and historical processes that have differently transformed me, Roch and Simitt, and many other migrants to the subcontinent.

To write the biographies of migrants from the sixteenth and seventeenth centuries, then, I have drawn on my own experience of becoming Indian. That experience is detailed here in a series of seven modern-day interludes that punctuate my tales of individual migrants. The interludes detail the vicissitudes of my encounters with Indian food and diseases, cityscapes and landscapes, nicknames, clothes, languages, weather, and so on. In other words, the interludes are mini-biographies in the sense I have suggested here—stories of how a body has been newly imprinted and changed by its time in India. I should stress that these are not exemplary success stories, let alone inspirational guides on How to Become Indian. The process of becoming Indian is not one that can ever culminate with finality in a pure Indian identity: I can no more erase all the mental and bodily habits of my middle-class New Zealand childhood, my English postgraduate training, and my twenty-three years in America as a professor of Shakespeare than I can give up my green eyes and easily sunburned skin. My body's previous histories in other parts of the world has made for some spectacular stumbles in India, actual as much as metaphorical. And I have no doubt that many more await me. But my own mini-biographies underscore how the tales of individual migrants to India in the sixteenth and seventeenth centuries are always also tales of the larger ecologies, physical and cultural, that have shaped and re-shaped them.

◆

What it meant to become Indian before the heyday of British colonialism additionally demands that we rethink the very ideas of 'India' and the 'Indian'. Of course, during the sixteenth and seventeenth centuries there was no single political entity called India. The subcontinent was divided up amongst a diverse collection of empires, sultanates, kingdoms, smaller colonial dominions, and tribal areas. These territories were not culturally, linguistically or religiously homogeneous: they differed within themselves as much as from each other. Nor were they uniform in terrain or climate. So to become Indian in the sixteenth and seventeenth centuries was not to become one monolithic thing. What one became varied on the basis of one's environmental as much as cultural and economic location. To become Indian in the coconut-rich hinterland of Goa meant something quite different from what it meant in the typhoon-drenched, mosquito- and tiger-dominated terrain of the Sundarbans or in the arid hills of the Deccan plateau. Likewise, to become Indian in the fakir-congested galis (lanes) of Ajmer meant something quite different from what it meant in the luxurious havelis of Agra or in the Mughal harem of Lahore. Each location prompted different bodily transformations.

For all their diversity, however, these locations did have one thing in common. To lesser and greater extents, and for different reasons, each was a multicultural space in which migrants found new homes. Although Portuguese Goa was the first major European colony in India, and had imposed the Inquisition in 1560 to prosecute non-believers, it was temporarily a haven for various religious dissidents—Sephardic Jews and English Catholics—from Europe. The Deccan sultanates were ruled by Persian and Turkish elites who brought foreign merchants, physicians and soldiers—including enslaved Africans or habshis—into cities such as Aurangabad, Ahmadnagar and Hyderabad. In addition to installing Central Asians as courtiers and retaining mercenary soldiers from Europe, the Mughals also welcomed Christian artisans, traders and priests into their main cities—Fatehpur Sikri, Agra, Lahore, Delhi, Ajmer. Other Portuguese-speaking zones outside the official Estado da Índia such as the pirate communities of the Sundarbans brought together Bengalis, Europeans and Burmese Arakans. And, as Amitav Ghosh's *In an Antique Land* shows, the Malabar Coast of south India may have been the most cosmopolitan zone of all, with cities like Cochin, Quilon and Calicut providing homes to Arab, Jewish and Chinese merchants and sailors. Each of these different multicultural spaces asked migrants to cultivate distinctive new bodily skills and habits.

Which is to say: these spaces not only offered migrants new homes. They also functioned as engines of bodily transformation. The foreigners who joined them altered their bodies in ways I have already discussed—by eating Indian food, wearing Indian clothes, succumbing to Indian illnesses and learning Indian languages. Just as importantly, their bodies were also transformed by the acquisition of new skills specific to the spaces. Those who joined local armies, such as Roch and Simitt or the Flemish captain Dillanai, often brought with them knowledge of how to handle firearms—a new yet devastatingly effective technology introduced to the subcontinent in this time. But they also had to master new bodily techniques: riding horses, enduring military manoeuvres in the heat, moving efficiently through intimidating terrain such as the rocky highlands of the Deccan, the parched deserts of Rajasthan or the Ghats of south India. The warrior sailors of Gujarat and Kerala, such as the Russian slave Malik Ayaz who became admiral of Diu and the Malaccan slave Chinali who joined a rogue Malabari navy, may have developed sea legs before coming to India. But in their new subcontinental locations they also had to adapt their bodily reflexes to tropical cyclones, Arabian Sea currents, and the predations of mosquitoes. Foreigners who joined communities of itinerants in Ajmer or Delhi, such as the English eccentric Thomas Coryate, had to train their bodies to perform rituals of prostration, to be satisfied with a meagre diet of rice and daal, and to endure extremes of weather in little or no clothing. Migrant medical practitioners, such as the French doctor François Bernier and the Portuguese physician Garcia da Orta, took unfamiliar body-altering (and sometimes mind-altering) drugs and herbal treatments before prescribing them to their patients. And foreign women living in Mughal harems, such as the Armenian Bibi Juliana Firangi and the Portuguese Bibi Juliana Dias da Costa, were expected to acquire an ensemble of new bodily techniques—dancing, singing, human chess-piece playing, robe-wearing, even weapon-bearing—depending on their rank and vocation.

The migrants whose tales make up this book were foreign yet not foreign. They came from elsewhere, yet they and their bodies also became Indian. Indeed, unlike other travellers who returned to their homes, all of them left their bones in the subcontinent. The most common term for these migrants in Mughal Hindustan was 'firangi'. This book is about the first firangis. By that phrase I don't mean the first foreigners in India, but rather the first people to live in the Indian subcontinent under the name of 'firangi'—which is to say those migrants who came to India during the first two centuries of the Mughal Empire. We might presume that the firangis were migrants from Europe: 'firangi', after all, was a Persian word derived from the Arabic 'farenji', a medieval Arabic rendering of 'Frank' or Frenchman—and 'Franks' had dominated the ranks of the Christian Crusaders from Europe, a land often known in the subcontinent as 'Firangistan'.

In pre-British Raj India, however, the firangi was not always a European. The term was applied variously to Christian migrants from non-European nations, such as Armenia and Georgia; to migrants who were native Christian converts from Portuguese Asian colonies such as Malacca; and to migrants who were Christian slaves from African territories. And 'firangi' was not applied exclusively to Christians. It was used also of Jewish migrants from Christian nations and even of some Muslim migrants who had served Christian masters. As this suggests, 'firangi' in its pre-Raj currency was something of an indeterminate term. It was not just a generic name for a foreigner. It referred more precisely to a migrant from a Christian land who had become Indian, yet continued, in a fundamental way, to be marked as foreign.

At times this liminal status could be a source of discomfort and alienation, not least in locations where the prevailing religious cultures, especially caste Hinduism, valued purity of body and belief. Yet it could also be a spur to extraordinary creativity. Amongst the migrants I consider, a remarkable number engaged in innovative thought-experiments—scientific, literary, military, architectural, artistic, artisanal, theatrical, spiritual, political, historiographical—that couldn't have happened anywhere but in India, yet couldn't have been produced by anyone but a migrant.

Here is a shortlist of these experiments, which I chronicle in more detail in the chapters that follow. The Portuguese physician Garcia da Orta, personal doctor to the sultan of Ahmadnagar, wrote a revolutionary treatise on tropical medicine based on his knowledge of Arabic and Indo-Islamic practice as well as his dialogues with local hakeems. The dissident English Goan priest Thomas Stephens wrote an 11,000-stanza Marathi poem—in traditional local styles derived from the Hindu Puranas—on the life of Christ. The Russian slave-turned-admiral Malik Ayaz and the Flemish war-captive-turned-general Dillanai devised ingenious fortifications to protect the Gujarati port city of Diu and the south Indian kingdom of Travancore. The East African slave-turned-soldier, regent and urban planner, Malik Ambar, designed and built the multicultural city, with its innovative water-supply system, which was to become Aurangabad. A mysterious European painter named Mandu Firangi combined elements of Western and Mughal styles in painting scenes from the Ramayana. The Basque jeweller Augustin Hiriart, known to the Mughals as Hunarmand, created ingenious devices in Agra using a mix of Hindustani and European techniques. The English fakir Thomas Coryate, based in Ajmer, performed an oration to Jahangir in Farsi that was a blend of Persian, Hindustani and English theatrical styles. The Armenian-Jewish yogi-qalandar Sa'id Sarmad Kashani, who migrated to Lahore, Hyderabad, and finally Delhi, wrote 321 Persian rubaiyyat (or quatrains) that amounted to a gloriously homoerotic manifesto for religious pluralism. The Portuguese salt-trader-turned-pirate Sebastião Gonçalves Tibau forged a unique island society in the Bay of Bengal that made fellows of European, Burmese and Bengali freebooters. And our old friend Niccolò Manucci, Roch and Simitt's victim, wrote a history of the Mughal emperors in Portuguese, Italian and French overlaid with Persian, drawing on indigenous chronicle and Western storytelling traditions. Even as they transformed their bodies, each of these migrants also helped transform 'India' into something more complex and plural than what we might usually understand by that term.

And that is why Manucci got it only half-right: Roch and Simitt weren't just 'English impostors'. In their artful border-crossings—which is to say, by resisting any purely foreign or purely local identity—they were also, in a very real sense, authentically Indian.

ON ARRIVING

I arrived in India. But it might be more accurate to say that India arrived in me.

Before my first proper visit, I had twice stopped in India en route to other destinations. I have no recollection of my first layover—touching down in Calcutta in 1965, when I was just two—but the second is seared in my memory. In 1987, I travelled from New Zealand to England to begin my doctoral studies. I arrived at Bombay airport in the dead of night, exhausted after a long haul from Perth. There I was confined to the Arrivals Lounge for three hours. I spent that brief time thrilling to the intense midnight heat and humidity: even in late September, the temperature was far sultrier than anything I had previously experienced, and the airport's odour of moist decay, sweat, and crushed areca nut—a mingled scent I found at once delightful and sickly—insinuated itself into my clothes, my hair and my mouth. I could still taste it on my lips and smell it on my pillow the next day when I woke up in London. It felt like the lingering trace of a one-night stand who had stolen away while I was sleeping.

A quarter of a century later, as an immigrant to India, I am still in Arrivals. And that's because India continues to arrive in me. Not just its heat, its humidity, and its odours. All kinds of Indian matter keep getting under my skin, for better and for worse.

In 2001, I finally visited India for more than a layover. By then, I'd been involved with an Indian for some time, and had been dreaming of India even longer. I'd glutted myself on Salman Rushdie's Bombay (in Midnight's Children*), Amitav Ghosh's Calcutta (in* The Shadow Lines*), and R. K. Narayan's south India (in* Malgudi Days*). But I had no sense of Delhi. Even though her family are originally from Kerala and Madras, my partner was, and is, a committed Dilliwali, and she wanted me to experience life in her city.*

And experience it I did. Arriving in Delhi felt simultaneously like falling in love and an unspeakable violation. If my brief Bombay layover had got under my skin, my stay in Delhi made me even more aware of my body as a permeable vessel bombarded by Indian matter, some welcome and some unwelcome. I swooned over my first taste of langda mangoes. I became a confirmed Limca addict. But I also spent much of my first two months in India flat on my back or seated on the pot, felled by Delhi Belly and the thousand natural shocks to which the intestines are heir. Each serving of ghar ka khana, no matter how tasty, seemed to prompt a typhoon in my guts followed by repeated visits to the bathroom. Though I was eating north Indian rather than Goan food, I found myself repeatedly recalling the somewhat xenophobic graffito I'd spied while studying in England: 'Is the Bottom falling out of your World? Eat a Vindaloo, and the World will fall out of your Bottom!'

Falling sick made me long for the cooler climates and blander foods of my native New Zealand. Yet it also saw me open up, in a fundamental way, to the city I now call home. It marked not just my arrival in Delhi, but also Delhi's arrival in my body—delivered, in viral or bacterial form, through the food and drink I consumed. What I have taken into my body here has changed me, altering my gastronomic preferences, my odour, my skin's chemistry, and (thank goodness) my immune system. So when I say that Delhi has arrived in me, I mean that it has seeped into me and colonized me at a molecular level.

To experience Delhi's arrival in my body—even in microbial form—not as a violation but rather as a welcome encounter is to dissent from the deep-seated fantasy that my body is an unchanging and self-contained fortress that cannot and should not be entered. It also means dissenting, at least implicitly, from my body's previous 'settings' in the West as the benchmarks for what I am or should be in India.

Perhaps that's why the experiences of Indian arrival I find most instructive are those of a pair of religious dissidents, both of whom landed in Goa in the sixteenth century. The pair not only dissented from the official religions of the countries in which they were born, they also welcomed the transformation of their bodies by unfamiliar Indian matter. The two men are unusual among the firangis in this book: they both left significant pieces of writing—a medical treatise, an epic Purana—that give us powerful clues about their transformative experiences of food and illness in India. Their dissident sensibilities also pushed them into border territories where they became, to lesser and greater extents, Indian. But in neither case was this transformation simply a product of strong intellectual conviction, emotional disposition or unorthodox religious faith. The men's bodies—or rather their noses, mouths and skin, through which they absorbed the transformative matter of their new homes—were central to their dramas of arrival. Because the two dissidents did not just arrive in India: India kept arriving in them.

This is the story of Garcia da Orta. Or rather, it is three very different stories, each nested within the others, like a set of Russian dolls. The first is an official story of a colonial Portuguese patriot; the second, a more unofficial story of an individual's physical transformation in India; and the third, an entirely surreptitious story of an underground international network that cuts across divides of geography and faith. Together these stories make up a firangi tale that has all the ingredients of a mystery novel: powerful state machinations, exotic drugs, covert religious dissidents, and tantalizing clues that lead to a startling climax. The mystery begins aboard a ship near the southwest coast of India.

It is the middle of the night in January 1538, a league off the Kerala shore. The night air is warm and eerily still: there isn't so much as a hint of a breeze. A Portuguese war galleon, sailing north from Cochin amid ongoing skirmishes with the Mappila pirates of the Malabar Coast, drifts lazily on the Arabian Sea. Despite the lack of wind and the distance from land, a strange, seductive fragrance suddenly fills the air. The scent finds its way into the nostrils of a passenger on board the galleon. The man, a relatively fresh arrival in India named Garcia da Orta, is so arrested by the experience that, more than twenty years later, he still remembers it, describing the fragrance as 'so strong and so delicious that I thought there must be a forest of flowers'.

The episode stands out not least because of its seeming disruption of the rhythms of war. In contrast to the purposeful speed of Portuguese military aggression, a moment of calm at sea sets Orta adrift in a reverie of perfumed air. The moment is something of a convention in firangi writing about India, which ritually notes how local smells—fair or foul—impress themselves on the new arrival. (Even Shakespeare, who probably never travelled out of England, dreams of the 'spiced Indian air'.) Yet the enchanting smells of India can accost the fiercest colonist and have no long-term impact on him, as was certainly the case for, commander of the galleon, Martim Afonso de Sousa, one of the most ruthless and unscrupulous colonial administrators in Portuguese India. We don't know what his immediate reaction was to the fragrance. But de Sousa's mission against the Mappilas culminated in the destruction of the pirates' camp in Vedalai, the burning of all their ships, and the death of 800 locals. Clearly there was no flower power epiphany for de Sousa.

How, then, to interpret the enchantment of Garcia da Orta? Though he served de Sousa as his ship's doctor, Orta's account of his experience makes no mention of his master or the mission against the Mappilas. Instead, his attention is devoted largely to the source of the mysterious fragrance. It came, he surmises, not from a forest of flowers on shore but rather from a cargo of cloves in a passing ship, en route from the Moluccas. (We might think again of Shakespeare, whose 'spiced Indian air' is full of the 'sails' of 'embarked traders'.) Here Orta implicitly acknowledges how his nighttime scented idyll, no matter how much it may have temporarily interrupted de Sousa's mission to decimate the Mappilas, was fully implicated within the larger drama of Portuguese eastward expansion. And that is because the Portuguese had come to India and the Spice Islands in large part to take direct control of the lucrative trade in pepper and spices, previously the preserve of Arab, Persian, Malabari and Chinese merchants. As Orta himself notes, 'the Chinese came in their ships' to the Moluccas, 'and took the cloves to their country and to India, Persia, and Arabia'.

Orta played a not insignificant role in this trade. As a firangi physician in sixteenth-century India, cloves were very much his business: European as much as Indian medical practitioners considered spices not just desirable foodstuffs but also miracle drugs. Writing of the clove, Orta remarks that it is used 'first as a medicine and for the scent, and then for culinary purposes'. But this is not simply a market-driven description of the clove's many uses. Orta's statement also hints at how, after arriving in India, he experienced the east arriving in him. His description of the clove is equally a description of what it does to bodies, including his own. Such attentiveness to the body's interactions with alien elements may be common among fresh arrivals. What makes Orta's description remarkable, however, is that it came more than two decades after he first arrived in India. Unlike de Sousa Orta remained curious about the physiological effects of eastern substances for the rest of his life. In other words, he repeatedly opened up his body to foreign elements in ways that destabilized his Portuguese identity.

We might see the strange incident of the night fragrance as entailing a collision between two rather different stories of the Portuguese presence in India. The first, a colonialist story, moves inexorably across the Arabian Sea towards the destruction of Vedalai as a prelude to Portuguese control of the eastern spice trade. The second, a story of tropical medicine and gastronomy, concerns the long-term transformation of firangi bodies by eastern drugs and foodstuffs. Hidden beneath these two stories, moreover, is a third, altogether more elusive tale of a religious dissident who felt at home with Indians and Indian cultures. All three stories converge in Garcia da Orta. Telling these stories, however, means halting the flow of chronological time and, in jerky high-speed reverse motion, hurtling back thrice from India to Lisbon, and then onward to Goa, Bombay, Ahmadnagar, and beyond.

Story 1: The Patriotic Physician

So let's begin by journeying back from India to Lisbon—but let's also sail forward in time. It is 1998, 460 years after that sweet-scented night off the Malabar Coast. Portugal is about to join the eurozone: its old coinage, established in 1911 after a revolution that deposed the constitutional monarchy, is on the verge of being superseded itself. Let's now step into the spice section of a Lisbon mercado to buy what the Portuguese call cravo-da-índia—or cloves—still smelling, as Orta described, like a forest of flowers. We purchase a large packet with a 500 escudo note, receiving as change a 200 escudo coin. Now let's take a close look at this soon-to-be-obsolete coin, a bimetallic brass ring encircling a copper-nickel alloy centre. Minted in 1991, the coin is one that most Portuguese handle on a daily basis: it is roughly the equivalent of a euro, for which it will be exchanged in a year. The coin's heads side features a particularly striking image. Where you might expect to see the mug of a king, queen, emperor, or president, there is instead a profile of a sixteenth-century doctor, wearing robes and physician's cap, clutching a book, and twirling a tropical plant. The 200 escudo coin commemorates a national hero for a republican age: not someone of royal blood, but a common citizen celebrated in Portugal and throughout Europe as the founder of tropical medicine. Now go ahead and slip Garcia da Orta, or his likeness, into your wallet.

For centuries, Orta was the leading character in a patriotic tale of global Portuguese expansion, one spearheaded not just by fidalgos or conquistadors but also by a relatively lowly physician. Orta is best known now for his authorship of fifty-nine dialogues entitled *Colóquios dos simples e drogas da Índia* ('Colloquies on the simples and drugs of India'), first published in Goa in 1561. This book played a crucial role in making India more liveable for its colonial European settlers. Outlining in extraordinary detail the medicinal properties of local plants (and some minerals), the *Colloquies* is both a practical guide on how to cope with the many illnesses of India, including cholera and a treasure trove of non-medical information about the subcontinent. Orta's treatise was much consulted—and imitated—well into the nineteenth century; it made its author a national hero. Statues of him were erected throughout Portugal, and his name came to grace the nation's public parks, streets, and hospitals.

Many aspects of Orta's biography seem to affirm his state canonization as a patriotic Portuguese physician. Born in around 1500 in Castelo de Vide, a village near the border with Castile, Orta was educated at the best medical universities in Spain—Salamanca and Alcalá de Henares—yet returned to Portugal to practice. He was so skilled and knowledgeable a doctor that he was awarded a chair of medicine at Portugal's premier university, the University of Lisbon, in 1533. But Orta gave up his academic post the next year to serve the colonial Estado da Índia. When Martim Afonso de Sousa led a fleet to Goa in 1534, Orta joined him as his personal physician. Orta's association with Sousa places him squarely in the mainstream of Portuguese global expansion. De Sousa, a fidalgo warrior-administrator, was the leader of the first Portuguese colonial expedition to Brazil in 1530; there he perfected the art of slash-and-burn river raids as a means of securing the submission of local peoples—an art deployed to lethal effect in his later campaign against the Mappilas. Orta accompanied de Sousa on various Indian expeditions, including the conquest of Diu and other military journeys to the Malabar Coast (where he smelled the cloves) and Sri Lanka. Although they were exactly the same age, their relationship was one of imperious master and respectful servant: Orta dutifully referred to de Sousa as his amo (lord), and dedicated his *Colloquies* to him. The physician stayed on in India after de Sousa returned to Lisbon in 1538. But when his amo was posted back to Goa in 1542 as the Portuguese Viceroy, Orta became servant to the highest authority in the colonial Estado da Índia. Following the expiration of his term in 1545, de Sousa again returned to Portugal—and Orta again remained in India. Yet the physician's star continued to shine brightly because of his prior association with de Sousa. In 1554 he was contracted to serve the new but elderly Viceroy Pedro Mascarenhas, who lasted less than a year in office before succumbing to illness. The ailing Mascarenhas clearly regarded Orta highly: upon assuming office, he awarded the physician the quit-rent (a lease with the promise of proceeds from the land) of the island of

Bombay—at that point a new Portuguese possession.

All these details suggest a life of patriotic devotion to Portugal as physician and colonial servant. That, at least, is how the colonialist version of Orta's story goes. It is reiterated in many brief biographical sketches of him: one of the most influential, outlined by the Goan historian José Gerson da Cunha in his *Origins of Bombay* (1900), claims that Orta led a long and happy bachelor life as a universally admired servant of Portugal before his death in Goa at the venerable age of 80. As we'll see, not one of these claims is true. Orta's position in India, and his relation to the Portuguese Estado da Índia, was considerably more precarious than da Cunha acknowledges. Other subterranean stories swirl beneath the surface of da Cunha's patriotic tale. To retrieve them, we need to sail back once more from India to Lisbon. But we need also to travel forward to 1552. That year witnessed events that would ultimately lead a famous Portuguese writer to an unusual Indian garden, a garden that had transformed the body of its even more unusual gardener.

Story 2: The Aam Aadmi

In 1552, Luís Vaz de Camões was a young man of 28, and something of a wastrel. He had been sent by his family to the University of Coimbra to study humanities. But he had dropped out, quite possibly to pursue his desire to be a writer but also to nurse a series of madcap love interests. Rumour has it that he (unsuccessfully) wooed a lady-in-waiting at the court, after which he set his sights (again unsuccessfully) on Maria, the sister of King João III. Whether because of these would-be trysts, or because he had made a potentially disparaging allusion to the king in a play—we don't know the precise reason—he was banished from Lisbon in 1548. In his four years away, Camões enlisted in the army, fought the Moors, and lost an eye; upon returning to Lisbon, he lapsed once more into a dissolute life. In 1552, after a public brawl with one of the king's servants, he was banished again, this time to Goa for three years.

Partly to rehabilitate himself during his Indian exile, Camões started writing an epic poem—*Os Lusíadas*, known in English as *The Lusiads*— about Vasco da Gama's journey around Africa to India. The poem, as befits its author's impaired ocular condition, is something of a one-eyed apology for Portugal's global ambitions. But it contains many haunting descriptions of India and the Orient, including the 'orchards of hot cloves/ Portuguese will buy with their blood'. These descriptions are clearly the product of first-hand experience. Indeed, Camões seems to have learned something of India's herbs and spices during a visit with Garcia da Orta in Goa. He was so impressed by Orta that he agreed to write a dedicatory poem for the physician's *Colloquies*, long before the publication of *The Lusiads* in 1572 made the formerly disgraced Camões a household name as the national poet of Portuguese imperialism.

'Orta' is also Portuguese for 'garden'. In the dedicatory poem he wrote for the *Colloquies*, Camões repeatedly puns on the physician's surname:

Favorecei a antigua
Sciencia que ja Achilles estimon
Olhai que vos obrigua
Verdes que em vosso tempo se mostrou
O fruto d'aquella ORTA onde florecem
Prantas novas que os doutos nao conhecem
Olhai que em vossos annos
Produze huma ORTA insigne varias ervas
Nos campos Lusitanos
As quaes aquellas doutas e protervas
Medea e Circe nunca conheceram
Posta que as leis da Magica excederam.

(Favour the ancient
Science which Achilles held in esteem;
Look, because you must see
What was created in our time
The fruit of a GARDEN where
New plants bloom, unknown to scholars.
Look, how in your lifetime
A remarkable GARDEN produces many herbs
In the Lusitanian fields,
Herbs which those wise sorcerers
Medea and Circe never found,
Because the laws of Magic outwitted them.)

As Camões's sustained pun on 'orta' suggests, Orta had created in Goa a garden full of marvellous plants, fruits and herbs previously 'unknown to scholars'—at least to western ones. Yet despite their Indian location, Camões situates the physician and the garden in 'the Lusitanian', i.e. Portuguese, 'fields'. In typical colonialist fashion, Camões presents Orta's

Indian garden as a purely Portuguese accomplishment, testimony to the ingenuity of a Portuguese native son. Yet what Orta planted in his garden didn't simply add to Portugal's fame. It also subtly transformed the gardener. Which is to say: the garden played a crucial role in Orta's becoming Indian. As Camões's sustained pun suggests, Portuguese doctor and Indian garden blurred into each other—and not just metaphorically.

Orta's garden was located in what was then still the relatively new colonial city of Goa, at the back of his house on the Rua dos Namorados ('Street of the Beloved'). Only a handful of cathedrals survive today in the haunted site now called Velha (Old) Goa; Orta's garden is long gone. But it is commemorated in Panjim, the capital of Goa, by a municipal garden that bears his name. Though perfectly pleasant, this new Jardim Garcia da Orta pales in comparison with the original. The modern garden is an orderly civic park with a well-mown lawn and a few park benches interspersed with palm trees. By contrast, Orta's garden was a teeming cornucopia of Indian trees, flowers, herbs, spices and fruits. We know some of its contents because of his *Colloquies*. The treatise proceeds semi-alphabetically, from aloes to zedoary, through an enormous number of Indian medicinal plants; presumably many if not all of them could be found in the garden. It certainly included a flower bed of mogra or jasmine flowers that, in the *Colloquies*, he claims 'smell sweeter than the orange flower' and give 'an agreeable scent to food'. And Orta speaks of a tart 'with a pleasant savour' made from carambola, or starfruit, freshly plucked from a tree in his garden.

As this might suggest, Orta's treatise often reads as a discourse less on medicine and botany than on gardening and gastronomy. The *Colloquies* list his garden's sweet-smelling and tasting foodstuffs, including chakka (jackfruit), tarbuz (melon), nirgundi (negundo), and imli (tamarind), even as it inventories the physiological effects of other medicinal Indian plants—areca nut, coconut, incense, opium; the list goes on and on. This suggests how Orta regarded his garden less as a colonialist map of Indian botany than as an experimental laboratory in which he could test the limits of his tolerance for Indian food and drugs. The *Colloquies* present the plants in his garden not just as exotic species in need of names or classification but also as transformative elements, which—like the cloves whose fragrance he inhaled that warm night off the Malabar Coast—have entered and changed him through his nose, mouth and skin. In India, then, Orta was one with his 'orta' in body as much as in name.

This isn't to say that Orta tried everything he saw locals putting in their bodies. He refused paan (whose betel odour he could not countenance) and bhang (though he is arguably the first westerner to offer a clinical description of that legendary affliction of recreational cannabis users: the munchies). Orta was well aware of the ways in which cultural factors affect the body's tastes: as he notes in the *Colloquies*, 'there is a good deal of habit in the matter of smells', and something that has 'a very nice smell' to an Indian can be 'very nasty' to him. But he displayed an unusual adventurousness in experimenting with Indian plants, fruits, spices and herbs. And what he put in his body led him, over time, to develop strong attachments to his new home. As his doubtless fictional interlocutor Dr Ruano (the name means 'man in the street') says of his first taste of Indian mangoes: 'it does not seem to me that I can now leave'. Ruano's remark may be a joke. But it's one that probably contained a kernel of truth: after reaching Goa in 1534, Orta never left India. Although other factors played a part in his staying, his body's transformed tastes and preferences probably made the proposition of living in India much more desirable. Those mangoes counted for a lot.

◆

How did Orta sustain his mango habit? In fact he had not one, but two gardens—the first in Goa, the other further north. As we have seen, he was awarded the quit-rent of Bombay in 1554 for his services to the Portuguese colonial state. At this time, Bombay was a far cry from what it was to become. Unlike the sprawling, polluted mega-city of today, in the 1550s it was a small island, one of seven that subsequent land-reclamation projects have turned into the peninsula now constituting the bulk of Mumbai. The island's land covered the small landmass extending from present-day Malabar Hill to the Castle, currently the headquarters of India's Western Naval Command; it was separated from Colaba (then a very small island) to its immediate south and Mazagaon (also then an island) to its immediate north. Unlike the smog of modern Mumbai, the island's air was famously clean. When it first came into the possession of the Portuguese in 1527, the island was initially given the name Ilha da Boa Vida, or Island of the Good Life. Orta, however, refers to it both as 'Bombaim' and 'Mombaim'. The first name may or may not be derived from the Portuguese bom bahia, or good bay; the second may or may not be derived from the Marathi Mumbadevi, the goddess Mumba. But Orta's slippage between the two names parallels the confusions of identity he came to embody, alternating between Portuguese and Indian worlds without ever belonging decisively to either one.

There seem to have been two villages on Bombay Island. The older settlement, Cavel, was in the same location as the modern-day neighbourhood of the same name; it was populated by Koli fishermen, many of whom were converts to Christianity. A second, densely populated village abutted the site now occupied by the Castle. This site is almost certainly where Orta's house and garden were located. The Castle's alternative name, Casa da Orta, pays homage to the estate of Bombay's early firangi tenant, though there is little if anything that survives from Orta's original property. Two gates of the manor are believed to remain in the INS Angre, a naval station in Mumbai. But there may have been another long-standing survivor from Orta's Bombay garden. In 1866, the *Bombay Saturday Review* noted that a Mrs Hough, living in Colaba, had a mango tree that fruited both at the normal time (May) and in Christmas. Orta claims in his *Colloquies* that he has 'a mango-tree in that island of mine which has two gatherings', in May and December. Was Mrs Hough's tree a descendant of Orta's eccentrically fruiting mango?

We don't know how much time, if any, Orta spent on the island of Bombay. It has been speculated that his wife and two daughters—who are not mentioned in the *Colloquies* despite Orta's abundant references to servants, colleagues, friends and masters—stayed there and that they inspired Camões's episode in *The Lusiads* about a magical Indian island populated by female nymphs. But the tenant of Orta's house was a Portuguese man named Simão Toscano. In his *Colloquies*, Orta notes the receipt of a basket of twenty mangoes from Toscano, picked from the biannually fruiting tree in the manor garden. Orta clearly enjoys their taste. He dutifully orders the best mangoes sent to the viceroy, but keeps six to serve in his house, requesting that they be sliced and soaked in sweet-smelling wine. Like any modern Indian who has passionate opinions about the best types of mango, Orta displays a connoisseur's knowledge—or partisanship—about the fruit. He is partial to the smaller mango of Gujarat but also likes the mangoes of Bengal and the Deccan. And he relishes mango pickle, conserved with vinegar and stuffed with green ginger and garlic. Which is to say: when it came to his preference in fruit, Orta had become a common Indian man, or what Hindi speakers call an 'aam aadmi'—and in that phrase's most literal sense: a mango man.

In the *Colloquies*, Orta typically converts his gastronomic enjoyment of mangoes into specialist medical knowledge. He draws in part on the conventional western medicine of the time, codified by the Greek physician Galen, which divided up all phenomena—including illnesses and their remedies—on the basis of their mix of cold, hot, dry and wet elements. So he regards the mango as a cold and damp fruit with juicy yet acidic properties, and he warns against the tendency of rotten mangoes to cause 'fevers, colics, bleeding, or erysipelas'. Yet Orta also sees mangoes as serving a medical purpose: the stones, when roasted, 'are good for the flux'. To which he adds, in an aside that typifies his highly embodied experience of Indian medicines: 'I have tried them and they seemed to me to be efficacious.'

◆

To know about the mango stone's curative properties, Orta had to depend on far more than just his empirical acumen or his training in Galenic medicine. He also had to become friendly with local medical experts and immerse himself in their cultural networks. This immersion evidently started at home, as can be seen in the *Colloquies*: Antonia, his servant-girl and possibly an Indian convert, is expert in the qualities of the Goan garden; and Malupa, a Hindu physician, appears in Orta's house and discusses how to reduce fever caused by inflammation, using turbit mixed with ginger. Malupa is supposed to be the first Indian doctor whose words are recorded in European writing. But the *Colloquies* refer also to numerous other Indian physicians, most of them Muslim, from whom Orta gleaned knowledge: among them, doctors in Cranganore who prescribe mercury for the cure of leprosy; a Gujarati physician who treats dysentery with opium and nutmeg; and one 'Mula Ucem'— probably Maula Hussein—an Ahmadnagar hakeem with expertise in the uses of zedoary as a remedy for joint pain.

As this suggests, Orta's initiation into Indian medical knowledge and practice was undertaken most extensively outside of the Portuguese Estado da Índia. Much of his learning was acquired during a long period of service, over many years, as personal physician to Burhan Nizam Shah (1503–53), the sultan of Ahmadnagar. The city, about 400 kilometres northeast of Velha Goa on the west bank of the Sina River, was founded in the 1490s by the Nizam's father, Malik Ahmad. By the 1540s, it had become a byword for opulence: the ever fragrance-conscious Orta notes in his *Colloquies* that while in Ahmadnagar he visited a sandalwood-scented pleasure house. Burhan Nizam Shah, who had ascended to the sultanate's throne when he was just 7, was an unusual and even contradictory figure. Nominally a Shi'a Muslim, he had married a dancing girl, liked to take bhang, and drank copious amounts of wine. Yet, under his rule, trade, culture and art flourished. The nizam's court was also highly multicultural: his favourite was Sancho Pires, a renegade Portuguese artilleryman and later captain of the Ahmadnagar cavalry who had at least outwardly converted to Islam and assumed the name Firangi Khan. It is uncertain how or when exactly Orta came to meet the nizam. But he seems to have gravitated into the sultan's service after his erstwhile patron, Martim Afonso de Sousa, had returned to Portugal upon the expiry of his term as viceroy in 1545. Indeed, Orta's work for de Sousa may have recommended him to the nizam, who had assembled a crack team of international physicians to serve him and his many sons. It is impossible to say why exactly Orta accepted the nizam's invitation to serve him, but the presence of both a lively medical community and a Portuguese connection (albeit an unconventional one) in Sancho Pires may have helped seal the deal. As may have the promise of substantial remuneration for his service: Orta says that he was paid handsomely.

Orta tended the nizam through multiple illnesses—a tremor, fevers, rashes—even though he protests in the *Colloquies*, perhaps a little too strongly, that he refused ever to be put on permanent retainer in Ahmadnagar. He seems nonetheless to have been fully integrated into the large, multicultural medical community of the court. In the nizam's service, he interacted with many distinguished Muslim hakeems, including a physician who had previously served Shah Tahmasp of Persia. Orta, by his own admission, had competitive relations with these hakeems, and on at least one occasion boasts of his supposedly superior abilities. But he evidently respected their knowledge of Indian medical materials and practices. Orta also speaks repeatedly throughout the *Colloquies* of the nizam as a close friend in possession of valuable local medical knowledge. Sometimes he dismisses this knowledge as crackpot, as when he laments the nizam's willingness to pay a huge amount of gold for a fake unicorn's horn whose powder was believed to have restorative properties. Yet he also learned much from his Ahmadnagar master. In exchange for teaching his sons Portuguese, Orta notes, the nizam 'taught me the names of illnesses and medicines in Arabic'.

It has been speculated that Orta was awarded the island of Bombay because of his brief period of service as personal physician to Pedro

Mascarenhas, viceroy of Portuguese India for a few months in 1554–5. It seems just as likely that the award was occasioned by the kind of linguistic exchange Orta performed serving the nizam and his sons. In the unstable geopolitics of the subcontinent, European nations were keen to cultivate alliances with various local powers. Firangi doctors who served royal Indian masters often operated less as renegades or turncoats (though that was sometimes the case) than as diplomats and trade negotiators. The English East India Company official Dr Gabriel Boughton, who is supposed to have cured Shah Jahan's daughter of burns in 1645, played a crucial role in negotiating Mughal support for an English settlement in Bengal. The Company actively solicited the help of other firangi physicians in gaining concessions from Indian rulers. A certain D'Estremon, French physician to the sultan of Golconda, was asked in 1684 to negotiate a farman from the sultan that would have allowed the Company to coin rupees. That same year the Company approached Johannes Poterliet, the Armenian Christian doctor to the nawab of Karnatik, encouraging him to seek a farman from the Mughal Emperor for English free trade in the Coromandel Coast. Orta was probably employed a century earlier in a similar unofficial capacity by the Estado da Índia, and his contribution to creating a Portuguese-speaking Indian court in Ahmadnagar must have won him commendation.

Yet this is to think about Orta's linguistic quid pro quo with the nizam only in terms of what the colonial Portuguese state may have derived from it. As his acquisition of specialist Arabic medical terminology makes clear, Orta's time in the Ahmadnagar court led him also to imbibe forms of knowledge that departed from and even undermined conventional Portuguese wisdom. Indeed, the *Colloquies* intimate how Orta was subtly engaged in a subversive project: refusing the global efficacy of European medicine. Throughout the treatise, he claims to value the evidence of eyewitness experience over that of bookish Greek authority. Even more subversively, he also repeatedly indicates a marked preference for Arabic knowledge and practice, particularly that of Avicenna, the tenth-century physician of Uzbeki-Persian origin known in Arabic as Abū 'Alī al-Ḥusayn ibn 'Abd Allāh ibn Sīnā.

Avicenna's medical theories derive in part from those of Galen. But Avicenna was also an intrepid cataloguer of Asian medicinal substances, and his profound intimacy with Central and South Asian traditions of knowledge—born in Uzbekistan, he learned mathematics from an Indian fruit wala—seems to have greatly impressed Orta. Avicenna's medical knowledge also shaped that of the cosmopolitan Arabic-speaking hakeems (the word means not only 'physician' in Hindi and Urdu but also 'wise man' in Arabic) who rubbed shoulders with Orta in the court of the nizam. Indeed, Orta bemoans as provincial the slavish submission of western physicians to classical Greek medical authorities who, he claims, knew nothing of India: 'I affirm that as regards India the Arabs are better authorities and err less than the Greeks.' This stance was tantamount to heresy at a time when Galen's word was sacred writ. Orta admits in the *Colloquies* that, when he was in Spain, he didn't dare say anything against Galen or against the Greeks. Yet, in India, after his time in Ahmadnagar, he repeatedly gave himself license to do just that.

How do we explain Orta's embrace of Avicenna and the Arabic medicine of the Ahmadnagar court, an embrace that led him to alter not just his beliefs but also his bodily habits, tastes and competencies? Indeed, it was arguably in Ahmadnagar that he acquired his knowledge of mango stones' medicinal properties and even his taste for mangoes themselves: he is fulsome in his praise for the Deccani aam. Was Orta just a remarkably tolerant individual? Or was his profession, at least as practiced in Ahmadnagar, one that conduced to multicultural curiosity? Both may well have been the case. But there was certainly another factor at play. I believe that the hints of becoming Indian in Orta's professional life—his willingness to open both his mind to Indo-Islamic forms of medical practice and his gastrointestinal system to desi drugs and foodstuffs—are related to a key detail that was for a long time suppressed in official accounts of his life. And in some ways it's no surprise that this detail was suppressed. Not only is it at odds with the triumphal narrative of the patriotic Portuguese hero, it is also something that Orta himself did his best to hide throughout his life, despite the fact that it arguably informed all his chief decisions—to migrate to Goa, to find service in Ahmadnagar, to embrace Muslim traditions of knowledge and (as we shall see) to marry the woman who became his wife. What is this suppressed mystery? Garcia da Orta, the quit-rent master of Bombay, was not quite the patriotic Portuguese Christian he seemed to be. He was in fact a Sephardic Jew named Avraham ben Yitzhak.

Story 3: The Judaeo-Muslim Hakeem

Let's hurtle back a third time from India to Portugal, but on this occasion let's also time travel to a momentous year with enormous implications for the entire globe: 1492. In this year, Christopher Columbus, looking for a westward passage to China and India, stumbles upon the Caribbean and the Americas; in the same year, following the reconquest of the Moorish emirate of Granada by the Christian King Ferdinand and Queen Isabella of Castile, Jews along with Muslims are officially banned from Spain.

The 'discovery' of America changed the course of world history. But so did the reconquista of Granada. It brought to an end a long age of multiculturalism in the area known as Al-Andalus or Andalusia, the ensemble of Muslim-ruled emirates that had been a vital part of Iberian culture for nearly eight centuries. Cosmopolitan and economically powerful, Al-Andalus had been a beacon of learning and cultural exchange between multiple traditions. Its main city, Córdoba, numbered among its most prominent thinkers the Muslim philosopher Ibn Rushd (better known in the West as Averroës, 1125–86) and the Jewish theologian Moshe ben Maimon (or Maimonides, 1135–1204). But to call either man simply a 'Muslim' or a 'Jewish' thinker is to finesse the cultural mixings that made his thought possible. Both were scholars of traditions outside their nominal religions—Averroës of Aristotelian philosophy as explained by Jewish exegetes, Maimonides of Islamic science and law. Al-Andalus, then, was a space in which Jews and Muslims were in close dialogue with, and transformed by, each other.

The term 'Judaeo-Christian' has been bandied around for some time to suggest a long-standing natural bond between the two religious traditions connected by that hyphen. In the US in particular, it has also been used more recently to imply that Muslims are natural adversaries of both Jews and Christians. Yet the long ugly history of Christian anti-Semitism makes clear that, for the better part of two millennia, Jews were bonded to Christians primarily as the latter's enemies. As the instances of Averroës and Maimonides suggests, the multicultural bond with the greater historical resonance was Judaeo-Muslim. Averroës's texts survive largely because of their transmission by Andalusian Jews. These Jews, like Maimonides, spoke, wrote and dreamed in Arabic; their cultural reference points, even the translations they read of Greek philosophy, were Arabic; and their gastronomic preferences were also profoundly influenced by their Moorish neighbours. As late as 1490, the Jewish population of the now substantially shrunken Al-Andalus, diminished to the Emirate of Granada by two centuries of Christian reconquest, were still deeply versed in Arabic language and culture. Even in Christian-ruled areas such as Castile and Portugal, Sephardic Jews were speakers of Ladino—a vernacular mixture of Spanish, Hebrew,

Aramaic and Arabic. In Ladino, for instance, Sunday is not 'domingo' (as it is in both Spanish and Portuguese) but 'alhad', derived from the Arabic 'alhat'. And the Ladino word for freedom is not the Spanish 'liberdad', but 'alforria'—derived from the Arabic 'hurriya'. Make what you will of that, but clearly Sephardic Jews did not associate the idea of liberty with Spanish Christian rule.

The mass expulsions of 1492 violently disrupted this Judaeo-Muslim nexus. But it did not end it. By and large, the nexus was simply dispersed to other parts of the world: many expelled families migrated to Morocco and cities of the Ottoman Empire such as Algiers, Cairo and Istanbul, where there were already communities of Jews and Muslims in close proximity. Those who stayed in Spain were forced to convert to Christianity. But even after conversion, they remained objects of suspicion and hostility. Muslim converts were derided as 'moriscos'; Jewish converts became known as 'nuevo Cristanos' or New Christians and, more derogatorily, as 'marranos', Spanish for swine. A considerable number of the moriscos and New Christians continued to practice their old faiths in secret. It was largely to ferret out covert devotees of the banned religions that the Spanish Inquisition was founded. Eventually, after open rebellions in Granada in 1568 and 1571, the moriscos were first deported to other parts of Spain and then, in 1614, banished altogether. The more compliant New Christians, at least those who survived the Inquisition, were allowed to remain. But in the decade following the official expulsion of the Jews, the threat of the Spanish Inquisition sent many New Christians fleeing to the relative safety of the kingdom of Portugal, where an Inquisition had not yet been instituted.

Among the refugees to Portugal were a couple known as Fernão da Orta and Lenore Gomes. Both had been born in the town of Valencia de Alcántara, near the border with Portugal; Fernão in 1456 and Lenore probably in the late 1470s. The town was something of a Jewish centre; to this day it boasts one of the best-preserved Gothic Jewish quarters in Spain. But it was populated also by Christians and Muslims, and one presumes that Fernão, who worked as a small trader, would have had to operate professionally in a multilingual environment that included Castilian Spanish, Ladino, and Mozarabic—a highly Arabized Romance vernacular spoken by Spanish Muslims as well as many Christians. With the threat of the Inquisition, Fernão and Lenore fled Spain and settled in the Portuguese border town of Castelo de Vide, a mere 28 kilometres away. Although they lived in the town's thriving Jewish quarter (which, in the years after the expulsion, was something of a way-station for émigré Spanish Jews), they both became New Christians, nominally converting to Catholicism in 1497. With this cover, they permitted themselves to raise a family: Garcia was born in 1500 or 1501, and his sisters Violante, Catarina, and Isabel were born in 1502, 1503 and 1504 respectively.

These, at least, were their New Christian names. But records indicate that the Ortas remained practicing Jews and retained secret Hebrew names. It seems that Garcia's was Avraham, or Abraham; we know that his father's was Yitzhak, or Isaac. In the Bible, Isaac is the son of the aged patriarch Abraham. But in the case of Fernão and Garcia, this relationship was reversed: old Isaac became father to Abraham. Who knows why Fernão/Yitzhak chose his namesake's father's name for his son—and whether he even had any choice in the matter. For all we know, Garcia/Avraham was named, as is frequent Jewish custom, after another dead relative. But it's tempting to imagine the freshly escaped Fernão and Lenore hoping for a new beginning, a new Abrahamic line, in Portugal and Castelo de Vide.

In 1500, when Garcia was born, his parents had reason to be at least guardedly hopeful. The situation on the ground was rather different in Portugal from what it was in Spain. Tens of thousands of Jews had fled to Portugal following the 1492 expulsion; in 1494, the newly crowned King Manuel declared the migrants free, though Spanish pressure following Manuel's marriage to Isabella of Aragon led to an edict in December 1496 that all Portuguese Jews convert (as the Ortas did). Still, despite local flare-ups, such as the 1506 massacre of Jews in Lisbon, the attitude of the crown remained relatively tolerant. Indeed, after some debate over whether to follow the Spanish example, the Portuguese authorities assured its New Christian communities that they would be protected. With the conversion edict of 1496, Manuel promised not to inquire into New Christians' faith for a grace period of thirty years; he renewed the pledge in 1504. After all, Portugal's growing maritime power was dependent not just on skilled Jewish labour—Vasco da Gama's navigator-astronomer Abraão Zarcuto, for example, was a Jew—but also on wealthy New Christian merchant families with international connections. These connections were often Judaeo-Muslim, tracing the trajectory of old affiliations from the dispersed culture of Al-Andalus, extending through North Africa and the Ottoman Empire to the Arabian Peninsula and the Indian Ocean.

Yet a chilling wind of change blew through Portugal as Spanish influence grew in the second and third decades of the sixteenth century. The signs were unmistakable: despite Manuel's previous promises of protection, the Inquisition was to be instituted after all. As part of the terms of his second marriage, to Isabella's sister Maria of Aragon in 1515, Manuel had consented to setting up a Portuguese Inquisition at the end of the thirty-year grace period, now scheduled to expire in 1534. Although the Inquisition wasn't formally instituted until 1536, and despite the nominal ban on New Christians leaving Portugal, many fled the country in the wake of Manuel's change of heart. Several decades later, after the 1579 decree of toleration was issued in Utrecht, a substantial number of Portugal's New Christians would land up in Amsterdam and convert back to Judaism; a grandchild of one of these refugees was the great Dutch philosopher Baruch Spinoza. Others fled to Morocco, Cairo, and Istanbul. But in the 1530s, as the spectre of the grace period's expiration loomed, another destination appealed to some New Christians even more: the Portuguese Indian colony of Goa.

◆

Given its timing, Orta's decision in 1534 to leave his post at the University of Lisbon and accompany Martim Afonso de Sousa to India was almost certainly motivated not by patriotism, but by a more pressing desire to save himself from religious scrutiny. Orta probably made the shrewd calculation that the upcoming Portuguese Inquisition would not chase him to India. Indeed, Goa was spared the auto-da-fé for nearly twenty-five years after the Inquisition came to Portugal. And though records are sketchy, Goa seems to have hosted a small yet significant exodus of New Christians looking for a place of refuge. Many were merchants. Some were relatively non-wealthy if respected physicians like Orta. And others were well-off New Christian families like the De Solises, cousins of the Ortas who arrived with their 17-year-old daughter Brianda in 1541. Eight years later, after the Inquisition in Lisbon had first imprisoned and then abruptly freed Orta's elderly mother, Lenore Gomes Orta, as well as two of his sisters, they too fled to Goa. It is likely that Orta used high-ranking contacts back in Lisbon—perhaps even Martim Afonso de Sousa—to rescue them.

For those New Christians who still secretly professed Judaism, Goa had much to recommend it. The city, originally a possession of the Hindu kingdom of Vijayanagar but captured and rebuilt by the Muslim sultanate of Bijapur in the late fifteenth century, already had a Jewish population prior to its conquest by Afonso de Albuquerque in 1510. Some of the Bijapuri Jews appear to have been Spanish speakers and therefore part of the larger transnational Judaeo-Muslim networks that connected the Iberian peninsula and North Africa to South Asia via the Ottoman Empire and the Arabian Peninsula. There is no reason to believe that these original Jews left after the Portuguese conquest: Albuquerque gained the support of local Hindus and Muslims by granting them their religious freedom, and it is likely that the Bijapuri Jews would have been given a similar promise. Indeed, their polyglot skills would have made them useful to the fledgling Portuguese Indian state as go-betweens with local Konkani, Marathi, and Arabic-speaking rulers. In the Inquisition-free years before and after Orta's arrival, Goa was a multicultural city where people of many ethnicities, tongues, and faiths mingled. For someone like Lenore Gomes Orta, it may even have seemed a little like the pre-expulsion multicultural community of Valencia de Alcántara.

Orta was able to lead multiple lives in Goa. He publicly served powerful Christian amos from Martim Afonso de Sousa to Pedro Mascharenas. In his professional dealings, he mingled with mostly Muslim hakeems and some Hindu physicians such as Malupa. But in his domestic life, he was part of Goa's undercover Jewish world. He married his cousin Brianda, the teenaged scion of the émigré de Solis family, in the 1540s; they required a special license to wed because of their close blood relation. Given the twenty-four-year age difference between them, they may not have enjoyed a strong emotional connection. Their families probably forced the match on both of them—or, at the very least, on Brianda—in the interest of maintaining the bonds of New Christian community. In any case, Orta makes no mention of his wife in the *Colloquies*, and he spent considerable time in Ahmadnagar away from their home in Velha Goa's Rua dos Namorados.

Over the decades from the 1540s to the 1560s, life for Goa's Jews gradually changed for the worse. Another New Christian physician, Jeronimo Dias, had been convicted of heresy, strangled, and burned in 1543. Two years later, Francis Xavier, the Jesuit missionary, requested the introduction of a Goan Inquisition. His ostensible target was 'rice Christians'—local Hindus who had converted only in name, and continued to engage in Hindu practices. When the Inquisition was finally established in 1560, however, the appointed inquisitors went after New Christians as well as crypto-Hindus. Overnight, a city which had provided a haven for Sephardic refugees became a deathtrap. The Inquisition set itself up in the old Bijapuri palace of the Sabaio Adil Khan, the grand building in which the viceroys had lived until 1554. (Orta no doubt visited the palace many times while serving de Sousa.) Among those killed were Orta's sister Catarina, who was burnt at the stake 'as an impenitent Jewess' in 1569, a year after Garcia's death. Orta's high standing with the authorities could no longer protect her, though he had succeeded in keeping the inquisitors away from his own door.

The looming threat of a Goan Inquisition may have been one of the reasons why Orta decided to spend considerable time in Ahmadnagar during the late 1540s and 1550s. Here he could do the Portuguese state some service, but also remain at a safe distance from it. And in Ahmadnagar, he found elements of the Judaeo-Muslim nexus which so distinguished Sephardic Iberian culture. These included not only the Arabic medical knowledge and practice of the nizam's court but also another New Christian renegade seeking shelter from the violence of the Portuguese state. We have already met him—Sancho Pires, known as Firangi Khan. This supposedly Portuguese Christian convert to Islam, wanted on a murder charge in Goa, was almost certainly born into an émigré Spanish marrano family. Pires's and Orta's shared background might help explain the surprisingly risky decision the physician made to plead the renegade's case for rehabilitation to the then Portuguese Viceroy of India, Afonso de Noronha. Pires had taken a leading role in the Ahmadnagar succession battle following the nizam shah's death in 1553; backing the eventual winner, Nizam Hosain Shah, he was mortally wounded one year later in a battle with Bijapuri forces at the Deccan fort of Gulbarga. In his petition to de Noronha, Orta claimed that Pires was not really Muslim at all, having willed much of his estate to Portuguese churches and charities. One might recognize in Orta's plea for Pires's good moral character—his spirited disavowal of the renegade's comfort with Islamic culture, his equally spirited insistence on Pires's true Christian devotion—a mirror image of the Indo-Sephardic physician's own public pretence to the Portuguese authorities.

It was a pretence Orta was unable to sustain, despite his initial burial in a Goan Catholic cathedral. A few months after Orta's death, his frightened brother-in-law—Catarina's husband—confessed to the Inquisition that the distinguished tenant of Bombay and servant of two viceroys had believed, among other abominable heresies:

...that the Law of Moses was the true Law; that they should live therein and keep the feast of Yom Kippur...and that they should keep the Sabbath on Saturdays, and change into clean shirts and linen on that day, and should light more tapers in the candlesticks than usual, and cleaner, and with more oil. That the [Old Testament] prophecies were not yet fulfilled. That Christ was not the son of God; that the Jews had not killed him, but he had died of old age, and he was the son of Miriam and Joseph.

We don't know how many of these claims were true; the fear of torture may have led Orta's brother-in-law to affirm things that were false. Indeed, Catarina da Orta renounced some of the claims she made in her own interrogation, including the assertion that Brianda had borrowed a shirt in which to wrap and dispose of her husband's corpse—an assertion she possibly made to hide the fact that Orta had been buried with Jewish rites. Yet this was enough for the Inquisition to order, in 1580, that Orta's remains be posthumously disinterred and incinerated, with the ashes thrown into the Mandavi River.

◆

How much, if at all, can we read Orta's Jewishness back into the *Colloquies*? And how might doing so contribute to our understanding of what it means for a firangi to become Indian? Like the eponymous letter in Edgar Allan Poe's *The Purloined Letter*, Orta's Jewishness is an open secret throughout the *Colloquies*: not immediately visible to us precisely because it is there in front of us, the last place we would look for it. Yet once we become aware of it, it's hard not to see it everywhere.

On the one hand, Orta goes through the motions of sounding like a dutiful, if not particularly religious, Roman Catholic. He refers to a Dominican friar as a member of 'our faith', welcomes the mass conversions of Tamil pearl fishermen undertaken by Miguel Vaz and Francis Xavier in south India, and refers critically to Lutheran Protestantism. On the other hand, Jews from all over the world make repeated cameo appearances in Orta's narrative as reliable first-hand sources of medical knowledge. His colloquy about the aloe is partly influenced by a conversation with some Jews from Jerusalem, his understanding of cardamom's etymological link to the Arabic hamama is derived from a Spanish-speaking Jewish apothecary, and his knowledge of certain medical materials is indebted to a Jewish trader from Turkey.

These divergent tendencies in the *Colloquies* suggest three things: Orta, like his fellow New Christians in Portugal, felt compelled to pass as a Catholic; despite the pressure to pass, there were many travellers and migrants in India at this time who self-identified as Jewish; and whatever pressure to hide their identities these Jews may or may not have felt in other Portuguese company, they didn't feel any such pressure when talking with Orta.

In addition to its many 'authentic' Jews, the *Colloquies* are also haunted by the spectre of what we might call 'not-quite-Jews'—peoples mistakenly regarded by Indian Muslims and Portuguese Christians as Jewish. Orta considers a distinctly non-Jewish ritual performed by a supposedly Jewish shoemaker community in the nizam shah's territories (soaking cows on one side and burning them on another). He also notes of Gujarati Parsis that although 'we Portuguese call them Jews', they 'do not circumcise nor are forbidden pork'. It is hard not to assume that Orta understood these 'not-quite Jews' through the prism of his own embodied experience of Jewishness, particularly in relation to matters of diet. And indeed, a Jewish dietary prohibition might subtly shape another of Orta's observations in the *Colloquies*. While discussing the mango, Dr Ruano abruptly asks him if it is true that Indians do not eat either fish or milk. Orta replies that the Gentios, or Hindus, do 'eat milk *with* some fish, but I do not know whether they say that it does so much harm.' The combination of eating milk with fish is a particularly odd detail to single out for attention—unless, of course, the person who does so has a heightened sense of, and even subscribes to, the Jewish dietary law that forbids meat and milk being served on the same plate.

But it would be a mistake to look for Orta's Jewishness in whatever hints the *Colloquies* might offer of a traditionally Jewish body and its habits. For Orta's was probably not the body of a typically orthodox Jew. Like most Portuguese New Christians born after the mass conversion edict of December 1496, it's unlikely Orta was circumcised. It's just as unlikely that he would have been able to observe Jewish dietary law, as a refusal to eat pork in Portuguese Christian company would no doubt have drawn suspicion. Instead, his was what we might call a migratory body: migratory both because it had travelled a great distance from Europe to India and because it had been forced to move away from the 'proper' bodily behaviours mandated by the religion he secretly professed. It was a body that, by virtue of the historical circumstances into which it was born and the multicultural spaces in which it lived, had been trained to inhabit otherness—whether understood gastronomically, culturally, linguistically, or religiously—as a basic survival strategy. It is in the apparently self-erasing embrace of India's otherness, I would argue, that Orta's Jewishness is paradoxically most visible in the *Colloquies*.

An embrace of otherness had distinguished Iberian Jewish culture for close to 500 years prior to the Spanish reconquista. As we have seen, to be Jewish in medieval Al-Andalus meant to be in close, culturally transformative proximity to non-Jews—in particular, to Muslims. A vestigial memory of this proximity pervades the *Colloquies*. Near the beginning of the treatise, Dr Ruano notes the recent degeneration of medical education in Spain, lamenting to Orta that 'now you have neither masters nor preceptors in Salamanca or Alcalá, for all are either dead or banished'. Ruano's reference to the 'banished' masters implicitly acknowledges how, in the wake of the 1492 expulsion, Spain had lost a rich Judaeo-Muslim corpus of medical knowledge with deep roots in Andalusian Arabic culture. This corpus derived not only from Averroës, author of the influential medical treatise *Kitab al-Kulliyat fi al-Tibb* (Book of Generalities), but also from Arab-speaking Jewish physicians such as Hasdai ibn Shaprut of Córdoba, Abraham ben David of Catalonia, and Joshua ben Joseph of Lorca. The university town in which Orta studied medicine, Alcalá de Henares, still boasts Moorish and Jewish quarters. Its name derives from the Arabic 'al-qal'a', meaning 'the fort' (compare the Hindi/Urdu qila); and within Alcalá's fort of medical study, Avicenna had once been the guiding light. Avicenna's five-volume treatise *Al-Kanun al-Tibb* (The General Canon), one of the cornerstones of Andalusian medical theory and practice, was avidly pored over by Jewish as well as Muslim physicians. Rather than performing a radical break with Iberian medical tradition, then, Orta's embrace of Avicenna in Ahmadnagar in fact marked a conscious return to it, at least in its Judaeo-Muslim form. Indeed, like his Sephardic medical forbears, Orta wrote with an Arabic-language edition of Avicenna on his desk in his Goan study.

As this suggests, the Judaeo-Muslim nexus Orta gravitated towards was linguistic as much as it was medical. What languages did Orta speak? Obviously Portuguese, the language in which the *Colloquies* were written—though his is a very Spanish-inflected Portuguese, bearing the trace of his parents' dialect and his education in Salamanca and Alcalá de Henares. He was clearly comfortable with Greek and Latin, which would have been de rigueur in his university studies. Perhaps Orta also spoke Ladino, the astonishingly hybrid language of Sephardic Jews in the

Iberian peninsula, Morocco, and Turkey. And he was certainly adept in a variety of Indian languages—the *Colloquies* show him to have at least some working knowledge of Malayalam, Konkani, Gujarati and Dakhni. But the language that connected Orta's Sephardic familial past to his Indian present was Arabic—the language of Judaeo-Muslim medicine in both Al-Andalus and Ahmadnagar.

Orta clearly knew enough Arabic to get by. In the *Colloquies*, he confesses that he reads the Arabic of Avicenna with the help of a Portuguese translation; but, as he notes, Avicenna's Arabic is the Syrian Arabic of the east, not the rather different western Arabic of the Maghreb, with which he seems to have had some basic familiarity. Orta clearly coveted a greater command of learned Arabic, and not just because it helped him better understand Avicenna. It was also the cosmopolitan lingua franca of sixteenth-century Muslim Indian sultanates, from the nizam's court in Ahmadnagar to the retinues of Sultan Qutb-ud-Din Bahadur Shah in Gujarat and Qasim Barid, ruler of the Bidar Sultanate. Bahadur Shah's Portuguese interpreter, a Parsi named Khwaja Percolim, taught Orta the Arabic names for aloe and other plants; and Orta was sufficiently fluent in written as well as spoken Arabic that he was able to dispense a prescription in Bidar for Qasim Barid's brother, Hamjam. Here we can witness the extraordinary multiculturalism of the Arabic-speaking Indian world. Hamjam was descended from a Turkish slave in Christian Georgia; yet in Muslim Bidar, he could converse in Arabic with a Spanish-educated Sephardic Jew from Portugal.

Orta's Arabic had a distinctively Jewish character, and not just because of its closeness to Hebrew. (Orta refers, for example, to the Arabic letters alif and ayn, which have more or less identical names in Hebrew.) Arabic was also one of the languages in which his discussions with Jews from other parts of the world were conducted. Many of these discussions took place in Spanish, but he and his Jewish interlocutors assumed that some mastery of Arabic was necessary to function as both a physician and an informed global traveller. Orta not only tells us that he learned the Arabic names of some Indian medicines from Jewish interlocutors; he also reports a discussion he had concerning the Arabic etymologies of Spanish place names with a Jew named Isaac of Cairo. This Isaac was a fascinating figure who exemplified the global Judaeo-Muslim networks that persisted in the wake of the Spanish reconquista. A relative of Orta's, he was something of a stateless double and even triple agent, working as a diplomat and spy for Portuguese, Ottoman, and Indian handlers.

Orta may not have led such a glitteringly glamorous life. But his state affiliations to a large extent mirrored Isaac of Cairo's, and in a fashion typical of migrant Sephardic Jews in the decades after 1492. Like Isaac, Orta could operate successfully within a variety of cultural locations. As a New Christian who had diligently leveraged the support of his political patrons in order to efface the 'newness' of his 'Christianity', he became a colonial householder in Bombay. But as a Sephardic physician deeply immersed in Judaeo-Muslim cultural networks that extended from the Iberian peninsula to India, he also found it easy to enter the Indo-Islamic world of the Ahmadnagar court as an Arabic-speaking colleague of Muslim hakeems. The turnstile between his Portuguese and Indian worlds swung both ways. And that is why he was not so much a colonial doctor or a quit-rent master as a hakeem of Bombay and Ahmadnagar, a Portuguese servant who had also become Indian. Orta's identity was not singular, but organized around fault lines that split and pluralized him. Just like the doubleness of the *Colloquies'* dialogues, where Orta's voice is divided between two different speakers (the character named Orta and the imaginary Dr Ruano), so was his lived identity not singular, but multiple.

Orta's secret Hebrew name, Avraham, turns out to have been particularly apt. The biblical Abraham was the father of two lineages— the Jews through his younger son Isaac, and the Arabs through his elder son Ishmael. In his story we can witness the mythical origin of the Judaeo-Muslim nexus in which Orta felt so at home. Yet Garcia/ Avraham also produced two other lineages: the official Portuguese story of a colonialist hero, which he himself worked hard to project, and the subaltern story of a hakeem of Bombay who became Indian through his immersion in desi food and Indo-Islamic culture. The *Colloquies'* only reference to the biblical Abraham seems to capture something of this subaltern story. Relating a tale he heard from a Dominican bishop who had spent considerable time in the Middle East and was fluent in Arabic, Orta reports that:

> Abraham, when God called him from Ur, a city of the Chaldees, went to Aleppo, the chief city of Syria, and took great quantities of cattle. He gave milk for all the necessitous and poor to drink, and they came for it every day. These poor people when they came asked for *yalep*, which means a question: 'order where we shall eat now'. This was the reason why that name was given to the land.

The Bishop said that this was the tradition of the old people of Aleppo, who believed that it was inhabited and ruled by Abraham.

This Abraham was less a patriarchal founder of lineages than a migrant, as too was the Avraham who wrote these lines. And the biblical Chaldean understood the transformative power of food in a new location, as too did the sixteenth-century firangi. Just like the plants from Orta's garden or the fragrant cloves he smelled off the Malabar Coast, the milk of Abraham's cattle in Aleppo did more than just restore health. It also prompted a sense of belonging to a new land. In this short story of new selves connected to medicinal foodstuffs and new homes, Garcia da Orta, the hakeem of Bombay and Ahmadnagar, pithily summarizes his own Abrahamic saga of becoming Indian.

| THOMAS STEPHENS/PÂTRI GURU,
THE KAVI OF RACHOL

What does it mean to say 'this is my body'? And what does it mean
to say 'this is my body' when the body in question has migrated from
England to India, lived there for forty years, and changed greatly from
the body it used to be? How might 'my body' have changed not just
in its appearance but also its skills, its pleasures, and its relations to the
local environment? Is it still 'my body' at all? These are the questions
posed by the extraordinary story of Father Thomas Stephens, also known
as Tomás Estêvão, also known as Pâtri Guru.

Stephens may have been among the first priests to frequent the
Bom Jesus Basilica. This grand Jesuit cathedral in Velha Goa, consecrated
in 1605, houses the mortal remains of St Francis Xavier. In recent
years, a prominent inscription—HI MHO JHI KUDD—has been placed
beneath the cathedral altar. The inscription is a Konkani translation of
the Latin 'hoc est corpus meum' (this is my body), the ritual formula
of the Eucharist spoken by the priest as part of the Roman Catholic
Mass. In its more familiar Western guises, whether Latin or English, the
words spoken by the priest as he holds aloft the Host or communion
wafer supposedly induce the miracle of transubstantiation, in which the
inert wafer is translated into the living flesh of Jesus. This first translation
enables a second. Once the priest has placed the wafer in the mouth
of the Christian believer, she receives the grace of God and becomes
part of the spiritual body of Jesus. The transformative power of the
Eucharist is, in other words, a doubly oral one. The act of speaking
translates dead matter into living flesh; the act of eating living flesh
translates an individual into a member of a spiritual community. Both
acts have been performed for over 400 years in the Bom Jesus Basilica.

The power of the Eucharist, however, doesn't quite capture all the
resonances of 'hi mho jhi kudd'. The Konkani inscription on the Bom
Jesus Basilica altar performs a rather different kind of translation, one that
has little to do with the translation of a wafer into the body of Christ
or an individual into a member of a larger spiritual community. The
inscription also translates something Western into an Indian form: most
obviously, the Latin 'hoc est corpus meum' is rendered into Konkani. In
the case of Thomas Stephens—a lifelong advocate for making Christian
ideas available in Indian tongues—the linguistic translation performed

by 'hi mho jhi kudd' also mirrors the more complex bodily translation of an Englishman into a Konkani kavi or poet.

As we will see, this second kind of translation again entails the transformative power of language and eating. But unlike the transcendent movement away from the flesh implicit in the conventional Eucharist formula of 'this is my body', the translation suggested by 'hi mho jhi kudd' hints at an altogether more worldly transformation—the firangi body that has morphed, through its everyday oral activity on the Konkan Coast, into something Indian. There is no assurance of transcendence here, no redemptive spiritual endpoint; instead there is simply an ongoing process of fleshly alteration. This process is the story of Stephens's firangi flesh. It is also a story of the transformative power of non-human flesh: the flesh of the coconut. If Orta was an aam aadmi or mango man, Stephens was a naariyal kavi—a coconut poet.

◆

Like most westerners for whom his name is at all familiar, I first encountered Father Thomas Stephens as a passing reference in a well-known sixteenth-century travel narrative about India and Southeast Asia. This narrative is often treated as the opening chapter in the history of British colonialism in the Orient, with its author lauded—or damned—as the 'pioneer' of English travel to India. The narrative chronicles the admittedly extraordinary adventures in Asia over a period of eight years, from 1583 to 1591, of Ralph Fitch, a gentleman merchant of London. The sections about India include accounts of Portuguese Goa, the sultanate of Golconda, Akbar's court in Fatehpur Sikri, a journey down the Yamuna River to Allahabad with a convoy of boats carrying salt, carpets and opium, and subsequent voyages down the Ganges to Benares, Patna, Hooghly and Chittagong. Fitch had travelled to Asia as a representative of the English Levant Company, some of whose directors were later to become primary shareholders in the East India Company chartered in 1600; his travel narrative about India and the East, much read in the 1590s, helped attract investors to the new company. Yet Fitch's journey came perilously close to ending before it had even started. Stephens played a crucial role in averting the disaster that befell Fitch upon his arrival in India.

In 1583, Fitch and four other Englishmen—two merchants named John Eldred and John Newberry, a jeweller named William Leeds, and a painter named James Story—had sailed from England to Aleppo on a ship called *Tiger*, with a plan to travel overland to Basra and then by sea to India. It was the beginning of a journey that seems to have captured the imagination of Fitch's countrymen. Even twenty years later Shakespeare remembered it in *Macbeth*: one of the witches talks of a 'sailor's wife' whose 'husband's to Aleppo gone, master o' the Tiger'. Shakespeare's decision to give these lines to a witch hints at how Fitch's Asian journey may have been regarded by some of his country people as something dangerous, even sinister. Indeed, no matter how much Fitch presented his travels as fuelled by a simple wish to 'see the countries of the East India', he obviously had more clandestine motives. He and his companions had set their sights on breaking into Portugal's lucrative trade with the Orient; in particular, they almost certainly had an eye on the illicit export of Indian precious stones, a practice outlawed by the Mughals and heavily policed by the Portuguese Estado da Índia in Goa. This might explain why Leeds, a jeweller rather than a merchant, was among the travellers. The Portuguese authorities certainly smelled a rat. Eldred had left the party at Basra; but when his four companions proceeded to Ormuz—a Persian Gulf island captured and fortified by Afonso de Albuquerque in 1507 for use as an Indian staging-post—they were arrested by the Portuguese, deported to Goa, and imprisoned on suspicion of commercial espionage.

Things looked grim for the four Englishmen. But after what Eldred describes as a 'long and cruel imprisonment', though it amounted to only a couple of weeks, they were suddenly released on 22 December 1583. Their good fortune was almost entirely due to the intervention of two Jesuit priests—Father Thomas Stephens, an Englishman, and Father Marco, a Fleming—both of whom bought the canard that Stephens's erstwhile countrymen were good Catholics in need of succour. The two Jesuits had generously posted a bond of 2,000 ducats as assurance that the Englishmen would not flee Goa. Despite the priests' efforts, Fitch, Leeds and Newberry stole away from the Portuguese colony. (Story, the painter, opted to stay in the Jesuit College of Saint Paul, where he briefly painted religious murals before decamping to marry a half-Indian woman.) The three English escapees went to Golconda, the site of the diamond mines, and then eventually made their way to the Mughal courts of Agra and Fatehpur Sikri, where Leeds proceeded to find employment with the emperor Akbar; we do not know what became of him after this. Newberry left for Lahore, after which he too disappears from the record, quite likely the victim of a robbery-murder in Punjab. Fitch, now alone, embarked on his river journeys to Bihar, Bengal, Burma and beyond, before returning to England, via Goa, in 1591.

The alleged English 'pioneer' in India tells us next to nothing about his Jesuit countryman who had reached Goa five years before him, and whose intervention saved him from prison and possibly worse. In his travel narrative, Fitch mentions only that Stephens was 'an English Jesuit'; in a private letter written from Goa in January 1584, he reveals a fraction more, saying that Stephens and Marco 'did sue for us unto the Viceroy and other officers', and 'if they had not stuck to us, if we had escaped with our lives yet we had long imprisonment'. Fitch's relative terseness about his Good Samaritan may have been born of either Protestant animosity or bad conscience, as Stephens's credit in Goa was in all likelihood somewhat compromised by Fitch and his colleagues' escape. Even if Stephens' motive for helping Fitch was less altruistic than it might seem—a Dutchman living in Goa at the time, Jan Hughen van Linschoten, claims that the Jesuits were interested in Fitch and his companions because they hoped to make money off them—it's hard to imagine Stephens not feeling burned by Fitch's default on a bond for which he had stood as surety. If not for the man whom Fitch characterizes curtly as the 'English Jesuit', however, it is conceivable that the East India Company wouldn't have come into being, for without Stephens's aid Fitch couldn't have finished the journey and written the travel narrative that prompted the Company's founding.

Yet Stephens's full story reveals him as less a foundational hero than a troubler of India's subsequent colonial history. And this is because his story crosses borders of language and culture in ways that complicate Fitch's reference to him as 'English'. Although Stephens appears only as a single passing reference in Fitch's narrative, we can still piece together his biography from shreds and fragments written in three different languages: English, Latin, and Portuguese. And we can supplement these with the evidence of a remarkable text in a fourth and a fifth language, written by Stephens himself.

Arguably the greatest work of English literature in the seventeenth century is John Milton's *Paradise Lost*, an epic twelve-book poem about the revolt of Satan and the other fallen angels, Adam and Eve's disobedience in the Garden of Eden, and the prophesied coming of Christ. The poem, in spite of its Christian theme, is a brilliant and unconventional meditation on political authority, free will and rebellion in which Satan, who curiously has to journey through the East Indies and

JONATHAN GIL HARRIS

Bengal to reach Paradise, assumes many of the qualities of an epic hero. Some sixty years before the publication of *Paradise Lost*, Stephens wrote an equally long poem on a similar subject—the Christian history of the world from Creation to the coming of Christ—with similarly unorthodox nuances. And like Milton's epic, Stephens's poem derives much of its force from its association, autobiographical in this instance, with a dissident traveller in an Indian Paradise. Stephens ought to be regarded as one of the great Renaissance English poets. But his accomplishment is more or less completely unsung, for one simple reason: he wrote his poem not in English, but in Marathi and Konkani.

So who was this Indian-language English predecessor of Milton?

◆

Stephens was born into a merchant family in the small hamlet of Bushton in Wiltshire, about 150 kilometres west of London, in 1550. We know little about his parents. His father, also named Thomas, was assessed in 1576 for personal goods worth £15, which suggests he was reasonably yet not exorbitantly well off. We know even less about the family's religious faith, although it is apparent from Stephens' later correspondence with his brother Richard that the latter was also an observant Catholic. Whether the brothers were brought up Catholic, or whether they came to the faith later, is unclear. Like many people at this volatile time when England's official state religion lurched repeatedly between Catholicism and Protestantism, Stephens's parents may have hedged their bets, at least publically. But it is safe to conclude that Stephens's adult religious convictions were forged in the crucible of England's mid-century sectarian tensions, over the course of which Catholicism shifted from being the nation's traditional religion into a vigorously suppressed species of heresy.

Stephens was educated at Winchester College, one of England's most venerable public schools, where he was elected fellow in 1564. It was founded in 1382 by the Bishop of Winchester, William of Wykeham, as a preparatory school for students at Oxford's New College, also founded three years earlier by Wykeham. At Winchester, Stephens would have received a thorough education in Greek and Latin; he would have also enjoyed an unusually good training in poetry. Christopher Johnson, who was appointed Master of the College in 1560 and almost certainly taught Stephens, was a gifted scholar of rhetoric as well as a Latin poet of some acclaim. Johnson's skills in Latin verse would have opened up Stephens to the arts of prosody—how to use rhyme and how to construct a metrically pleasant line on the model of Plautus, Horace and Virgil. Johnson's classes would have also made Stephens feel more at home in the language of the Roman Church. While Winchester may not have been a seething hotbed of Catholic activity during Stephens's time there, the Protestant authorities had moved to ban the college from teaching Latin graces, now considered too Catholic a ritual. Perhaps there was still a hint of the old faith in the air when Stephens was at Winchester: the college produced an unusual number of students who went on to become militant Catholics dedicated to overthrowing the Protestant Queen Elizabeth, including the Gunpowder Plot conspirator Henry Garnett and the polemicist priest Nicholas Sander.

Like many of his fellow Winchester College graduates, Stephens was groomed to study at New College in Oxford. Robert Parsons, a Jesuit dissident who came to know him some years later in Rome, claimed that Stephens had not only studied at New College but was also on very close terms with the famous Catholic martyr Edmund Campion, who took his master's degree there in 1564 and taught at Oxford until 1569. We cannot be sure, however, of the truth of Parsons's claim. Campion was ten years older than Stephens, so hardly university-friend material. And Campion was at that time not yet a Jesuit, or even a confirmed Catholic; indeed, in 1564 he received holy orders as a deacon in the Church of England. Further complicating Parsons's claim is the fact that Stephens's name does not appear in any of the Oxford University records from the 1560s. He himself states elsewhere that he only ever studied humanities privately. Still, if Stephens did indeed go to Oxford, and was already a devout Catholic at that time, it would have been very hard for him to continue his studies there: in a show of conformity with the avowedly Protestant Queen Elizabeth upon her accession to the throne in 1559, Oxford University had vigorously purged itself of Catholics. Perhaps Stephens had gone up to Oxford in the mid 1560s as a closet Catholic of only mild conviction, but felt forced to leave and commence private studies as his faith grew stronger and the purges became more insistent. Yet for Stephens, as for many of his Catholic peers, Campion must have seemed a glamorous role model after his dramatic resignation from Oxford in 1569. It is quite conceivable that the charismatic Campion's post-Oxford career inspired some of his former fellows and pupils—perhaps Stephens among them—to follow his path into Jesuit orders.

In about 1572, Stephens became attached to Thomas Pounde, a nephew of the Earl of Southampton and, like him, a graduate of Winchester College. Pounde had been a favourite of Queen Elizabeth's at court but had been expelled in 1571, quite possibly for dissolute behaviour. After licking his wounds for some time at his family estate, he got religion and became an underground proselytizer for Roman Catholicism. Stephens reportedly travelled throughout England with Pounde for two years disguised as his servant, helping him to cultivate a secret Catholic network. Together they drifted towards the Jesuit path in which Campion had already begun to take an interest. Pounde in particular had become excited by letters from India about Francis Xavier and the Jesuit mission's success in converting Hindus. Together, Pounde and Stephens seem to have hatched a mad dream of going together to Goa to join the mission and continue its work.

But the dream turned to dust in 1574, when Pounde was abruptly arrested and imprisoned. He was to spend thirty years in jail as a religious dissident. Immediately after Pounde's capture, Stephens fled to Rome—we don't know how—and enrolled as a novitiate in the Society of Jesus. One of the other students was his fellow Winchester graduate and the later-to-be-notorious Gunpowder Plot martyr Henry Garnett. Stephens did not forget Pounde. He wrote a petition on behalf of his friend to the Society of Jesus, requesting that Pounde be formally admitted to the society as a layman; in the petition, which was granted in 1578, he praised Pounde for his asceticism, saying that 'for most of the time in which I lived with him he led a most austere life and used no bed, but slept on the ground'. And Stephens continued to nurse Pounde's dream of India. In 1579, the Society finally granted him permission to go to Goa to aid the Jesuit mission there. Stephens travelled first to Lisbon, from where he set sail with twelve other Jesuit missionaries as part of a fleet of five ships on 4 April 1579. The fleet voyaged around the Cape of Good Hope and arrived in Goa on 24 October.

◆

Seventeen days after Stephens's arrival in India, he wrote a letter to his father describing the long sea journey. It is a fascinating document, not least because it is the only surviving piece of writing by Stephens in his native English. Surprisingly, given the religious zeal that had prompted his relocation, there is little in the letter that sounds like it comes from the pen of a dissident Jesuit missionary. There are occasional mentions of the providence of God with regard to Stephens's health and the good winds that propelled the ship to India. But these are perfunctory inshallahs, and no more zealous than anything we'd expect even from a mainstream English Anglican. Stephens begins the letter by giving commendations to his mother; his tone of filial obligation trumps all religious piety, suggesting that perhaps his parents were not thrilled by his mission—or, perhaps more likely, that he was watchful about what he wrote back to a country where Catholics in general, and Jesuits in particular, were now regarded as seditious enemies of the state.

Foregoing any display of missionary zeal, then, the letter cleaves more closely to another genre: the fabulous travelogue. Much of Stephens's letter is devoted to detailed descriptions of exotic marvels that he saw during his sea voyage around Africa and the Cape of Good Hope—the stuff of John Mandeville and other medieval travellers' tales. He tells his father about his sighting of what seems to be a Portuguese man o' war or Medusa jellyfish, which he characterizes as 'a thing swimming upon the water like a cock's comb…almost like the swimmer of a fish in colour and bigness, and beareth underneath in the water strings which save it from turning over'; he describes 'strange kinds of fowls… some of them so great that their wings, being opened, from one point to the other contained seven spans'; and he talks of a miraculous fish 'as big, almost as a herring, which hath wings and flieth, and they are together in great number'. In all these instances, Stephens effaces himself; invisible in the marvellous scenes he describes, he offers each as an occasion 'to glorify Almighty God in His wonderful works and such variety in His creatures'.

Even as Stephens steps out of frame throughout this slideshow of exotic marvels, we can see another tendency lurking in the background of his letter. He also observes how the journey to India pathologically transforms the flesh of sea voyagers: Stephens explains, in what seems to be a description of the symptoms of scurvy, that those who undertake such a long journey are likely to 'fall into sundry diseases, their gums grow great and swell, and they are fain to cut them away, their legs swell, and all the body becometh sore and so benumbed, that they cannot stir hand or foot, and so they die for weakness'. And he talks also of the experience of crossing into the 'burning zone' near the equator, where sea voyagers suffer 'so many inconveniences of heats and lack of winds that they think themselves happy when they have passed it'. In other words, Stephens had begun to note the transformation of firangi bodies in foreign environments. He was not simply watching a marvellous spectacle of a new world: he recognized that this new world was, more accurately, an environment that had permeated his body, in the form of disease and heat.

Early modern European travellers' encounters with torrid Indian climates repeatedly made them aware of how their bodies were not unchanging, self-contained entities, but protean nodes in thermodynamic ecosystems. No matter how strong their cultural differences, Portuguese as much as English travellers to India had a common experience of exposure to a completely alien *heat*. And this exposure transformed their flesh. As the Portuguese priest Sebastien Manrique noted in 1640, to travel in India was to be 'heated by ague or by the heat which the titanic and glowing Planet causes'. According to the humoral understanding of their bodies that most European travellers brought with them to India, moreover, heat was not just a matter of the climate. It was also a property of certain types of food. The Italian traveller Pietro della Valle notes of four Carmelite monks he met in Goa: 'They came almost all sick, having suffered much in the Deserts of Arabia and other places of the journey, where they had felt great scarcity; and for all this they would needs observe their Lent and Fasts by the way, sustaining themselves almost solely with Dates, which is a very hot food; and withal the alteration of the air, both very hot, and unusual to them in the height of Summer, was the occasion of their being all sick.'

By contrast, Stephens claims to have arrived in Goa in good health, 'contrary to the expectation of many'. In his letter to his father he voices the hope that 'God send me my health so well in the land, if it may be to His honour and service'. Here we can see him nursing the hope that his identity, along with his health, might remain stable in the new environment: he believed that, unlike the other sick travellers, he might pull off the feat of arriving in India without India's pathogenic matter arriving in him. But his hope was quickly dashed. In a letter he wrote to his brother Richard in 1583, Stephens notes that he was 'tried by a serious illness' shortly after he reached India. We do not know what illness it was—quite possibly dysentery, the plague of many a new arrival—but it obviously felled him with particular force, given that he could still recall its gravity four years later. This was but the first of many bodily transformations that he was to undergo in Goa.

Stephens's letter to his brother makes clear that he had absorbed, upon arrival, Goa's bacteria or viruses. But his letter to his father, so sparse on detail about his Indian destination (he seems to have become exhausted describing the events of the journey), does show that his attention had already been arrested by another form of Indian matter he took into his body—a new plant he had not seen before: the coconut. He writes at the very end of the letter that 'the drink of this country is good water, or wine of the palm tree, or a fruit called cocoas'. Stephens had clearly already sampled coconut water, a powerful antidote to the loss of body salts caused by sweating in India's extreme heat. As we will see, this was the beginning of a long and profound relationship that transformed his body and its habits.

Stephens's passage to India, therefore, entailed the passage of India's physical elements through his flesh. To this extent Stephens's trajectory out of Europe parallels that of Garcia da Orta, who was equally enchanted and transformed by the new matter his body encountered in India. Also like Orta, Stephens opened up too to the languages of India, and in no small part because of his dissident religious convictions—an opening up that, as we will see, likewise transformed his flesh. But whereas Orta's dissident Jewishness directed him, via Arabic, towards the Indo-Islamic community of Ahmadnagar, Stephens's dissident Catholicism directed him, via Marathi and Konkani, towards a specifically Goan cultural syncretism that we might describe as Christo-Hindu.

◆

The Goa in which Stephens landed in 1579 was a somewhat different city from the one in which Garcia da Orta had first arrived in 1534. After three decades of relative religious tolerance following Portugal's conquest of the city from the Bijapur Sultanate, it had become an increasingly bellicose beacon of Christianity. The Inquisition had been set up in 1560 partly at the request of St Francis Xavier, the Jesuit priest whose name is now commemorated by a thousand schools and colleges in India. Thanks to Francis Xavier's aggressive work in converting Konkan Hindus—especially Brahmins—after he came to India in 1542, the Jesuit mission in Goa became a major force in shaping the culture of the region. Francis Xavier bequeathed to the mission a distinctive legacy of intolerance. Horrified by what he regarded as the idolatrousness of Goa's Hindus, Francis Xavier took little care to study their customs or learn their languages; his aim was to save souls. If Hindu temples needed to be destroyed to bring the word of God to the infidels, that was simply a grim necessity.

Stephens initially fitted in well with the mission. Despite the serious illness to which he succumbed in his first year, he moved smoothly to ordination as a priest six months after his arrival. His Jesuit masters, expecting him to take a prominent role in guiding native heathen souls to the light of the gospel, promptly dispatched him to the frontier parish of Salcete, south of the island of Goa and at the border with the Bijapur Sultanate. Salcete was at that time ground zero in the Jesuit conversion drive. When the Jesuits first arrived in there in 1560, they encountered a land of fifty-five villages ruled largely by Brahmins. Among a population of more than 80,000, there were just 100 Christians; the overwhelming majority worshipped the local deity Shantadurga (or Shanteri). Most of the Salcete Christians lived in or next to the fortress of Rachol, which had been wrested from the sultan of Bijapur in 1520 by the Portuguese, in league with the Vijayanagar Hindu king, Krishnadevaraya. Despite this Portuguese–Hindu partnership, the Jesuits advocated for a more aggressive stance against local religious practices. In 1569, with the full support of the Jesuits, the Portuguese razed a Brahmin temple in Rachol and more than 300 other temples throughout the rest of Salcete. The sultan of Bijapur, spying an opportunity to get back at the Portuguese, retaliated by burning down the Jesuit college and hospital in Margão, the main town in the parish. The Jesuits quickly rebuilt, however, adding for good measure a new seminary in Rachol with a beautiful baroque church, still functional today. They also persuaded the viceroy to ban all idolatrous practices in Salcete, including worship of Shantadurga.

By 1580, the year Stephens reached the parish, the Jesuits had succeeded in growing the local Christian community eight hundredfold to 8,000—most of them converted Brahmins. The Jesuit missionaries seem to have felt that, because of the Brahmins' priestly culture, they were proto-Christians, riper for indoctrination than the Bijapuri Muslims, who were deemed to be infidels and idolaters beyond the pale. Even as the Portuguese razed Hindu temples and banned local religious practices, they also allowed Brahmin converts to retain the signs of their caste, including the yajnopavita or sacred thread, provided these were blessed by a Catholic priest. Indeed, Goan Catholics descended from Brahmins are to this day still known as Bamonns. The Christianization of caste identity is symptomatic of a lethal distinction the Portuguese drew between good and bad Indians, one that played out in the religious violence that followed Stephens's arrival in Salcete. The ban on all idolatry in the parish led locals to make a formal appeal to the Spanish King Phillip

II, the widower husband of Mary Tudor who was also now ruler of Portugal; when the appeal was denied, tensions were further inflamed. After a Jesuit priest slaughtered a cow outside a temple, a number of missionaries were killed in retaliation.

The incident happened just before Stephens received news from his brother Richard of Edmund Campion's execution in England. Stephens's reply, composed in Latin, glorifies both the missionaries and Campion as martyrs, citing a fellow Jesuit who averred 'how beautiful it is to lay down one's life for the Faith'. But far more striking than his admiration for the gory deaths of his fellow missionaries, which he passes over quickly, is his delight in the behaviour of a Brahmin convert named Bernardo, whose story he tells at great length. This Bernardo had been entrusted to Stephens's care; he had made good progress in Latin and was sent from Salcete to Goa to continue his studies, but was kidnapped en route by his Brahmin family. Despite their best attempts to bring him back to the Brahmin fold, he resisted. Eventually he escaped, and returned to the Jesuits by running through dense forest and finding a boat that allowed him to cross the river to the Rachol seminary, where Stephens was based. To row the boat, Bernardo fashioned an oar from the leaf of a local tree of particular interest to Stephens, one that he already associated with deliverance from adversity: the coconut.

Stephens's story so far is entirely of a piece with Francis Xavier's mission to rescue Hindus from idolatry. But one can detect in it a hint of another disposition. In his letter, he notes how Bernardo's family was approached by an 'apostate' who had relapsed into Brahminism. Bernardo's brother and mother had resorted to violence in the hope of bringing the boy back to idolatry. According to Stephens, however, the apostate warned them against such a strategy, pointing out that 'gradually were we won over to the Christian religion and gradually did we leave it. This is not to be wondered at, seeing as the Fathers themselves do not prevail upon one the very first day, but attract people little by little... if you do him violence, you will only make him more obstinate.' The apostate failed to persuade the exemplarily devout Bernardo. But one can glimpse here an intriguing act of ventriloquism on Stephens's part, one that entails an unexpected identification with the apostate. Rather than the violent programme of suppression authorized by Francis Xavier, Stephens implicitly advocates for a moderate incrementalism, a tactic that he has the apostate attribute to 'the Fathers'.

This hints at how Stephens approached the Jesuit mission rather differently from Francis Xavier. Unlike the latter, Stephens took considerable pains to learn local customs and tongues in the hope of attracting his largely Brahmin target constituency 'little by little'. Clearly a gifted linguist—he quickly became conversant in Portuguese, and was known in Goa by the Portuguese version of his name, Tomás Estêvão—he also acquired Konkani, the local language of both Goa and the northern Malabar Coast. In the densely forested frontier village of Rachol, where he lived for most of his four decades in India before his death in 1619, speaking Konkani was a necessity; even as rector of Rachol, a position to which he was appointed in 1610, he preached and took confession in the local vernacular. Indeed, he became so fluent that he wrote the first Konkani grammar book, the *Arte da lingoa Canarim*, which was published posthumously in 1640. We do not know who his teachers were, but he evidently spent considerable time in the company of Konkani speakers.

Just as impressively, he devoted himself to learning Marathi, the language of 'high' literature among the Brahmins. It was in Marathi, sprinkled with some Konkani, that Stephens composed—probably after his appointment as rector of Rachol—his epic 11,018-line poem about the history of the world from Creation to the coming of Christ. He called the poem the *Kristapurana* (Story of Christ); in it, he styled himself as 'Pâtri Guru,' Marathi for 'Father Teacher'. His narrative reworks tales from the Old and New Testaments, as well as some apocryphal stories; it also includes a dialogue between Pâtri Guru and a Brahmin. The *Kristapurana* was first printed in 1616 on a press at the Rachol seminary. Although printed in Roman type, it became enormously popular with the local community of Brahmin converts and, subsequently, with Malabari Christians and even Marathi-speaking non-Christians.

Does Stephens's ability to write Christian literature in an Indian language (or two) make him a compellingly unconventional figure or a lethally effective colonist? It's hard not to assume the latter. Stephens adopted many predictably colonialist positions: he supported the conversion of Indians, and his writings are only ever obliquely critical of Portuguese violence against Hindus. Moreover, learning native languages to better disseminate the Word of God was increasingly part of an official Jesuit policy called 'accommodation', or inculturation. The New Christian Portuguese Jesuit Henrique Henriquez, something of a role model for Stephens, had written and published Christian doctrine and catechisms in Tamil in the 1560s. The Italian Jesuit Roberto de

Nobili continued Henriquez's efforts, also composing catechisms in Tamil; during his nearly fifty years in Madurai in the first half of the 1600s, de Nobili went further than Henriquez by adopting local customs such as shaving his head, wearing a thread across his torso, and sporting a dhoti around his waist. Similarly, the Italian Jesuit Costanzo Giuseppe Beschi—also known as Veeramamunivar—went native in the early 1700s, living as a sanyasi or holy man and writing Tamil poetry. Yet Beschi remained a fiercely dogmatic Catholic all his life. Stephens may have been influenced too by the example of Jerome Xavier, a Jesuit priest in Lahore who in the 1590s wrote a Persian 'life of Christ' called the *Dastan-i-Masih*. Stephens's *Kristapurana* was arguably part of this Jesuit tradition of inculturation.

But it's important to remember that even if the Jesuits initially worked with the sanction of the Portuguese colonial state, they weren't identical to it. Although King João III had appointed Francis Xavier as his Apostolic Nuncio in Portuguese India, the Jesuits didn't operate straightforwardly within the machinery of colonialism and empire. Stephens's mission to translate the Word of God into local vernaculars may have not fallen afoul of state law in his lifetime, but it did later, as did indeed the Jesuit order in general. After several years of sustained pressure, the colonial authorities banned the use of vernacular languages in 1684 and declared Portuguese the sole official language. Stephens's *Kristapurana* suddenly became a problematic text. The poem went even further underground with the (temporary) suspension of the Jesuit order in 1773, as a result of which many texts associated with the Society of Jesus were destroyed. This might be the reason why not a single copy of the first three editions of the *Kristapurana* survives today. But in the wake of the vernacular language ban and the suspension of the Jesuits, the *Kristapurana* survived in largely secretive oral form amongst Goan and Malabari Christians. In the process, it became a powerful rallying point for anti-colonial sentiment; it was still recited with pride by Marathi-speaking Indian freedom fighters at the height of Gandhi's Quit India Movement in the 1940s.

As an instance of the Jesuit policy of inculturation, the *Kristapurana* arguably achieved its quasi-colonial end—bringing Christian lore to the locals. But its subsequent history makes clear how the *Kristapurana* also became a venerated text in communities that did not coincide with, let alone submit to, the colonial project. It is tempting to see the poem's anti-colonial history as stemming from Stephens's unusual and fractured identity; as a dissident Catholic who had gone underground in his native country, he was used to operating outside the strictures of official authority, and he continued to do so in Rachol. Although he assumed the name of Tomás Estêvão, he repeatedly showed a willingness to move beyond the bounds of Portuguese national, religious, and linguistic community. In addition to helping out Ralph Fitch and his English Protestant countrymen, Stephens was most comfortable living in the Indian-majority hinterland of eastern Salcete, and he evidently chafed at the Portuguese colonial authorities' refusal to create movable typeface in Devanagari characters so that the *Kristapurana* could be printed—as he had recommended—in the native Marathi script. But the anti-colonial history of the *Kristapurana* also has much to do with the power of translation to transform what is being translated. Stephens didn't simply dress up Jesuit Christian doctrine in workman-like Marathi. He also demonstrably fell in love with the language, in a way that Indianized both the Christianity he sought to preach and his own body.

◆

In his letter to his brother, Stephens expresses his admiration for the linguistic structure of local languages, which to his ear is 'allied to that of Greek and Latin'. On the one hand, Stephens maps Indian languages back on to familiar authoritative European models that he first learned at Winchester. On the other, he opens up to the nuances of their unfamiliar sounds. As he remarks to his brother, 'Their pronunciation is not disagreeable… The phrases and constructions are of a wonderful kind. The letters in the syllables have their value, and are varied as many times as the consonants can be combined with the vowels and the mutes with the liquids.' Note the sensory pleasure Stephens takes in the complex acoustic textures of the local languages: his is not just an intellectual appreciation but also an embodied delight. Clearly he loved how Marathi felt in his mouth.

This delight is apparent in the best-known section of the *Kristapurana*, in which Stephens praises the beauty of Marathi:

Zaissy puspã mazi puspa mogary
Qui parimallã mazi casturi
Taissy bhassã mazi saziry
Maratthiya

Paqhiã madhe maioru

Vruqhiã madhe calpataru
Bhassã madhe manu thoru
Maratthiyessi

(As the mogra among flowers
As musk among perfumes
So among languages is the beauty
Of Marathi

As among birds the peacock
As among trees the kalpataru
So among languages is
Marathi)

We might read this passage as a strategic tour de force. Stephens's praise of Marathi is judiciously pitched at the Indian reader or listener with images that evoke the local landscape. He thus brings Christian lore to his Indian readers in not just a language but also images that recognizably belong to their world. Yet Stephens's use of Marathi is not simply a means to a Christian end. As this passage suggests, he did far more than simply drape a Western theological message in a rough-cut indigenous fabric. To become a Marathi kavi, Stephens also had to master the intricacies of the language's highly sophisticated literary forms.

Christopher Johnson's classes on Plautus and Virgil at Winchester College doubtless provided Stephens with a solid platform for his poetic labours in India, including an intuitive sense of prosody and rhetoric— the sound of a well-honed line, the evocative power of a well-chosen image. But there is little that is Latinate about the form of poetry he uses in the *Kristapurana*. Again, we don't know who his Marathi teachers were. But they must have been highly conversant with literary Marathi. Stephens had carefully studied not just the medieval Marathi Puranas— epic stories of creation, gods, and kings—but also appropriated one of Marathi's most distinctive poetic forms. He had become adept in the use of the ovi stanza, which consists of three longer rhyming lines of between eight and fifteen syllables followed by a short unrhymed line. The ovi, a little like the haiku, allows for the exfoliation of an idea through a kaleidoscopic sequence of diverse images: it lends a distinctive musical and visual power to otherwise abstract religious concepts.

For example, the ovi is used to particularly strong effect in the *Dnyaneshwari*, a thirteenth-century Marathi commentary on the Bhagavad

Gita by the legendary poet Dnyaneshwar. He expanded the 700 slokas of the Gita into 9,999 ovis with the intention of making spiritual ideas accessible to readers and listeners unfamiliar with Sanskrit. The ovi is also the poetic form favoured by the Brahmin Marathi poet-saint Eknath (1533-99), a contemporary of Stephens who became renowned in western India for his attempt to revive Marathi literature in general and Dnyaneshwar in particular at a time of Muslim rule in the region. Eknath journeyed though much of what is now Maharashtra reciting bhajans and other religious poems in public; he also critiqued the caste system, embracing Dalits and bathing in water reserved for them. As a result, the ovi became associated with a kind of evangelical Marathi Brahminism that was at one and the same time literary yet popular, spiritual yet worldly, traditional yet glamorously anti-establishment. In other words, it represented everything to which Stephens's brand of Indian Catholicism aspired.

Stephens doubtless heard of the exploits of Eknath; he probably closely studied his ovis before writing the *Kristapurana*. He may have even regarded him as a potential source of competition for his Brahmin constituency. But in appropriating Eknath's distinctive style, he wasn't simply speaking to people in the language and the poetic form of the region. He was also lending voice to powerful personal experiences of his attachment to his new home. He may or may not have known about Eknath imparting his touch to that which was deemed untouchable. But with his ovis, Stephens too opened up his body to the touch of a world supposedly alien to him. For the landscape Stephens describes in his praise of Marathi isn't designed simply to hook his Indian readers; it also bears the imprint of his own sensuous interactions with it. Here, if briefly, we can glimpse Stephens's own delighted body in Goa, smelling mogra flowers, hearing the cry of the peacock, gazing upon the kalpataru tree. And this body is the missing point of connection between landscape and language, a language that seems to have induced in him a similar delight. Which is to say: speaking Marathi changed Stephens.

First and foremost, it changed Stephens' bodily habits. Pronouncing Marathi's different consonants and vowels, and what he calls its 'liquids' and its 'mutes', would have required him to transform how he used his facial and labial muscles. His eccentric yet systematic Romanized spelling of Marathi in the *Kristapurana*, with its use of italicization and diacritical marks to distinguish between different vowel sounds and its meticulous distinction between different dental consonants that sound identical to most English speakers (d, dd, dh, ddh, t, tt, th, tth), shows how much attention Stephens had paid to the nuances of Marathi pronunciation and to getting these right. But speaking Marathi also changed the Christianity he attempted to bring to his readers. The *Kristapurana* retells stories from the Old and New Testaments. Yet the Christianity he explains is one that has been adapted to Indian, and even Hindu, concepts. He calls Jesus, for example, a swami. But the Hinduization of Stephens's Christianity is perhaps most clear from one word choice in the above passage: 'calpataru', or kalpataru tree.

◆

Throughout the *Kristapurana*, Stephens invokes the 'calpataru'. This represents an ingenious exercise in inculturation. Here he adapts a traditional Hindu motif for Christian purposes: the kalpataru is, in Sanskrit mythology, a divine tree that has the power to grant all wishes, as a result of which Indra the god-king takes it with him to Paradise. Consequently, 'calpataru' provides Stephens with a powerful translation for the Tree of Life in the Garden of Eden, which is how he uses the word at the poem's beginning. This typifies how Stephens—unlike Garcia da Orta, who felt a profound affinity with Indo-Islamic culture—gravitated towards Hindu concepts. He probably did so less out of a deep sympathy than a pragmatic sense of the main constituency for his poem, Brahmin Hindus who had converted to Catholicism.

There was another shrewd calculation behind Stephens's adaptation of the kalpataru. As his paean to Marathi suggests, his use of the word serves to localize the Edenic tree in Goa. Throughout the subcontinent, the kalpataru was identified with local trees. In Uttarakhand, locals venerate a mulberry tree as the kalpavriksha, another term for kalpataru. In Bengal and elsewhere, the kalpataru is the banyan tree. But the inhabitants of the Konkan coast equate it with the coconut tree, because of its ability to provide for a wide spectrum of human needs.

This was a tradition with which Stephens was evidently familiar. In the letter he wrote to his brother, he remarks of the coconut tree that:

> It gives oil, liquor (*vinum*), toddy (*lac*), syrup (*mel*) sugar and vinegar. Coir-rope is also made from it to tie with, and its branches are used to protect huts from rain. It gives fruit all the year round, which are rather nuts than dates, resembling a man's head. When the exterior rind has been removed, they rival the size of two

fists. Inside, the fruit contains water like light beer and good to quench one's thirst. It is so plentiful that, after drinking from one fruit, you would not look for another. In the interior of the nut is a kernel lining it all over like a covering and forming a prized article of food. The shell furnishes the blacksmith with charcoal. Those that live near the sea not only load their boats with the tree, but also utilize it for making ropes and sails. You will find hardly any piece of writing except on its leaves.

Here we can see Stephens not so much describing the Goan kalpataru as rehearsing an oft-repeated local narrative about it. Yet it is clear that, like his relation to spoken Marathi, his relation to the kalpataru was embodied as much as it was conceptual. As we have seen, the long letter Stephens wrote to his father in 1579 refers to the 'drink of this country' derived from palm trees: here he invokes either coconut water or toddy, the zesty alcoholic brew he mentions in his letter to his brother. Each drink has a significant impact on the body. Coconut water is an excellent guard against dehydration; electrolyte-rich, it has a cooling effect in the heat. And its alcoholic derivative toddy is a fine protector against the cold. It is difficult to imagine Stephens having done without either drink during his four decades in India. In the last three years of his life before his death in 1619, most of them spent in the infirmary next to the Bom Jesus Basilica, he struggled to take food because of a chronic stomach problem; it's likely that coconut water would have been a regular part of his sickbed diet. It is likewise difficult to imagine Stephens earlier in his life avoiding the multiple uses of the coconut in its many other forms. Eating the coconut's white flesh by itself or mixed into tasty dishes such as the kishmur fish curry that is so plentiful in the region; using its husk as coir for rope; employing it as charcoal for cooking; sheltering under its leaves in the monsoon; even writing on it as a substitute for paper (indeed, it is tempting to imagine drafts of the *Kristapurana* written on the leaves of kalpataru)—Stephens must have been familiar with all these.

In other words, Stephens's 'calpataru' is not simply a Marathi term that translates a Christian concept. It is the catalyst for an entirely new ensemble of bodily habits, habits that differ from how Stephens had used his body in England or Rome. If Stephens imbues the kalpataru with miraculous properties in the *Kristapurana*, it is partly because the coconut also helped transform him from Thomas Stephens the English religious dissident into Tomás Estêvão the Goan migrant and Pâtri Guru the Marathi poet. The coconut was for Stephens the secular version of a consecrated communion wafer: it was the agent by means of which he could not only say 'this is my body' in Konkani but also experience his as a Konkani body—that is, as part of a larger ecological and cultural network specific to the Konkan Coast. After all, 'hi mho ji kudd' is a phrase that would come most naturally only to someone habituated to interacting with Goan coconuts in a variety of ways.

The coconut may have provided Stephens with an illustration of the workings of divine providence and the principle that God makes everything for some use—or, in the case of the kalpataru, for potentially infinite use. That is certainly how the coconut was regarded back in England by the great seventeenth-century religious poet, George Herbert: 'The Indian nut alone/ Is clothing, meat and trencher, drink and kan,/ Boast, cable, sail and needle, all one.' Yet the coconut does not always function in such straightforwardly theological fashion in the *Kristapurana*. When Stephens invokes it, he doesn't do so simply to translate key concepts of Christian doctrine for his Marathi-speaking readers. He also localizes those concepts, displacing and transforming them in ways that vividly conjure the details of the Salcete landscape. When, for example, Stephens describes the rebuilding of Jerusalem, he writes that

Draqhe vely puspa taru bhina zahale
Zuna taddamadda bhumy paddale
Teanche tthai vruqhe vaddhale
Apaisse

(Grape vines, flowers and trees fell apart
Old high coconut and palm trees fell to the ground
In their place trees grew
Naturally)

Here Stephens imagines a Jerusalem that has fallen from its former glory, a glory associated not just with vines and flowers but also with the coconut tree. However, his term for the latter in this passage is not the heavenly kalpataru of Sanskrit mythology. Instead he uses the memorable word 'taddamadda'—a local Konkani term that, describing the soaring height of mixed groves of coconut and palmyra trees, helps Stephens re-imagine the original Jerusalem as a version of the contemporary Konkan Coast. As a result, the paradise that Christian doctrine associates with a lost past is subtly outsourced to Stephens's and his readers' Indian present. We may have lost Jerusalem, Stephens seems to say. But we have gained Salcete now. Or, rather, Salcete has gained us—and transforms us with its marvellous coconuts.

Describing the animals afflicted by the waters of the Great Flood, Stephens again evokes the local coconut-rich landscape with a word that points to neither Christian doctrine nor Hindu mythology but an actual experience of a Salcete coconut tree:

Veagra bocaddiyã saue põuaty
Zalli siha sardhalla craddaty
Zallachare manuxanssi mellaty
Nariyelli vari

(The tigers swim with the sheep
In the water the lions play with smaller cats
Those living in the water meet men
Atop the coconut tree)

Stephens here describes the devastation wrought by the biblical Flood as an inversion of cosmic order: its water levels the hierarchical distinctions between species and between heights, placing mighty and weak animal, treetop and submarine seascape, in unexpected proximity. For modern readers, this might sound less like the Flood as conceived in the Bible than a description of the tsunami that crashed into India's coconut-lined Coromandel Coast in 2004. But the stanza has a more specifically Goan resonance. Stephens's concluding line invokes the nariyelli, a commonplace Marathi term for the coconut; the image he conjures with the nariyelli, of men atop the coconut tree, is a powerful one in Goa even today. For the coconut trees of the region are scaled daily by agile men who tap the fruit for water and toddy. During his forty years in India Stephens may not have adapted his body to clamber up coconut trees in search of libations. The nariyelli, however, was the agent of numerous other recalibrations of his body and its flesh.

Indeed, the Marathi name Stephens assumed in the *Kristapurana* suggests as much. 'Pâtri Guru' means 'Father Teacher'. But 'patri' also means, in Sanskrit, both 'letter' and 'leaf of a palm tree'. It is hard to imagine that Stephens, so adroit with languages, was not aware of this pun. Was his choice of name a subtle homage to the coconut leaves on which he most likely wrote—a homage, indeed to the tree that was in so many ways his guru? Pâtri Guru is the man who teaches from palm tree leaves, with palm tree leaves, from the vantage point of palm tree leaves. In this name, then, we might see Stephens recalibrating his flesh not simply *with*, but also *as*, the Konkan coconut tree.

◆

These recalibrations of the flesh are why we cannot dismiss Stephens as simply an instrument of European colonial power. He certainly operated at the confluence of two of the strongest currents of pre-British colonialism in India: the Portuguese Estado da Índia and the Jesuit mission. But even within that confluence, we find eddies and counter-currents that do not flow in predictable directions.

It would be a mistake to assume that the coconut alone could generate those counter-currents. Countless firangi settlers until Independence had their bodies transformed by naariyal paani, but in ways that reinforced rather than undermined the stark asymmetry of colonial power relations. A Bengali friend tells me about how a family from her well-to-do South Calcutta neighbourhood had a servant, Ramani, who had served in the home of a British family in the city before Independence. This Ramani was a great raconteur. One of his stories was about how his British masters would call out for him—the khansama (cook) or 'Johnny'—and offer him one penny if he could crack open a coconut for them: 'Johnny Johnny, one penny,' was their refrain. And when the water was extracted, the white sahibs would drink it and say 'good water, good water'. Ramani's story about the British officer calling for a coconut and assuming the willingness of Indians to cut it for him, speaks volumes. No matter how much the coconut may have transformed the officer's body, it was delivered to him courtesy of a colonial economy in which the British were served by menial Indian labourers. A similar situation may have obtained for Stephens. If he did not himself clamber up coconut trees to retrieve coconuts, who did? Who cracked his coconuts for him? Who laboured to safeguard his health? In telling the story of the miraculous powers of the naariyal, it is perhaps too easy to forget the stubborn power of an economy in which labour was divided in entirely colonialist ways. Stephens was doubtless the beneficiary of an early version of this economy—which is to say, like Ramani's British officer of Calcutta, he was a gora sahib served by Indian peons.

Yet there were other economies at work in Stephens's career, in which power was not organized in quite so predictable a fashion. From whom did he learn local languages, including vernacular Konkani and high Marathi? From whom did he learn the complexities of the ovi form? From whom did he learn about Eknath? He immersed himself in local literary tradition in a way that few other Jesuit practitioners of inculturation did and as a result, mastered Konkani, Marathi, and their poetic forms. But his education would have demanded that he submit to other local masters. Perhaps this submission did not take the overt political form of Orta's employment by the sultan of Ahmadnagar. But Stephens certainly had to submit to Indian teachers, and in ways that would have recreated something of the relation he had with Christopher Johnson, his master at Winchester College. How much did he have to submit, not just intellectually, but also physically to his Indian gurus? How, for example, did he sit during his Marathi lessons? How did he turn the pages of Marathi Puranas—perhaps inscribed on coconut leaves—such as Eknath's? How, in short, might his body have adapted not only to the plant life but also to the classrooms of the Konkan Coast? How did his body change in ways that not only served the ends of the Portuguese colonial state but also traced the outlines of rather different modes of contact between firangi and desi?

If we look aslant at the Konkani phrase on the altar of the ancient Bom Jesus Basilica in Old Goa, we might see another subtle story of transformation that no longer points in the same spiritual direction as the Eucharist's miracle of transubstantiation. For 'hi mho jhi kudd' not only translates the formula of the Catholic Mass, 'this is my body', it also transforms it. The Romanized Konkani phrase is part of Thomas Stephens's native language Christian legacy to Goan Indians: to this day, his name is associated with the flowering of Konkani as a literary language, thanks to the Thomas Stephens Konknni Kendr in the Goan parish of Bardez, which houses an extraordinary archive of Konkani texts by Stephens and other non-Portuguese Goan writers of the past four centuries. He has also recently become a figurehead for the indigenous Romi Konknni Movement, whose objective is to have Roman-script Konkani declared one of the official languages of Goa. And Stephens has additionally served as a standard-bearer for Goa's other indigenous languages: in the mid twentieth century, at the height of the Quit India movement, his praise of Marathi from the *Kristapurana* was posted widely in non-Christian venues throughout Goa, such as the Saraswat Brahman Samaj's Library in Margão. The phrase 'hi mho jhi kudd', then, hints at the transformations that have accompanied and complicated Stephens's legacy. In particular, it gestures towards the work performed by Indian agents, human and non-human, in refashioning Christian orthodoxy into something anti-establishment, an instrument of colonialism into something anti-imperialist, and firangi flesh into something Indian.

Because firangis did not just arrive in India. India—and its tasty fruits—kept arriving in them.

ON RUNNING

A running body is not just a body that runs. It's a transformative element, both adapting to and subtly altering its environment with each stride.

In Delhi, I am part of a fifteen-strong running group. We are a diverse if solidly middle-class bunch: lawyers, corporate types, a doctor, an NGO worker, a mountaineer, a professor; Hindu, Sikh, Parsi, Christian, Jew; Tamil, Malayali, Sindhi, Punjabi, Bengali, Nepali, English, Australian and, of course, Kiwi. Together we run three times a week, either in one of South Delhi's many forested parks or along the leafy roads of Lutyens' New Delhi. It's best to run first thing in the morning, before the sun gets too hot and the streets get too congested. This is important during the week, when we usually run 8 kilometres in advance of the rush hour. But it's especially important during the weekend, when we run for twice as long and are out later in the day. In the summer, when we start our morning run, the temperature may be 35 degrees Celsius; it can be as high as 40 when we call it quits.

But the hot sun is not our only obstacle. Next to the Rashtrapati Bhavan, the president's residence, lives a large colony of monkeys. The alpha male is an ugly, muscular piece of work who bares his fangs every time we run past him; on at least one memorable occasion, he has chased after us. And when angry simians don't pursue us, there are other challenges. In a dark glade of the Deer Park of Hauz Khas, there is a protruding root that catches every tenth runner's toe—and can break it, as I once discovered to my immense discomfort. Then there's the problem of the running surfaces. After a steady regimen of soft clay trails in forested parks, a sudden shift to the hard asphalt of Lutyens' Delhi proved too much for my 50-year-old left Achilles tendon, which refused to last the course and packed up for three months after that.

Negotiating all these obstacles means we have to map our courses with care. And we don't just map them mentally. Over time, as we repeat our routes, our bodies get to know them in ways that our minds can't. Based on their past experiences, our legs make crucial split-second decisions about when to speed up and speed down, where to turn, how to place our feet to avoid drains, roots, potholes, passers-by, rickshaws or monkeys. Our muscles flinch, coil, engage and contract because of a library of reflexes stored in them.

And, over time, our bodies change profoundly in response to the terrain.

71

Running up the Delhi Ridge—the forested spine of the city, an extension of the Aravalli mountain range that cuts across Rajasthan and Haryana—builds up the glutes, quads, hamstrings and calves. Pounding the asphalt of Lutyens' Delhi changes the soles of the feet: blisters turn into calluses, bloodied toenails fall off and regenerate. Repeated exposure at speed to Delhi's heat and humidity makes us sweat more, changing our habits of hydration and diet, but also helps us absorb the oxygen from the city's polluted air more efficiently. And it isn't just our individual bodies that remember, and are altered by, our running routes. It is also the collective body of the group. Running together, stepping and breathing in synch even when we're making our way in silence, we move as one, responding to a shared bodily imprint of the terrain and our past trajectories through it.

Running in Delhi has been part and parcel of my experience of becoming Indian.

It has also, counter-intuitively, helped me imagine the biographies of a special class of firangi migrant: the warrior slave. Slavery in sixteenth-century India was a somewhat different institution from its counterpart in colonial America. Many people from other parts of the world—Russia, Malaya, Holland, East Africa—were taken captive so they might serve in semi-military capacities, as guards, soldiers and sailors. Yet these warrior bondsmen were much more mobile, socially as well as physically, than the agricultural labouring slaves of the West: a few even rose to positions of political as well as military authority in India. And their authority was granted to them in large part because of their expertise—acquired through repeated exercises with their regiments—in navigating difficult Indian environments, whether on land or at sea.

My running group is a world apart from the armies and navies in which these foreigners served. Its membership is elective rather than coerced, its activity middle-class pastime rather than bonded subaltern labour. But my group shares two vital features with the earlier military slave associations. Our bodies' collective physical exertions in Indian terrain have engendered unexpected affinities across borders of religion and culture. And in mapping that terrain, our bodies have been transformed by and become part of it.

| MALIK AYAZ, THE NAUSENAAPTI OF DIU;
CHINALI, THE NAVIKAN OF KOTTAKKAL;
AND DILLANAI, THE VALIYA KAPPITHAAN
OF KANYAKUMARI

An old Sufi fable tells us that Sultan Mahmud of Ghazni fell in love with a beautiful slave boy named Ayaz. One day, the sultan asked his beloved whether he knew of any king as great as he. Pat came the reply: 'Yes, I am a greater king than you.' 'But how on earth can that be?' thundered Mahmud. 'Because even though you are a king,' said Ayaz, 'your heart rules you, and this slave is king of your heart.'

As is typical of Sufi tales, Mahmud's master-slave relation with Ayaz is an allegory of desire. The (here) reversible bond between ruler and slave, between the sultan-turned-slave and the slave-turned-king, models the transformational force of erotic captivation—a captivation understood as a state of joyous submission to a higher power, even for those who are themselves powerful. Sufis repeatedly transform the material relations of slavery into the language of exalted love for Allah: the primary Persian and Urdu Sufi term for a religious devotee, 'abd', is Arabic for 'slave'. Yet abd—like its other common Persian-Urdu synonyms ghulam (meaning boy as well as slave) and bandhwa (bonded person or galley slave)—doesn't quite describe the unique slave status of Ayaz in this tale. Ayaz is, rather, a mamluk, another Arabic word that refers to a captive of war retained as a slave loyal to his conquering sultan. This adds to the tale's vision of desire a further, powerful dimension. A mamluk is by definition a foreigner, alienated from his country of birth. The migrant captive who captivates the sultan and commands his erotic surrender suggests the border-crossing nature of desire, which drives lover and beloved alike into new worlds, disorienting and reorienting them both.

But one needn't read the fable simply as an allegory of desire. This would be to move simply from the domain of the social (Mahmud and Ayaz's master-slave relation) to that of the erotic. The tale can be read also in the opposite direction: its vision of desire's border-crossings brings into view otherwise oblique social realities of pre-Raj India. The fable deals with actual historical figures. Mahmud of Ghazni was the first Muslim ruler in India, the son of a Turkic soldier-slave, who from 997 to 1030 CE conquered much of what is now Afghanistan, Pakistan, and Indian Punjab; Ayaz was a mamluk of Georgian origin who rose to the rank of general in the sultan's personal army, and was eventually awarded the governorship of Lahore. In other words, Ayaz was an early instance of what the Mughals would call a firangi—a foreigner from a putatively Christian land who had come to live in India. And, as we will see, he was just one of many firangi captives who served Indian masters in a military capacity.

What the fable of Mahmud and Ayaz doesn't tell us is how a firangi slave might adapt to his new land. It suggests that the intimacy Ayaz enjoyed with his master was crucial to his becoming Indian. But it is silent about the larger warrior community the historical Ayaz operated in, or the new terrain he had to familiarize himself with as a soldier in order to earn his appointment as the governor of Lahore. And that is too bad, as the true-life story of how a firangi slave crossed borders and came to be Indian—and a successful, socially mobile Indian at that—is every bit as remarkable as the Sufi fable of a king in erotic thrall to his slave.

This chapter teases out the elusive biographies of three firangi warrior captives who came from different parts of the world: Russia, Portuguese Malacca and Flanders. They found homes in different Indian locations: Gujarat, Calicut, Travancore. And they lived at very different times: the end of the fifteenth century, the end of the sixteenth century, the middle of the eighteenth century. But there are striking continuities between their stories, continuities that flesh out the border-crossing subtext of Ayaz's story. Several elements are common to the three warriors' diverse biographies, sketchy as the surviving details are. Each was alienated from his place of birth. Each extended his loyalty neither to kin nor countryman but to an Indian master. Each enjoyed an unusually close bond with his master, who conferred on him significant privileges and status. Each worked closely with a community of fellow warriors serving the same master. And each was, along with the members of his warrior community, transformed by the unique environment in which he fought.

These warriors' stories might not have the poetry of a Sufi fable. Yet in their minor-key prose, they might still unsettle some of our assumptions about firangis and slavery.

◆

Mere mention of the word 'slavery' is likely, at least in the West, to evoke the spectre of the American plantation: brutal agricultural labour confined to an ethnicity regarded as subhuman, children born into bondage, and no hope for social advancement without liberty. But in India, as in many parts of the world, slavery hasn't always coincided with the American model. Different political, economic, and cultural factors have resulted in a wide array of forms of bondage and servitude specific to the subcontinent. Something like American plantation slavery was pervasive in the heyday of British colonialism, when poor people were forced out of Bengal and Bihar—usually as a consequence of debt default—and shipped to Mauritius, Fiji and the Caribbean as indentured agricultural labourers. Prior to the nineteenth century, however, Indian slaves tended to do other types of labour, some more demeaning and some less: domestic work, singing and dancing, sex work, temple duty and, perhaps most commonly, military service. Notably, these pre-colonial Indian slaves often had more hope of social advancement than the later indentured agricultural labourers. This was particularly the case with slaves retained in a military capacity as swordsmen, archers, cavalry soldiers, sailors and, later, bombardiers and artillerymen.

India's military slaves were sometimes, like their American counterparts, 'chattel' slaves—that is, they were purchased by private masters and middlemen in the busy slave markets of the Middle East and Central Asia. In many cases, however, they were—like Ayaz—mamluks captured in war. The word 'mamluk' might evoke visions of powerful medieval Muslim sultans, from the Mamluk dynasties that ruled Persia from 1077 to 1231 and Egypt and Syria from 1250 to 1517. But it also refers to an Arabo-Persian institution of slavery that, as the phenomenon of the Mamluk sultans might suggest, diverges greatly from the colonial American version. 'Mamluk' is Arabic for 'property'. Yet mamluks were property in a rather different sense from their counterparts in colonial America. They were a military caste of warriors belonging to a sultan; they were also ethnically diverse, having been captured from battlefields throughout Asia, Africa and Europe. Unlike slaves in America, mamluks were usually accorded a high status, often higher than that of local nobles—some were granted positions of considerable military and even political authority. This social mobility was in no small way due to a deep-seated suspicion throughout the Middle East and Central Asia of local soldiers, whose kin and clan loyalties were likely to bond them more closely to private lords than to the sultan. Because mamluks had been alienated from their nations and families, it was supposedly easier to inculcate in them a deep and abiding loyalty to their new master.

In return, the sultan would repose great trust in the mamluks, a trust that was often understood as the love of a father to his sons.

This paternal love is evident in the astonishing success of the mamluks of Delhi, who followed their Persian counterparts in ascending to the sultanate throne. After the last Ghurid sultan of Delhi, Muhammad Ghori, died childless in 1206, the kingdom was divided between his mamluk generals. The generals had emerged from the ranks of more than 10,000 Turkic slave troops from Afghanistan and the Central Asian steppes; Muhammad Ghori legendarily regarded them as his surrogate sons. When confronted about the problem of succession due to his childlessness, he is supposed to have retorted: 'Other monarchs may have one son, or two sons; I have thousands of sons, my Turkish slaves who will be the heirs of my dominions, and who, after me, will take care to preserve my name.' And so it came to pass upon his death: the Afghan slave-general Muhammad bin Bakhtiyar Khilji assumed power in the sultanate's eastern territories, violently subduing Bengal and Bihar (in taking the latter, he destroyed the centuries-old Nalanda University and massacred its students, having failed to understand that it was a university and not a militarized fortress). Nasiruddin Qabacha, a Kipchak slave-general from what is now Kazakhstan, took control of Multan. And Qutubuddin Aybak, an Uzbek slave-general, assumed power in Delhi itself, building the legendary Qutub Minar during his brief four-year rule. Although the last of the Delhi mamluk sultans surrendered power in 1290, the legacy of Muhammad Ghori's Turkic slaves endured throughout the pre-colonial era: until the eighteenth century, many states in the subcontinent retained a cadre of slave warriors of mostly foreign origin, some of whom rose to positions of considerable authority.

'Turuksha'—meaning 'Turk'—was initially a synonym for mamluk. Over time, however, the ethnic composition of India's military slaves diversified. In the fifteenth and sixteenth centuries, an increasing number came from Christian areas at the borders of Asia and Europe. Qasim Barid, previously the wazir and chief confidant of the Bahmani Deccan king Mahmud Shah, founded the Deccan Bidar Sultanate. Like Ayaz, he was a mamluk from Georgia, though it has been argued he was Hungarian. Other mamluks came, via the Constantinople slave market, from European Balkan and Slavic nations at the frontiers of Ottoman expansion. Indeed, the English word 'slave' derives, via the medieval Latin 'sclavus', from the Slavs, who were repeatedly sold into slavery by conquering peoples from Iberia to Turkey. Many kings of the Egyptian

Mamluk dynasty were of Balkan and Slavic origin; so too, as we'll see, was one of the captive warriors in Gujarat. In the two centuries after the arrival of Vasco da Gama in 1498, the Portuguese also found their way into India's captive foreign warrior regiments, where their supposed command of artillery was a valued commodity. By the end of the sixteenth century, there were other non-Turkic slave-troops serving Indian rulers: East Africans (habshis from Ethiopia) in the Deccan and at least one East Asian (from Portuguese Malacca) in south India. But European firangi warrior captives, from the Iberian peninsula to the Netherlands, also remained part of the mix well into the eighteenth century.

Most of these firangi captives weren't called mamluks. But they operated within military associations that were in key respects similar to the Delhi mamluk troops. A version of mamluk slavery, for example, featured prominently in the powerful military factions of the Deccan sultanates, including the so-called firangiyan regiments. Again, the relation of sultan to captive foreign soldier was a paternal one: we have already met Sancho Pires, also known as Firangi Khan, the Portuguese captain of the Ahmadnagar cavalry who was the favourite 'son' of the nizam shah. Similarly paternalistic ruler/soldier relations obtained in other militarized states of pre-colonial India, including Calicut, Vijayanagar and Travancore. Although the armies of south India entailed something closer to arrangements of contracted labour, it is hard in the final analysis to distinguish these completely from the older Arabo-Persian mamluk systems, inasmuch as they often featured foreign captives bonded emotionally as well as legally to a local potentate.

That we do distinguish the 'contracted' from the 'bonded' warriors probably has to do with the fact that a surprisingly large number of Mughal, Deccan, and south Indian soldiers were, like Ayaz or Sancho Pires, firangis. Europeans—or so it is assumed in the West—are not meant to be slaves, and slaves are not meant to be socially mobile. Yet many of the Europeans who fought in Indian rulers' armies were captives; and some did quite well for themselves. It is easier, and consorts more with conventional Western understandings of slavery, to call these bonded European soldiers 'mercenaries' or 'renegades' rather than 'slaves'. The habit starts with the early seventeenth-century Portuguese historical chronicles. In his *Decades*, for example, Diogo do Couto speaks admiringly of the 'renegade' firangi warrior Pires. He understands the latter's close bond with his royal Indian master as having emerged not from a local tradition of warrior slavery but, rather, from Pires's superior military prowess and valour. In the process, Couto disregards the fact that Pires was, in effect, the property of the nizam shah—a status that Pires chafed against even as he materially benefited from it.

But the social mobility of India's firangi warrior captives was not just a consequence of the intimate bonds they enjoyed with their masters. It was the outcome also of their intimate relations to the physical environments in which they successfully fought—relations that demanded new skills and reflexes of their bodies. As members of military associations that roamed the distinctive local terrains of the western Indian coast with the specific objective of repelling foreign invaders—primarily the armies and navies of the Portuguese—the firangi warriors had to adjust to demanding conditions radically different from those of their home countries: scorching heat made all the fiercer by the sandy deserts and all the muggier by the coastal marshlands of Gujarat; torrential monsoon rain, thick jungle, and endless waterways in the lush lands of the Malabar Coast; precipitous coast-to-hill climbs in the waterfall-rich Ghats dividing southwest India from Tamil Nadu. Over the course of repeated military operations in these extreme environments, the warrior firangis adapted their bodies to their new Indian landscapes. Or, more accurately in the case of the three warriors we are about to meet, they adapted their bodies to their Indian waterscapes.

How can a firangi war captive be most at home when he is most at sea? This conundrum is due partly to the transformation of the maritime spice trade from the sixteenth to the eighteenth centuries. Once a stable global network controlled by Chinese, Indian and Arab merchants, it was increasingly disrupted by heavily militarized European powers—first the Portuguese, then the English and the Dutch. As a consequence, the vulnerability as well as strategic importance of the Arabian Sea ports of India's west coast grew. It became imperative for Indian rulers to guard these ports with well-drilled navies; but because of caste Hinduism's conviction that the kaala paani, or the ocean, was impure, recruitment of local warrior sailors was often a difficult task. Non-Hindus and foreigners were needed, and the mamluk system provided a ready pool of warriors, some of whom already had experience at sea. But even when they had acquired military prowess in forms of land combat, they could still be pressed into naval service, as was the case in Gujarat with an archer of Russian origin. Enter Malik Ayaz, the fifteenth-century mamluk namesake of Ayaz, the slave who ruled his sultan's heart.

The Slavic Slave: Malik Ayaz

The original Ayaz, as we have seen, was beloved by his royal master, Sultan Mahmud. Five hundred years later, another mamluk warrior named Malik Ayaz (c. 1450–1522), turned the head of a second sultan named Mahmud—in this case Mahmud Begarha, the sultan of Gujarat. And like his mamluk namesake, Malik Ayaz enjoyed unusual privileges and status: he was promoted to the rank of nausenaapti (admiral) in the Gujarati navy, and became governor of the island of Diu. (The 'Malik' of his name is also a title of high rank, meaning 'lord'.)

The second Ayaz may have received his name in honour of the first: when the sultan took possession of his young slave, the latter-day Mahmud was probably aware of the popular Sufi legend and invoked it when naming his Ayaz. Tempting as it is to read the pair as poster-boys for same-sex desire in medieval Gujarat, the slave's name may have been conferred on him simply because he hailed from more or less the same region as the original Ayaz. There are conflicting reports about Malik Ayaz's place of birth—one suggests Java, others Persia and Croatia—but most contemporary references to him agree about his firangi provenance. Specifically, he seems to have come from southern Russia, near the Georgian frontier with the Ottomans. We do not know his birth name. It has been speculated that he was a Tatar Muslim, one of the huge swath of people in the Eurasian steppes descended from Turks, Mongols and Bulgars. But the sixteenth-century Portuguese chronicler João de Barros claimed, after close consultation of official Gujarati records, that he was a Russian of the 'heretic sect'—probably Eastern Orthodox—captured by Turks and sold into slavery in Istanbul.

If this is true, Malik Ayaz was one in a long tradition of Slavic slaves. Many were, like him, taken to and sold in Turkey, especially during the period of Ottoman expansion into the Caucasus, Ukraine and the Balkans. We might think of Slavs as Europeans. But Russia was also very much part of an Asian network that connected it to India. This network wasn't routed just through Istanbul and the Ottoman Empire. Its links were often more direct, tracing overland paths through Central Asia. Anthony Jenkinson, the English explorer of Persia, visited the chief slave market of Asia, Bukhara in Uzbekistan, in the 1550s. There he reported seeing Indian slaves, but also many 'Russians'—a term that could equally refer to Tatars as well as ethnic Slavs. It seems that a good many were bought by people headed to Indian courts, where Russian slaves were desirable because of their skill as fighters and, in particular, as archers. In the Tatar regions of Russia contested by the Ottomans, especially Crimea, Chechnya, and Dagestan, as well as in the kingdom of Georgia, the locals had become reputed for their pinpoint skills in archery, modelled on the Ottoman style.

Malik Ayaz seems to have been a particularly gifted archer. This was no doubt a skill valued by his new Turkish master; maybe it is what the latter had in mind when he allegedly described the slave as a 'jewel of great price'. Following his purchase in Istanbul, Malik Ayaz was taken by his master to Basra, at that time still part of the Abbasid Caliphate. The coastal city was a cosmopolitan entrepôt in the Arabian Sea trade network (its name in Persian means 'where many paths meet'); Arab, Chinese and Indian ships carrying fragrant cargoes of spices from Malabar and the Moluccas often berthed there, and Malik Ayaz's master may have been involved in the trade. Basra's major industry was salt, extracted primarily from mines worked by slave labour. But Malik Ayaz wouldn't have been dispatched to the mines; most of the salt-worker slaves were captives from the east African coast. Instead, he was probably employed to provide security to his master in what was an often lawless region. In the blisteringly hot and humid delta marshlands of Basra, Malik Ayaz would have had to adapt his archer's reflexes to terrain radically different from that of his native Russia. Although archery is primarily a form of land combat, he doubtless had to learn how to traverse rivers and streams, quite possibly protecting not just caravans but also ships carrying valuable cargo. And although Malik Ayaz had been accustomed to shooting at enemies from elevated locations in the hilly terrain of the Caucasus, he now had to hone his archer's eye in an area that was more or less completely flat.

If, as I have speculated, Malik Ayaz's master was a spice merchant, this might help explain why the pair travelled to Gujarat in the early 1470s. At this time, Gujarat was a central node in the international spice trade network, with mercantile connections extending west to Arabia and east to the Spice Islands. Indeed, there was a Gujarati merchant colony in the Moluccas long before the Portuguese gained a foothold there. Malik Ayaz probably accompanied his master to Gujarat to provide security to him and his cargo. In any case, he certainly had his bow and arrows at the ready, for it was his archer's skills that brought him to the attention of Sultan Mahmud Begarha. According to popular legend, he is supposed to have fired an arrow into a hawk that had landed on

JONATHAN GIL HARRIS

the sultan's head. This William Tell-like exploit led his master to offer him as a gift to the sultan. And once in Mahmud Begarha's service, he continued working in a military capacity.

Malik Ayaz quickly benefitted from the paternalism of the mamluk system. With the loving patronage of Mahmud Begarha, he became a general rather than a simple soldier. The sultan, long embroiled in ongoing skirmishes with the neighbouring Rajputs, employed Malik Ayaz to oversee them. After many successful campaigns against the Rajputs, the former archer led a famous campaign, in 1484, against their stronghold of Champaner in the hinterland of Gujarat. Upon capturing the town, he and his army then laid siege to the neighbouring hill-fort of Pavagadh; they prevailed after twenty long months, despite the odds against them. It is not too fanciful to imagine that Malik Ayaz's victory drew on his embodied experience of his native land: his capture of Pavagadh might not have been possible without knowledge of how to fight on hilly terrain such as that of the Caucasus.

But in Gujarat he also had to adapt to a physical environment very different from anything he had experienced in Russia. It was not for nothing that Sultan Mahmud Begarha was known as Sultân al-Barr, Sultân al-Bahr—'Sultan of the Land, Sultan of the Sea'. Gujarat in the late fifteenth century was an Arabian Sea superpower, its influence extending over oceans as well as land. Following the first Portuguese attempts to wrest control of the spice trade, conflict over control of the Arabian Sea ports demanded that Gujarat create an effective naval force. Malik Ayaz was charged to lead it; indeed, it was as a navy admiral (or nausenaapti) rather than as an archer or land general that he became most famed for his tactical nous. But, as we will see, his naval skill was not honed on the open sea. It was, rather, the island-riddled, delta-and-desert marshland of coastal Gujarat that he mastered. Perhaps his experience in Basra, whose climate and marshy terrain is similar in fundamental ways to that of coastal Gujarat, gave him an advantage, one that Mahmud Begarha recognized in promoting him.

In 1478 when he was still probably only in his twenties, and as a reward for his early military successes, Malik Ayaz was awarded the governorship of the relatively humble port island of Diu. The island was only 40 square kilometres in area; it was part of a delta complex on the southern fringe of Gujarat's Kathiawar peninsula, separated from the mainland by a murky creek connected to the Chasi River. The terrain was arid, sandy and windswept; the island's northern side, facing the creek, was a tidal salty marshland, while the south was rocky, with limestone cliffs. Yet, under his rule, Malik Ayaz turned this unpromising terrain into the most prosperous city in Gujarat. Diu became a critical entrepôt in the international spice trade, to which both Hindu and Muslim merchants as well as many foreigners were invited. As governor, Malik Ayaz led a flamboyant lifestyle, opening up his palace to the residents of Diu for sumptuous feasts. But this was no descent into the luxuriousness of an idle despot: he simultaneously toiled to make the city a military stronghold, devising ingenious strategies for fortifying and defending it. Employing a technology similar to that of the Ottomans in the Golden Horn, he erected a tower on a rock in the Chasi River harbour; from this, he drew a massive iron chain across the mouth of the harbour at the south and east of the island. The chain was raised to admit trading vessels; but it served primarily to block the entry of enemy ships into the harbour. Malik Ayaz also built a bridge over the creek lying between island and the mainland. Together, the chain and the bridge made Diu almost invulnerable to attack from the sea.

Malik Ayaz's innovative safeguards were designed to protect Diu from the Portuguese, who were looking to seize ports on India's west coast. They had already taken Cochin. But they were keen to muscle into Gujarat in order to take fuller control of the spice trade. To defend the Gujarat coast, Malik Ayaz forged an extraordinary, multinational tactical alliance. He extracted from Circassian ex-slave Al-Ashraf Qansuh al-Ghawri, the Egyptian Mamluk sultan, a promise of a fleet. He also received promises of support from Venice and the Zamorin of Calicut, both partners with the Mamluks in the spice trade. These alliances speak to Malik Ayaz's unusual transnational affinities. Just as his embodied experiences of combat in Russia and Basra may have helped him defend Gujarat's hinterland and marshlands, so may his multiple Gujarati/firangi/mamluk identities have proved a potential asset in dealing variously with Indian, European and Egyptian rulers.

In 1508, the Mamluk fleet that Malik Ayaz had requested finally reached India's west coast. But it turned out to be woefully ill-prepared for combat with the Portuguese. Because the Mamluks were not a naval power, they had obtained a dozen Ottoman galley ships which they had had to disassemble in Alexandria and rebuild in the Red Sea. The galleys were manned mostly by Greek soldiers and Ottoman slaves, many of them archers who were no match for the superior firepower of the Portuguese warships. The Mamluk fleet first engaged the Portuguese at

Chaul, about 60 kilometres south of Bombay on the Maharashtra coast. During the skirmish, Lourenço de Almeida, son of the Portuguese viceroy, was killed. His father, Francisco de Almeida, threatened violent retaliation; Malik Ayaz quickly sought to appease him, but the Portuguese viceroy retorted that 'I will take your city, to pay for everything, and you, for the help you have done at Chaul.' The Portuguese fleet that descended on Diu on 3 February 1509, was a veritable machine of destruction: it consisted of eighteen warships armed with state-of-the-art grenades, artillery and cannons. Although the Mamluk flotilla—which included ships dispatched by the Zamorin of Calicut—numbered a hundred, most of its vessels were small dhows that did not allow its occupants to board the taller Portuguese galleons. They proved sitting ducks for Almeida's navy, who sprayed them with cannons and grenades at will. The Gujarati/Mamluk/Calicut fleet capitulated within a matter of hours.

After this crushing defeat, Malik Ayaz offered the Portuguese viceroy a fortress at Diu. But much to his surprise, Almeida refused it, thinking it would be too much trouble to maintain a land presence there. For him, what was more important was the Portuguese display of utter naval superiority on the open sea. Diu's complex network of delta marshes and creeks were, in his eyes, a strategic liability for his navy. The Portuguese therefore resolved to turn their attention to the better-harboured Goa instead, which they captured the following year. And so Malik Ayaz lived to fight another day. In this phase of his life, we might conclude that his skills were less the product of sharp-shooting archery or able-bodied seamanship than of pure luck coupled with a canny instinct for political survival. We can certainly see him chopping and changing his loyalties after the battle of Diu. He abandoned the alliance with the Mamluks, and briefly considered siding with the Portuguese. Then, sensing their rapacity, he sent out feelers to the Ottoman emperor, renewed his alliance with the Zamorin of Calicut, and spent the rest of his life resisting the Estado da Índia. The Portuguese were to capture Diu only some ten years after Malik Ayaz's death in 1522.

Despite the disastrous losses suffered by the joint Gujarati/Mamluk/Calicut fleet in 1509, we shouldn't underestimate the extent to which Malik Ayaz's political survival skills were built on his mastery of the distinctive terrain and waterways of Diu. He succeeded not just because he had received the patronage of Mahmud Begarha, or because he had cultivated canny alliances with other powers. Malik Ayaz also worked closely with his physical environment, acquiring an intimately embodied knowledge of its river harbour, creeks and marshlands. His was no doubt a knowledge built partly on his individual experience of Basra. But his experience of Diu's environment was also collective; he would have had to traverse the island's waterscapes repeatedly with other sailors to learn the river tidal patterns, to identify where the submarine rocks were located, to determine the best spots to berth ships. Malik Ayaz may have been a fair-weather friend in his military allegiances. But in crucial ways, his principle allegiance remained the same for forty-four years: to the land and waters of Diu. And that's part of the reason why this Slavic slave has gone down in history as a principled 'Indian' resister of the Portuguese.

The Chinese Captive: Chinali

In the centuries immediately before Malik Ayaz's alliance with the Zamorin of Calicut, there had been a significant Chinese presence on the Malabar Coast—one that has left faint yet still visible traces. We might think of the Chinese fishing nets in Cochin; former Chinese districts such as the Silk Street of Calicut; and the ruins of Chinese temples near Quilon. The Chinese traded for several centuries with Arab merchants in Quilon, and the famed eunuch admiral Zheng He led his great fleet seven times to the Malabar Coast between 1405 and 1433. But by the time Malik Ayaz fought the Portuguese, the once thriving trade between China and the Malabar Coast, driven by the import and export of spices, had all but ended. There was still a community in Calicut called the Chinna Kribala, the descendants of Chinese and Malays who had intermarried with locals. But by and large, the Chinese had vacated Kerala.

Chinali, who lived in the Calicut kingdom fort of Kottakkal in the last decades of the sixteenth century, was a notable exception. Some have speculated that he was a member of the Chinna Kribala community. But Diogo de Couto, the author of the seventh Decade of the Portuguese chronicle *Decades of India* (1603), tells us that Chinali was a Chinese sailor who, prior to moving to India, had been enslaved by the Portuguese. There's little reason to doubt Couto: he had personally interrogated Chinali in 1600, just days before his execution in Goa. We do not know if Chinali was from mainland China. He may have been a native of Macau, the Portuguese colony in south China. It is more likely, though, that he was born in Malaya. Couto claims that Chinali had been a slave in Malacca, the fortified Portuguese city on the western coast of the Malayan peninsula. Previously a way station for Zheng He's fleet en route to India, it was home to a small but sizeable Chinese diaspora community.

The Portuguese had many slaves in their Asian colonies, though most in Goa and Macau were from Africa. These African slaves were often forced to convert to Christianity: in Macau, they constituted a kind of Christian mamluk caste, stoutly defending the colony from attacks by the Dutch. As I noted in the introduction, they seem to have been regarded as firangis by Indian rulers: the African Muslim João de Santiago, who had been forced to convert to Christianity by his Portuguese masters, embraced his old religion when he entered into service with the Gujarati Sultan Bahadur Shah. Yet he assumed the name of Frangi Khan. Many native slaves from Malacca would also have been forced to convert to Christianity. Ferdinand Magellan was accompanied in his circumnavigation of the world by a Malaccan slave who had been baptized and given the name Enrique. It is quite possible that Chinali had also been baptized and given a Christian name. And because he had spent time as a slave of the Portuguese, it is likely that Chinali would have registered for many Malabar natives as a firangi.

Chinali was supposed to have been 'liberated' by the Kunhali Marakkar, a naval warlord-cum-pirate based in Kottakkal who (sometimes) served the Zamorin of Calicut. But we know little about the circumstances of the boy's transfer from the Portuguese to the Kunhali. Our knowledge of Chinali is drawn entirely from two accounts by Europeans: Diogo de Couto's *Decades*, in which Chinali is mentioned only in passing, and a remarkable narrative published in 1611 by the French traveller François Pyrard de Laval. It is largely because of the latter that some might think of Chinali as a 'freed' slave.

Pyrard's is a swashbuckling tale. He was part of the first French expedition in the early 1600s to the Malabar Coast; although the French were relative latecomers to India, they—like the Portuguese—were eager to break into the lucrative spice trade. But the expedition's hopes were dashed after Pyrard's vessel was shipwrecked in the South Maalhosmadulu Atoll of the Maldives in the Arabian Sea and its crew taken captive. Malaria quickly reduced the Frenchmen's numbers from forty to four. Although the survivors were treated well by their captors, they were stuck on the island for four years, during which time Pyrard learned the local Dhivehi language and customs. His ethnographic observations make up the bulk of his narrative. But it is lent considerable flavour by what happened to him subsequently: he somehow managed to escape the Maldives aboard a Bengali ship, was taken to Chittagong, made his way back to Cochin, was imprisoned and tortured by the Portuguese, and then succeeded in travelling to the Moluccas before returning to France. Pyrard's experiences of imprisonment and torture in Cochin predisposed him to regard the Portuguese as the principal villains of Asia. And his horror of the Portuguese, along with his own experience of escaping captivity, arguably coloured his account of the Kunhali Marakkar and Chinali.

The story of the Kunhali and his Chinese slave had evidently become something of a folk legend in Portuguese Cochin by the time Pyrard reached there in 1607, seven years after Chinali's death. Pyrard derives much of his information from Couto. But he gives Couto's report a somewhat different spin, based in part on his dialogue with the Kunhali's nephew, with whom he stayed for twelve days in 1607. Pyrard writes that 'Chinali, a Chinese…had been a servant at Malacca, and said to have been the captive of a Portuguese, taken as a boy from a fusta, and afterwards brought to Kunhali, who conceived such an affection for him that he trusted him with everything'. Because Chinali had been the slave of the dreaded Portuguese, Pyrard assumed that his new Indian master had liberated him. And because both Chinali and the Kunhali were mortal enemies of the Portuguese, Pyrard saw them as fellow opponents of Portuguese tyranny. But his account leaves things a little unclear. Chinali, he tells us, was taken from a fusta—a small galley boat conventionally rowed by twenty-four to thirty-six slaves. This was not the standard Portuguese merchant ship, but rather a vessel favoured by the North African corsairs of the Mediterranean as well as by Portuguese pirates in the Orient. We don't know if Chinali was one of the fusta's galley slaves. But that he should have been captured from a fusta rather than a merchant ship or galleon makes sense: given that he operated primarily out of dhows and fustas himself, the Kunhali would not have been able to board and loot one of the large Portuguese ships. Chinali, in short, was probably the booty of a cross-pirate raid.

As such, he would have been not so much liberated as passed on to a new owner. Once he became the property of the Kunhali, however, Chinali was bonded to him in ways redolent of the mamluk system into which Gujarati slaves such as Malik Ayaz and Frangi Khan had been assimilated. First of all, he was given a new name and religion that, like the name 'Frangi Khan', signaled his integration into a local

JONATHAN GIL HARRIS

Indian community even as it marked him as foreign: 'Chinali' is a Muslim name—Chin Ali—which means 'Chinese Ali'. Second, Chinali became the Kunhali's trusted lieutenant. According to Couto and Pyrard alike, the two men enjoyed an unusual intimacy, with the Kunhali treating Chinali as his son and confidant. Which is to say: their relation reproduced the paternalism of the mamluk bond. Their intimacy translated also into a shared antipathy to the Portuguese. In the rather intemperate words of Couto, both the Kunhali and Chinali were 'fanatical Muslims' committed to driving the infidel Portuguese out of the Malabar Coast.

The Kunhali, whose full name was Muhammad Kunhali Marakkar IV, was already a powerful and much-feared figure on the Malabar Coast. He was the scion of a powerful line of Muslim naval warriors: the Marakkars derive their name from the Malayalam word for boat. For a century they had served the Hindu Zamorins of Calicut, but their origin is uncertain. They have been linked to the Mappila pirates, but there is some evidence to suggest that they were descended from Egyptian Arabs. They had long played a leading role as middlemen in the rich spice trade between the Malabar Coast and the Red Sea. With the incursions of the Portuguese in the early sixteenth century and their capture of Cochin in 1503, the Marakkars were employed to defend Cochin's traditional enemy Calicut. Their brief was to use their naval power to protect the Zamorin's monopoly on the spice trade; the trade-off was that they were granted a near-royal status. The title of 'Kunhali' was hereditary, and passed down for four generations. But in the 1590s, as Muhammad Kunhali Marakkar acquired more power, his relation with the Zamorin soured. It was pushed to breaking point after the Zamorin covertly partnered with Calicut's long-standing enemy, the Portuguese, to try and destroy the Kunhali. This served to make the Kunhali an even more redoubtable foe of the Portuguese. It also transformed him into a rogue ruler of his own small dominion: as Couto said, he 'was so proud as to forget that he was but a vassal, and to hold himself out for a king'. His 'kingdom', described by Couto, was a heavily fortified camp on the Kottakkal peninsula next to the Kotta River; its walls, four paces thick, enclosed a citadel and a dungeon crammed with Portuguese prisoners.

At the Kunhali's side, Chinali became the scourge of the Malabar seas in the 1590s, with Couto claiming that he was responsible for killing or torturing numerous Portuguese. According to Pyrard, Chinali's malice derived principally from religious reasons: 'he was the greatest exponent of the Moorish superstition and enemy of the Christians in all Malabar, and for those taken captive at sea and brought thither he invented the most exquisite kinds of torture when he martyred them'. Here Pyrard's tone of mild admiration for fellow opponents of the Portuguese shades into a more conventional Islamophobia. Yet he also clearly sees Chinali's violence as a response to the cruel period of captivity that he, like Pyrard himself, had supposedly endured with the Portuguese.

For all its brevity, Pyrard's narrative lends Chinali some complexity. He was not just a religious fanatic; he was also, Pyrard notes, a master on water. Chinali had obviously acquired his sea legs aboard the Portuguese fusta on which he had previously served. But he operated with yet more skill on the Kerala backwaters, thanks to his experiences with the Kunhali and the other pirates. He helped capture other fustas and small boats from the Portuguese. But most of all, he acquired considerable skill in river navigation and combat. The Kunhali's camp at Kottakkal, whose invincibility scared the Zamorin and the Portuguese alike, was not a coastal fort; its power derived from its river location, which afforded access only to small vessels lower than those used by the Portuguese in war. In such river craft, which are not unlike the tourist houseboats that ply the Kerala backwaters today, one is less confined than is the case in bigger ships. These river boats allow quick movements from the deck to the river bank, or from boat to boat. To capture Portuguese ships, Chinali must have become adept at clambering, running, jumping, and grappling across vessels; he must have honed his sense of balance on water, and on fusta decks soaked with monsoon rain. Yet even as Couto and Pyrard cast Chinali in a leading role in the Kunhali's sea and river raids, he was no doubt accompanied by other similarly-abled pirates in the capture of Portuguese fustas. The Kotta River was, in Couto's words, a 'nest' for pirates who captured and operated these smaller vessels. The word 'nest' suggests a teeming pirate collectivity. And it is within this collectivity that Chinali had become a navikan—Malayalam for skilled sailor.

Through the machinations of the Zamorin of Calicut, however, acting in concert with his supposed Portuguese enemies, Chinali was finally captured in 1600 along with the Kunhali. The Zamorin had promised the pair safe passage if they surrendered; but when the Kunhali, accompanied by Chinali, surrendered his sword to the Zamorin, they were promptly arrested by the Portuguese. Both were tortured and asked to convert to Christianity. The Kunhali refused, and was gruesomely executed. But Chinali consented, taking the name of Bartolomeu. Following his interview with Couto, he was accompanied to the scaffold by Jesuits from the Brotherhood of Holy Misericórdia and orphan children who prayed for him, after which he was executed and buried in consecrated ground in Goa: quite the send-off. But why did Chinali accede to this last-minute conversion and change of name? Was he simply younger and more impressionable than the Kunhali? Was his conversion an act of defiance against his humiliated master? Or had he felt compelled to return to a religion he had previously been forced into, in the forlorn hope of saving himself by acknowledging a shared Christian past with his firangi captors? Bartolomeu may have even been his earlier Christian name as well: Saint Bartholomew was believed to have been, along with Saint Thomas, one of the original evangelists in India. His name was thus associated with bringing the light of gospel to Asia, and it was a popular name for Indian and East Indian converts.

With Muhammad Kunhali Marakkar's execution, an overlooked chapter in the history of 'authentically Indian' resistance to European colonialism was brought to an end—a chapter partly spearheaded by a Chinese slave navikan. Chinali's leading role in the Kunhali's raids against the Portuguese complicates the inscription on the memorial to the Kunhali Marakkars at Kottakkal, erected by the Indian navy: 'The Kunhali Marakkars occupy a special position in the history of the Malabar Coast. They symbolize native resistance to foreign rule, and made lasting contributions to our seafaring traditions.' In this instance, at least, both 'native resistance to foreign rule' and 'our seafaring traditions' were the product of complex border-crossings. And Chinali was not the only foreign captive warrior who helped defend a south Indian spice-trading territory from European invaders.

The Flemish Renegade: Dillanai, aka Eustachius de Lannoy

It is easy to assume that the mamluk system was simply a Muslim institution, a backward custom imported from the Arab and Persian worlds to an India where the idea of a slave-troop caste was alien, even abhorrent. Of course, the Hindu caste system meant that there was already a local warrior jati—the Kshatriyas and, in the case of Kerala, the Nairs. But something like the mamluk system had been a feature of Hindu kingdoms prior to the arrival of Islam in India. The Chola Kaikkolars, for example, were a military caste that seems to have been comprised at least in part of war captives. And like the mamluks, they enjoyed a special proximity to and intimacy with the ruler.

A counterpart to the mamluk system was to be found also in the Hindu-ruled state of Vijayanagar, which had a huge number of foreign gunners on its payroll in the 1500s. These soldiers were vital in defending the Hindu kingdom and its startling rocky terrain from incursion by the Deccan sultanate armies. Although the Vijayanagar system seems closer to the modern wage-based model of the mercenary, the soldiers were in many ways mamluks: they were forbidden from leaving the kingdom, and were in effect glorified captives. We do not know precisely from where these foreign soldiers came. Some were clearly Portuguese. And judging from travellers Domingo Paes's and Fernão Nunes's descriptions of the Vijayanagar soldiers' clothes, which included 'Moorish' tunics, some were Muslims—quite possibly from the multinational forces of other Indian states, and most likely Central Asians or Afghans. Others may have been African: the Siddi Hindus and Muslims of Karnataka, often assumed to be the descendants of Goan runaway slaves, may partly trace their origins to African Vijayanagar soldiers. And the presence of archers in the Vijayanagar army suggests some others may have been, like Malik Ayaz of Gujarat, from the Caucasus region. That the soldiers were allowed to practice their own 'religions', plural, indicates that Christians as well as Muslims were likely among them.

A mamluk system, albeit a singular instance rather than a sustained tradition, can be seen also in the Hindu-ruled kingdom of Travancore. The system dates from a period technically outside the historical ambit of this book. But it is interesting to consider briefly inasmuch as it shows how, even in colonial-era India, the 'Muslim' mamluk warrior slave culture I have examined here persisted in—or was replicated by—a 'Hindu' state, albeit in transformed geopolitical circumstances. It also shows how, despite the sometimes pronounced Hindu antipathy to firangis as impure or untouchable, the 'foreigner' could still be valued if not fully embraced in military situations. Perhaps this was not despite but because of the logic of caste. So long as the sea and those who sailed it were considered impure, it was expedient to outsource local naval operations to firangis and non-Hindus, as the Zamorins of Calicut had done with the Kunhali Marakkars and then Chinali. Whether this motive played a part in the strange story of Eustachius de Lannoy, also known as Dillanai, we can only speculate.

Once again, as with Malik Ayaz and Chinali, the story of a captive firangi warrior's relocation to India is tied up with the vicissitudes of the global spice trade. Eustachius de Lannoy was a Flemish sea captain; born in 1715 in Flanders, he was sent by the Dutch East India Company in 1740 to help set up a factory at Colachel, near Kanyakumari in what is now Tamil Nadu. The Company, like its Portuguese and French predecessors, had hoped to crack the spice trade. But it had sought also to compete with the English, whose strength was growing in the region. After some initial success in claiming land around Kanyakumari for the Dutch, de Lannoy and his crew were defeated and taken captive in 1741 by the Travancore army, under the command of the redoubtable Maharaja Marthanda Varma. Under the maharaja's rule, Travancore had become an anti-colonial power to be reckoned with. Marthanda Varma had expanded his territories against the advances of the Dutch and the English. And he had shrewdly extended his patronage to the sizeable Syrian Christian community of southwest India, whose international trading connections allowed him to bypass the networks increasingly dominated by European colonial powers. Marthanda Varma was a canny military tactician as well as politician: he reduced the influence of feudal Nair lords and their private armies and created a new standing army loyal to him and the Travancore state. In short, he created the conditions in which something like the old mamluk system of the north could take root.

After the defeat of the Dutch at Colachel, Marthanda Varma offered de Lannoy a position as a commander in his army, with the request that he reorganize it on the Dutch model. De Lannoy accepted the offer; along with some twenty other soldiers in his regiment, he spent the rest of his life—nearly four decades—in India. Perhaps the Dutchman made a 'free' choice to serve Marthanda Varma. But he was in effect the maharaja's military captive. As such, de Lannoy enjoyed some of the privileges of a mamluk general. He displayed unswerving loyalty to, and earned the enduring trust of, Marthanda Varma, who granted him a comfortable house at Udayagiri Fort near Kanyakumari. He worked closely with Marthanda Varma and his diwan, Ramayyan Dalawa, to devise Travancore military and naval policy. And in the process, he came to be called Dillanai, a Tamil version of his name.

Dillanai's success is all the more remarkable given the odds against it. These odds were in large part cultural. As a non-Hindu who lacked caste, he wasn't allowed to set foot in the maharaja's palace. Dillanai's meetings with the piously Brahmin yet evidently pragmatic Marthanda Varma had to take place in other, 'neutral' locations; even there, the Dutchman must have borne the brunt of various caste-related proscriptions, which were enforced more strictly in Travancore than elsewhere in the subcontinent. Dillanai would have had to take considerable care, for example, about the water and food he touched and in whose company he touched it. The imperative to re-train his body's habits, however, was not just cultural or religious. It was also ecological. To succeed as Dillanai, he also had to adapt his body—as had his mamluk predecessors—to the land and waterscapes of his new country.

Dillanai fought mostly on land, helping Marthanda Varma win territory as far north as Cochin. But his achievements extended also to the sea, though less as naval officer than as maritime fortification strategist. For example, he designed and constructed an elaborate circular sea fort, Vattakottai, off the Kanyakumari coast. He also designed and constructed a 40-kilometre-long defensive wall at Travancore's northern boundary, the Nedumkotta, which led up to the Western Ghats from Vypin Island in the Cochin harbour estuary. The wall prevented land and sea attacks by the English and the Dutch. In later decades, it also kept out Tipu Sultan, the expansionist ruler of the kingdom of Mysore. These two constructions not only speak to Dillanai's Dutch tactical acumen; they also indicate his keen feel for the lie of the Indian land. To build Vattakottai and the Nedumkotta, he clearly spent considerable time with his troops trawling the coast and climbing the Western Ghats, becoming sensitive to their points of vulnerability, but also allowing the terrain itself to serve as the best security against invaders. His comfort with fortifying Travancore's coastal zones may have derived in part from his earlier familiarity with the low-lying Dutch and Flemish flatlands, themselves protected against the predations of the sea by well-designed dykes. But in the kingdom's inland areas, Dillanai's body also would have had to adapt to a decidedly alien activity, at least for a Dutchman: scaling steep mountains, quite possibly at speed and sometimes in the pouring monsoon rain, with well-drilled regiments who had acquired an intimate knowledge of the Western Ghat's many precipices, hidden passes, and waterfalls.

This combination of tactical skill and collectively embodied geographical knowledge is one reason why Dillanai earned the title of 'valiya kappithaan' or 'great captain'. It is a nice portmanteau title: half Malayalam, half Dutch (the Dutch word for 'captain' is 'kapitein'), it embodies his split identity as a firangi who had become Indian. And his identity remained split for the rest of his life. With the strong encouragement of Marthanda Varma, Dillanai had introduced specifically Dutch technologies—especially artillery and gunpowder—to the re-organized Travancore army, which helped make his new country a bulwark of 'Indian' resistance to foreign invasion and colonial rule. Indeed, he played a major part in making Travancore one of the most independent kingdoms in the subcontinent; alone among the states of south India, it retained a monopoly on its spice trade even after the British annexation. The inscription on Dillanai's Christian grave at Udayagiri Fort is, fittingly, in both Latin and Tamil; it notes that 'for 37 years he served the king with utmost fidelity'. In other words, the valiya kappithaan's grave memorialized him as both Eustachius de Lannoy, a loyal devotee of his European religion—Roman Catholic, as indicated by the Latin inscription—and Dillanai, an equally loyal Tamil-speaking patriot of Travancore.

Although they were separated by two centuries, it would have been fascinating to hear a conversation between Dillanai, the valiya kappithaan, and Garcia da Orta, the firangi hakeem, about their diverse experiences of south Indian wind. Orta smelled the fragrant spices of the Malabar Coast at sea in the night air, air that ultimately filled the sails of his master Martim Afonso de Sousa's war galleon and blew it towards victory over the Mappila pirates at Vedalai. If Sousa's wind-assisted campaign gave the Portuguese an upper hand in the global battle for the spice trade, the campaigns of Dillanai insured that the sea air could also blow the spice trade the other way, back to India and to Indian control. And he facilitated that wind-change by coming to know and working closely with the distinctive features of his southern Indian environment: in effect, he embodied the sea breeze that blows from the ocean back to the land, caressing the coastal shores and making its way up the waterfall-webbed Western Ghats. In this way, Dillanai was even closer than Malik Ayaz or Chinali to Ayaz, the firangi slave with whom I started this chapter. For 'Ayaz' means, in Persian, 'night breeze'—a name that suggests how much the mamluk or captive warrior might embody his new Indian environment and its unpredictable turbulences.

Perhaps there *is* some poetry, then, lurking in the prosaic lives of India's captive firangi troops.

In the previous chapter, I suggested that the biographies of India's foreign mamluks are fitful prose-poems. Yet the life-story of one migrant slave who lived in the Deccan during the late sixteenth and early seventeenth centuries might seem more reminiscent of an extended action movie. And that's because his biography is also the saga of how an Indian martial art was born. Without this art, it's arguable that one of the most powerful modern understandings of what it means to be authentically Indian couldn't have taken shape.

This slave's saga is the prequel to another, more famous military tale that has acquired considerable potency in post-independence Maharashtra and India: the tale of Chhatrapati Shivaji Bhosale, the great Maratha warrior king of the 1670s. Because Shivaji successfully overcame the supremacy of the Muslim Mughals to set up his independent Maratha kingdom, many now valorize him as an authentically Indian nationalist—a Hindu defender of the Maharashtra soil, valiantly protecting it from foreign peoples and religions. Yet this authentically Indian nationalist was greatly indebted to a martial art developed by a Muslim migrant. That migrant, Malik Ambar, is the subject of this chapter. And so is the martial art he perfected.

Any martial art entails training the body to a superior degree of physical ability. And martial skill is acquired through endless repetitions of moves—punches, kicks, pushes, grapples, springs—which instil in the warrior a set of reflexes that bypass his or her conscious decision-making processes. A warrior whose fighting reflexes are so deeply ingrained can seem like a singular automaton or machine. But the machine that motors a martial art is not a singular human body. It's a vast ensemble of elements, human and non-human. First, the martial art machine is a collective human entity. This entity is constituted not just in space—in the shape of an army of warriors who train and fight together—but also over time—as a martial 'school' of practitioners whose knowledge has been passed down over generations from teachers to students. Second, the martial art machine binds humans to inanimate elements. The warrior works in concert not just with his or her weapons but also with a larger physical environment in which she or he has learned to fight. Learning a martial art means adapting one's body to the distinctive features of a specific terrain: hard and soft surfaces, throughways and obstacles, slopes and their gravitational effects. In the process, the warrior's body develops an intimate muscle memory of its environment, and in a way that exceeds simple cartographical knowledge. Cartography functions in two dimensions by mapping points on a flat plane. By contrast, the martial art practitioner's embodied knowledge of his or her terrain is topographical. Unlike cartography, topography functions in three dimensions, plotting the vertical elevation variations as well as horizontal extensions of a landscape. The martial art that Malik Ambar helped invent, and that enabled Shivaji and his Maratha warriors' military successes, was particularly attuned to the topographical details of his environment.

To grasp the fundamental principles of Malik Ambar's innovative martial art, and the legacy he bequeathed to Shivaji, we need first to visit the scene of a battle on the Deccan highlands in the early seventeenth century—and from there, voyage back in time to the highlands of another country, another continent and another century.

◆

May 1621. The Mughal emperor Jahangir has been fighting a long, grinding war in the Deccan against the rebel troops of Ahmadnagar. Although Jahangir's father Akbar invaded the sultanate in 1600 and deposed its infant sultan Bahadur Nizam Shah, Ahmadnagar's soldiers have refused to accede to Jahangir's rule. In the months following the conquest, a rebel general named Malik Ambar had installed a second boy, distantly related to the sultan, as the new nizam shah. When, in 1610, the boy died, he crowned yet another child as puppet-sultan in the rebel troops' new stronghold of Khadki. For eleven years, Malik Ambar and his troops have fiercely defended Khadki and Ahmadnagar against the Mughals in the name of this now teenaged sultan, Burhan Nizam Shah III.

Jahangir's army has had to contend with a redoubtable enemy. Malik Ambar, now in his seventies, is still a crack military tactician. Despite the Mughals' numerical supremacy, superior artillery and greater cavalry strength, Malik Ambar and his troops have stubbornly managed to maintain their ground. But 'ground' is perhaps not the right word. And that's because the terrain the rebels occupy is anything but solid. Although the Mughals have succeeded in sacking Khadki, they come unstuck on a sticky wicket: Malik Ambar, having spirited the young sultan to the fort city of Daulatabad, has led his troops into a zone that Jahangir, in his memoir, the *Tuzuk-i-Jahangiri*, calls 'chihla u jamjama'—marshes and quagmires. This murky terrain confounds the much more regimented Mughal army, used to campaigns on solid battlefields. From the marshlands, Jahangir tells us, the rebels have 'scattered in all directions', disappearing into the rocky hills of the Deccan to fight another day. It is a miraculous vanishing act and, for Jahangir, a massive disappointment. Although he praises his 'victorious army' and brags that Khadki will not regain its splendour for 'twenty years', Jahangir will in fact never be able to get the better of Malik Ambar and his troops. The Mughal emperor may have won the battle, but he has lost the war: Malik Ambar—with whom Jahangir has become so violently obsessed that in 1616 he commissioned an official portrait of himself shooting arrows into the Ahmadnagar general's decapitated head—quickly rebuilds Khadki and successfully resists the Mughals until his death in 1626.

When the news finally reaches Jahangir's court of Malik Ambar's long-awaited death (albeit from old age rather than decapitation), the ageing Mughal emperor is himself too ill to write about his joy at having outlived, if not outfought or outsmarted, his great adversary. By this time, the composition of the *Tuzuk-i-Jahangiri* has been outsourced to a hired Mughal court scribe, Mu'tamad Khan. And unlike his choleric master, Mu'tamad Khan offers a decidedly sober, even admiring account of Malik Ambar. 'In warfare, in command, in sound judgment, and in administration', he writes, 'he had no rival or equal... He well understood that predatory warfare, which in the language of the Dakhin is called bargi-giri.'

'Bargi-giri': what an utterly sublime word. Its very sound might seem to evoke the bruising physicality of fierce hand-to-hand combat. One can imagine a modern Hindi action film of that name starring a shirtless Salman Khan or a mustachioed Rajinikanth as Malik Ambar, somersaulting in slow motion as he kick-boxes, karate-chops, and scimitar-scythes his way through a battalion of Mughal dupes. But unfortunately, at least for modern directors and film stars, the art of bargi-giri is not the stuff of today's action movies. It is instead a guerrilla martial art concerned less with muscular face-to-face combat than with long-term tactical battles of attrition in the Deccan's challenging terrain. Malik Ambar's vanishing act in the chihla u jamjama near Daulatabad is a perfect illustration of bargi-giri. It no doubt demanded a measure of military athleticism; but it primarily entailed using the soft Deccan marshlands to wrong-foot the overly regimented Mughal troops.

Malik Ambar's command of bargi-giri bespeaks an extraordinary intimacy as much with the rocky ranges as the swampy bogs of the Deccan plateau. But it hints too at topographical knowledge gleaned from a life that had traversed nations and continents. For Malik Ambar was not originally from the Deccan. He had been born in the highlands of East Africa, in a land ruled by the Christian kingdom of Ethiopia. And he was not originally a malik or lord: he had arrived in India as a slave destined for military service. So how do we locate Malik Ambar? Was he Ethiopian? Indian? Both? Neither?

These questions shape my narrative of the border-crossing life of Malik Ambar. His biography is part of a larger, often neglected story about Indian Ocean trade and forced African slave migration to the subcontinent. It is also part of another story about an African military and political culture that shaped the medieval Deccan sultanates and, more indirectly, modern Maharashtra. As I have suggested, acolytes of Shivaji regard as authentically Indian a military art that owes a huge debt to a Muslim from Africa. But it isn't just the latter-day foot soldiers of Shivaji who are wrong-footed by Malik Ambar's identity—as if his bargi-giri was a form of war waged against not just the Mughals but also certain modern ideas about what it means to be Indian. I too struggle to place him. Might we better understand Malik Ambar's life, and his relation to his new land, through the prism of the firangi?

◆

In his haunting AIDS memoir *My Own Country*, the physician-novelist Abraham Verghese briefly describes his often confusing experience growing up in Ethiopia as the son of expatriate Malayalis. One of Verghese's reminiscences stands out in particular. Though he considered himself a local, Verghese was, throughout his childhood, taunted with a xenophobic Amharic epithet: 'ferengi', or foreigner. To be called a 'ferengi' was, of course, doubly estranging for an Ethiopian native of Indian origin who, habituated to the identical-sounding 'firangi', could not help but hear in the Amharic term of abuse a reminder that he was *neither* Ethiopian *nor* Indian. Such is the destabilising lot of the Indian expatriate in East Africa, and indeed of Indian diaspora populations in many parts of the world. But what if Verghese's trajectory of migration were to be reversed? What would an East African migrant to India be called? How would he or she react to being characterized as a firangi?

And can we even call an East African in India a firangi?

Malik Ambar, at least during his Deccan life, was not what most Indians would now think of as a firangi. He was not from Europe; he was not Christian; he was not white. Unlike some other Africans who earned the soubriquet of 'Firangi', Malik Ambar didn't ever serve a Christian master, as did the one-time Portuguese slave Frangi Khan, the African Muslim bondsman of the Gujarat sultan Bahadur Shah. And it is highly unlikely Malik Ambar was born a Christian. He was indeed sold into slavery in a Christian country, the kingdom of Ethiopia. Yet his sale there was almost certainly due to his *not* being a Christian: because Ethiopian orthodox Christians were prohibited from enslaving co-religionists, they tended to recruit slaves from the pagan kingdoms and provinces to its south. Even for those Indians who may have understood Malik Ambar to be a migrant from a Christian land, his identity was understood regionally rather than religiously. After coming to India, Malik Ambar was known not as a firangi but as a habshi—the local Dakhni term for an Abyssinian. And in the habshi Deccan regiment to which he was initially assigned as a military slave, he and his compatriots were pointedly distinguished from the specifically firangiyan troops.

Yet, to consider Malik Ambar a firangi is, I believe, a rewarding thought experiment. Because he was not from the kingdom of Ethiopia proper but from an annexed territory, Malik Ambar—like Verghese—could well be called a ferengi by native Amharic speakers today. But the Indian rather than the Amharic version of the word, and its distinctive ambivalences, is perhaps a more accurate description of the vagaries of Malik Ambar's identity. Despite its referential slipperiness throughout the sixteenth and seventeenth centuries, the word 'firangi' tended to name one phenomenon in particular: an often poor foreigner from a Christian-ruled land who has become local, but was still in some ways marked as a foreigner. As an enslaved native of a province at the periphery of the greater Abyssinian region, Malik Ambar was both an Ethiopian and not an Ethiopian, both an alien and not an alien. This ambivalence was something that stuck with him throughout his subsequent migrations to and within India, where he was always both a foreigner and not a foreigner, an Indian and not an Indian. As such, Malik Ambar's tale does much to illuminate the paradoxes of pre-colonial firangi identity.

Malik Ambar's tale also sheds more light on the long, complex history of military slavery in the subcontinent: in particular, the twin marginality and political centrality of the migrant mamluk or captive warrior. And his tale is again a biography in the radical sense I teased out in my introduction—specifically, a story of how a migrant body was imprinted by the unique ecologies and topographies of India. Unlike the maritime military slaves of the previous chapter, Malik Ambar experienced his new country as an exclusively landlocked one. Yet like them, he also worked creatively with water, albeit in a dry terrain where abundant sources of potable water were often hard to come by. His creative labours—inspired in equal part by his body's adaptation to India and his experiences outside of it—is why the biography of this East African ferengi resonates so powerfully with the stories of the first firangis.

◆

Much of Malik Ambar's early life remains veiled to us. Some commentaries claim that he was born a slave in Harar, a largely Muslim city in eastern Ethiopia. But a seventeenth-century Deccan record reports that he was born free and only later sold into slavery as a child by his impoverished parents. Although he certainly passed through the slave market of Harar, his origin there is questionable. One commentator claims his family came from a town called Alhura in the Wej province of the Muslim Adal Sultanate, near what is now Somalia. This is unlikely given that he was almost certainly not born a Muslim. Pieter van den Broecke, a Dutch traveller to Yemen and India, described Malik Ambar as 'a black kafir from Abyssinia with a stern Roman face'; remarkably, some have taken Malik Ambar's supposedly 'Roman face' as evidence that he must have been born in the Muslim and Christian areas of northeastern Ethiopia, whose inhabitants are more visibly descended from Semitic ancestors. But Van den Broecke also noted that Malik Ambar's birth name was Chapu, a fact confirmed by Deccan records in which he is called Shambhu and Shan-bu. As the Indian Ocean historian Richard Eaton has pointed out, the name—which is unmistakably both non-Muslim and non-Christian—indicates a point of origin in the pagan Kembata region, some 350 kilometres south of Addis Ababa, the modern capital of Ethiopia.

We do not know how old Chapu was when he was enslaved. So it is hard to ascertain how much his African years left an impression on him. He was born in 1548 or 1549; we know he had arrived in India by 1575 after living for some years in the Middle East, which makes it likely he was enslaved as a youth. His birth name stayed with him, if only as a memory, which suggests that he retained at least some of his native language in India. If he grew up in Kembata, his first tongue was probably a version of Kambaatissaata, one of the Cushitic dialects of the south, which belong to a very different family from the Semitic Amharic language of the north. In the Deccan, he would have had to acquire at least some fluency in the local Dakhni dialect as well as Marathi, Persian and Arabic. Still, as we will see, he may have had occasion to speak his native Cushitic tongue too. In India, Chapu additionally could have drawn on his experience of Kembata's social organization. The province was one of the more hierarchical societies of the larger region, with strongly demarcated distinctions between nobles, free commoners, artisans and slaves; Chapu was probably born into the second or the third class. A vestigial memory of this hierarchy may well have prepared him for the distinctions of caste and rank that were a vital part of the Hindu and Muslim cultures of the Deccan.

A third experience of his childhood also probably stayed with him throughout his migrations: living in arid highland territory. Kembata is on the lip of the Great Rift Valley, which cuts a swathe through Ethiopia. It is situated at considerable altitude, with a climate that is relatively mild and even chilly at night. The terrain is considered fertile by Ethiopian standards, which is why its population density is unusually high. But Kembata also endures long periods of no rain and, as a result, frequent drought and famine. Its rocky hills and seasonal creeks make it difficult to sustain good soil for subsistence farming, and annual crop yields vary considerably from year to year. Working what arable land there is poses significant physical challenges: scaling the hill slopes at altitude demands enormous athleticism and aerobic strength. As a result, anyone whose livelihood depends on farming these highlands runs the constant risk of depleted body salts, especially in times of drought. The chronic seasonal lack of water is partly offset, however, by the area's main crop, ensete, a potassium-rich cousin of the banana that is a good antidote to dehydration. Kembata's altitude, climate and ensetes may provide good training conditions for modern Ethiopia's many long-distance runners. But in the sixteenth century, Kembata was also a good training ground for a man who was to spend most of his adult life as a guerilla warrior on the highlands of the Deccan plateau. One can imagine the young Chapu skilfully scaling steep slopes, negotiating the boggy soil of silted creeks, and acquiring an intuitive sense of the patterns of rain and water flow through the hills and ravines. All these skills would serve him well later in his Indian life.

This is not to suggest that Chapu's life before his enslavement was some kind of romantic idyll. On the contrary: Kembata at this time was a highly dangerous place to live in. The area had been annexed by the Ethiopian Christian kingdom in the fifteenth century. But from 1529 to 1543, incursions by forces of the Adal Sultanate loosened the Ethiopian hold on Kembata and other southern provinces. Following the death in 1543 of the powerful Adal general, Amam ibn Ibrahim Al-Ghazni, the Oromo tribe invaded much of northern, eastern and central Ethiopia. Until 1554, the Oromos made a policy of enslaving the inhabitants of the areas they pillaged, turning them into gebrs—a term that literally means tax-paying serfs. It is not beyond the realm of possibility that a 5-year-old Chapu was one of those enslaved by the Oromos. But the southern provinces, including Kembata, largely resisted the Oromo supremacy. Instead, they became embroiled in civil wars of their own, fragmenting into small kingdoms. Amid this turmoil, Kembata also became the target of raiders in league with slave traders from Harar. Wars and raids conspired to bring many in Kembata to abject poverty—including, it would seem, Chapu's parents. Several sources claim that the parents sold their son to slave traders, though he may have been captured in war. In any case, Chapu's journey to India begins in Harar, the staging post of the Ethiopian slave trade.

Chapu's journey was not an isolated or individual event. It was part of the larger political economy of the Indian Ocean, in which Ethiopia was linked, through trade, to the Middle East and India. As Richard Eaton has noted, royals at the Abyssinian courts of the sixteenth century greatly valued Indian silk, a tendency remarked on by several European visitors. It appears that these silks were often bought from Indian traders in exchange for local slaves. The exchange was driven by a growing demand in the Deccan sultanates for military slave labour, a demand met partly by the political instability and economic deprivation of the southern kingdoms in the wake of the Adal Sultanate incursions. Tens of thousands of habshis from Kembata and its troubled neighbouring regions were enslaved and relocated to the subcontinent in the mid sixteenth century. Most were non-Christian and non-Muslim pagans: just as Christians could not be enslaved by Ethiopian Christians, so too did Quranic law prohibit Muslims from selling other Muslims. Indeed, the kingdom's Indian silk-wearing Christian rulers probably collaborated with Harar's Muslim slave traders to insure a ready supply of pagan habshi warrior-slaves for their Deccan trading partners.

Chapu was not initially bought by an Indian-bound trader, however. Van den Broecke reports that he was taken from Harar and re-sold in the Red Sea port of Mocha, in what is now Yemen, for eighty guilders. Chapu's owner, Qazi Hussein, converted him to Islam, as a result of which he was given the name Ambar (meaning 'ambergris' or 'precious jewel'). Becoming Muslim did not exempt him from being the property of another Muslim: according to local tradition, a Muslim could be a slave if he had been born a pagan. Soon Qazi Hussein re-sold Ambar for twenty ducats; he was then taken to the Baghdad slave market, where he was bought by a Shariah jurist from Mecca. We do not know how long he was in the jurist's possession, or what kind of work he was made to do. But after some time, Ambar was sold again, this time to a leading Baghdad merchant named Mir Qasim al-Baghdadi. Ambar's return to Baghdad proved to be something of a turning point for him, as his second stint there laid much of the foundation for his eventual life in India.

Mir Qasim al-Baghdadi didn't treat Ambar as a menial slave. For whatever reason—maybe he spied some talent in him, maybe he needed someone to perform clerical work for his businesses—he had Ambar formally educated in Arabic. And in Baghdad, the young slave also received other forms of education. Ambar again had an experience of water in a dry climate, but one radically different from what he had encountered in the highlands of Kembata. The city had been conquered by the Ottomans in 1534, and had begun to fall into a period of decline. But it still retained much of the old functional infrastructure of the Abbasid caliphate period from half a millennium earlier. In particular, the Abbasids had successfully negotiated the considerable challenges of Baghdad's near-desert location by building numerous aqueducts and canals that conveyed water from the Tigris and Euphrates rivers to all parts of the city. Only one of these aqueducts, carrying water to the shrine of Abdul al-Qadir, survives today; in the sixteenth century, however, most of the system was still operational. Indeed, medieval Baghdad was the exemplar of a modern, well-watered city. After the chronic water shortages of Kembata, this must have left a strong impression on the former Chapu.

A second major turning point came in 1575, when Mir Qasim took Ambar to the Deccan, presumably on a business trip. There he sold his Abyssinian slave to a nobleman named Chingiz Khan, the peshva (prime minister) of the nizam shah of Ahmadnagar. Ambar must have blinked twice upon meeting his new, powerful master. For Chingiz Khan, unlike many other local lords, was not a Persian or a Deccani. Like his new slave, he too was a habshi.

◆

The medieval Deccan ruling class was not ethnically homogenous. It included two dominant groups—Iranians or 'westerners', and Deccanis or 'locals' descended mostly from the royal Turkic and Afghan dynasties of northern India. In Ahmadnagar and Bijapur, these two groups were supplemented by a number of Maratha chiefs, mostly regional rajas and landlords who paid tribute to the sultans. But there was also a significant African presence among the lords or maliks. Chingiz Khan—known additionally as Malik Dabir—was typical of the Deccan's African lords: all of them were, in mamluk fashion, former military slaves from Kembata and Ethiopia who, having enjoyed royal patronage, had been granted high political offices. In other words, like firangi mamluks such as Malik Ayaz of Gujarat, the habshi slaves were not denied social mobility. Indeed, they constituted a vital part of the Deccan political culture and lent it much of its distinctly military character.

This key role arose partly in response to sporadic outbursts of factionalism between the Iranian 'westerners' and the Deccani 'locals'. The African lords represented a supposedly neutral party; they were often called upon to mediate conflicts between the two factions. In practice, however, they often identified with the Deccanis inasmuch as they too tended to see themselves as locals, having no active ties with their Ethiopian homeland the way the Iranians did with family members in Persia. The Africans' loyalty to the Deccan sultanates had usually been established through extended periods of service in the habshi military slave regiments. Chingiz Khan, for example, had worked his way up the ranks of one such regiment—eventually being appointed a general—before becoming the peshva of Ahmadnagar. There were habshi lords in other Deccan states too: among them were the immensely powerful Ikhlas Khan, a general who briefly became regent of Bijapur in the 1580s, and former slaves such as Hamid Khan and Dilawar Khan, both of whom played crucial roles in the Bijapuri succession struggles of that time. That these lords could become such a force in Deccan politics had much to do also with the implicit challenge represented by the habshi slave armies they commanded. In the Deccan, it was presumably a strategic error for the 'Western' and 'local' lords to disrespect generals of large regiments, especially the habshi regiments in which soldiers were fiercely bonded to their leaders through collective experiences not just of warfare but also, perhaps, of a common Cushitic tongue such as Kambaatissaata.

Ambar followed a career path similar to his new master's. In Chingiz Khan's service, he was initially just one of many habshi slaves serving the peshva. We do not know what prompted Chingiz Khan to favour Ambar, though it is quite possible that the slave had received a strong recommendation from Mir Qasim al-Baghdadi. Ambar's formal training in Arabic, for long one of the official languages of Ahmadnagar court—as demonstrated by the experience of Garcia da Orta—would have given him another significant advantage. In any case, Chingiz Khan soon began to treat Ambar as a confidante and surrogate son. Khan's wife even found him a bride, an African woman named (as far as we can tell) Karima Bibi, though we do not know if she too was Abyssinian. Perhaps Karima Bibi, Ambar, and Chingiz Khan were all part of the larger Kambaatissaata-speaking sub-community in Ahmadnagar. After Chingiz Khan died, Ambar was not formally manumitted; but he seems no longer to have been considered a slave. For reasons that remain unclear, he decided to leave Ahmadnagar and seek his fortune in the sultanate of Berar. It was here he received the title of 'Malik', or 'lord', in honour of his military and administrative skills. Here too he put together an African army loyal specifically to him—though in this case the African troops were immigrant Arabs rather than habshis. A dispute with other lords over the composition of his army led to his leaving Berar in the 1590s and returning, with a number of Arab soldiers, to Ahmadnagar, where the power of his retinue suddenly made him an influential player in the sultanate's ongoing political and military struggles.

Malik Ambar's return to Ahmadnagar coincided with the Mughal assaults on the Deccan under Akbar. The emperor had asked all the sultanates to acknowledge his supremacy; in 1595, the Ahmadnagar sultan, Ibrahim Nizam Shah, was killed in battle with the Mughals, and his infant son Bahadur—after a period of uncertainty and heightened tension between the Iranian and the Deccani lords—was named the new nizam. Following Bahadur's accession, the political affairs of Ahmadnagar were taken over by the former regent of Bijapur, the brilliant warrior queen Chand Bibi. The daughter of the former Ahmadnagar sultan Hussain Nizam Shah, Chand Bibi had been married to Ali Adil Shah I, the sultan of Bijapur. Upon her husband's death in 1580, a series of murderous succession struggles led to her briefly becoming de facto ruler of Bijapur. In 1595, amidst the Mughal wars, she added the regency of Ahmadnagar to her CV. Importantly, she won the position by cultivating the support of various habshi nobles, including Ikhlas Khan. The latter extended his patronage also to Malik Ambar, who rose quickly in the ranks of the Ahmadnagar ruling class. He led his Arab-habshi regiment at the Mughal siege and conquest of Ahmadnagar in 1600, which followed hard on the heels of Chand Bibi's murder by enraged Deccan troops who thought she had betrayed the sultanate to Akbar's sons. Malik Ambar fled to the hills, but then he pulled off the feat that led to all his future successes: in the Maratha fortress town of Paranda, he uncovered an infant grandson of the former Ahmadnagar ruler, Bahadur Nizam Shah I, and declared him the new sultan. By 1607, Malik Ambar had had himself appointed vakil-us-sultanat, or regent of Ahmadnagar, a post that he was to hold till his death in 1626.

In the wake of the Mughal conquest of Ahmadnagar, and his leadership role in organizing the resistance to Akbar and then Jahangir, Malik Ambar's ensemble of political and civic responsibilities radically expanded. Most notably, he turned to urban planning, designing the city of Khadki, which became the sultanate's new capital after the sacking of the Ahmadnagar fort. In hand-picking the new nizam shah, Malik Ambar became more than a kingmaker; he also took pains to cement his family's place permanently in the Ahmadnagar ruling classes. He installed the puppet boy-sultan, Murtaza II, as the nizam shah on condition that the boy marry his daughter—a remarkable development for a foreign slave who was suddenly now related, by marriage, to his adopted country's royal family. Malik Ambar's 'low' African origin was not forgotten by his new relatives, however. The habshi princess was apparently bossed around by the nizam's elder wife, a Persian, who taunted her for being no more than a slave girl. But both the nizam and his elder wife had to answer to Malik Ambar. Some commentators have suggested that when Murtaza and his Persian wife got too uppity, Malik Ambar had them poisoned. There is no firm evidence to confirm any such skulduggery; however, Murtaza did die surprisingly young and Malik Ambar moved quickly to replace him with a new, more compliant boy-sultan, Burhan Nizam Shah III.

As the vakil-us-sultanat, Malik Ambar was Ahmadnagar's de facto king. And during his nineteen-year supremacy, he introduced significant economic as well as political innovations that transformed the sultanate.

His experience in Baghdad serving Mir Qasim and, in all likelihood, attending to details of his master's business affairs seems to have come in good use: with great skill, he substantially reformed and streamlined the Ahmadnagar revenue system, making it fairer as well as more profitable. Interestingly, one of the key planks of his reforms was the abolition of fixed rents based on volume of land. He resolved instead to peg taxes to the annually variable conditions of crops, and decreed that the size of land allocations shouldn't be uniform, but should rather be bigger or smaller according to how fertile the land was. It is tempting to see this policy as the brainchild of a man who, as a boy in the variably arable and arid lands of Kembata, had seen his parents reduced to poverty because they couldn't produce a sufficient crop yield to offset their tax burden.

Malik Ambar groomed his wastrel son Fateh Khan as his dynastic successor. When the habshi ruler died in 1626, Fateh took over as the vakil-us-sultanat of Ahmadnagar. One of the new ruler's first orders was to rename Khadki 'Fatehpur' as a tribute to himself. But his vain decree didn't have any long-term effect, for Fateh Khan was not half the politician or military tactician his father had been. Within three years he had lost control of Fatehpur; by 1636, the entire Ahmadnagar Sultanate had been re-conquered by the Mughals. When the victorious prince Aurangzeb entered Khadki-urf-Fatehpur, he took a page from Fateh Khan's book and renamed the city for himself. It has been known as Aurangabad ever since. Despite its long-standing Mughal name, Aurangabad retains much of its habshi urban planner's character. In particular, it is a city whose distinctive architectural features everywhere reveal Malik Ambar's military knowledge. The knowledge that shaped Khadki's construction was not just of war, but more specifically of bargi-giri—which demanded in turn an embodied knowledge of the difficult Deccan highland terrain. To understand the city Malik Ambar built, then, we need to gain a better understanding of this embodied military knowledge and how he acquired it.

◆

Bargi-giri has been translated as guerrilla warfare. In the *Tuzuk-i-Jahangiri*, Mu'tamad Khan characterizes this kind of warfare as 'predatory'—as if it were animal-like. But bargi-giri's predatory nature involves not so much animal brutality as invisibility: in this form of feral encounter, the hunter doesn't allow himself to be seen until the moment of attack. Bargi-giri works through stealth and surprise. It entails not large battalions of troops marching in strict formation, but small bands of guerrillas reliant on improvisation. Its key tactic is not the carefully choreographed battle but the ambush. For guerrilla bands to be effective in bargi-giri, they needed to know the local terrain well: its hiding places, points of vulnerability, and escape routes. The skilled bargi-giri guerilla was either someone who already knew the Deccan terrain like the back of his hand—or a foreigner whose experiences of his native land had habituated him to the specific challenges of the Deccan highlands.

The Ahmadnagar regiments Malik Ambar commanded after his return from Berar in the 1590s initially consisted just of Arab and habshi troops. At this point, he is alleged to have had 1,500 men under his command. Most of the habshis serving in the Ahmadnagar regiments would have come from the mountainous highlands of the south of Ethiopia. Though it is likely that they spoke Dakhni, they may well have spoken with Malik Ambar in his native Kambaatissaata. Whatever language they spoke, it is clear that the habshi troops felt an extraordinary loyalty to their general, one that was based not just on military discipline or on racial, cultural and linguistic solidarity. One imagines that they had also cultivated a strong sense of community grounded in a shared topographical endeavour. The habshis, like Malik Ambar accustomed since childhood to scaling hills at altitude, collectively plotted the highways and the byways of the Deccan landscape, getting to know its every rocky nook and cranny in order to defend it against the Mughal forces.

As Malik Ambar's power grew, so did the size of his regiments. By 1610, he is supposed to have had 7,000 men under his control; by 1621, over 20,000. This dramatic increase can be attributed to an exponential rise in the number of habshi slaves exported from Ethiopia to the Deccan in the early seventeenth century. But Malik Ambar's regiments were swollen in large part by his vigorous recruitment of local Maratha chiefs and warriors. Like the habshis, the Marathas had acquired a special aptitude for dealing with the Deccani landscape. Their knowledge, of course, was a more local one, gleaned from lives spent in the rugged, dry highland terrain of what is now eastern Maharashtra at the northwest tip of the Deccan plateau. Indeed, Malik Ambar seems to have clicked with the Marathas as fellows not just in arms but also in skills of highland survival. Working with this shared knowledge of the Deccan, he trained them to be successful practitioners of bargi-giri, setting the scene for the later Maratha dominance in the region.

One of the Maratha warriors with whom Malik Ambar worked closely as he perfected the art of bargi-giri was an upper-caste patil (or landlord) from the Bhosale clan of Pune. His name was Maloji. Born in 1552, Maloji migrated from his village to Sindkhed in the Ahmadnagar Sultanate, where he found service as a cavalry man of Lakhuji Jadhav, a jagirdar (or local chief) in the Ahmadnagar political administration. Maloji and his wife, Uma Bai, remained childless for many years. After praying for children during the Mughal siege at the Ahmadnagar city dargah of Shah Sharif, a local Sufi saint, the couple had two sons in 1601, whom they named Shahaji and Sharifji in honour of the saint. By this time, Maloji evidently had come to the attention of Malik Ambar, who gave him a military promotion and also awarded him the jagir (or chiefdom) of Pune. Maloji fought alongside Malik Ambar through many of the initial campaigns against the Mughals. He died in 1606 during a skirmish with the Bijapur army; his son Shahaji—just 5 years old at the time—inherited the Pune jagir, but also remained closely associated with Malik Ambar, who seems to have served as something of a godfather to him.

Early in his life, Shahaji was trained in Deccan guerrilla warfare, possibly under the tutelage of Malik Ambar himself. He married Jija Bai, the daughter of Lakhuji Jadav, which bonded him even closer to the ruling classes of Ahmadnagar. Like Malik Ambar before him, Shahaji briefly left Ahmadnagar to serve in the army of another Deccan sultan— in this case, the Adil Shah of Golconda. But Shahaji soon returned to Ahmadnagar where, under Malik Ambar, he was the chief general in the legendary Battle of Bhataudi against Jahangir's son Khurram (later Shah Jahan). While Shahaji commanded 20,000 troops, Khurram's vast army numbered 200,000, and was equipped with state-of-the-art artillery and fighting elephants. Despite this numerical disadvantage, Shahaji defeated Khurram in spectacular fashion, resorting to one of the most fundamental principles of bargi-giri: using the local terrain to overpower his enemy by stealth. Because Khurram's massive army needed an equally massive victualling and watering apparatus, they had set up their base camp next to the Mehkari River, a short distance from a large dam built by Ahmadnagar engineers. Shahaji punctured the dam, which resulted in a flash flood that engulfed the Mughal army. Thousands of men drowned, as did many fighter elephants; in the battle's aftermath, Shahaji captured no fewer than twenty-five Mughal chiefs. And an enduring guerrilla legend was born.

Shahaji is best known as the father of Shivaji, the great Maratha warrior and nationalist hero. Shivaji was born in 1630, four years after Malik Ambar's death. But his life was very much shaped by the tradition of bargi-giri in which Malik Ambar had trained his father and grandfather. The innovative guerrilla warfare methods associated with him—Shiva sutra and ganimi kava—were refinements of strategies that also distinguished Malik Ambar's bargi-giri. Shivaji, like Malik Ambar and his troops, specialized in judicious use of local geography and surprise ambushes to lead his Maratha forces to victory over much larger Mughal armies. Although Shivaji has often been cast as a committedly nativist Hindu (he was supposed to be an avid student of the Mahabharata and the Ramayana, and promoted the use of Sanskrit rather than Persian as the official court and administrative language), he was in fact deeply tolerant of other religions and ethnicities. Shivaji admonished Aurangzeb for failing to recognize that Hinduism and Islam are 'terms of contrast' that pay homage to the same 'Divine Painter'; he claimed that 'Frankish Padres' are good men; and he numbered among his closest military aides habshi naval lords such as Ibrahim Khan and artillery specialists such as Siddi Ibrahim. All this testifies to how Shivaji's family history as much as his military tactics were very much the products of a multicultural, multidenominational Deccan culture.

We might ask: with so many thousands of habshi troops serving in the Deccan armies along with the Maratha soldiers, how did this pan-religious African-Indian collective morph into a seemingly regional Hindu movement? By the early eighteenth century, the habshis had all but disappeared: because the vast majority of East African immigrants were male slaves, they did not maintain an ethnically separate sub-culture in the way that African-American slaves and their descendants have done in the US. For the most part, the habshis intermarried with local women. Although some pockets of people descended from Africans (the so-called Siddis) live in Maharashtra and Karnataka, these are most probably descendants not of Malik Ambar and the habshis but of Goan runaway slaves. In all likelihood, Ethiopian genes might survive instead in some people who think of themselves as Maratha. More importantly, however, Malik Ambar's legacy in the region is cultural rather than racial. Having trained Maratha warriors in the art of bargi-giri, many of them became leading figures in subsequent insurgencies against the Mughals. In addition to Maloji and Shahaji, Malik Ambar numbered among his lieutenants Maratha chiefs such as Sharifji (Shahaji's brother),

Parsoji, Mabaji, Nagoji, Hambir Rao, and Chavan. Their fellows and descendants shaped the military culture of the Maratha kingdom. It is one of Indian history's ironies that a movement sometimes associated with Hindu nativism and a virulent antipathy to foreigners was, at its inception, so deeply indebted to Muslims and African migrants, as well as to a form of warfare that emerged from cross-denominational, trans-continental solidarities that to some might now seem unthinkable.

Which is also to say: bargi-giri was a collective craft, based on the constant movement of bands of warriors over the land of the Deccan. Because Malik Ambar's mixed habshi-Maratha army spent days and even weeks at a time out in Ahmadnagar's wild highlands, they would have had to have become skilled at finding nourishing food on the fly. Here Malik Ambar and his fellow habshis probably drew on their past experiences in Africa, looking for dehydration-beating kelas, or bananas related to the ensete with which they had grown up. (And the Maratha corner of the Deccan is banana territory. Jalgaon, a town in the northwest Deccan plateau established by the Marathas, is also known as 'Banana City'; it contributes half of Maharashtra's banana production and 3 per cent of the world's.) Even more, Malik Ambar and his men must have become skilled in finding water in a dry climate. This would have entailed far more than simply knowing the locations of springs, lakes and clean streams. It would have also required repeatedly tracking the flow of water down hills and through ravines and valleys—and, in the process, developing a strong sense of the lie of the land and its gravitational planes. In other words, while roaming the Deccan highlands, Malik Ambar and his soldiers must have honed not just their geographical but also their topographical skills. These skills certainly came in handy for the urban planner of Khadki.

◆

Malik Ambar's most lasting legacy is the city of Khadki—now called Aurangabad—which he himself designed and built in 1610. From its inception, Khadki was a modern, multicultural city not unlike Hyderabad, built at much the same time by the Adil Shah of Golconda. Khadki, like Hyderabad, boasted attractive masjids, mandirs, and even a church. Also like Hyderabad, Khadki was designed to withstand Mughal aggression. The city thus featured not just striking public buildings, but also extensive fortifications and well-armed city walls. Most notably, Khadki also offered its citizens state-of-the-art civic amenities, including an innovative water system of Malik Ambar's own design called the Neher—also known in Dakhni Urdu as the Nahr-e-Ambari—which survives to this day. At a time when the citizens of Ahmadnagar had long endured chronic water shortages in the arid highlands of the Deccan, Malik Ambar's design was nothing short of a miracle of civil engineering.

When its initial phase of construction finished in 1612, the Neher was already one of the most sophisticated water-supply systems in the world, consisting of an elaborate network of canals, conduits, waterfalls, underground channels, aqueducts and reservoirs. Although Khadki had a small perennial stream flowing through it—the Kham—this was insufficient to provide for a city of the size that Malik Ambar had imagined, especially with its enormous military garrison. So he had to devise other ways of bringing water to Khadki, via routes that were not susceptible to attack from the outside. When he first shared his design for the Neher with the other lords of Ahmadnagar, it provoked scorn from some of them, including the wazir, Mulla Mohammad, who derided Malik Ambar's plan as 'imaginary and preposterous'. The wazir had a point. The local hilly terrain around Khadki made it extremely difficult to build raised aqueducts on pillars; instead, the water had to flow through a combination of elevated and underground tunnels employing a variety of technologies relying on gravity and water pressure. Despite its doubters, Malik Ambar's plan worked, providing enough water to meet the needs of Khadki's 700,000 inhabitants.

To distribute its water so widely among the residents of the city, the Neher had to be planned not as a centralized singular water body with one origin and one destination but as an entire network with multiple points of input and output. A map of the Neher's various tributaries and channels looks uncannily like a modern Metro Rail plan: it consists of twelve lines with numerous 'stations' and 'interchanges' designed to reach as much of the city as possible. The main line was a canal that branched in two directions, the first providing water to the Naukhanda Palace on a hill in the centre of the city (Malik Ambar's headquarters, again built by him), the nearby Juna Bazaar and several wealthy suburbs; the other supplied the Shah Ganj area. This line was criss-crossed by numerous other lines, mostly ceramic water-pipes that drew water from tanks fed by external wells, dams, and mountain springs. Of the twelve original lines, four still function today. Others were added over time, building on the foundations of Malik Ambar's elaborate network. Arguably the most striking feature of the Neher is a water mill called the Panchakki, situated

1 kilometre outside old Aurangabad, and connected via an underground channel and water pipe to a spring in the mountains more than 8 kilometres away. The mill, which grinds grain into flour for pilgrims, adjacent to the dargah for the Sufi saint (and migrant from Bukhara) Baba Shah Musafir, is powered by an artificial waterfall; it also contains a mosque surrounded by dancing fountains—an extraordinary integration of religious devotion with sophisticated water-flow technology. The mill, waterfall and fountains date from the time of Aurangzeb and are rightly regarded as feats of Mughal engineering. But each of these eye-catching innovations depends on an ingeniously designed subterranean water-relay system initially laid out by Malik Ambar in 1612.

Many might see the Neher simply as a feat of civil engineering. I prefer to characterize it as an exercise in migrant firangi poetry using not language but water, not verse but pipes. The Neher was every bit a creative exercise in becoming Indian as was Thomas Stephens's *Kristapurana*. Stephens employed a language foreign to him and made it flow in beautiful lines; Malik Ambar did the same with the mountain water of the Deccan. Stephens organized his clusters of Marathi and Konkani words into elegantly compressed ovi stanzas; Malik Ambar organized his own mixed media (elevated aqueducts, open-air channels, underground ceramic pipes) into equally elegant networks. If the *Kristapurana* had a utilitarian aim—assimilating Christian stories into Hindu traditions—so too did the Neher, a public utility designed to bring water to all Khadki's residents. And, most importantly, both the *Kristapurana* and the Neher derived their innovative power from a migrant's embodied knowledge of a new Indian landscape. Stephens's poem pays covert homage to the transformative effects of the Goan coconut on his English body; Malik Ambar's creation pays homage to his experience of water in the Deccan plateau.

Malik Ambar's skill in water-supply design had probably been honed during his years in Daulatabad, the Ahmadnagar stronghold, where he had been based on and off in the first decade of the 1600s. The city, just 16 kilometres to the northwest of the Khadki, was a hill fortress in a strategically important location. Built on top of a tall conical slab of basalt, Daulatabad was accessible only through a narrow path hewn through the rock and a bridge that could fit no more than two people standing abreast. In other words, it was close to unassailable. But it also suffered from serious water-supply shortages. Muhammad bin Tughlaq, the Delhi sultan, had made Daulatabad his capital in the 1300s because of its defensive capability; but he soon had to abandon it because of the difficulty of obtaining water there. The Ahmadnagar Sultanate faced similar problems.

In the early 1600s, Malik Ambar devoted considerable time and energy to designing and constructing a basic water-supply system for Daulatabad, some of which—an aqueduct and a long ceramic pipe encased in stone—has only recently been rediscovered in an orchard near the city. For whatever reason, however, Malik Ambar and the Ahmadnagar ruling class decided to follow in Muhammad bin Tughlaq's footsteps and abandon Daulatabad. Perhaps Malik Ambar had concluded that the task of providing sufficient water to the hill-city was too difficult; perhaps too he had conducted a thorough investigation of the region and decided that Khadki was better located for the kind of extensive water-management project that was necessary to support a city of 700,000. But his early experiments with water supply in Daulatabad provided him with an excellent platform for what he later achieved with the Neher. These experiments may have owed something to age-old Deccan engineering technologies employed by earlier Buddhist, Jain and Hindu cultures in the nearby Ellora and Ajanta caves, a mere 10 kilometres from Daulatabad. But Malik Ambar also drew on his experiences of water in other parts of the world, from Africa to the Middle East. These experiences are legible in the design features of the Neher.

At one level, the Neher is the design of a migrant to India familiar with the Baghdad aqueduct system. Indeed, much about the Khadki city plan is redolent of medieval Baghdad. That Malik Ambar was able to pull off the feat of civil engineering that is the Neher testifies to more than just his skill as an administrator or urban planner. It also suggests a vivid first-hand experience of Baghdad's water supply, one that he communicated powerfully to Ahmadnagar's engineers (some of whom too may have been familiar with the Arab technologies of water conveyance). But the Neher is the design also of someone who had spent considerable time in the wilds of the Deccan surveying its topography—not with modern surveying instruments, but with his body and the bodies of his habshi and Maratha troops. Malik Ambar had developed a keen sense of where water came from, which way it flowed, where it was most and least vulnerable to outside attack. And his topographical knowledge was in turn the consequence of years of body knowledge acquired in the highlands of Abyssinia, scaling its slopes and tracing its creek-beds. Which is to say: Khadki was designed by a man accustomed to Deccan water patterns, Baghdadi aqueducts, and Kembata droughts. If, as the African saying goes, it takes a village to raise a child, sometimes it takes a globe to make a city.

This seemingly paradoxical combination of cosmopolitanism and localism, of homelessness and rootedness, is the recurring theme of Malik Ambar's story. The habshi vakil-us-sultanat was a Deccan nationalist who had successfully made a foreign land his home; he did so by drawing on his experiences of African and Middle Eastern terrain even as he adapted to the distinctive topography of the Ahmadnagar highlands. Yet within his new land he was also curiously homeless, and this condition was crucial to his military and political success. The art of bargi-giri entailed constant nomadic motion—like the flowing water whose movement he so carefully traced—over mountainous and inhospitable terrain. Perhaps this constant movement was encoded in the very word bargi-giri. In the Dakhni term, Jahangir and his Persian-speaking courtiers may have heard an echo of another word, one freighted with meaning. Describing the effects of chasing Malik Ambar over the desolate Deccan landscape for many years, Jahangir claimed that the Mughal troops had suffered considerable hardship from a condition that he calls, in Persian, 'bi-jagiri'. The term means 'want of a settled home or residence'.

For Jahangir and his Mughal troops, long separated from the nomadic lifestyle of their Turkic and Mongol ancestors, this homelessness was a disabling condition. Indeed, it was part of what made Malik Ambar and his army so foreign to them. Despite the much-vaunted multiculturalism of the Mughals, who welcomed migrants from many parts of the world to their principal cities and championed religious syncretism, Jahangir persisted in regarding Malik Ambar as irredeemably alien, as illustrated by his repeated rants in the *Tuzuk-i-Jahangiri* against the 'black-faced Ambar'. Though Jahangir understood Malik Ambar racially, his animus was also driven by a perception that his adversary refused to stay in one place, that his nomadism refused the rootedness Jahangir associated with Mughal civilization. But for Malik Ambar—the Indian who was not an Indian, the ferengi who was not a ferengi, the firangi who was not a firangi—this restless movement was an empowering precondition of his ascendancy. Chapu/Ambar/Malik Ambar moved a long way in his life, from Africa to the Arabian Peninsula to Mesopotamia to India. And even in Ahmadnagar, he kept moving across the hills, ravines, and marshlands of the Deccan. His bi-jagiri was crucial to his bargi-giri; his homelessness was crucial to the foundation of the 'authentically Indian'

Maratha homeland. And this paradox, of moving yet settling, is at the heart of what it meant to be a firangi in sixteenth- and seventeenth-century India.

Because Malik Ambar's constantly moving body was not just a body that moved. It was also a transformative element, both adapting to and subtly altering its environment with each movement.

ON RENAMING

What's in a firangi's Indian name?

In most parts of the world, nicknaming is a common practice. In India, it is a compulsion. And not just on the part of those who liberally bestow pet names on their family members and friends. Indian nicknames themselves are bearers of compulsion, forcing those who acquire them to do things they wouldn't otherwise do.

Shakespeare's Juliet thinks a name is immaterial—that 'a rose by any other name would smell as sweet', that her Romeo would still be Romeo whether he was surnamed Capulet or Montague. The play, of course, proves Juliet dead wrong: our names do matter, sometimes with lethal consequences. Our names position us within larger social networks of clan and community, dictating who we can fraternize with but also who we should regard as mortal enemies. And they determine the scope of what our bodies can and cannot do. Romeo Montague is compelled to bear arms against Juliet Capulet's beloved cousin, the man who killed his kinsman Mercutio; if his own last name had been Capulet, another, perhaps equally deadly, set of embodied compulsions would apply.

The shaping power of names in relation to bodies is especially apparent in India. Throughout most of the subcontinent, last names are markers not just of region but also of religion and caste. They thus play a role in diversely marking who can and can't be touched, what can and can't be eaten, who can and can't be loved. Attempts to dispense with caste-specific names notwithstanding, Indian surnames represent a contract of legibility between members of a community and those who don't belong to it. This is just as true of Indian nicknames, though in less obviously restrictive ways.

In India, nicknames often tie one to smaller, more ad hoc communities: school classes, groups of friends, sporting fraternities, workplaces, celebrity circles. Most commonly, they tend to tether one to immediate family rather than to a larger clan. Indian nicknames seldom have anything to do with one's real name. Just think of Bollywood stars such as Kareena Kapoor, otherwise known as Bebo, or Hrithik Roshan, also called Duggu. Both Bebo and Duggu are family nicknames, even if 'family' in these two instances has, for the purposes of branding and marketing, expanded to include the stars' fans. As such, nicknames still mark a seeming divide between an intimate circle of insiders and those excluded from it. This intimacy can be a stranglehold as much as an embrace: it lays a claim to one's ownership by a larger community. But can a nickname dictate a body's behaviour in the way a patronym, clan title, or caste name can?

Indians sometimes give foreigners new nicknames. A Punjabi friend, for example, has dubbed me both 'Gilinder' and 'Gillu'. The monikers are affectionate acknowledgements of my partial Indianization. But they are also much more than that. Each is specific to a different context: Gilinder is the party version of me, Gillu the sporting version. So what happens to me when I am addressed as Gilinder or Gillu? It isn't just a matter of being called something different, something Indian. Each nickname is also a summons to use my body differently as part of a new community. The Sikh-sounding Gilinder, for example, is expected to dance bhangra-style in a way that Gillu isn't. And, as my running group knows, Gillu—like a gilahari (Hindi for 'squirrel')—is given to darting and frantic scurrying, especially when chased by the angry alpha monkey of Rashtrapati Bhavan. These nicknames don't simply describe who I am. Whether I like them or not, they incite me to use my body in ways that I don't in other parts of the world.

We have already seen how warrior slaves were given new names by their Indian masters. But the practice of renaming firangi migrants was not confined to mamluks. In the Mughal Empire it was extended to any foreign servant of the emperor. Though some foreigners were retained in military capacities, a number who had artistic talents were seconded to the karkhana (the royal artisanal workshops). In the process, these firangi artisans received new names and titles that transformed them from humble migrants into imperial servants. Their new names weren't just signs of membership in a new community. They often evoked specific physical skills: indeed, one firangi artisan who served in the Mughal court was given a new name that meant 'skilful' in Persian. Such titles served as summons to make one's body conform to the demands of sophisticated Mughal artistic practices—painting, jewel-cutting, throne-designing. And to master these practices, the firangis had to modify physical talents they had cultivated in their former homes and adapt these to Indian conventions. Which is why renaming was, and still is, a vital instrument of becoming Indian.

What's in a firangi's Indian name? A palimpsest of old and new bodily aptitudes.

Sometime around 1618, the Mughal court painter Bichitr finished an
unusual portrait. In it, the emperor Jahangir sits on a throne shaped like
an hourglass. A large golden halo surrounds his head; two little angels
fly above him, while two more cavort at the throne's base. Four men
stand beneath him. The first is a Sufi sheikh, to whom Jahangir presents
a book; the last is the painter himself, canvas in hand. In between these
two figures stand an Ottoman sultan and, astonishingly, a firangi: King
James of England and Scotland.

Bichitr's portrait is testimony to the grandeur of the Mughal Empire
in its seventeenth-century pomp. But he has captured that grandeur
through what we might call a sustained experiment in the subjunctive.
And by that I mean a painting which represents not the world as we
know it but a parallel reality. Bichitr has us enter a fantastical world of
winged angels and a haloed Muslim emperor; he celebrates the global
sway of a Great Mughal who will never set foot out of Hindustan;
and he populates it with subservient foreigners, including a firangi
king who will never set foot in it. In sum, the painting says: Names
Matter. Bichitr pretends that Jahangir is—as the Persian meaning of his
name would have it—'Conqueror of the World', with a British king
and a Turkish sultan paying homage to him. (Malik Ambar, of course,
is not allowed to trouble this scene of triumph.) Bichitr underscores
the pretence by including himself in the painting, holding a canvas.
This seems like a sly wink to the painting's spectators, recognition that
Jahangir's world-conquering power is less reality than artistic fiction. But
Bichitr's portrait is not quite a flight into the patently unreal. Rather,
it proposes a hypothetical reality that might, under certain conditions,
become true or at least credible.

Under Jahangir's father Akbar, the Mughal Empire had grown
territorially—annexing Gujarat and Bengal—and economically. It
exported goods to China, Arabia, Abyssinia and Europe. In particular,
Akbar promoted textile manufacture for foreign markets, building roads
that connected Mughal weavers' workshops to seaports and abolishing
inland tolls and duties. The American silver with which European traders
bought Indian cotton and silk greatly enriched the empire's chief cities:
a Jesuit priest who visited Lahore in 1581 claimed that 'it is not second

to any city in Europe or Asia'. Under Akbar and then Jahangir and Shah Jahan, the Mughal Empire was increasingly a global force. In the subjunctive fantasies of its art, however, it was not just a force. It was world-conquering—even firangi-conquering.

Bichitr's painting partakes of this fantasy at several levels. Not only does it present King James beneath Jahangir. It also takes possession of firangi techniques and technologies. The angels that fly above Jahangir are in fact putti—little baby Cupids—meticulously painted in the style of Renaissance Italian artists. And Jahangir sits atop a throne that incorporates firangi technology: the hourglass was a French invention. Lest this seem like a cosmopolitan embrace of the Christian world, however, Jahangir trains his attention on the Sufi sheikh alone. The message is that firangi artistic practices and artful inventions are all well and good, but they must submit to an unambiguously desi Great Mughal. But what about firangi artists themselves? Did they too submit to the Great Mughal?

This brief chapter considers a firangi artist who worked for Akbar as part of a cross-cultural experiment designed to bolster Mughal power. To find favour, the artist not only had to bring coveted skills with him from Europe to India, he also had to adapt these skills to the artistic traditions and practical needs of the Mughal court. In the process, he acquired a new name that—like Jahangir's own—had a subjunctive power: the name proposed that the artist's body become something other than what it had been, something Indian. This required him to adjust his hand-to-eye coordination, his posture in new work spaces, his comfort with unfamiliar artisanal implements. But this artist is an unusually shadowy figure: his life is shrouded in mystery, as he makes only the most fleeting appearance in Mughal archives, and there is no trace of him in any Western records. How to recover his story? Perhaps the art of the subjunctive is the best way to access the lives of artists who dealt in the subjunctive. So let me begin with a 'what if' scenario involving another firangi painter.

◆

When Ralph Fitch journeyed to India in 1583, he took with him two artisans—William Leeds, a jeweller, and a painter named James Story. Fitch and his fellow travellers, bankrolled by the English Levant Company, had set out in the hope of visiting Mughal Hindustan and extracting a trading agreement from Akbar. In a team whose members we might have expected to consist simply of merchants and diplomats, the inclusion of the two artisans is puzzling. Story never made it to the Mughal court: as we have seen in Chapter 3, he remained in Goa after the imprisonment and release of Fitch's party. By contrast Leeds, journeying out of Goa with Fitch, soon found employment with Akbar, who (Fitch claims) gave him no less than a house, a horse and five slaves. But would Story the painter have been as fortunate if he had accompanied Leeds the jeweller to the Mughal court in September 1584?

Commentators on Fitch's journey have speculated that Leeds was included in his party because the English Levant Company had high hopes of busting into the lucrative Indian jewel trade. While no doubt true, this is to understand the mission from an entirely Anglocentric perspective. Story's and Leeds's inclusion in the travelling party was as much the result of Mughal policy as of English trading ambition. Fitch's journey was made possible by a Mughal state that had become one of the principal engines of cultural as well as economic globalization. Akbar's apparent willingness to add a foreign jeweller to his staff was symptomatic of an expansive imperialist culture that, while praised for its cosmopolitanism and religious tolerance, sought to advance its sphere of influence by adapting and refining other cultures' skills in new technologies. But would the Mughals also have wanted to employ a firangi painter like James Story? What would have happened if Story had accompanied Leeds and the English party to Fatehpur Sikri?

◆

It is a scorching September day in 1584 at the edge of a hill-city approximately 40 kilometres north of Agra. The August monsoon has come and gone, failing to deliver the relief the residents of Fatehpur Sikri have been hoping for. The large artificial lake immediately to the city's northwest has more or less dried up, triggering the water-supply crisis that, just under a year later, will permanently drive Akbar and the city's nearly 100,000 inhabitants to the more abundantly watered Lahore. William Leeds and James Story are parched after a long journey from the Deccan. They have—much to Leeds's interest—visited the diamond-rich sultanate of Golconda; but their aim has always been to meet Akbar. So they have trudged north in the summer heat, first to Agra, and then to the Mughal emperor's planned city. The Englishmen's first glimpse of Fatehpur Sikri is from a distance: a flash of red on top of a hill. With its highly visible battlements, it is in some ways a typical north Indian fort city, testimony to the might as well as the wealth of the Mughals.

Even Fatehpur Sikri's name has a hint of military swagger—'fateh' is Persian and Arabic for 'victory', to commemorate Akbar's triumphs over the local Rajputs.

Approaching Fatehpur Sikri from its southern side, Leeds and Story climb up a long flight of steps that leads to the city's entrance: the massive Buland Darwaza, a 54-metre-high archway attached to the large Jama Masjid and inscribed with Arabic characters on one of its pillars. Because the Englishmen can't read the inscription, they don't know that it spells out a quote about the transience of life ('the world is a bridge: cross it, but build no houses on it'; an ironically prescient pronouncement given that Akbar will abandon the city in just eleven months). The archway, the inscription and the Jama Masjid all suggest to Leeds and Story that they are entering a conventionally Muslim city. Nevertheless, the Buland Darwaza also contains subtle signs that the city isn't quite what it might seem. Story, with his painter's eye, immediately notes the gateway's distinctive hues. The Buland Darwaza has been constructed out of the plentiful red alluvial sandstone that is a feature of so much north Indian and Rajasthani Hindu architecture. Indeed, Fatehpur Sikri's principal architect, Tuhir Das, has pointedly designed the city as a multicultural blend of Persian and indigenous Hindu styles. But Story is oblivious to another potentially multicultural detail of the Buland Darwaza: although the gateway's inscription invokes a prophet of Islam, this prophet—Isa—is, in fact, Jesus Christ, with whom the Mughal emperor has recently become fascinated. Indeed, if the Englishmen had visited two years earlier, they would have met two priests named Father Antonio de Montserrat and Father Rodolfo Acquaviva, frequent visitors to Fatehpur Sikri ever since Akbar first invited the Jesuit mission to his court in 1579.

At the opposite end of the Jama Masjid square is the gleaming jaali-work (lattice) of a brand new building. This is the dargah of Shaikh Salim Chishti, a recently deceased Sufi saint who correctly predicted the birth of a son to the previously childless Akbar, and who is worshipped by Muslims and Hindus alike. Workmen are still adding finishing touches to the building. Indeed, everywhere Leeds and Story look, they see stone-carvers hard at work. The shapes the carvers cut are not the non-representational forms the Englishmen have seen in stricter Islamic cities. Fatehpur Sikri's red sandstone columns, walls, and ceilings instead teem with the shapes of living creatures—birds, animals—as well as incorporating stylistic features that Story has seen elsewhere in Hindu and Jain temples. After spending ten months in India, Leeds and Story quickly conclude two things about Fatehpur Sikri: first, this is a city that employs many artisans; and second, these artisans are not exclusively beholden to the styles of Islam. Other religious and cultural traditions are welcomed, even fashionable, here.

The Englishmen cannot see the most distinctive buildings inside the emperor's royal residences. But if they could, these would only confirm their intuition about Fatehpur Sikri. The small palaces of Akbar's queens—at least one of whom, Harka Bai, is Hindu despite her better-known Persian name of Mariam-us-Zamani—are festooned with Hindu designs that include Vishnu in his Rama incarnation. Akbar's own apartments in his Mahal-i-Khas are repeatedly carved with the chandrashala motif, long used in pre-Islamic Indian architecture; his hall of private audience, or Diwan-i-Khas, features a huge, richly carved column modelled on Vishnu's tree or pillar of the universe. And on a Thursday evening, Leeds and Story along with other residents of Fatehpur might hear yogis and mullahs debate theological issues in the Ibadat Khana. In its precincts, Akbar has begun to lay down the foundations of Din-i-Ilahi, a syncretic universal religion that contains elements of Islam, Hinduism, Jainism, Buddhism, Christianity, and even Zoroastrianism.

Crossing from the vicinity of the palaces to the immediate east of the Diwan-i-Am, or the Public Audience Hall, Leeds and Story spy another, large complex of apartments. These are the karkhana, the royal workshops that house the emperor's most skilled artisans. It includes Muslims and Hindus; once he enters Akbar's employ—presumably to cut and polish precious stones—Leeds will probably work here too. The only prerequisite for admission is advanced skill in an art or craft favoured by the emperor. Chief among these skills is painting in the Mughal style: every week the works of karkhana painters trained in Mughal conventions are laid before Akbar for his evaluation. As Akbar's chronicler Abu'l Fazl notes in the *Ain-i-Akbari*, 'His Majesty, from the time he came to an awareness of things, has taken a deep interest in painting and sought its spread and development.' And Story is a painter. But can he be admitted to the karkhana, especially if he is not versed in local styles? How can a firangi become a Mughal painter?

◆

What we call Mughal painting was in fact resolutely multicultural, grafting to its Persian roots a rich array of other cultural elements. As the distinctive architecture of Fatehpur Sikri makes clear, local dastkars (the Persian, Urdu and Hindi word for craftsmen) had been given a free hand in assimilating Rajput and other Hindu traditions. Mughal painters too drew on local styles. But they also turned their gaze even further afield. In the late sixteenth century, they began an extended dialogue with European art, thanks to a sudden influx of prints that arrived in India with Portuguese traders and missionaries. Akbar retained a royal kitabkhana or atelier of over a hundred painters who, studying print copies of Italian paintings, developed skills of perspectival illusion, sfumato (or blurred lines), and chiaroscuro shading; the putti in Bichitr's portrait of Jahangir were one outcome of this extended conversation with Italian art. Akbar's own interest in painting techniques from around the world, including Europe, was partly personal and even spiritual. Abu'l Fazl records him as saying, in opposition to strict Muslims who thought painting an abomination, that 'a painter is better than most in gaining a knowledge of God'. But Akbar also understood the political utility of learning other cultures' skills. The acquisition of foreign techniques and technologies stood to increase Mughal global power.

Which is to say: a firangi painter like James Story, no matter how outlandish his training and his style, would almost certainly have been welcomed into the royal karkhana to demonstrate and share his talents with local artists like Bichitr. Indeed, housing a firangi artist would also have been very much of a piece with the two great projects Akbar authorized his Fatehpur Sikri painters to pursue in the 1580s.

In 1581, Akbar commissioned his royal kitabkhana to produce 168 illustrations for a Persian translation of the Mahabharata, or as it was known, the Razmnama—Persian for 'The Book of War'. Its translation was intended to shore up support for Akbar among his Hindu subjects as well as insist, in Persian, on the points of convergence between Islam and Hinduism. Martial opportunist that he was, Akbar also believed that Hindu 'war' texts such as the Mahabharata contained secrets that could be of use to the Mughal military. The Razmnama was no one-off project. As it was nearing completion, Akbar commissioned his royal painters to begin work on an illustrated Persian translation of the Ramayana. It was finished in 1588; by this time Akbar had relocated his court and karkhana to Lahore. Largely untouched by scholars, and now inaccessible, the manuscript and its illustrations are housed in the Maharaja Sawai Man Singh Museum in Jaipur. The Mughal Ramayana, like the Razmnama, was an extraordinary experiment in trans-culturalism.

Hindustan's greatest Sanskrit and Persian scholars collaborated on both translations. One illustration in the first edition of the Razmnama, as a kind of meta-commentary on the translation process, depicts Muslim and Hindu scholars sitting together, poring over text diversely written in Nasta'liq (the Persian version of Arabic) and Devanagari (i.e. Sanskrit) scripts.

But it is the illustrations of the Ramayana translation that give the most telling evidence of Akbar's and the Mughal painters' committed multiculturalism. There are 176 full-page miniatures in the Mughal Ramayana. Like most Mughal painting of the time, each of the miniatures entails collaboration between several artists. In a striking departure from previous tradition, the pictures are signed by their painters. This innovation might have been inspired by the copies of signed European paintings that circulated in the Mughal court and karkhanas in the 1580s. But the Mughal Ramayana's signatures also advertise the work of a multi-denominational ensemble. A surviving list of the 59 artists who contributed to the 174 paintings in the Mughal Ramayana includes both Muslim and Hindu names. The list makes clear that a collaborative team of two and sometimes three painters worked on each picture— one doing the outlines, a second looking after the colouring and, on occasion, a third attending to the faces. But here's the surprise: at least two paintings were worked on by a Christian foreigner. James Story's subjunctive history in Fatehpur Sikri is, in many ways, this elusive firangi painter's real story.

◆

The list of artists who contributed to the Mughal Ramayana includes the name of one Mandu Firangi. He is named as a contributor to two of the paintings; but it is almost certain that he had a hand in several more. There are two other Mandus in the list, responsible for a further six paintings: a plain Mandu, who worked on four, and a Mandu Kalan (or 'Mandu Senior'), who assisted with two. All three figures may be the same person. But it's possible that only the non-surnamed Mandu is our Mandu Firangi, distinguished from an older painter of that same name. Most of the names on the list appear in other records of the time, including Abu'l Fazl's catalogue in the *Ain-i-Akbari* of the leading painters in the Mughal court. Tellingly the three Mandus do not figure in any other records of the time, which suggests they were one person who was commissioned specifically to contribute to the project.

We know absolutely nothing about Mandu Firangi or his life, beyond the fact that in the mid 1580s he was possibly resident in Fatehpur Sikri and then in Lahore, as were his paintbrushes. It is unclear which country he originally came from, in which artistic traditions he had been trained before coming to India, and whether he came as a lone wolf or as a representative of a nation, a guild, a religious mission or (like Story) a trading company. Was he an economic refugee? Was he a criminal on the run? Or was he an art student on (say) a Jesuit-sponsored equivalent of a study-abroad programme? His last name indicates that he was a foreigner, and almost certainly a Christian. It's not impossible that he was a native of Armenia, as 'Firangi' was a common last name for Armenian migrants to India. But circumstantial evidence from the paintings strongly suggests Mandu Firangi had been born and trained in Europe, though we cannot identify where. He certainly wasn't the Portuguese painter who came to Lahore with a Jesuit mission and a much-studied painting of the Madonna and Child; this painter visited in 1595, seven years after the Persian Ramayana was completed. And tempting as it is to suspect that Mandu Firangi was, in fact, James Story, the evidence overwhelmingly indicates that the English painter—despite the subjunctive tour on which I have taken him—never set foot in either Fatehpur Sikri or Lahore, and was living in Goa when Mandu Firangi was commissioned to begin work on the Ramayana paintings.

Mandu Firangi's first name yields even fewer clues about his place of birth. Many painters were named for their city or region of origin: among the list of contributors to the Ramayana are Kesav Gujarati and Meghav Gujarati, as well as Nand Gwaliari. Mandu is a fortress city in the Malwa Sultanate in what is now Madhya Pradesh. It was something of an artistic centre; Malwa painting was renowned in the late fifteenth and sixteenth centuries. Perhaps Mandu Kalan, the senior painter mentioned in the list of Mughal painters responsible for the Ramayana manuscript, was from Mandu; and perhaps Mandu Firangi had been seconded to him as his apprentice. But we should not assume that Mandu Firangi's first name has anything to do with Mandu the city. As the above examples make clear, painter's surnames rather than their first name tended to indicate their place of origin. And there is also a distinct possibility that Mandu is a misnomer. It could be a mis-rendering of Maddu or Madhu, meaning sweet or honey. Or perhaps Mandu is a shortened version of a European name such as Manuel or Armand, just as Maddu might be a transliteration of Matthew or Matthieu. But there is simply not enough surviving evidence for us to know.

For the most part, the list of fifty-nine painters who contributed to the Mughal Ramayana doesn't include the name 'Naqqash', the common appellation for skilled painters throughout Persia and Mughal Hindustan, quite possibly because it was assumed that they all answered to it outside the royal kitabkhana. A single contributor to the Ramayana, one Hussein Naqqash, is given this title. The great illustrator of flora and fauna in the *Baburnama*, for instance, was named Mansur Naqqash; even the well-known twentieth-century Pakistani artist Syed Sadequain Ahmad Naqvi was also known as Sadequain Naqqash. Most of the Mughal Ramayana's contributors would have answered to the title of 'Naqqash'—including, most likely, Mandu Firangi after his initiation into the kitabkhana. The naqqash was not a rang saaz, a commonplace painter, but an artisan who had been trained to execute specific skills—burnishing paper, grinding pigments, outlining, colouring, and also calligraphy—according to specific conventions. He also used a variety of implements different from those employed by other painters: a porous bag containing charcoal for outlines, a needle to puncture the lines of a master drawing consisting of a tracing, goat-hair and squirrel-hair qalams (or brushes) for applying paints. As such, 'Naqqash' was not just a term for a trade, but also a name that called forth certain types of skilful embodied behaviour.

We tend to think of skill now as the attribute of a single artist or craftsman. In pre-modern Europe, by contrast, skill referred not to an individual attribute but a relation to an artisanal community. To acquire the skill of painting, as James Story and Mandu Firangi had, one had to enter into an association with a skilled community of painters rather than a community of skilled painters. The difference may seem merely semantic; but it is significant. The acquisition of painterly skill demanded initiation into a set of bodily aptitudes specific to the community in which one was trained. This was equally the case with the naqqash of Mughal Hindustan. The skilled painter was less an individual with a rare talent than a member of a skilled collective. (That is why Mughal paintings, at least initially, were attributed not to individuals but, if at all, to the kitabkhana or painting community that had produced it.) And many of these collective skills would have been alien, at least initially, to a firangi painter like Mandu Firangi. How did he deal, for example, with the challenges of painting a Nasta'liq script that read from right to left? And how did he cope with the Mughal naqqash's distinctively stylized representations of animals, birds, and trees?

One of the Ramayana illustrations to which Mandu Firangi contributed is a generic exercise in conventional Mughal style. This painting, ascribed to Mandu Firangi in collaboration with another painter named Miskin, is a portrait of a reclining Bharat clutching Sita's foot as Ram waits beside her. It includes highly stylized birds and trees that are a commonplace in Mughal paintings of the sixteenth century. Five women stand on one side of the tableau, seven on the other, and two behind Bharat; all are depicted in full or three-quarter profile, as is also common for the time. And a caption, in Nasta'liq script, refers to the moment in the Ramayana when Lakshman learns of the departure of Ram and Sita to the forest. But as the art historian Nuzhat Kazmi notes, the painting offers scattered hints of European techniques. The buildings in the background, while reminiscent of Indian-style domed towers, also include structures that recall the Gothic castles of Renaissance landscape painting. And the illustration employs Italian techniques of perspective and chiaroscuro, especially in the fabrics draped around Bharat and some of the women. None of these details are evidence of a firangi artist's hand: they could all be the work of an Indian naqqash who, like Bichitr, had studied print copies of European paintings. One such naqqash was Mandu Firangi's collaborator Miskin, a painter in Akbar's royal kitabkhana listed in the *Ain-i-Akbari* as one of the best painters of the age and renowned for his command of firangi techniques and ingenious portraits of animals. So it is quite possible that most details in this painting about Bharat, Ram and Sita—including its experiments with European techniques of perspective and chiaroscuro—were his work, and Mandu Firangi, playing a junior role, was only secondarily responsible for its execution.

But there is another, arguably more arresting painting featuring Bharat, Ram and Sita in Akbar's Ramayana manuscript. In it, Bharat is depicted meeting Ram in the forest. Again, as Kazmi observes, most of the iconography is conventionally Mughal: two stylized birds sit in a tree above Sita, while Bharat's retinue fills the space between two stylized hills. One striking trans-cultural detail stands out. Ram and Sita both have blond hair, as does Lakshman, who stands at the side of the picture. In all other Mughal illustrations, Hindu gods' hair is invariably black. In other words, the colourer of this painting—possibly using what the Mughals called peori, a yellow pigment derived from the urine of a cow fed mangoes for a week—has given the gods a firangi makeover. Or, more accurately, he has made them over in the image of the golden-haired Virgin Mary and Jesus of many Italian Renaissance paintings, such as Raphael's famous *Niccolini-Cowper Madonna* (1508).

This painting of blond Hindu gods is attributed to Tarhi-Mandu and Amal-i-Bhagwan. In Persian, 'tarhi' means 'design' and 'amal' means 'application of colour', which suggests that Mandu was responsible for the painting's outlining and Bhagwan for its colouring. Perhaps Bhagwan gave the painting's subjects unorthodox hair-colouring at his firangi collaborator's request, or in winking homage to him. In light of this, it is tempting too to wonder whether Miskin's collaboration with Mandu also offered tribute to the European naqqash: Miskin may have produced that illustration's chiaroscuro effects and Roman-style buildings in order to acknowledge his collaborator's artistic traditions.

We cannot know what the intention behind Bhagwan and Mandu's golden-haired Hindu gods may have been. But we can speculate about its effect. If Tarhi-Mandu is, indeed, Mandu Firangi—and it is hard to imagine he wasn't—the painting not only furthers the Indian conversation between Hinduism and Islam that had been the driving force behind Akbar's commission. It also borrows knowingly from Christian-Italian convention to illustrate a Persian translation of a Sanskrit story. As in Bichitr's painting of Jahangir, firangi conventions are appropriated for Mughal imperial purposes. That the hair colour in Mandu's painting was not 'corrected', and that the painting was included in the final manuscript version of the Mughal Ramayana, shows how Mandu Firangi, Bhagwan and Akbar's royal kitabkhana had daringly enlarged the range of possibilities for what it could mean to paint an authentically Mughal painting. This enlargement might strike us as exemplarily cosmopolitan. But it is also hints at the global aspirations of a Mughal state looking to expand its sphere of influence by mastering foreign cultural styles and techniques.

◆

Aside from the list of contributors to Akbar's Ramayana, there is not one reference to Mandu Firangi in any Mughal or Western archive. We do not know how fully he was integrated into the multicultural world of Fatehpur Sikri and later Lahore. But to participate in the project he would have had to closely study the techniques of the Mughal artists in Akbar's royal kitabkhana. In all probability, he also got to know some of them intimately well. Perhaps he also became friends with William Leeds, another firangi dastkar assigned to Akbar's karkhana in the mid 1580s. And we can assume that, if he first joined Akbar's service in Fatehpur Sikri, he moved to Lahore in 1585 with the other drought-stricken residents; his contributions to the Mughal Ramayana were almost certainly completed in 1588 in the northern city.

But the stark reality is that we know nothing about the content and chronology of Mandu Firangi's life: how and when he entered Akbar's service, how long he stayed in the subcontinent, whether he returned to his country of origin. Nor do we know which languages he spoke in Hindustan, whether he wore Mughal clothes, whether he had an Indian lover or wife and children, or when and how he died. In this respect, the scant artistic fingerprint he has left is perhaps more typical of the firangis in the Mughal period than those left by the fleshed-out figures I have been able to chronicle in other chapters. His life is a vapour-trail as elusive as the evaporating water of Fatehpur Sikri in the mid 1580s.

But despite the dearth of surviving information about Mandu Firangi, we can still recover important aspects of his Indian biography in its most literal sense—the way in which his body was imprinted and transformed by his time in Hindustan. And a significant number of these transformations were occasioned by the artisanal work he performed in Fatehpur Sikri and then Lahore, in accordance with what I have suggested was his Indian artisanal name. I refer here of course not to 'Mandu Firangi', a name designed to disclose his origin, but to 'Naqqash', a name that summoned him to a unique set of skills. To serve in Akbar's kitabkhana, Mandu Firangi Naqqash would have had to adapt his physical techniques in a variety of ways. He wouldn't have stood at an easel but sat on the ground as he worked. He would have had to train his body to master several new arts: grinding pigments for use as paint, preparing the rough surface of a paper canvas with a piece of smooth agate, piercing the thin charba (vellum) of a khaba (master tracing) with a fine needle, dusting charcoal through the pierced charba onto a page from a small porous muslin bag, applying a coat of red paint with a squirrel-brushed qalam to fix the charcoal. And if he worked in the sun-blasted, water-deprived location of Fatehpur Sikri, he would have had to train his body to perform all these skills with scant hydration. How would the lack of water have changed not just his body, but also the consistency of the ground pigments he used as paint? Without water, how much would he have been able to clean his workspace and himself after a painting session? After Akbar and the royal kitabkhana moved to Lahore, did Mandu Firangi Naqqash again have to change his bodily habits and painting materials in a new city abundantly supplied with water by the Ravi?

In other words, Mandu Firangi's biography—for all its glaring absences and for all the questions it leaves us with—is ultimately a tale of ongoing skilful bodily adaptation to ecological as much as cultural imperatives. He had to adapt to the different climates and water-supply environments of Fatehpur Sikri and Lahore. But he also had to adapt to the specific skill-sets of the Mughal painters' kitabkhana. And these processes of adaptation not only changed him and his body into Mandu Firangi Naqqash, they also subtly transformed the meaning of what it meant to be an authentically Mughal dastkar.

Tourists who visit the Taj Mahal in Agra almost invariably find themselves standing before Shah Jahan's and Mumtaz Mahal's tombs. Located in the heart of the complex, the tombs are a remarkable sight, nearly as memorable as the more famous outside view of the Taj. Unlike the anonymous cenotaphs in older Mughal monuments such as Humayun's Tomb in Delhi, the Taj Mahal's tombs spectacularly broadcast the identities of the royal pair they commemorate. An octagonal enclosure of intricate jaalis encircles them; at the centre of the enclosure lies the tomb of Mumtaz Mahal, for whom the Taj was built. To the tomb's left is the cenotaph of Shah Jahan, added later and clearly off-centre in relation to his wife's—though his status is reaffirmed by its greater height. But the tombs' most striking feature is their colourful decoration, which both complements and contrasts the sheer white of the Taj exterior. The marble surfaces of each tomb—both sarcophagus and supporting plinth—are festooned with dazzling inlay patterns of flowers made of shimmering precious stones: brownish-red carnelian, blue lapis lazuli, green turquoise. We could call the style Mughal psychedelic.

The local term for precious stone inlay is parchin kari, meaning 'driven in'. In the West, it is called pietra dura, the Italian for 'hard stone'. The technique had been honed by Florentine artisans in the late sixteenth century. But pietra dura artifacts, widely circulated throughout Europe and the Ottoman Empire, began to find their way to Mughal Hindustan in the early seventeenth century. Just as the artists of Akbar's royal atelier had studied and adapted the styles of Italian Renaissance painters, so did Mughal court jewellers emulate and reimagine the techniques of Florentine pietra dura stoneworkers. In the nineteenth century, after the British captured Agra, the Taj Mahal's exquisite parchin kari work struck them as decidedly non-Indian—so much so that they began to believe that it had been designed by a European artisan, working in consultation with the building's Persian and Turkish architects. Sir William Henry Sleeman, the British resident at Gwalior, went even further: he argued that the entire Taj Mahal had been designed by a French jeweller named Austin of Bordeaux.

The man Sleeman called 'Austin of Bordeaux' certainly did not design the Taj Mahal. But he did live in Agra during the reigns of Jahangir and Shah Jahan. And he was a designer and artisan of considerable skill. He had developed his talent in jewel-cutting as a young man in France, and it was this talent that won him the attention of the Great Mughals. Just as importantly, he was also a skilled counterfeiter. This was arguably an even more decisive factor in the jeweller's success. Not only did his work as a counterfeiter lead him out of Europe and to India; it was also responsible for his most impressive creations in the Mughal court. For counterfeiting need not be simply a craven deception designed to dupe people into believing that an object is what it is not. It can also be a brilliant exercise in creative adaptation, in refashioning material normally associated with one form and making it bear the distinguishing marks of something completely different.

The migrant jeweller's counterfeit masterpieces included artworks and contraptions that he produced for Jahangir and Shah Jahan. But they also—perhaps chiefly—included himself. A firangi who has become Indian is a counterfeit in the best sense: not a lamentable deception but an artistic and uncannily accurate reinvention as something different. Yet the jeweller's counterfeit masterpieces also bore telltale signs of his past European lives. These past lives meshed with elements of Mughal Agra in two ways. First, they meshed at the level of artisanal skill. The Mughal desire for beautiful art, especially art that makes creative use of precious stones, gave the French-trained jeweller access to Jahangir's and Shah Jahan's courts in ways that many other foreigners could only dream of. Second, his past lives meshed with the Mughal culture at the level of his name. The jeweller acquired a new title in Agra that, when combined with his old French name, gave him a new identity. His new name not only made him a firangi Mughal servant, it also demanded that he transform his European body's skills in ways that conformed to Mughal traditions of artisanal aptitude.

Of course Austin of Bordeaux never designed the Taj Mahal. The claim that he did is a British fiction. But the man who Sleeman called 'Austin of Bordeaux' (a name that is also a British fiction) was himself responsible for many other beautiful creations. In particular he designed eye-catching royal thrones that suggest much about the hybrid aesthetic culture of the Mughal court. In making his counterfeit creations, this firangi designer of Indian thrones produced a subjunctive Mughal world similar to that of Bichitr's painting of Jahangir and King James or Mandu Firangi's painting of a golden-haired Rama and Sita—a world that subordinated European techniques and bodies to the imperatives of Mughal power. But whereas Bichitr and Mandu Firangi created this subjunctive world with paint, the so-called Austin of Bordeaux did so with precious stones. These stones are part of a larger tale of becoming Indian amid increasing global traffic in jewels.

◆

If Mandu Firangi's life is a vanishing vapour-trail, we are equally in the dark about the fate of William Leeds, the English jeweller who accompanied Ralph Fitch to India and was employed by Akbar in Fatehpur Sikri. What would have happened to Leeds after Akbar made the decision to abandon the city on 22 August 1585? Would he have accompanied the emperor and the other members of the royal karkhana on the long trek from Fatehpur Sikri to the Lahore? And how might the work of a firangi jeweller in the Mughal court have contributed to the cultural expansionist programme represented by the Ramayana project?

For all we know, Leeds was no longer even alive when Akbar relocated. There is no record of him after Fitch's account in either English or Mughal archives. But if he survived the great Fatehpur Sikri water shortage of 1585 as well as the bouts of dysentery, heatstroke and epidemic disease that routinely afflicted firangi visitors from this time, he was probably retained in Akbar's khankana. Here he would have worked for what was, in effect, the Lahore public relations bureau of the Mughal court, shaping its image on the global stage. The Mughal javaheris, or jewellers, toiled long and hard to make Akbar, his omrah, and his harem look powerful, and this included bedecking them in an astonishing amount of jewellery: turban clips, tiklis, earrings, nose studs, necklaces, chains, finger-rings, toe-rings, bracelets, clasps, and anklets. Most of these items were fashioned out of gold and silver, but they were set with diamonds from Golconda, rubies from Badakhshan, and emeralds from Ajmer and Udaipur. Akbar was also a dedicated follower, and supporter, of international jewel fashion. The Mughal javaheris were enlisted to cut precious stones entering from other parts of the world, including emeralds from the Muzo mines in Colombia. Leeds too may have been encouraged to adapt European styles for Mughal fashions. We know that a Mughal jeweller produced an emerald turban clip that resembled the French aigrette fashionable among women in Queen Elizabeth's court. Using European skills of enamelling and a distinctive floral Western design, one of Akbar's jewellers made a series of rings inlaid with precious rubies, sapphires and garnets. Perhaps this jeweller was a firangi like Leeds.

Flash forward to 1603. Although Lahore is the bigger city and closer to the powerful Silk Route linking Mughal Hindustan to China, Persia, the Levant, Turkey and Europe, Akbar has not been able to stay away from Agra, the traditional Mughal seat of power since Babur's invasion in 1526. From 1598 onwards, he has resided there almost exclusively. The city has not yet entered its mid-seventeenth-century heyday: hallmark structures such as the Taj Mahal, Itmad-ud-Daulah's tomb, the Chini ka Rauza, and Akbar's sublime Sikandra Complex are all yet to be built. Agra is, nonetheless, a beautiful city where—in contrast to the hustle and bustle of Lahore—life is a little more sedate. Pleasure gardens, including Babur's Ram Bagh, dot the east side of the Yamuna River. On the river's west side, Akbar—in between his taxing campaigns against the Deccan sultanates—invests considerable energy in refurbishing and expanding the Agra Fort, which by the time of his son Jahangir and grandson Shah Jahan will have become one of the architectural marvels of Mughal Hindustan.

If Fatehpur Sikri is a monument to a cross-cultural Mughal aesthetics exemplified by its architecture and paintings, Agra Fort is a display case for another Mughal art form: exquisitely designed jewellery. Precious stones are to be seen throughout the fort—on the persons of the emperor and the Mughal omrah (high-ranking officials); on royal thrones encrusted with rubies, emeralds, and diamonds; on the walls and ceilings of the imperial buildings, which gleam with inlaid jade, amethyst, turquoise and mother of pearl. As early as 1584, Leeds's travelling companion Ralph Fitch notes that Agra has 'very much merchandise…of precious stones, both rubies, diamonds and pearls'. These precious stones are already on their way to becoming a metaphor for the power of the Mughals. Akbar has dubbed nine exceptionally talented courtiers his navaratnas (nine jewels); the mosques that Akbar's son and grandson will build inside the Agra Fort will be named Nagina Masjid (Jewel Mosque) and Moti Masjid (Pearl Mosque).

But Mughal jewel power is most apparent in Akbar's carefully crafted political spectacles. At court, he liberally bestows jewels on his omrah, vassal kings and visitors, who are obliged to gift him even more in return. And twice a year, on the first day of the solar and the lunar calendars, he weighs himself or one of his sons on a set of scales against piles of gold, silver and precious gems, which he then donates to the poor. This spectacle necessitates a large army of javaheris, or jewellers.

Many are retained in Akbar's karkhana in order to cut and mount the endless procession of precious stones that flow daily into the Mughal coffers. Upon Akbar's death in 1605, according to a Flemish visitor's calculations, his 'diamonds, rubies, emeralds, sapphires, pearls and similar jewels' will be valued at '60,520,521 rupees'. A century later, when Persian invaders raid the Agra Fort treasury, they will find an enormous stash of precious stones that once belonged to Noor Jahan, the wife of Jahangir. Noor Jahan's treasure bears witness to the many functions of a well-cut jewel. It is at one and the same time an objet d'art, a luxury commodity, and a badge of power. All these communicate Agra's status as the cultural, commercial, and political capital of one of the world's richest empires.

And many visitors take note of its power. Agra is now, in 1603, a major destination for firangi migrants from other parts of the world: Akbar has invited the Jesuits to set up a permanent mission; he has also authorized the building of a Portuguese church as well as a church serving the city's large Armenian trader community. They are just one of many Christian nations represented among the city's merchants. When the English trader William Finch visits Agra in 1611, he will be greeted by an English mercenary, three French soldiers, a Dutch engineer, and a Venetian merchant. For Akbar, these visitors represent not just a resource from which he can commercially profit. They also are a global audience, beholden to his spectacular theatre of jewels. Later firangi visitors in the time of Jahangir and Shah Jahan seem to have been personally invited to view the matchless splendour of the imperial Mughal jewels. The French traveller, Jean-Baptiste Tavernier, devotes an extended sequence of his *Travels in India* to describing the precious stones he was shown in Agra by the Mughal treasurer, Akil Khan, including the famed Koh-i-Noor diamond.

In 1603, sixty years before Tavernier will gaze upon the Koh-i-Noor, another firangi is involved in a scene of political theatre starring the Great Mughal's jewels. On this occasion, though, the scene is partly stage-managed by the firangi, an Englishman named John Mildenhall. And the scene is spectacular. Mildenhall has learned during a stint in Lahore that one cannot gain access to Akbar without an impressive gift, and that the emperor has a strong predilection for jewels. So he has arrived in Agra from Lahore with a substantial present for Akbar—twenty-nine horses and 'diverse jewels, rings and earrings to his great liking'. Lavish jewellery as well as horses summarily presented, Mildenhall informs Akbar of his business: he is representing his queen in the hope of acquiring special trading privileges for England with the Mughals. Akbar takes well to his visitor and receives him several times over the next few months. It is quite easy to imagine Akbar initially asking Mildenhall if he is indeed from 'Angrestan' and, after Mildenhall has affirmed that this is so, the Great Mughal delightedly crying out the name of his former English employee and marvelling aloud at the stones William Leeds polished for him. And we might also imagine Mildenhall making a mental note to himself: this is a good place to be a jeweller. With the help of a skilled gem-cutter whose work would please Akbar and solicit certain concessions from him, one could make a very tidy profit here.

Indeed, Mildenhall is a profit-hound. And that is because he is something of a crook. Mildenhall is in India not, as he claims, to represent the queen, but to steal a march on the newly founded East India Company, which had announced in 1599 its intention to send a fleet to India. Mildenhall hopes that, by brokering an advance trading agreement with Akbar, he can leverage his position for significant personal gain. By 1609, he is back in London, petitioning to be given special trade-negotiator status by the East India Company for the then-astronomical retainer fee of 1,500 pounds. Astonishingly the Company agrees, perhaps because of his extraordinary personal connection with Akbar. But Mildenhall then ups his fee to 3,000 pounds. This time the Company shareholders refuse, and his plans are dashed. When a merchant enlists him to serve as his agent in Persia, however, he begins to scheme again.

At some time during his year back in London, Mildenhall has made the acquaintance of a young Frenchman who, he is told, has a rare skill in counterfeiting precious stones. Perhaps their first exchange goes something like this. Mildenhall informs the Frenchman about his upcoming mission to Persia; the Frenchman looks slightly bored. Mildenhall boasts about his previous journey to India and his friendship with Akbar, the Great Mughal; the Frenchman still looks bored. But when Mildenhall tells him about the precious stones he has seen in Agra Fort, and the special status Akbar's English jeweller had enjoyed in the emperor's karkhana, the Frenchman sits up and pays attention. Mildenhall tells him that, to gain an audience with the Mughal emperor and to receive his generosity, one must have a ready supply of expensive-looking jewels. The Frenchman says that he might be able to help out. He tells Mildenhall that he would be interested in coming with him to India; if they become business partners, they would stand to make a tidy profit. 'What is your name, sir?' asks Mildenhall. 'Austin of Bordeaux,' replies the Frenchman. 'Or, in my language, Augustin—Augustin Hiriart.'

◆

Augustin Hiriart was born in the French port city of Bordeaux in the early 1580s. His last name indicates that he was of Basque origin. Although Bordeaux is somewhat to the north of the Basque territories of southwestern France and northeastern Spain, the city had a large Basque community in the sixteenth century. How much would Hiriart's ethnicity have been a shaping factor in his youth and adult life? At this time, Basque culture and language was regarded with suspicion and even hostility by the majority Francophone population. Because Protestantism had made some inroads into the Basque territories, the community was often the target of religious intolerance: they attracted the attention of the Inquisition in Spain, and in France they were accused of witchcraft. Hiriart may have grown up speaking Basque, but all his surviving communications are in French. How did this affect his sense of himself? It is striking that many firangi migrants to India—including Garcia da Orta and Thomas Stephens—were, like Hiriart, members of a persecuted minority community in their places of birth. In each case, this seems to have generated a sense of not quite belonging that prompted them to keep crossing borders. Belonging to a stigmatized minority community can also make one adept in the art of passing as something else to escape persecution. It can, in short, make one a skilled counterfeiter of identity.

The details of Hiriart's life prior to his arrival in India are scarce. What we know about him is in large part dependent on four letters, written in French, that he sent from India to Europe. These indicate that he was literate. But we don't know where he was educated, or to what level. He probably joined the jewellery business in his teens; the trade was a common one for Basques. Distinctive rosary rings dating to the 1500s, known as Euskal arrosarioa, were crafted by Basque jewellers in northeastern Spain and southwestern France. These rings display a high degree of artisanal sophistication: each includes ten delicate prayer knobs, ornate filigree, and intricately carved motifs such as crowns of thorns, rosebuds, and fleurs-de-lis. To produce them, the Basque artisans would have needed to cultivate bodily skills of sharp eyesight, superior hand-to-eye coordination, and steady fingers. Perhaps Hiriart was trained in the Euskal arrosarioa tradition. In one of his letters from India, he asks that his regards be sent to a 'Monsieur Castaniac marchant jeolier, a la plaso du pales a Bordeux [Mr Castaniac merchant jeweller, at the Place du Palais in Bordeaux]'. This merchant jeweller shares his surname, Castaniac, with a Basque village in the French Pyrenees; perhaps he was once Hiriart's employer or master, and Hiriart his apprentice. Hiriart's letter places Castaniac in the Place du Palais, one of the oldest streets of Bordeaux and the location of the old Château de l'Ombrière, from which the English once ruled the kingdom of Aquitaine. It was a posh address; the upper-class French philosopher and essayist Michel de Montaigne was based there between 1557 and 1570. Castaniac had obviously done well for himself.

Despite his association with the well-to-do Castaniac, Hiriart left Bordeaux for England in 1601, when he was only 19 or 20. There had been maritime links between Bordeaux and London from the days of English rule in Aquitaine, and a merchant jeweller could easily find passage to a city where the demand for high-quality precious stones, especially in the ageing Queen Elizabeth's royal court, was strong. Yet there may have been other reasons for Hiriart's move. It's not inconceivable that he was a religious refugee. In the mid sixteenth century, Protestantism had swept from Geneva through the southwest Basque regions of France; there was considerable tension between Catholics and reformists, which further to the north culminated in the infamous 1572 St Bartholomew's Day massacres of Huguenot Protestants in Paris. The Edict of Nantes in 1598, when the Protestant king Henri of Navarre converted to Catholicism, supposedly brought an end to the tension. But it also drove many French Protestants to England. Perhaps Hiriart was among them.

But there was probably another, more clandestine, reason for Hiriart to go to England. Many years later, in 1625, he wrote from India to Charles Cauchon de Maupas, the Baron du Tour. The baron was a French diplomat whom he had met in London in 1603. It is clear from the letter that Hiriart is a little anxious Baron du Tour might not remember him: he starts by reminding the baron of their first meeting. He then proceeds to say, as if offering a further aid to the baron's memory, that 'Entre autres choses i'ay esté expert pour contrefaire les pierries [Among other things I was expert at counterfeiting precious stones].' On the one hand, this may suggest merely that Hiriart had been contracted to produce pleasant-looking imitations of expensive gems; the English royal court, for example, was often in need of fine costume jewellery. But he may have been also indirectly admitting to a skill that had got him into serious trouble. A surviving correspondence between Hiriart and Robert Cecil, the director of England's spy network, strongly suggests the latter. In 1601, shortly after Hiriart came to England, Cecil met him and asked if he knew how to make a 'balas ruby'—a red spinel cut to look like a ruby. At the time, Hiriart said it was impossible. But in 1603, he wrote to Cecil and confessed that he had worked out how to manufacture such a stone 'to the greatest possible perfection', so much so that a stone actually worth 300 pounds would be mistakenly valued at ten times that amount. We do not know what prompted this second letter. At the time, however, there was a major counterfeit scandal unfolding in the London Goldsmiths' Company, involving a master jeweller named Thomas Sympson who had presented fake stones to the governor of the Turkey Company as precious gems from France. Hiriart and some other Frenchmen seem to have come to England specifically to join Sympson's counterfeiting ring; and Hiriart may have been pressured by Cecil for information, upon threat of imprisonment, deportation or worse. Whatever the truth, the taint of counterfeiting seems to have rubbed off on Hiriart.

Hiriart's subsequent association with the shady Mildenhall only sullies his case further. After the two men decided to travel east together, they journeyed overland: by Hiriart's own account, they went through Arabia, Mesopotamia, Babylon and Persia. They may have travelled with a larger party. Hiriart notes in a letter how 'all the Frenchmen I brought with me died' in the Asian heat; we do not know if they were fellow members of Sympson's counterfeiting ring. But their travels were disrupted when Mildenhall, rather than selling his consignment in Persia as he had been instructed, carried on in the direction of India. One presumes that he, together with Hiriart, had hoped to take advantage of the trading privileges Akbar had supposedly granted him by offloading his consignment in Agra at a profit. Mildenhall, however, was hauled down near the border of Persia by a couple of English agents representing his employer; here he was made to surrender the consignment, valued at 9,000 pounds. We don't know if Hiriart was with him at this point. Mildenhall proceeded to Lahore; shortly after arriving, he fell sick. He doggedly pressed on to Ajmer, where Jahangir was holding court. But his condition continued to deteriorate, and he died in June of 1614, in a house he was sharing with Hiriart. In the days before his death, he had made Hiriart his legal heir on the condition that the

Frenchman marry Mildenhall's half-Indian daughter. He also bequeathed Hiriart his papers, which apparently included a diary recording his observations about their travels. It is unclear whether Hiriart accepted Mildenhall's condition. But we do know from East India Company records that Hiriart proceeded to burn Mildenhall's papers. Why? Did they contain incriminating evidence about Mildenhall and Hiriart? If so, what might this evidence have been—did it mention Hiriart's past counterfeit dealings? Or did it mention a plan, perhaps, to offload fake jewels manufactured by Hiriart as precious gifts at the Mughal court?

In any case, Hiriart soon moved from Ajmer to Agra. It is quite possible that it was he who made arrangements to have his English friend's corpse conveyed to the city: Mildenhall's grave is still visible to this day at the old Agra Catholic Cemetery, just behind the Bhagwan Talkies Cinema near National Highway 2. By the time the firangi jeweller was settled in Agra, however, he had already come to the attention of Jahangir.

◆

Of Hiriart's first years in Agra, we again know little. But he seems to have quickly gained employment with Jahangir, perhaps as early as his stay in Ajmer. An English ambassador to Persia, Sir Robert Shirley, visited Ajmer in September of 1614—just two months after Mildenhall's death—and an East India Company record states that he left 'carrying the Frenchman's elephant with him'. We can assume this Frenchman was Hiriart: he remarks in a letter written in 1620 that he had some years previously 'mandis un ellefant por Perse avec don Roberto Charly [sent an elephant through Persia with Sir Robert Shirley]', in anticipation of gaining leave from the king. This suggests Hiriart had already been in Jahangir's service for some time. Perhaps the ailing Mildenhall, who had met Jahangir on his previous visit to Agra, brokered their meeting. And perhaps Hiriart immediately impressed Jahangir with gifts of (fake) rubies. That Hiriart was in a position to gift Shirley an elephant means that he had been not simply employed, but also preferred.

After entering Jahangir's service, Hiriart took an Indian wife. Writing in 1625, he says: 'My wife's mother and her sister when their husbands died, burnt themselves alive, embracing the bodies of their dead husbands, but that was before I was connected to the household.' This 'wife' was definitely not Mildenhall's daughter, who in 1614 was eleven at most: it is also impossible that the Indian Mrs Mildenhall committed sati on her husband's pyre, as his body was spirited away to be buried in Agra. So Hiriart either reneged on the supposedly binding condition of Mildenhall's declaration of him as his heir, or took a second wife. What prompted Hiriart to marry another woman? Did he fall in love? Or, more likely, given the custom of Mughal emperors picking wives for their favoured servants, was she chosen for him by Jahangir? We know next to nothing about Hiriart's nameless wife: she was clearly born a Hindu, though he claims that she converted to Christianity. The evidence indicates that they had two and maybe three children. In 1620, Hiriart refers to a son who had been born two years earlier, and who was at that time his only child. He notes in a 1625 letter that Jahangir has named the child 'Servant of Christ', or Abdul Masih—further circumstantial evidence that Jahangir had had a hand in the match. Hiriart also says that he has held off on baptizing his second son, as he hopes to come back to France to have him baptized by King Louis XIII himself. Interestingly, a letter written in 1630 by a Monsieur Alvarez of Paris to 'Augustin Herryard gentilhomme Francois au service du Roy, le grand Mogor [Augustin Hiriart, French gentleman in the service of the King the great Mughal]' refers to Hiriart's son, Loys or Louis; perhaps this was the second son, named for the king of France in anticipation of what Hiriart hoped would be a glorious return to his native country.

But Hiriart was to be disappointed in this hope, and in others. He never returned to France. In a letter written from Chaul in 1632, just a year before he died, Hiriart expresses his great longing to see his native country again. And he also mentions, with more than a hint of sadness, his 'wife and one child, who is left to me from the affliction'. In other words, Abdul Masih or Louis, or both boys, died during one of the bouts of plague that swept through Agra and Lahore in the 1620s. Hiriart makes no reference to a daughter, but the surviving child could have been a girl: an old document records an inscription found on an Agra Christian gravestone commemorating 'Iane [Jane] de Hiriart, filia [daughter] de Augustin'. We do not know how old Jane was when she died; it is quite possible that she or one of the brothers may have survived to adulthood and had children of their own. For all we know, Hiriart may still have Indian descendants living in Agra or Lahore today.

Hiriart evidently tasted disappointment in his family life. But he prospered professionally. His talent had quickly impressed itself on Jahangir: acknowledging that Hiriart had no peer in the 'arts of a goldsmith and a jeweller, and in all sorts of skill'—the Persian word the *Tuzuk-i-Jahangiri* uses for 'skill' is hunarmandi—the Mughal emperor renamed him 'Hunarmand', or skilful, early in his Indian career. Hiriart welcomed the title, and used a version of it in his letters back to France, which he signed variously as 'Augustin Houaremand' and 'Augustin Houaroud' (some of those 'u's in the second names may in fact be his version of 'n's). He himself glossed the meaning of his name in French as inventeur des arts—inventor of arts. His gloss is quite accurate: to be hunarmand is the distinguishing trait of the Mughal dastkar. Hiriart's artistic invention led him to be widely admired in much the same way any Indian IIT engineering graduate is today: indeed, a German visitor to India called him the Ingenieur des Grossen Mogouls, or Engineer of the Great Mughals. But Hunarmand (as he was now known) didn't win his Indian name for his engineer's skill. It had been given to him some years prior for his superior artisanal skill in working precious stones and designing beautiful objects.

Hunarmand probably impressed Jahangir first with his skill in manufacturing and cutting imitation 'balas rubies', a precious gem clearly dear to the emperor. The Frenchman notes that the 'he alone has more of these than all the men in the world'. But it is more likely that Hunarmand won his name for his talent in creating beautiful objects for his Mughal master. He seems to have been contracted in 1616 to work on a major piece, which took three years to complete: a new throne for Jahangir. It was presented to the emperor as part of the lavish Navroz celebrations organized by his prime minister, Itmad-ud-Daulah, in March 1619. Jahangir describes the throne as made of 'gold and silver, much ornamented and decorated, the supports of which were in the form of tigers'. He estimated its cost at an astonishing 450,000 rupees. But this wasn't all. At the same festival, Jahangir notes, Hunarmand also 'offered the value of Rs 100,000 in jewelled ornaments and cloths to the Begums and the other ladies of the Palace'.

Perhaps it is the Navroz-celebration throne that Hunarmand describes in a letter to Baron du Tour in 1625, although the 'tigers' that Jahangir attributed to it are described differently by its creator. Its visual impact rivals that of Bichitr's imaginary hour-glass throne:

> I have prepared a design for the construction of a royal throne
> for the King on which he sits once a year for nine days (which
> they call the new days), when the Sun enters the sign of the
> Ram, when their year commences. This throne is supported by

four lions weighing 150 quintals of silver covered with beaten gold leaf, and the canopy is supported by 12 columns in which there are 12 thousand ounces of enameled gold. The canopy which is in the form of a dome has been covered by me with 4 thousand of my artificial stones, but the genuine stones corresponding to these are of inestimable value, for the King has a great number of pearls and it is certain that he also has more large diamonds and large rubies than all the princes of the universe. On the ascent which has four steps I made 4 'Suisses' like those which are at the gate of the Louvre, with halbards in their hands but no wine in their stomachs.

What is most striking about this description is how it explicitly combines local and foreign design features. The lion must have been familiar to Hunarmand as a staple of European iconography. But it probably acquired a different meaning for him in Mughal Hindustan. Not only did he see, for the first time, great cats such as tigers and leopards. Surely he would also have been aware that the principal imperial standard of the Mughals—the alam—featured a golden lion with a sun rising from its back. Yet in front of the throne's legs, right next to Hunarmand's four replicas of the Mughal golden lion, stand the figures of four Swiss halberdiers. This eccentric detail might be the creation of a homesick Frenchman pining for Europe. But it is also testimony to the persistent will of Mughal art to incorporate other cultures—a will that we might see here as of a piece with Jahangir's aspirational global power. After all, as Hunarmand himself informed Baron du Tour, Jahangir's name means 'Conqueror of the World'.

This cross-cultural masterpiece artfully combined not just Mughal and European design features (though who knows what Jahangir really made of those teetotaller Swiss guards!) but also Hunarmand's skills in cutting both real and fake stones. As his 4,000 'artificial jewels' demonstrate, he had turned to account the counterfeiting skills that probably drove him out of England. Indeed, one might read the entire letter as an attempt to persuade Baron du Tour—who may have had to intervene with Cecil to bail the Frenchman out of whatever trouble he had got into in 1603—that Hiriart's skill in creating fake stones is a skilful art, or hunarmandi, rather than a crime. No wonder Hiriart signed his letters to the Baron as 'Hunarmand'. And Jahangir certainly enjoyed his firangi javaheri's ingenious use of precious stones, counterfeit or not. He claims in the *Tuzuk-i-Jahangiri* that 'from the beginning of the reign of the late king (may the light of Allah be his testimony!) until now, which is the fourteenth year of the rule of this suppliant, not one of the great Amirs has presented such offerings'. For his efforts, Hunarmand was rewarded with 3,000 darb (1,500 rupees—a huge sum at the time), a horse and an elephant; subsequent rewards included 'a house valued at eight thousand livres', a hat with a 'likeness in gold' of Jahangir, and tigers, leopards, and rhinoceroses. Not uncoincidentally, Hunarmand also became an early exponent of the Indian tradition of re-gifting: in one of his letters, he speaks of trying to fob off some of these feral 'presents' onto another visitor, who unsurprisingly wasn't keen to take them.

In the *Tuzuk-i-Jahangiri*, Jahangir makes clear that Hunarmand's name refers not just to his skills in jewellery but also to his other *hunarmandi*, including his powers of invention. Hunarmand describes some of his inventions in his letters back to France. Take, for example, an innovative machine that he boasts about in a letter he wrote in 1625: 'I have got a great reputation for the military machines which I have made…for this country. I have made a carriage which without risking the life of a man shoots arrows and burns everything which it meets or which comes near it.' This early version of a tank, both an artistic creation and a feat of engineering, was a cultural cross-over. Even as it was clearly designed to comply with the scorched-earth policy employed by Jahangir in his Deccan campaigns against Malik Ambar, it also incorporated recent Western pyrotechnical innovations: its power to 'burn everything' was almost certainly modelled on that of European artillery. In other words, the machine was a hybrid that matched foreign technology to local military demand. Jahangir took a deep personal interest in acquiring such technology. The German traveller, Heinrich von Poser, travelled with Hunarmand from Agra to Lahore in January of 1622. The two men had an audience there with Jahangir; von Poser reports that, during the unveiling of a new throne 'made of gold and about a foot high, constructed after Mr Augustin's designs', Jahangir asked the German through a translator 'what countryman I was, and why I had come there, what I had learnt, and whether I had with me anything rare and special in the nature of firearms'.

Hunarmand devised another innovative military contraption. Faced with the practical problem of corralling fighting elephants gone wild in the course of daily battles staged for Jahangir, the Frenchman claims to have 'invented a machine by which the person in charge, were it even a child, can by a contrivance which he holds in his hands bind and unbind [an elephant] with large iron chains a hundred times an hour and let him run about as much or as little as he likes'. The mechanics of Hunarmand's pachydermic remote-control device are unclear. But it probably drew, like the fighting carriage, on elements of European technology—perhaps the chains used to bolts the sides of vessels under construction, which the young Hiriart may have encountered in the ship-building docks of Bordeaux—in order to meet the military demands of the Mughals: their elephants needed to be controlled carefully in real war campaigns as much as mock battles.

It is hard to imagine that Hunarmand could ever top these creations, especially after the death of his biggest supporter, Jahangir, in 1627. Hunarmand was suspicious of Jahangir's son and successor Shah Jahan; he feared the new emperor's overt animosity to the Portuguese in particular and Christians in general, and declared that 'he is hated by high and low'. Yet Shah Jahan retained his services. In a letter he wrote in 1632, Hunarmand claimed that he had been 'employed these two years at Agra in making plans for a new throne which the King had ordered before he left Agra for the Deccan'. Shah Jahan, Hunarmand says, had demanded 'that two hundred times a hundred thousand livres should be spent on this throne in gold, diamonds, rubies, pearls and emeralds'. Circumstantial evidence indicates that this design was for Shah Jahan's legendary Peacock Throne, or Takht-i-Tavus, which is supposed to have included the Koh-i-Noor diamond. François Bernier saw the throne in the 1650s or 1660s; he asserted that its eponymous jewel-encrusted peacocks 'were made by a workman of astonishing powers, a Frenchman by birth...who, after defrauding several of the Princes of Europe, by means of false gems, which he fabricated with peculiar skill, sought refuge in the Great Mogul's court, where he made his fortune'. Although Bernier doesn't name the shadowy Frenchman, the biographical details he mentions about the throne's creator are eerily close to what we know about Hiriart/Hunarmand.

More fanciful is William Henry Sleeman's notion that 'Austin of Bordeaux' was the chief architect of the Taj Mahal, a baseless claim that one still finds routinely repeated on many Indian websites. The canard was probably born of a condescending European conviction that such a beautiful building couldn't have been designed by a non-westerner. As we have seen, the failure of nineteenth- and early twentieth-century

British art historians to recognize the extent to which Mughal artisans had artfully experimented with foreign aesthetic techniques also led them to misattribute some of the Taj's most striking European features—such as its pietra dura inlay patterns, which are a feature of much Mughal architecture of the seventeenth century—to firangi creators. Hunarmand is not the only European artisan to whom the design of the Taj has been credited. In 1640, the Portuguese Jesuit Sebastian Manrique claimed that another migrant who lived and worked in Agra and Lahore during the 1630s, the Venetian goldsmith Girolamo Veroneo, drafted the building's original plan. Manrique's canard was revived in the 1800s by an English antiquary, and the rumour grew legs in 1910 with the rediscovery in Lahore of Veroneo's grave. Of course the grave proves nothing about the Taj's provenance. But it does suggest once again how migrant firangi artisans were able to find work, and make new lives for themselves in Mughal Hindustan.

Hunarmand did not design the Taj Mahal. Nevertheless, he may have been commissioned to design the mausoleum's original silver doors, a dominant feature of the Taj Mahal before they were melted down and looted by Jat marauders in 1764. Apparently Hunarmand was contracted to do similar metalwork in the Agra Fort, though he didn't live to complete the commission. He died in his early fifties in about 1632, allegedly poisoned in Cochin while negotiating for the Mughals with the Portuguese. Hunarmand makes clear in his last surviving letter that he had been threatened by Shah Jahan, who feared that his talented jeweller was planning to leave the Mughal court. Perhaps Hunarmand was killed at the emperor's orders.

◆

The artisanal skill that Hunarmand embodied in his name as well as his nature was certainly a rare, even unique individual talent. Yet it was one that entailed a collection of bodily aptitudes gleaned from diverse artisanal communities in diverse locations. Hunarmand most likely acquired a talent for miniature precious stone detailing—one that entailed nimble finger work and attentive hand-to-eye coordination—from artisans trained in Basque tradition. And he probably learned how to counterfeit rubies—a quasi-alchemical practice that demanded heightened manual sensitivity to the tactile properties, including surface temperature and weight, of artificial as well as genuine stones—from other French jewellers in Bordeaux and London. But he learned the art of royal throne design and construction—an art that demanded not just a creative intelligence but also new physical skills in precious stone inlay work and animal-form metal sculpture—from watching Mughal artisans. The name 'Hunarmand' might have represented royal recognition of his abilities. But it also raised the bar of expectation: to remain worthy of the name, he would have had to insure that he was up to date with Jahangir's and Shah Jahan's tastes. And this would have meant staying well versed in both traditional and innovative techniques employed by other local jewellers. If the name 'Hunarmand' recognizes Hiriart's skills of counterfeiting, it captures more than just his ability to transform a humble spinel into the spitting image of a ruby. It also pays tribute to his ability to transform himself from a firangi jeweller into a Mughal dastkar.

For Hiriart to become Hunarmand, and for Mandu Firangi to become Naqqash, each man had to do more than just acquire an Indian dastkar name or title. They also had to submit to a demand implicit in their titles—a demand that their firangi bodies adapt to the unique skill-sets of Mughal arts. This adaptation entailed overlaying diverse aptitudes acquired from different parts of the globe with new Indian skills. As a result, Augustin Hiriart Hunarmand and Mandu Firangi's bodies became versions of their cross-cultural creations: Indo-European palimpsests in which Hindu gods have blond hair and Mughal thrones feature golden Swiss halberdiers. On the one hand, the hybrid skills of Mandu Firangi and Hunarmand challenge us to enlarge our understanding of what it means to be a Mughal dastkar producing Mughal art. On the other, we should see this enlargement not as a radical transformation of Mughal aesthetic tradition but, rather, as that tradition's very lifeblood. The emergence of European cultural forms within the mainstream of Mughal art during the reigns of Akbar, Jahangir and Shah Jahan doesn't quite model an exemplary cosmopolitanism, nor does it anticipate the firangi ascendancy of later centuries. Rather, as Bichitr's painting of Jahangir preferring a Sufi sheikh to foreign kings suggests, it bolsters an Indian aspiration to occupy a position of power and influence on the global stage. The work of firangi dastkars proposes, subjunctively, that we be in awe of world-conquering Great Mughals.

What's in a firangi's Indian name? A palimpsest of old and new bodily aptitudes. And that palimpsest helped expand the cultural and imaginative terrain of the Mughal Empire.

ON RE-CLOTHING

'Clothes do not make the man', the saying goes. But this is a peculiarly Western conviction. The assumption that who we are is utterly independent of what we wear is anathema in many other parts of the world.

In India, clothes often identify you as part of a community. I am speaking here not just of obvious badges of identity, such as the Muslim taqqiya or skullcap, the saffron robes of a Hindu sanyasi, or even the upavita or sacred thread worn by Brahmin men. Clothes often signify in more subtle ways. In Kerala, how a woman ties her sari often indicates if she is Hindu, Muslim, or Christian. And as this suggests, what you wear might not just broadcast your identity but also direct you to use your body accordingly. The five mandatory articles or kakaar worn by observant Sikh men are a good case in point: for example, the kesh—long hair covered with a turban—means you cannot go near a razor or barber's scissors; the kangha—a small wooden comb—requires you to groom your uncut hair regularly; the kacchera—a holy undergarment—demands that you abstain from sexual excess.

It is more helpful in India, perhaps, to think not of clothes but of clothing. Clothes are mere commodities that can be easily discarded. Clothing your body, by contrast, transforms it. Clothing marks your body as belonging to a specific community and obliges it to perform certain acts. At an even more basic level, clothing changes your body. Donning handspun khadi cotton lowers your body's temperature in summer, but it also raises it in winter. Wearing chappals puts less pressure on your toes than pinched Western shoes might, but their flat soles can also diminish your arches. Dressing in a sari, blouse, and petticoat requires you to comport your body and hold your arms in distinctive ways.

In the fifteen years I have been visiting and living in India, I have taken to wearing local clothing. Short-sleeved cotton kurtas were my gateway habit. I liked their colours and patterns; even more, I liked their feel on my skin and their lightness in the summer heat. I then graduated to long kurtas and churidars. After years of belts and elastic waistbands the churidar ka naada—the string with which you tie the churidar pants above the hips—took some getting used to: I always managed both to garrote my waist, leaving a deep red weal around it, and to end up with my churidar crotch sagging somewhere near my knees. Yet there was something about the flow of the long kurta, the way in which it anchored my body yet admitted air as I walked, that I found deeply satisfying. Its length also changed my posture, allowing my 6'3" frame—often slightly hunched at the shoulders because of too much time huddled over laptop and desk—to rise to its full height. My current favourite piece of clothing is my black Pathan suit, a two-piece that consists of a long fitted cotton kameez and salwar. In it, I not only stand tall: my billowing salwar lowers my body's centre of gravity, allowing me to dance at parties with absolute freedom of movement.

But my Indian clothing is far more than a collection of comfortable or enabling accessories. It has also locked me into a culture of gift-giving. Many of my clothes have been given to me as presents by friends and relatives. When I wear them my body changes not just in its posture or its movements. It changes also in relation to other bodies, becoming part of a larger body based on bonds of reciprocity and obligation. In other words, the fabrics I wear delineate a social fabric. This social fabric's warp and weft is not always as comfortable as the fabrics on my body. Gifting clothes can be a democratic act; but it can also be deeply feudal. And sometimes it can be both. My cook wears several of my discarded shirts and jackets. I am pleased that I can give him clothes he needs; but even as my gifts have created an intimacy between us, they have also cemented our class difference. By re-clothing him, I bind him more firmly into a hierarchal relationship of obligation to me.

The ambivalences of gifting clothes are a feature of the biographies of two firangi women who lived in the Mughal harem. They were both obliged to participate in rituals of gifting robes and fabrics, as both givers and receivers. These rituals gave them decent, even stunning, garments to wear. But it also enmeshed them in complex hierarchical relations of service and obligation. Like the renaming of firangi artisans, the re-clothing of firangi harem women summoned them to use their bodies in accordance with the often stern prescriptions of the Mughal court. And that is why the harem might be seen not just as a physical space but, more particularly, as an engine of bodily transformation.

Clothes, then, do make the man. In Mughal Hindustan, they also made the woman. Or rather, they made the firangi woman become Indian.

How can we retrieve the stories of firangi women from Indian and European archives overwhelmingly dominated by male figures? The life stories of firangi men prior to the British Raj tend to be elusive; yet they are downright commonplace in comparison to the few surviving stories of firangi women in India from this period. And the scale of the problem is only underscored by how difficult it is to recover the lives even of native Mughal women. This is nowhere more apparent than in the controversy surrounding Akbar's legendary wife Jodha Bai. Immortalized in myth and modern film as the love of Akbar's life and as a co-creator of the much-vaunted Mughal culture of Muslim-Hindu syncretism, there is in fact no verifiable trace of a real Jodha Bai. When we seek her flesh-and-blood form, the lady (to quote Alfred Hitchcock) vanishes.

Salman Rushdie comments on this predicament in his novel *The Enchantress of Florence*. Jodha Bai is a major character in the novel's opening pages; but she is merely a sequence of disembodied echoes in a Fatehpur Sikri palace. As such she is invisible to everyone in the Mughal court, even the emperor, save for one person: the Persian naqqash Abdus Samad, who has painted her 'from the memory of a dream without ever looking upon her face'. This, Rushdie seems to imply, is the historical lot of Mughal women. We hear their voices only as faint echoes within the thrum of others' stories, and we fashion their portraits only by dipping a brush into the paint-box of our fantasies. Rushdie suggests how the supposedly 'real' women of Mughal history are tales—or, rather, tales about tales. And like Scheherazade's stories in *A Thousand and One Nights*, our tales about Mughal women lead us not to real people but to other stories. Jodha Bai is herself a skein of stories rather than a real person, a legend stitched together from the half-remembered threads of other yarns—of Akbar's real wife Harka Bai, of Jahangir's wife Jodh (spelt without the 'a' in historical texts) Bai. She herself seems never to have existed.

Rushdie's case is no doubt overstated. Take, for example, Gulbadan Banu Begum (1523-1603), the daughter of Babur and the sister of Humayun. We have direct access to Gulbadan's distinctive voice throughout the *Avhal-i Humayun Badshah* ('Circumstances of Emperor

Portuguese 200 escudo coin, depicting
Garcia da Orta

כנה כנינוביתזבל לך מכן לשב
עולמיס שנה נדול יהיהכבורהבית
הזה האחרון מזהראשון ליצירההים
בשלישיבשבתחמשהלכסלובוא

THE INSCRIPTION ON THIS
SLAB BELONGED TO
THE SYNAGOGUE IN KOCHANGADI
IT WAS BUILT IN 1344
THE OLDEST SYNAGOGUE IN COCHIN

Orta visited Cochin in Kerala in 1538 and
may have visited the synagogue there

The altar in the Bom Jesus Cathedral, Old Goa

The Rachol Seminary, Salsette, Goa, where Stephens was rector from 1610

Navy memorial in Kottakkal, Kerala, to the Kunhali Marakkars, the fourth of whom was Chinali's master.

Photo courtesy Marzook Bafakyh and P. S. Sudheer.

Diu Water Fort jail, near where Malik Ayaz constructed the cross-harbour chain to protect the port from foreign invaders

Diorama depicting Eustachius De Lannoy's surrender after the Battle of Colachel in Travancore; at the Padmanabhapuram Palace in Thuckalay, Kerala

De Lannoy's tomb, Udayagiri Fort,
with inscriptions in Latin and Tamil

Door to Malik Ambar's tomb in Kuldabad,
near Aurangabad

Photo courtesy Jasmine Luthra

Photo courtesy Freer Gallery of Art, Smithsonian Institution, Washington, DC
Purchase, F1942.15a

Bichitr, Jahangir Favouring A Sufi Shaikh Over Kings (c. 1618)

The Buland Darwaza, Fatehpur Sikri

Mumtaz Mahal's and Shah Jahan's tombs featuring colorful bejewelled pietra dura or parchin kari inlay, Taj Mahal, Agra

Jaali of harem quarters in Lahori Fort, from where Juliana Firangi may have peered at the river Ravi

Underground women's apartments, Lahore Fort

The Rang Mahal in the Lal Qila (Red Fort),
where Juliana Dias da Costa probably spent time

Juliana Dias da Costa, from a portrait reproduced in Francois Valentijn,
Oud en Nieuw Oost Indien, *Amsterdam 1724*

Photo courtesy Lebrecht Music & Arts

Sign for Delhi Development Authority flats in Sarai Jullena, a district in southeast Delhi named for Juliana Dias da Costa

The village of Jogabai, on the Yamuna riverfront in Okhla district, Delhi; once part of Juliana Dias da Costa's jagir

Photo courtesy Ulises Ali Mejias

Photo courtesy Ulises Ali Mejias

A Kos Minar on the highway to Ajmer;
Coryate probably guided his way from Agra by following these milestones

The fakir-ridden road leading to Ajmer Dargah Sharif of
Moinuddin Chishti in Ajmer

THOMAS CORIATE
Traueller for the English
VVits : Greeting.

From the Court of the Great MOGVL, *Resident at the Towne of* ASMERE, *in Easterne* INDIA.

Printed by W. Iaggard, and Henry Fetherston.
1616.

The frontispiece to Coryate's Traveller for the English Wits,
depicting him (at his request) riding on an Indian elephant

The entrance to the Akbari Fort, Ajmer;
Coryate begged here before Jahangir, sitting in his jharoka

Inside Sarmad's dargah in Meena Bazaar, Delhi

The Charminar of Hyderabad, the centre of the then-new city in which Sarmad and Abhai Chand lived for nearly a decade

Burmese screen painting supposed to depict the Portuguese mercenary-cum-Irawaddy delta potentate, Filipe de Brito e Nicote, about 1600

Photo courtesy Sayam U. Chowdhury

Sandwip, the island in the Bay of Bengal to which Tibau relocated in 1609 with his band of pirates and declared himself 'raja'

Broadway in Chennai, at the division between Fort St George (left) and Black Town (right). This is the site of Manucci's first house in Madras

View of Chennai from Parangi Malai, or St Thomas Mount.
Manucci had another house and garden here

Siddha medicine dispensary, including a jar of lingam—one of Manucci's
favourite medicinal substances

Humayun'), her vivid memoir of the reigns of her father and brother. And we know a lot about the lives of other Mughal queens and princesses. But it is certainly true that most of the women of the Mughal chronicles—if they are mentioned at all—are more often than not just passing references in stories told by, and about, men. What, then, of firangi women in the Mughal Empire? If even the royal Jodha Bai is nothing but a series of echoes, what hope can we have of recovering the biographies of humbler firangi women who migrated to Hindustan? How do we begin to track down their footprints in an age when firangi as much as Mughal women were so often the effaced and nameless possessions of men?

Very few firangi women travelled to Mughal Hindustan. No firangi woman artist joined Mandu Firangi or Augustin Hiriart Hunarmand in the Mughal karkhana; no firangi bandit queen accompanied Thomas Roch and Raben Simitt in their rogue expeditions through Haryana. This reflects on not just Mughal but also firangi patriarchal customs. Although Portuguese women settled in Goa, Diu, Cochin and Hooghly, they by and large remained confined there, unlike those roving Portuguese men who became mercenaries in the armies of the Deccan sultans and the Mughal emperor. And in the first decades of the seventeenth century, the English East India Company actively banned women from journeying to India by sea. Other seafaring parties to India also excluded women: the Jesuit missions to the Mughal Empire were, unsurprisingly, all-male affairs. And those firangis who travelled to Hindustan via the overland Silk Route likewise tended to travel in all-male caravans.

Yet there were a handful of firangi women who not only visited but also settled in Mughal India. They didn't have many options about where to live. At least two of them, both named Juliana, found a home in the royal female apartments of the emperor's palace, known variously as the zenana, the mahal and the haram. We cannot plot with accuracy the full life-stories of the two Julianas—when they did what, and where, and with whom: those details are stubbornly elusive. As I've suggested throughout this book, however, biographies in the pre-colonial era become more legible when we re-imagine the nature of 'biography' itself. If we understand biography to be less a chronologically ordered narrative of an individual's life and more a story of bodily transformation in response to the specific challenges of new ecological, cultural, and economic environments, then we can learn a lot about the lives of firangi women in the subcontinent—and a lot more than their marginality in

Mughal and European archives might suggest. The world of the zenana offers us much on this score.

The zenana reshaped the bodies of its foreign and local inhabitants in a variety of ways. Life there demanded certain physical aptitudes. And these went far beyond the sexual talents that the Western Orientalist imagination has traditionally attributed to it. Women acquired skill in highly stylized Mughal forms of physical comportment—dancing, singing, playing. These skills were accompanied by two types of makeover. Like the male artists who served the emperor, women in the zenana were usually given new names. Just as importantly, they were also given new robes. Both makeovers firmly embedded them in Mughal culture and summoned them to adapt their bodies accordingly. The faint whispers of women's lives that emanate from Mughal and firangi traveller archives hint at ways in which migrant women were literally re-clad as authentically Indian. Rushdie's Jodha Bai in *The Enchantress of Florence* may suggest the obstacles in the way of those who seek to write biographies of women in pre-colonial Hindustan. Yet for all their apparent fictiveness, some stories about Mughal women offer us revealing points of entry into the labyrinth of migrant firangi history. And that labyrinth keeps returning, with the force of gravity, to the harem.

◆

What exactly is the harem? Perhaps the most accurate answer is that it is a space of Western fantasy. 'Harem' is the English rendering of the Arabic 'haram', meaning sanctuary; haram is also related to 'harim', meaning the female members of the family, and 'haraam', meaning forbidden. But the connotations of the Arabic term 'haram' have been displaced by the rather different referent of the English word 'harem', which names not just a physical space but also the large female retinue owned by a Muslim sultan or emperor for his sexual pleasure. As a result, the space of the harem has morphed into something rather different in the Western imagination from what the haram was in reality. This is as true of the Mughal harem as it is of the even more famous Imperial Harem of Topkapi *Palace in Istanbul*. Like Rushdie's Jodha Bai, the Mughal harem has largely been fleshed out in the colours of men's dreams.

Foreign men were barred entry into the Mughal harem. As a result, it became the object of fevered speculation among them. Travellers to Hindustan widely supposed the harem to be a space in which nymphomaniac wives and slave-girls, overseen by eunuchs, serviced the gargantuan sexual needs of the emperor. The Englishman William Finch imagined Jahangir in the harem 'like a cock of the game', where he 'may crow over all'; his countryman Thomas Coryate believed that Jahangir kept there 'a thousand women for his own body', while others estimated the figure to be closer to three or even five thousand. Such fantasies conjured up a sexually overheated den of vice. But other Europeans imagined the Mughal harem as a temperate paradise more in the vein of Shangri-La or the Garden of Eden. The French Jesuit François Catrou claimed that the Mughal harem had 'running streams, shadowy groves, fountains and subterraneous grottos', all built with the purpose of 'securing a delicious coolness'. His assessment was based on several other European visitors' reports. Yet in both guises—as den of sexual depravity and as idyllic paradise—the harem was supposed to be completely external to the male world of politics and, indeed, history.

Such assumptions were based largely on surmise and bazaar gossip. After all, very few firangi men ever got to see the harem. One or two foreign physicians were admitted to treat ailing Mughal women; but even their supposedly eye-witness accounts draw more on others' fantasies than on actual observation of the culture of the harem. Niccolò Manucci, who briefly served as a physician in Shah Alam's retinue, notes that the custom was for eunuchs to lead an attending doctor into the royal female apartments with his head and eyes fully covered by a shawl. As a result, Manucci never saw the women he treated. But he offers for his readers' titillation the news that the harem women would 'kiss...and softly bite' his hand. Similarly, Aurangzeb's French physician François Bernier says that he was led into the harem with a Kashmir shawl covering his head, which prevented him from seeing anything. Nevertheless, he confidently asserts, like Catrou, that the space was full of 'gardens, delightful alleys, shady retreats, streams, fountains, grottoes'. Such descriptions helped reinforce the Western canard that the harem was an over-sexed paradise for the emperor's private enjoyment, completely cut off from the public sphere.

Yet the historical evidence indicates that the Mughal zenana was neither simply a nest of sexual vice nor a self-enclosed private space. Nor was it an institution immune to historical change. In the time of Babur and Humayun, when the Mughals still retained vestiges of the nomadic culture of their ancestors, the haram, like the court, was a collection of portable tents that housed the emperor's royal female relatives as well as wives and slave-girls. It was only in Akbar's time that it transformed into a permanent bricks-and-mortar structure incorporated into a royal palace. Humayun's tent-haram was much smaller than Akbar's palatial zenanas in Fatehpur Sikri, Lahore and Agra; Abu'l Fazl claims that these housed up to 5,000 women. But the Mughal emperor hadn't suddenly discovered the pleasures of unbridled promiscuity. The sharp increase in the zenana's population was because Akbar, in a deliberate programme of empire-building, married numerous women from Persia, Rajasthan, and elsewhere to secure political alliances with potentially troublesome warlords and rajas. Not all of these 'wives' ended up sharing Akbar's bed. Yet all of them came with their own female family members and servants. And many of the wives, sisters, and mothers of Akbar's high-ranking courtiers were also housed in the royal zenana.

In other words, most of the women in Akbar's zenana weren't the emperor's wives or concubines, let alone playthings. Rather, they were themselves players within larger networks of political as much as familial relations. As the early Mughal historian Ruby Lal has shown, the women in the royal zenana were part of a complex social fabric that blurred the boundary between the public and the private. It wasn't just that the emperor's wives—or, more specifically, junior wives egged on by their senior counterparts—were tasked with producing heirs to the Mughal line. They and other members of the royal zenana, especially the older higher-ranking women, played a key role in brokering familial bonds, generating state policy, and mediating political conflicts. If there were 5,000 women in Akbar's zenana—the total claimed by Abu'l Fazl—they were comprehensively assimilated into a larger project of knitting together, and socially ordering, the multicultural empire of the Mughals. It is indeed the case that the women's bodies were to a large extent the possessions of the emperor, and expected to submit to Mughal expectations. But the bodily behaviours mandated of royal zenana women were connected to the larger web of political activity that Ruby Lal describes, and were by no means simply sexual.

Take, for example, zenana women's recreational pastimes. The image of the harem as a pleasure-palace is doubtless enhanced by the fact that Mughal women danced, sang, and played musical instruments. Yet these pastimes weren't just pleasurable diversions. The Dhrupad classical music of Akbar's court, in the syncretic fashion so typical of Mughal culture, deliberately combined elements of local Hindu and foreign Turko-Persian musical traditions. The emergence of the Dhrupad style was connected to Akbar's larger project of forging shared multicultural bonds across an ethnically, religiously, and linguistically diverse territory. This project helped spawn a distinctively Hindustani musical identity: indeed, the late sixteenth century was when 'authentically' Indian instruments such as the sitar and the sarod emerged into the musical mainstream. Yet these instruments were both cultural hybrids. The sitar is a fusion of long-necked lutes from Turkic Central Asia and the Indian veena; its name derives from the Persian 'sehtar', or thirty strings. The sarod also has a mixed lineage: loosely based on a Central Asian and Afghan instrument called the rubab, the sarod's name is the Persian word for 'beautiful sound' or 'melody'. Many Mughal musicians were male, such as the legendary vocalist Tansen, whom Akbar regarded as one of his navaratnas or nine jewels. But zenana women too acquired considerable skill in the arts of singing and playing instruments. Both arts entailed the cultivation of specific physical talents: holding the unwieldy sitar or sarod while sitting cross-legged, plucking and strumming their many strings, controlling and modulating the movement of vocal chords while singing, syncopating fingers and voice with the distinctive multi-layered rhythms of the tabla.

Musical performances at court were also accompanied by dancing girls from the zenana. These were not yet the more sexualized nautch girls of later times. Although some of the Mughal dancers were concubines and slave-girls, many were royals such as Jahanara Begum, the daughter of Shah Jahan. And although they probably practiced several forms of dance, the dominant style was the Mughal version of the Kathak tradition. Kathak's roots date back to ancient performances by Hindu storytellers (Kathak is related to the Sanskrit 'katha', meaning 'story'). But the multiculturalism of the Mughal court and zenana prompted Kathak dancers to absorb elements of Persian and Central Asian forms. Indigenous Hindu techniques, including the tribhanga (thrice-bent) formations, remained part of the Mughal Kathak dancer's repertoire. But other foreign innovations were introduced. Whereas most Indian dance forms demand bended legs (or what ballet practitioners call the demi-plié stance), the Mughal form of Kathak appropriated the straight-legged position of Persian dancers. This enabled the dancer to devote more attention to her feet, with which she tapped out intricate percussive patterns—emphasized by scores of ankle-bells—in response to the rhythms of the tabla. Under the influence of Sufi dervishes, Kathak dancers also incorporated the chakkar (spin), which again required skilful footwork, including turning on the heel. We might see this footwork as a metaphor for the biography of the harem woman. Her feet were trained to move in ways that not only transformed her individual body but also integrated her into a larger entity—Mughal culture in all its syncopated diversity. The body of the zenana Kathak dancer, after all, was as much a multicultural palimpsest as the body of a firangi dastkar such as Hunarmand: it collated aptitudes from various parts of the world.

In Fatehpur Sikri, these artistic forms of expression were supplemented by other physical pastimes. Zenana women played extended games of ankh-michauli or hide and seek, which consisted of one woman having her eyes covered by a cloth while the others hid. A quarter was built in the women's apartments for the purpose. Women also took a special role in Mughal games of pachisi, an Indian form of chess. The traditional game involved a cross-shaped board and small playing pieces; but the zenana women of Fatehpur Sikri played on a gigantic, open-aired chequered board in a pachisi courtyard constructed by Akbar in the early 1570s. These games featured Akbar and his queens directing the movements of harem women who functioned as the board's human pieces. As frivolous as these games might seem, they served a serious social function. Not only were they part of what seems to have been a comprehensive and robust programme of physical exercise for the zenana women—or at least its younger members; they may well have resonated too with a larger pattern in the zenana's physical activities: outlining social hierarchies in and outside the harem. One imagines, for example, that Akbar's games of human pachisi traced power relations not only between the royals and the human pieces, but also within the harem itself.

Social hierarchies were most sharply articulated in elaborate harem rituals of gift-giving designed to reinforce the superiority of the senior women. Chief among these was a ritual known as khil'at or honorific robing, derived from the Arabic word for 'dress'. The ritual was employed to honour foreign visitors but also to demarcate rank internally. Members of the Mughal court customarily presented expensive robes to visiting ambassadors and dignitaries; but senior women in the zenana would also be the recipients of khil'at from their juniors. The ritual was supplemented by other forms of gift-giving. In her memoirs, Gulbadan Banu Begum recalls an intricate series of instructions from her father to gift four trays, one plate of jewels and a dancing-girl first to his 'elder relatives', followed by lavish if smaller-scale gifts to 'my sisters and children and the harams and kinsmen, and to the begums and aghas [lords] and nurses and foster-brethren and ladies, and to all who pray for me'. As these instructions make clear, the women of the court were expected both to comport themselves and clothe each other according to very precise prescriptions based on family, age, rank and profession.

We may see the khil'at ritual as excessively, perhaps even obsessively, formal. But it was also part and parcel of a larger Mughal investment in not just demarcating social hierarchy (or vertical relations) but also stitching together bonds of reciprocity (or horizontal relations) between different factions, clans and, importantly, ethnicities and linguistic groups. As we have seen, Akbar's was a formidably multicultural court, as was the country he ruled. He had introduced Persian as a 'neutral' court language that would smooth the differences between the omrah's Turkic Muslims and its Rajput Hindus. But rituals such as khil'at were equally important in establishing social bonds according to mutually agreed upon visions of rank and cross-cultural obligation. The khil'at gifts clad court women in garments that befitted their status and function within the Mughal polity: libas-i-darbari or public robes for the highest-ranked women with official titles, jama or jacket for wives and daughters of courtiers, angarkha or dancing costume for Kathak performers.

If the court was multicultural, the harem was even more so. The royal wives, family members, and courtiers' wives included Mughals, Uzbeks, Rumi Turks, Persians, and Rajputs. But the zenana also included occasional firangis—usually the wives of foreign men retained in the court. Humayun's tent-haram, for example, briefly housed the wife and children of a visitor from Poland. The zenana slave-girl culture, like that of the mamluks, was more multicultural still. A number of firangi slave-girls in Shah Jahan's time were Portuguese, captured during the Mughal conquest of Hooghly in 1633. Foreign slave-women, trained to a high degree of martial sophistication, also served as zenana guards. Known as urdubegis, they were outfitted—in a slave-class counterpart to khil'at—with bows, arrows, and daggers. Gulbadan mentions one such urdubegi in Humayun's zenana, Fatima Bibi, who seems to have been of Turkic origin. But later Mughal emperors also employed habshi, Russian, and Circassian slave-guards. The latter weren't confined to the space of the zenana: the urdubegis often escorted royal women as they travelled by palanquin on hunting trips and other excursions. In sum, pre-colonial firangi women could find a place in the Mughal harem as wives, guests, or slaves.

The task of stitching together such a diverse zenana community demanded a concerted policy of linguistic cohesion to supplement the social bonding rituals of khil'at. As in the court itself, Persian became the lingua franca for a community of women whose many mother tongues must have rivalled that of Babel. A related, equally effective strategy was the wholesale renaming of the women in the zenana—both royals and slave-girls—with Persian titles. Most of the royals received names that were, in effect, honorifics. Akbar's mother, herself a Persian, was known as Maryam Makani (Mary of Both Worlds). His Hindu wife became not only Jodha Bai in subsequent storytelling tradition, but also Mariam-us-Zamani (Mary of the Universe) in the court and harem. These Persian names were indicators of seniority and rank. By contrast, some royal titles made statements about physical beauty: after marrying Jahangir, Noor Mahal (Light of the Palace) was renamed Noor Jahan (Light of the World). By contrast, concubines were often named according to the palaces to which they were supposed to belong: Shah Jahan's favourites were named Akbarabadi Mahal (Palace of Agra) and Fatehpuri Mahal (Palace of Fatehpur). And many women who performed specific functions in the zenana received names that designated their skill. Anka, meaning wet-nurse, was a common name or title. Banu, used of both royals and women of lower rank, indicated the position of a senior matron, which came with certain responsibilities. Like the new names acquired by painters and jewellers in the royal kitabkhana, harem women's names summoned them to use and clothe their bodies in certain ways. And these physical aptitudes were integral to relations not just within the harem itself but also within the larger Mughal state apparatus.

We cannot recreate the full life stories of individual women in the royal harem. But by paying attention to Mughal rituals such as khil'at, we can partially reconstruct the diverse ways in which harem women's bodies were imprinted and transformed by their experiences there. Even Rushdie's disembodied Jodha Bai can be fleshed out in this more literally biographical sense, and in a fashion that does not just utilize the colours of our fantasy. Indeed, 'Jodha Bai' is itself a name that emerges partly from the traditions of the Mughal court and harem. The title 'Bai' was reserved for either an older or a senior woman; as such, it presumed of its bearer and her companions distinct forms of clothing and bodily comportment in relation to others, depending on their relative rank. We can retrieve similar bodily experiences from the titles of firangi women in the harem. As with Jodha Bai, though, we first have to reckon with the white noise of male stories and fantasies about Mughal-era women.

♦

In fact popular Indian legend gives us a firangi counterpart to Jodha Bai: a woman named Bibi Juliana. Like Jodha Bai, she is really several conflicting stories, most of them unmoored from any evidence that might lead to a single historical figure. Also like Jodha Bai, Bibi Juliana appears as a character in a romantic story about her supposedly royal husband. This man's story masquerades as historical fact. But it has been constructed using all the ingredients of a swashbuckling adventure novel: oceanic journeys, pirates, kidnappings, and fair damsels in distress. Our hero, cut from the same manly cloth as Errol Flynn, is a dashing prince named Jean-Philippe Bourbon de Navarre.

According to an early twentieth-century version of the story by the Armenian-Indian historian Mesrovb Jacob Seth, Jean-Philippe Bourbon de Navarre was born in 1526 into the French royal family. After a duel that went wrong when he was only 15 years old, Jean-Philippe fled Europe with the family priest aboard a ship. But his woes had just begun; shortly after he set sail he was captured by Turkish pirates in the Mediterranean. The pirates took him to Egypt for sale in the slave market of Cairo. But there, in Seth's words, 'the young prince soon gained, by his affable manners, the esteem of the sovereign of the country who took him in his service and gave him a command in the army'. He was imprisoned once more during an Egyptian campaign in Ethiopia. Yet, Seth tells us, 'his Christian religion, his noble lineage, his lively intelligence and his great learning soon raised him to a high position in that Christian country'.

At some point in the mid 1550s, Jean-Philippe sailed with an Ethiopian fleet to India. After reaching the Coromandel Coast, he left his ever-faithful family priest on shore and proceeded to Bengal. But learning about the magnificence of the Mughal court in Agra, he journeyed there and sought service with Akbar. The Great Mughal, always curious to make the acquaintance of foreigners, was—according to Seth—'struck by his gracious manners, his novel bearing, and his vivid intelligence'. (Foreign monarchs' attraction to Jean-Philippe's superior breeding is clearly one of the recurrent leitmotifs of the story.) Akbar offered the French prince a position of command in his army, subsequently appointing him master of the artillery and promoting him to the rank of mansabdar or governor. Jean-Philippe, as 'befitted his noble blood', proved himself a loyal servant and fine warrior-administrator. Akbar was so desperate to keep him in his court that he richly rewarded him with many gifts. And this is where Bibi Juliana enters the story.

Depending on which version of the story one reads, Juliana and her sister Maria were either Armenian or Portuguese. They were captured in the mid sixteenth century by Arabian Sea pirates and deposited in India. (Evidently pirates are this adventure-story's equivalent of travel agents, allowing Europeans package deals to places they would otherwise never have visited.) The two sisters then came to the Mughal court; Akbar, falling in love with the elder sister Maria, took her as one of his wives and renamed her Mariam-us-Zamani. At the same time, Juliana was wooed by the dashing and debonair Jean-Philippe de Bourbon. Eager to offer every inducement to his favourite firangi prince to stay in Hindustan, Akbar encouraged the union and presided at their wedding. Jean-Philippe was now the Great Mughal's brother-in-law. After his marriage to Juliana, Jean-Philippe received a further promotion from Akbar: he was appointed a nawab, and his family was entrusted, in perpetuity, with the defence of the Mughal harem. Seth explains that Juliana, 'on account of her skill and her knowledge of the European system of medicine', was appointed the harem's chief physician. Together, Nawab Jean-Philippe and his Bibi Juliana remained diligent Christians. They provided the money to construct the first Christian church in Agra, which was completed in 1604. Both were buried there, though their graves can no longer be found as the church was supposedly destroyed by Shah Jahan in the 1630s during his stand-off with the Portuguese.

The union between Jean-Philippe and Juliana is also supposed to have resulted in a line of firangi-descended Indians surnamed Bourbon. Granted special privileges by the Mughals, the Bourbons claim to have been cruelly displaced from their hereditary office as defenders of the harem by Nadir Shah's invasion and sack of Delhi in 1737. Yet they prospered in Madhya Pradesh. Jean-Philippe's supposed great-grandson, Francis de Bourbon (1718–78), took up residence in Narwar, near Gwalior, upon land that had been supposedly granted to his French ancestor as a hereditary fief by Akbar. Although the Bourbons retained their French surname, the sons repeatedly married Armenians; several members of the family are supposed to be buried in the Armenian cemetery in Agra. The family's sense of connection to their alleged ancestors from the age of Akbar grew stronger still in the nineteenth century, when they were among the richest of the royal families in Gwalior State. At the time of India's First War of Independence in 1857, a Lucknow branch of the Bourbons claimed to own a version of the Persian translation of the Bible that priests from the first Jesuit mission to Fatehpur Sikri had given to Akbar in 1580, and which had then been passed on by the emperor to the Bourbons' Christian ancestor, Bibi Juliana. The Bourbons retained their princely status into the first half of the twentieth century; however, the abolition of royal rank since Indian Independence has affected their position, and they are now part of the working middle classes. The family's current scion, a plump moustachioed lawyer named Balthazar Napoleon Bourbon, lives in Bhopal. He made news in May of 2013 when he was visited by the French ambassador to India, who declared that 'it is extraordinary to have a Bourbon here today!' Pictures of this very Indian 'royal', posing somewhat awkwardly with his wife and children, were circulated around the world.

It's a wonderful story, with a stirring *Slumdog Millionaire*-type conclusion that catapults a humble Indian to a position of national and even global prominence. The only problem with it is that it is patently untrue. There isn't one shred of historical evidence to indicate that Jean-Philippe Bourbon de Navarre ever existed: he has left no trace in either the Mughal chronicles or the French archives. A recent novel, *Le Rajah Bourbon* by Michel de Grèce, suggests that Jean-Philippe was the secret Italian-based son of Charles de Bourbon, the so-called 'Constable of Bourbon'. But nothing lends credence to this surmise. Juliana Bourbon and her sister Maria, the supposed wife of a Mughal emperor, are likewise missing from the record. Akbar probably married a Christian—Abu'l Fazl claims as much—but she was not, as modern Indian guides at Fatehpur Sikri suggest, Mariam-us-Zamani. Visitors are repeatedly told that Mariam's palace is the palace of Akbar's Christian wife; as evidence, they point to a supposed painting of the Annunciation on her palace ceiling. Yet as we have seen, Mariam-us-Zamani was probably the Persian name of a Hindu Rajput princess, Harka Bai; and the 'Christian' painting in her palace is most likely of winged figures from Persian mythology. The more one scours the archive, the more Jean-Phillipe, Juliana Bourbon and her sister Maria vanish into thin air. Indeed, it is impossible to trace the Bourbon lineage back beyond the Francis de Bourbon who settled in Narwar after 1739. His supposed great-grandfather and great-grandmother are, like Rushdie's Jodha Bai, stories fleshed out in the colours of our dreams.

Thanks to a passing reference in the *Tuzuk-i-Jahangiri* and a letter written in 1626 by a Jesuit priest, however, we do know that Lahore was home in the 1580s and 1590s to an Armenian migrant named Juliana. We also know of another woman named Juliana who, some one hundred years later, served Aurangzeb's wife Nawab Bai and then their son Bahadur Shah. It's almost certain that the Bibi Juliana Bourbon of popular legend is a composite of these two figures, and that the descendants of one of these women invented a myth of royal firangi ancestry to add extra lustre to their line. I turn now to the first Armenian Juliana, less to arrive at the 'truth' behind the legend of the Indian Bourbons than to get a better understanding of the lot of firangi women in Mughal Hindustan. Even as Juliana Bourbon's stories subdivide into other stories, they all return to the harem—and to the ritual of khil'at.

◆

In the *Tuzuk-i-Jahangiri*, we hear about a Mughal courtier named Sikander Zul–Qarnain who has been made faujdar (commander) of Sambhar, a lake-town in Rajasthan. Zul–Qarnain, we are told, is the Christian son of Iskandar, an Armenian who had served Akbar; he has inherited his command from his father, the previous faujdar of Sambhar. The *Tuzuk-i-Jahangiri* tells us too that Akbar had given Iskandar in marriage to the daughter of one Abdul Hai Firangi, also an Armenian Christian. ('Hai' was a common Mughal term for Armenian.) All we are told of Abdul Hai Firangi's daughter is that she 'was in service in the royal harem', and that 'by her', Iskandar had 'two sons'.

Some more light is cast on Abdul Hai in the *Ain-i-Akbari*. Here, if it is indeed the same Abdul Hai, he is referred to as the qazi of the Imperial Camp—in effect, Akbar's chief justice. He is also referred to as khoja and amir, titles that roughly translate as 'sir' and 'lord' and indicate his high status in the multicultural Mughal court. But there is no mention of his daughter in any of the Akbar-era chronicles of the Mughals. To obtain information about her, we have to turn instead to a Latin letter written in 1628 by the Italian Jesuit priest Francesco Corsi to his handlers in the Vatican. Corsi lived in Agra from 1604 until his death in 1635; he is a fairly reliable reporter, as he evidently had come to know Abdul Hai Firangi's family well. Unfortunately, he never met the Armenian's daughter, who died before Corsi's arrival in Hindustan, and he tells us next to nothing about her. But Corsi does tell us her name: Juliana.

As the daughter of a high-ranking courtier, Juliana must have been housed in one of the plusher apartments of the royal harem. This would have made her, if not a surrogate member of Akbar's family, then a part of the larger network of wards for whom he took responsibility. And it was probably in this capacity that Akbar offered her as a bride to her fellow Armenian Christian, Iskandar, in about 1590. Corsi refers to Iskandar as 'Mirza Sikander': the Persian honorific mirza means 'prince', a title befitting Akbar's award to Iskandar of the faujdari of Sambhar, a strategically important town located next to the Mughal Empire's largest salt mine. 'Sikander' is the Persian version of Alexander the Great, though Iskandar was not a warrior like his namesake but a merchant. According to Corsi, Iskandar was born in Aleppo. But he had also lived in various cities of India—possibly including Goa, as he was proficient in Portuguese. Indeed, Akbar's strong support for the émigré Armenian Christian community had much to do with the transnational web of trading connections that Armenian merchants had established from the Levant through Persia to Portuguese India. Once he found service with Akbar, Iskandar may have used these connections to help turn the salt mine of Sambhar into a profitable venture for the empire as well as himself. In any case, Akbar valued Iskandar's abilities sufficiently to match him with Abdul Hai Firangi's daughter. It is quite possible that this firangi 'prince', from a faraway land and bearing the name of a great royal, was the germ of inspiration for the legend of Jean-Philippe Bourbon.

After her marriage to Iskandar, Juliana Firangi had two sons. The first, Mirza Sikander Zul-Qarnain, was born in 1592; the second, Mirza Iskandrus, three years later. (As an adult, Zul-Qarnain was to provide money for the upkeep of the church in Agra; this may be the source of the myth that Juliana Bourbon built the church in that city.) Notably both boys were given names that, like Iskandar's own, are Persian versions of Alexander. In other words, they were seen as sons and heirs of their father. We do not know what kind of relationship Juliana had with her children. But Corsi tells us that Akbar, 'of his special affection for Bibi Juliana', gave both the boys to one of his childless queens to be adopted and educated as her own children. Mughal and Jesuit documents about Mirza Zul-Qarnain indicate that Juliana's two boys were raised in the harem alongside Jahangir's son Khurram, the future Shah Jahan. What Juliana herself thought of this arrangement, Corsi does not say. Although he represents it as a special gift to Juliana on Akbar's part, it's hard for us now not to think of it as a deprivation—though it was a common practice to farm out children born in the harem to wet nurses and surrogate mothers. Juliana's health may have played a part in the decision; she was dead by 1598, which we know from a letter written that year in Lahore by the Jesuit priest Jerome Xavier. He talks about a recent court scandal involving an Armenian man who, having just lost his Christian wife, wished to marry her sister; although Akbar supported the new union, Jerome Xavier—with the support of Jahangir—damned it as incestuous, and stopped it from happening. Corsi's letter confirms that this man was Iskandar: 'King Akbar tried to marry M. Sikander with a sister of Bibi Juliana now dead, but…Fr Jeronimo Xavier and the rest of the Fathers objected.'

In sum, we know next to nothing about the details of Juliana Firangi's life, other than what she did at the bidding of others before her early death: live in the harem, marry a man chosen for her, have two sons named for him, and surrender them to one of Akbar's queens. Is it possible to flesh out these bare facts with more substance?

Some details of Juliana Firangi's life will remain forever elusive. We don't know, for example, where she was born. Nor do we know which part of Armenia her family was from—and whether her father migrated directly from Armenia or from another location such as Tabriz in Persia, where there was already a large diaspora at a time when Turkish and Persian hostilities in the Caucasus had forced many Armenians out of their homeland. We are also in the dark about when Abdul Hai Firangi and his family came to Lahore. One record reports that, after meeting an Armenian merchant named Hakobjan in Kashmir in the 1560s, Akbar had encouraged him and his fellows to settle in Agra. Abdul Hai Firangi was quite possibly part of this first wave of migration; given his rank in the Mughal court by the 1580s, he may have come to Akbar's attention in Agra before the capital was relocated to Fatehpur Sikri. If so, Juliana—who was probably in her teens when she married Iskandar sometime in or shortly after 1590—would have been born and raised in Akbar's new capital of Fatehpur. But it is equally possible that she was born in Persia or even Armenia itself. If Abdul Hai Firangi migrated to Hindustan and joined the Mughal court only after it had relocated to Lahore in 1585, then Juliana would have been raised outside of the subcontinent.

We also don't know what Juliana Firangi was called in the harem. It was common for Armenian Christians in Mughal Hindustan to have both a Persian and a Christian name. Juliana's son, Sikander Zul-Qarnain, had three sons; they were known alternately as Mirza Observam/John

Baptist, Mirza Eres/Gaspar, and Mirza Danyal/Michael. Juliana was known to Corsi by her Christian name, which probably honoured Saint Juliana of Nicomedia, a fourth-century virgin martyr popular in Eastern Orthodox Christianity. (Saint Juliana was martyred because she refused the husband chosen for her; in this respect, the Armenian Juliana differed from her sainted namesake.) Like her grandsons, Juliana Firangi probably answered to another Mughal name. She may have been called 'Jullena'—a local Persianised version of Juliana. But in the hierarchical world of the Mughals, she would have been addressed by names or titles that indicated her status. Even Corsi refers to her as 'Bibi', a respectful Turkic/Urdu title that recognizes her rank. She was almost certainly called begum, or 'lady'—a term that derives from beg or bey, a Turkic word for a higher official. Any woman who was the wife or daughter of a beg was entitled to be addressed as begum: Bibi Juliana Firangi would have qualified on both scores.

◆

What would Juliana Firangi's harem life have been like? And how would it have left its imprint on her body?

It is not inconceivable, given her father's rank, that Juliana was educated. Many of the royal harem women were highly literate: some, such as Gulbadan Banu Begum, wrote poetry. If Juliana could read and write, she would have had to learn how to hold the traditional kalam or reed pen used by Mughal courtiers, which needed to be dipped into a roshandani or inkwell. She would have also got used to sprinkling what she had written with sand. These writing accessories were often consolidated in a pen box, or kalamdan, traditionally the preserve of official scribes but often presented as gifts to Mughal female as well as male aristocrats. One worked with a kalamdan not on a desk but sitting cross-legged—a position that Juliana must have got used to as a matter of course: this is how she would have watched performances of Kathak dance and listened to, or even participated in, performances of Dhrupad music. Whether or not Juliana Firangi was taught to read and write, she would doubtless have learned to speak court Persian. She probably spoke Armenian too, especially if she had lived with her father and mother—about whom we know absolutely nothing—before relocating to the harem. But it was in Persian that Juliana would have interacted with the other harem women, both informally and formally.

The physical space of the royal zenana in the Mughal fort of

Lahore would have demanded that Juliana Firangi use her body in other distinctive ways. Tourists who visit the fort are guided to an old harem at the northwest of the complex, dominated by the spectacular Sheesh Mahal, or Palace of Mirrors. Yet this lavish structure was built after Juliana's death by Shah Jahan, who was always seeking to correct what he regarded as the architectural bad taste of his father and grandfather. Akbar's and Jahangir's earlier zenana, spurned by Shah Jahan, had been located at the fort's northeast end. It consisted of palatial apartments painted by members of the royal kitabkhana for Akbar's wives, including Mariam-us-Zamani, smaller apartments for other senior ladies, and adjoining cells for junior harem members. These apartments would probably have flanked a large open courtyard criss-crossed with water channels. But we cannot be sure, as hardly any of the Akbari zenana's original structures survive. One of the few remaining sections is the fort's external wall, which features distinctively Mughal red sandstone bay windows covered with intricate jaalis. The jaalis stop outsiders from looking in; peering through the lattice-work, however, Juliana and the other harem women could stare at the bustling street life of Lahore as well as savour the cool breeze blowing off the river Ravi, which flowed next to the fort wall. Juliana enjoyed other Mughal cooling technologies. The Lahore zenana of Akbar featured a maze of subterranean apartments and corridors—some of which still exist—to which the women retreated during the hottest summer months. An elaborate series of tunnels connected the apartments to the fresh air of the outside world, which was cooled by a network of chadars, or narrow sloping chutes, conveying water from above. These tunnels may have let in air, yet they admitted very little light. The summer apartments would have been illuminated instead by candles; they were darkened places in which Juliana and the other harem ladies spent much of their time sleeping, eating, bathing in hamams, and congregating during the evenings in larger subterranean halls for Dhrupad and Kathak performances.

But Juliana Firangi would not have been entirely confined to the Mughal harem. For example, she most likely accompanied other harem ladies on some of Akbar's and Prince Khurram's many hunting trips. Sheikhupura, some 30 kilometres northwest of Lahore, was the favourite hunting ground of Khurram; he was joined there by the royal women, some of whom took an active part in the hunting. Indeed, his later-to-be wife Noor Jahan acquired a reputation as a gifted sharpshooter. It is faintly possible that Juliana travelled out of the harem too in the company of her husband, Iskandar, on a journey to Sambhar, though as a Mughal harem woman it is unlikely that she ever journeyed far from Lahore. But at least some of her activities outside the Lahore Fort would have demanded that she conform to the demands of certain firangi rituals. The city was home to a large Armenian Christian merchant community; its members worshipped at a church constructed with the permission of Akbar. Juliana Firangi and her sister most likely visited the church on Sundays and holy days, maybe travelling in a palanquin escorted by a female Circassian or habshi guard.

In the church itself, she would have observed rituals of bodily behaviour expected of Armenian worshippers in general and of Armenian women in particular. She would have kneeled to accept Communion, and eaten bread soaked in consecrated wine on high holy days. When the priest pronounced the words of consecration, Juliana like other churchgoers may have fallen on the ground and kissed the earth. Armenian women were traditionally barred from approaching the altar, but certain rituals were expected of them on various dates of the Armenian Christian calendar. On Hambartsum or Ascension Day in May, for example, young women were expected to walk freely in fields and sing songs. It is impossible to know whether Juliana Firangi was allowed to do this before her marriage, let alone as a woman of the Lahore harem. She would probably have fasted in the forty days before Zatik or Easter, however, and maybe even observed the traditional Armenian ritual of putting lentils on a thin piece of cotton so that they might sprout in time for Easter Day itself. And, like other Armenian women, she may have put on her best clothes for Tsaghkazard, or Palm Sunday.

What would have these best clothes have been, however? Would they have been Armenian-style garments? Or were they Mughal clothes much like those she and other harem women would have worn on Sheikhupura hunting expeditions? It is most probable that, as a resident of Akbar's harem, she exclusively wore fabrics given to her in rituals of khil'at. Chief among these would have been long-flowing jamas or jackets. Jamas were worn by both Mughal men and zenana women: they were long-sleeved, fitted tightly over the chest and laced up at the sides, and flared into a large skirt beneath the waist. The jama normally covered an ankle-length petticoat or vest; women also accompanied it with a veil of some kind and, in cold weather, with a Kashmiri shawl or qaba. The woman's jama could make quite a fashion statement. A painting survives of Noor Jahan hunting armed with a flintlock—quite possibly at Sheikhupura—and her hunting costume ensemble includes a fine translucent cotton jama with intricate stitch-work. Another painting depicts her in a turquoise jama with a recurrent paisley pattern. Noor Jahan may have had her jamas especially commissioned according to her taste. But it's quite possible that they were first presented to her in cloth form as khil'at gifts. As a begum, Juliana Firangi too would have received gifts of fabric for jamas, though doubtless less grand than those sported by Noor Jahan. Juliana would have worn her gifted clothes at large, formal gatherings—including performances of music and dance. The jamas she was gifted were not only designed to strike the eye, they also afforded her freedom of movement—far more than that enjoyed by, for example, the kimono-clad female courtiers of Japan and Korea.

But the khil'at ritual gifts included other accessories that were more constraining. Juliana may have received the ornamented head-dress known as the sisphul, a large belt made of gold from which hung a cluster of pearls and other precious stones. Those who wore the sisphul would have had to hold their necks very straight and turn their heads slowly. At official ceremonies, Juliana may have presented with—and expected to wear—all sorts of other bejewelled accessories. The karna-phul, or ear-flower, is described by Abu'l Fazl as a popular ornament amongst Mughal harem women in Akbar's time: it consisted of precious metals and jewels and hung almost to the shoulders. Juliana may have also had to wear elaborate nose rings, heavy necklaces, two inch-wide bajuband or armlets, and colourful kangan or bracelets. These heavy items would have forced her to adapt her posture and gestures, making her move with more care than the jama alone demanded.

Ritual gifts of khil'at insured that Juliana Firangi was fully implicated in the elaborate social networks of the zenana and the Mughal court. They demanded that she adapt her physical comportment, both in giving gifts and in wearing them. They also stitched her into the rich fabric of a larger social body. It would be anachronistic to assume that hers was a companionate marriage: it is likely that Juliana spent most of her time apart from her Sambhar-based husband, and apart from her sons. But this arrangement would not necessarily have condemned Juliana Firangi to a life of loneliness. The formal obligations of a harem woman of stature in gift-giving and other social rituals would have meant she was always surrounded by people. Still, it is hard not to see her early death in or before 1598 as the end of an unfulfilled life. Unlike the firangi men I have discussed so far, Juliana did not leave behind a treatise on medicine, an epic poem, a fortified city, a water-supply system, a memorable painting, or a beautiful throne. Other than her two sons, the only legacy of Bibi Juliana Firangi, the begum of Lahore, are distorted Jodha Bai-type stories cherished by her possible Bourbon descendants in Madhya Pradesh and by Armenian Indians. In sum, she was re-clothed in the threads not just of khil'at robes but also of popular yarns.

9 | JULIANA DIAS DA COSTA, THE JAGIRDAR OF JOGABAI

The mythical Bibi Juliana Bourbon's story is woven from the disparate loose threads of two real lives—the lives of two women named Juliana. We have already spun the yarn of Juliana Firangi. This chapter teases out the tale of Juliana Dias da Costa.

Stories and clothes are, if only metaphorically, closely related. As my phrasing in the previous paragraph suggests, stories are woven and unwoven; we say we spin a yarn, or tease out a tale, or lose the thread of a narrative. The relation can be glimpsed also in the common etymologies of 'text' and 'textile', from the Latin 'texere', meaning to weave. In modern consumer society we are likely to think of both texts and textiles simply as commodities, as things that we can buy and own. But as their shared artisanal etymology suggests they are also deeply social acts, and in ways that are perhaps more obvious in the public rituals of the Mughal world. A dastan performed at court is not just a story but a dynamic transaction between a dastango or storyteller and his listeners. Khil'at is not just a robe of honour but, again, a ritualized transaction between a gift-giver and a recipient. And just as the act of listening to a tale can change a person, unravelling and re-seaming how she thinks about the world, so is identity altered by the act of re-clothing. I may be telling the story of Juliana Dias da Costa in this chapter. But her personal story is ultimately a more general story of how identity is repeatedly re-woven both in narrative and in clothing. Within the fabric of Mughal society, Juliana Dias da Costa's character was un-stitched and re-stitched, just as it was in the many diverse narrations of her life.

As we have seen, the Armenian Bibi Juliana Firangi who lived in Akbar's Lahore during the 1590s matches many of the attributes of her namesake in the myth of Jean-Philippe Bourbon de Navarre. Like Juliana Bourbon, Bibi Juliana Firangi was a Christian immigrant to India in the sixteenth century; she had a sister; she married a foreign 'prince'; and she lived in the royal harem. But three elements in the Juliana Bourbon myth don't square with what we know of Bibi Juliana Firangi. Juliana Bourbon was one of the most powerful ladies in the Mughal harem, worked as a physician, and was (in at least some versions) Portuguese. Each of these elements seems to have been imported from diverse narratives about the life of a third Juliana, Juliana Dias da Costa, who was born about sixty years after the death of her Armenian predecessor. These narratives offer us glimpses into royal harem life in Delhi's Lal Qila, which in the age of Aurangzeb and Bahadur Shah differed quite markedly from what Bibi Juliana Firangi had experienced in Akbar's Lahore harem.

Among the differences are the relative status and influence of foreign harem ladies not related to the royal family. Bibi Juliana Firangi was a largely silent and even sidelined figure in Akbar's zenana. By contrast, her later Portuguese namesake enjoyed an altogether more prominent role as a political counsellor to the Great Mughal. It was not always this way: Juliana Dias da Costa began her service in Aurangzeb's harem working in a very menial position. The high rank she eventually held in the harem of Aurangzeb's son and successor Bahadur Shah, moreover, was not due to the status of her father or husband, as it had been for Bibi Juliana Firangi. Remarkably, Juliana Dias da Costa's rank was something she achieved on the basis of merit, without ties of family or marriage. It led to her becoming a significant jagirdar or landowner in Delhi. It also led to her being re-clothed. In the later decades of her life, she wore striking robes on formal and ceremonial occasions. These robes were made of an expensive fabric whose exchange was a crucial part of the larger Mughal social fabric fashioned out of rituals of khil'at. And the robes demanded of Juliana Dias da Costa modes of comportment that diverged from what had been expected of her when she first served in the harem.

So who exactly was this rather different firangi Juliana? As we will see, the second real-life counterpart to the storied Juliana Bourbon herself subdivides into yet more stories. Yet the various stories of Juliana Dias da Costa hint once again at the bodily adaptations a foreign woman had to undergo to live in the Mughal harem.

◆

What we 'know' about Juliana Dias da Costa is derived from a diverse ensemble of eighteenth- and nineteenth-century accounts written in Portuguese, Italian, Dutch, French, English and Persian. As Taymiya R. Zaman has shown in a sublime profile of Juliana Dias da Costa, these various accounts offer wildly conflicting information about her. They agree in only the broadest of particulars: Juliana Dias da Costa was of Portuguese descent; she was in the service first of Aurangzeb's wife Nawab Bai and then their son, the future emperor Bahadur Shah; she rose to a position of unusual political influence under the latter; she was granted, before her death in 1734, substantial land holdings near Delhi that she bequeathed to her descendants; she possessed some medical knowledge; and she lived much of her life in the royal harem. Within those broad outlines, the different surviving accounts add colour to the life of Juliana Dias da Costa in very different ways, depending on the fantasies and predispositions of their authors. But like Salman Rushdie's Jodha Bai, Juliana Dias de Costa emerges as a composite of men's dreams about her.

There is the Juliana Dias da Costa of the Portuguese Estado da Índia records, consisting largely of letters written by a sequence of Goan viceroys during the reign of King João V of Portugal (1706-50). These letters project Juliana as a Portuguese patriot who represented the Estado as a 'procuradora' or lobbyist at the Mughal court. According to the correspondence, Juliana's efforts on behalf of the Portuguese state were valued with the award of a village in Goa, though it is unclear whether she ever visited there. Included in the records is the one surviving document in Juliana's own hand. It is a letter from 1711, written in Persian. Juliana's Persian lines are accompanied by a Portuguese translation, possibly in another hand. The letter is addressed to King João of Portugal; in it, she acknowledges gifts exchanged between Portugal and the Mughal court, and prays for the glory of the Portuguese throne. Although this letter potentially fits the viceroys' presentation of Juliana as a loyal Portuguese patriot, it reads somewhat ambiguously. That it is written in Persian suggests that Juliana was more comfortable in the language of the Mughal court than in Portuguese; and even as she plays the part of a loyal servant of Portugal, she is evidently aware of the material benefits that Bahadur Shah and the Mughals stood to gain from that performance.

Then there is the Juliana Dias da Costa limned in eighteenth-century writings by Jesuits and other European visitors to India. These present her as a model, even saintly, Christian. The Italian Jesuit missionary Ippolito Desideri, who visited the Mughal Empire in 1714 en route to setting up a mission in Tibet, met Juliana in Delhi. In his Latin account of his journey, he describes her as the 'support and ornament of our Holy Faith in the Empire'. She emerges as a lobbyist not for Portugal but for Christianity in general: according to Desideri, Juliana had even come within a whisker of converting Bahadur Shah. In his account, she becomes a miracle-worker in the manner of a conventional medieval Christian saint. Desideri says, for example, that she extinguished a potentially dangerous fire in the Mughal court with the branch of a Palm Sunday tree, as a result of which Bahadur Shah was moved to send each Palm Sunday for a consecrated branch that he kept in his room for the year.

Juliana's exemplary piety is stressed also by the Dutchman François Valentijn, whose account of the Dutch Embassy to Lahore in 1711 again depicts her as a model Christian, although of a somewhat military inclination. Riding on an elephant alongside Bahadur Shah in battle, she is supposed to have claimed that he would not lose because the prayers of all Christians were with him. He also accompanies his written portrait with an engraving of Juliana supposedly based on a drawing done in India: I say 'supposedly' as there is very little that looks Indian about the scene, including a palm tree that one would be hard-pressed to find in Lahore. In the portrait, Juliana stands imperiously in a public setting: apart from a possible sisphul that extends from her hair to her forehead, her head is not covered—an unlikely detail in Mughal Hindustan. Her dress faintly resembles the masculine jama worn by Mughal lords at the time, though it has been pleated and given a cowl that makes her look both more feminine and more Christian—an impression reinforced by the picture's dominant detail, a large crucifix that hangs from her neck on her partially exposed chest. Valentijn's virago Christian emerges with even more alacrity in a late-eighteenth-century French-language account of her life by Jean-Baptiste Gentil (1726-99), who had served in the military and the court of Shuja-ud-Daulah, the nawab of Awadh. Gentil's Juliana is an Indian Joan of Arc who rides into battle bearing the standard of the cross, is declared the 'Protector of Christians', and crowns Bahadur Shah on the feast day of John the Baptist.

Gentil's account is revealing also because it is one of several such portraits by supposed relatives and descendants of Juliana. He had married Teresa Velho, Juliana's grand-niece, in 1772; Gentil's recollection of Juliana takes its place in what was to become a concerted family project of glorifying their ancestor. He claims, for example, that Juliana was granted the title of 'khana' or princess, and was granted Dara Shikoh's palace. In the nineteenth century, the English-speaking scion of a wealthy Christian Indian family, J. P. Val D'Eremao, claimed that he was the great-grandson of Juliana and that the family still possessed the jagir or title to several villages near Delhi granted to her by Bahadur Shah. The D'Eremaos also claimed that their seemingly Portuguese family name was derived from a title granted by Bahadur Shah to Juliana, Durr-i-Oman (pearl of Oman), although there is no record of such a title in the Mughal archives. And they trotted out a slightly different version of the Bourbon canard, claiming that Juliana Dias da Costa had been married to a second son of King Henri IV of France, Jean-Baptiste Gaston de Bourbon, who had escaped to India and found service in the Mughal court—this despite the fact that Gaston de Bourbon had died in France in 1660, when Juliana was only two years old.

Finally, there is the altogether more prosaic version of Juliana Dias da Costa that emerges from Persian-language Mughal records. She is mentioned in a chronicle called the *Tarikh-i-Muhammadi* as 'Jullena', a 'firangi woman who was the favourite of the late Bahadur Shah', and who died in Delhi in 1734. Other Mughal documents confirm that several villages near Delhi were indeed granted to Juliana and passed to her descendants in the D'Eremao family. These brief references indicate that no matter how much she may have been perceived by the Portuguese as their political procuradora, by other Europeans as a model of Christian piety, and by her descendants as the heroine in a story of transoceanic royalty, the Mughals saw her as a powerful if slightly unremarkable lady of the court, favoured by and receiving gifts from the emperor himself.

Is it possible, amid these conflicting perspectives, to recreate Juliana Dias da Costa's life story? Many of the details are blurry, though we certainly have a better sense of what she did, and when, than we do with her Armenian namesake. But other key elements remain tantalizingly elusive.

◆

Juliana Dias da Costa was probably born in 1658, the year Aurangzeb deposed his father Shah Jahan. We do not know her birthplace. Some accounts suggest Bengal; others Cochin, which was a Portuguese possession until its capture by the Dutch in 1663. But Juliana may have been born in Delhi. Her father, Agostinho Dias da Costa, was Portuguese. He seems to have lived in Hooghly before moving to Agra and then Shah Jahan's new capital in Delhi, where he served the Mughal court as a medical attendant. A Jesuit missionary who lived in Delhi between 1648 and 1654, Antony Botelho, intimates that Agostinho Dias da Costa was a 'renegade' or Muslim convert who had been captured by Shah Jahan's army during the Mughal sacking of Hooghly and brought to Agra as a prisoner in 1633.

If Botelho's testimony is true, Agostinho Dias da Costa was part of the surprisingly large Portuguese Indian population who lived outside the bounds of the Estado da Índia. Some of these were pirates, operating out of river ports in the dangerous Bengal delta region. Others were mercenaries who served in the Deccan firangiyan regiments. Many of these fugitives converted, if only nominally, to Islam. If Agostinho was indeed a renegade convert, he may have served a Muslim master. Perhaps his medical expertise dates back to such a period of service; it appears that there was something of a vogue among high-ranking Indian Muslims to retain the service of a firangi doctor on the assumption that they had a special skill in medicine. Many foreigners took advantage of the fashion to pose as hakeems. But if Botelho is right and Agostinho was captured by Shah Jahan's forces in Hooghly, his conversion—and his medical practice—might date only from his time in Agra. He would have had little opportunity to become a renegade in Hooghly: it was a Christian town, even though it owed tribute not to the Estado da Índia but to the Mughal Empire. It was also a nest of Portuguese slave-trading pirates who had intermarried with Bengalis and Burmese women; the pirates' raids in Mughal territories were what prompted Shah Jahan to sack Hooghly in 1632. Agostinho was probably only a child at this time. We don't know what his parentage was; for all we know, his mother may have been not Portuguese but local. And we don't know either who Agostinho married in Mughal Hindustan. But it is likely that she was a Christian; even if Agostinho was a renegade convert, his daughter was a devout Catholic all her life.

By the time of Juliana's birth, Agostinho was probably working for Aurangzeb: Niccolò Manucci, fleeing in 1659, claims to have met in Multan one 'Agostinho Dias', who seems to have had insider knowledge of the Great Mughal's plans. This Agostinho—who was almost certainly Juliana Dias da Costa's father—warned Manucci that Aurangzeb had issued an order for the eunuch's death. If Agostinho was working as a medical attendant in Aurangzeb's court in 1659, it's quite possible that his wife was also living in the royal harem and Juliana was born there. But we can place Juliana Dias da Costa in the harem with certainty only in her adult life. We know nothing about her childhood years.

The Mughal zenana under Aurangzeb in Delhi was a rather different institution from what it had been in the time of Bibi Juliana Firangi. A strict Sunni Muslim, Aurangzeb is often believed to have banned music and dance. The Delhi harem's inhabitants may still have trained in Dhrupad and Kathak traditions, but could not perform as they once had—although Aurangzeb was apparently captivated by the musical skills of his favourite concubine, Heera Bai. But other arts were encouraged, especially literature: Aurangzeb's favourite daughter, Zeb-un-Nisa, was a talented poet, as was his sister Roshanara Begum, the harem's chief lady. Juliana Dias da Costa may not have written poetry. As her letter to King João of Portugal indicates, however, she was literate in Persian. We don't know if she read any of the great Indo-Persian medical treatises of the time. Nur al-Din Shirazi, court physician under Shah Jahan and chief officer of the royal houses in Agra under Aurangzeb, authored several influential medical works in Persian, including the *Ilajat-i-Dara-Shikohi*, an encyclopaedia that synthesizes Islamic and Hindu Ayurvedic medical traditions, and the *Alfaz-al-Adwiya*, a dictionary of drugs. Juliana's father—who quite possibly met Shirazi—may have been familiar with both. But perhaps she browsed them too: several sources refer to Juliana's considerable medical knowledge, which she appears to have put to use in the harem. If she was sufficiently fluent in Portuguese, she may have been familiar also with Garcia da Orta's *Colóquios dos simples e drogas da Índia*.

In the harem, Juliana Dias da Costa served Nawab Bai, the mother of Aurangzeb's son Shah Alam. Nawab Bai, also known as Rahmat-un-Nisa, was Aurangzeb's second wife; she had been born a Kashmiri princess, the daughter of Raja Raju of Rajauri. Her marriage to Aurangzeb was a testy one. He began to distrust her because of the rebellion of their elder son, Muhammad Sultan. Shortly after Aurangzeb's accession to the Mughal throne, he had Muhammad Sultan imprisoned; the son died in Salimgarh Prison after more than fifteen years in confinement. Aurangzeb and Nawab Bai's second son, Shah Alam, also fell out of favour with the father and was taken into custody. Shortly after this, Nawab Bai followed her son into prison; she died there in 1691, emotionally and mentally wrecked by the experience. Letters written by Portuguese viceroys indicate that Juliana Dias da Costa also briefly fell out of favour with Aurangzeb and was imprisoned for some time. This may well have coincided with Aurangzeb's seven-year imprisonment of Shah Alam at Daulatabad from 1687 to 1695, following the latter's criticism of his father's decision to go to war with the Deccan sultanate of Golconda. Upon Juliana's release, she continued to serve in the household of Shah Alam who, upon his father's death in 1707, became the emperor Bahadur Shah. He clearly regarded Juliana highly, consulting her often on affairs of state until his death in 1712. According to one record, she was given a rank higher than that of most nobles in the court; this entitled her to special robes and a retinue of 5,000 men when she rode out of the Lal Qila. Despite her sudden promotion from servant to royal confidante, she is said to have retained a reputation for iffat and taqwa (modesty and piety). Perhaps this is why she remained an influential advisor to subsequent emperors until her own death in 1734, at the ripe old age of 76.

♦

So much for the scant chronological details of Juliana/Dias da Costa's life. But what about her biography, at least in the specifically embodied sense that I am using that term? How was her body imprinted and transformed by her experiences of service with Nawab Bai and Shah Alam/Bahadur Shah?

The harem in Delhi's Lal Qila, built by Shah Jahan when he transferred the capital from Lahore to Delhi in 1638, was a space in which Juliana Dias da Costa must have cultivated specific bodily habits and skills. Some of these may have been occasioned by the qualities of the space itself. The harem's Mumtaz Mahal, where many of the court women lived, was cooled through jaalis by the Yamuna river; and the famous Rang Mahal (Palace of Colours) for the Mughal royal women was cooled by a long water channel, the Nahr-i-Behisht (Stream of Paradise). Juliana could have taken advantage of the pleasant temperature of either building to read medical books like Shirazi's and write her letter in Persian to King João of Portugal. In her earlier years as a servant of Nawab Bai, she would also have cultivated more menial physical skills of cleaning and cooking that were adapted to the space of the harem. She may have shopped at the Lal Qila's crowded Chhata Bazaar (Covered Market) for cooking materials. Even as Juliana trained her body to perform certain domestic tasks, she must have also attended to others' bodies: her medical practice—most likely a trans-cultural composite of Persian, Ayurvedic Indian, and Portuguese skills—would have entailed administering food, drugs, and liquids to harem women.

There are no explicit references to Juliana or her medical practice by Nawab Bai's or Shah Alam's firangi visitors. But Niccolò Manucci, who served Shah Alam as his physician from 1680 to 1685, tells an intriguing story that hints at traditions of female medical workers among the Mughals. According to Manucci, Shah Alam was desperate to retain him in his service, fearful that he might leave for Europe. To that end, the prince plotted to find him a local firangi wife who would keep him in Hindustan. One day, Shah Alam told Manucci that 'there was a European in the palace'. At that moment there appeared, in Manucci's words, 'a very pretty girl, dressed as a man in European style, with a gold-mounted sword at her side'. Of course, this was a ruse on Shah Alam's part; a girl in his service could not appear in public, which is why she was disguised as a man. Manucci, seeing through the ruse, addressed her in French and made to kiss her, at which she fled. Shah Alam, laughing, asked Manucci what he wanted to do. Manucci told him that he 'wanted to embrace and kiss the would-be young man'. Shah Alam replied that 'the firangi…was not a man but a woman', and that if Manucci wished he could marry her. Interestingly, Shah Alam also told Manucci that 'she could serve to carry my medicines to the mahal'. This last suggestion proved to be the deal-breaker; Manucci, no longer aroused, angrily replied that 'she was no use for that, as medicines administered by a woman's hand produced no effect'. And he complains that, for a long time after, Shah Alam joked about Manucci's response.

Shah Alam's offer to Manucci indicates how women were often expected to do medical work in the harem. It is tempting to speculate that the 'pretty girl' he employed in his trick on Manucci was Juliana Dias da Costa, by this stage already used to conveying and administering medicines in the zenana. She was in her early twenties in 1680, and perhaps still unmarried. And she was in the service of Shah Alam's mother, and therefore accessible to the prince. There may, of course, have been other European women in her service or the prince's. And the fact that Manucci spoke French to the cross-dressed 'pretty girl' suggests that she may not have been the Portuguese-origin, Persian-speaking Juliana. But the incident still suggests three ways in which Juliana might have been physically affected by her experiences in the Lal Qila harem. First, as we have seen, she had to deal in medicines. Second, she had to submit to dramas of re-clothing in accordance with her royal masters' will; this included dressing for audiences in a male public sphere (and here we might recall Jean-Baptiste Gentil's description of Juliana as a cross-dressed virago, riding out with Shah Alam—now the Emperor Bahadur Shah—into battle). And third, she had to endure attempts to match her with possible husbands, not to mention unwanted advances from lecherous men like Manucci. It may have been because of one such match—or advance—that she became a mother.

So what of Juliana Dias da Costa's children? We know of her nineteenth-century descendants, the D'Eremaos. But her more immediate descendants remain unknown to us. In correspondence between the Goan viceroys and Portugal following Bahadur Shah's accession, mention is made of her married grandson Joseph Borges da Costa and his brother-in-law Diego Mendes. 'Habits of Christ'—an honorific title normally awarded to pure-blooded Portuguese not descended from Jews or Muslims, though occasionally awarded to mixed-blood Portuguese Indians—were given to both men in 1715; it seems the award was on account of Juliana's status at the Mughal court. But no mention is made anywhere of either her husband (the patently false D'Eremao claim about her marriage to Jean-Baptiste Gaston de Bourbon notwithstanding) or her children. One letter by a Portuguese official says that Juliana arrived at the Mughal court with her husband, a Portuguese surgeon. But this letter most likely confuses her father for her husband. Given her considerable status in the Mughal court and the many mentions of her, how are we to explain the baffling absence of her husband's and children's names from Indian and European records? One possibility is that Juliana Dias da Costa was unmarried and childless, and the 'grandchildren' who inherited her holdings weren't, in fact, her own, but descendants of a sister or a cousin. But there is also another possibility. Despite the hagiographic tone of Jesuit, European and family accounts of her model Christian piety, Juliana Dias da Costa may have entered the Mughal court not as a servant but as a harem slave-girl, and may have had one or more children out of wedlock.

Lending weight to this speculation is an extraordinary document—an unpublished account of Juliana Dias da Costa's life, written in Persian in the mid 1700s, by a mysterious man named Gaston Bruit. The account is called *Avhal-i-Bibi-Juliana* (The Circumstances of Bibi Juliana). Bruit was associated with Gentil, the Frenchman who married Juliana's niece, and may himself have been a descendant of Juliana: it seems as if the *Avhal-i-Bibi-Juliana* draws on some family lore that was still fresh in her immediate descendants' memory. Bruit gets some basic facts wrong: he claims that Juliana was captured as a child by the Mughals during their conquest of Hooghly in 1632 and brought to Agra, which would have made her over a hundred years old at her death; he was probably confusing her early life here with that of her father Agostinho. Yet if Agostinho had been enslaved by the Mughals, it is entirely possible that his daughter was also born a slave.

Despite getting Juliana's date of birth wrong, the *Avhal-i-Bibi-Juliana* includes many vivid details that are not present in other accounts. Chief among these is Bruit's prevailing sense of Juliana as a possession 'given' to various Mughal royals. He writes that both Juliana and her mother were gifted to a begum of the royal household; after her mother's death, she was given to 'a man of her own people' in marriage, but he died in battle shortly after. Then, Bruit claims, she was handed over to Aurangzeb's wife Nawab Bai, the mother of Shah Alam. When Aurangzeb arrested Shah Alam, he also imprisoned Nawab Bai and dismissed all her servants, including Juliana. But Bruit writes that Nawab Bai finally prevailed on Aurangzeb to find her a maid; hearing of this, Juliana 'offered her services and settled on a price of purchase' by Nawab Bai. The language here strongly suggests that Juliana was not simply a servant but, more accurately, a slave-girl.

If what Bruit writes is true, and Juliana Dias da Costa was indeed a slave, it is highly likely that she was unmarried. And if she had had a child, it would have born out of wedlock. Who could the child's father have been? Before we rush to speculate that the future Bahadur Shah had had a secret love child with his favourite firangi slave, we might do well to remember that, although many Mughal princes had children with slave-girls to whom they were not married, these children's identities were never disguised. Two of Akbar's three sons, Murad and Danyal, were born of his liaisons with concubines; and Jahangir had two sons, Jahandar and Shahryar, born in 1605 of two different mothers who were not his wives. There was no shame attached to these children. Likewise, an 'illegitimate' child of a Bahadur Shah would not have been expunged from the record, nor would the emperor's paternity have been hidden. But perhaps the offspring of a liaison between an unmarried Christian woman and her unknown lover might have been a little more scandalous to her Christian descendants. We do not know whether Juliana had a lover and, if she did, whether he was Muslim or Christian. But if Joseph Borges da Costa was indeed Juliana's biological grandson, his Portuguese name suggests that the father of her child may have been a firangi rather than a Mughal courtier. Was the canard of Juliana's marriage to an émigré Bourbon a family legend designed to divert attention from a potential scandal involving her? Gaston Bruit— despite the first name he shared with the man the D'Eremaos supposed to be Juliana's Bourbon prince husband—sheds no light on this: he mentions neither the Bourbons, nor any child of hers.

Bruit's account of Juliana's life is more revealing on another score. He offers vivid descriptions of her life in the women's royal apartments in Delhi. Bruit presents her as a version of a medieval European anchorite, performing Christian rituals with admirable devotion. According to Bruit, she would begin her day early, spending four hours in her ibadat khana, or place of worship, engaged in rituals of self-purification—presumably prayer and holy ablutions. Then she would join the other women of the household in the royal kitchen, where she would spend another four hours preparing Mughlai food: we are told that she made a particularly good dish of daal aur chaawal (lentils with rice), which was Bahadur Shah's favourite. Finally, she would dress up in her libas-i-darbari or formal attire and devote herself to court matters. Whether or not Bruit's account of Juliana's activities is accurate, it captures with some insight the ways in which Mughal harem culture consisted far less of the sexual recreations many have attributed to it than of quotidian physical chores: prayer, cooking, dressing. We can see how these chores transformed Juliana's body, training it in a variety of aptitudes. We can see too how these habits were, again, not simply 'domestic' in the traditional sense. Most of them were intimately connected to the realm of the public sphere. This is why her transformation from a court-girl with a 'price of purchase' to a senior advisor of the emperor was, in some ways, not at all remarkable: it was a logical outcome of Mughal harem life, in which the domestic repeatedly blurred into the political.

Nothing underscores this more than Bruit's image of Juliana in her libas-i-darbari. The robes point not just to Juliana's participation in the political culture of court; they also signal her rank within the harem, a rank that would have been formally acknowledged in the presence of other women through rituals of khil'at, out of which her libas-i-darbari were most likely fashioned. Her formal dress was no doubt visually impressive. The standard khil'at gift for Mughal courtiers of the highest rank was seven sarapas, or full robes. These were flowing garments made of cotton or silk, and often embroidered in gold with patterns that included the alam or Mughal lion. Khil'at for men of the highest rank also included a turban; we don't know if this was part of Juliana's libas-i-darbari, but she would have doubtless worn headwear of some kind in the presence of male courtiers. Her formal attire would also have demanded that she comport her body with care, according to physical as much as cultural demands. How would she have sat? And stood? How would she have gestured in the robes? We cannot know for sure, but she would have had to carry herself with care, not just in accordance with her rank, but also to protect her expensive garments from wear and tear. In her public appearances—after all, libas-i-darbari literally means robes of the court, meaning she ventured out of the harem into spaces normally considered 'male'—Juliana Dias da Costa was an actress in a specifically Mughal form of political theatre. In this theatre, her robes played an important role in shaping not just her body but also a larger social body. As we saw in the last chapter, the rituals of khil'at were crucial in stitching together the fabric of the Mughal harem and court and, beyond them, of Mughal society in general.

◆

Juliana's rank was recognized in the space of the harem through her clothes. But it was recognized publicly too. As we have seen, she operated in public spheres normally considered male. Juliana had enough political pull to convince the state to exempt Christian 'dervishes' in Agra from the jazia, or poll tax for non-Muslims. The award of several villages to her just outside of Delhi was further material evidence of her considerable stature. The land was supposed to amount to 97 bigha—a unit of measurement designating around 7,000 square metres, which means the entire grant was approximately 170 acres or 70 hectares—and included five wells. In other words, Juliana Dias da Costa had, by the time of her death, shed her status as a purchased woman and become a female jagirdar or landowner.

This was perhaps the most masculine privilege extended to Juliana. It is unclear how much time she spent on her land, and whether she was obliged as a jagirdar to make regular appearances before her tenants. That a substantial church was built there indicates she left her physical imprint on her property. The church was almost certainly built at her request, and maybe even to her specifications. Christians claiming to be her descendants—including some of the D'Eremaos—lived on the land into the twentieth century; they were part of the church's congregation. It is possible that Juliana attended services there too, riding by horse or sailing by river boat down the Yamuna from the Lal Qila to her jagir.

Any such visits to her estate would have been public semi-ceremonial events. Juliana may not have worn her libas-i-darbari but she would have certainly worn clothes appropriate to her rank as a jagirdar. In these semi-public appearances, Juliana would have had to comport herself in ways that skilfully negotiated the potential perils that confronted a woman entering a male sphere and performing her power within it. Presumably she would have been expected to wear a veil of some kind. But she would have also needed other props or accessories to perform successfully her role of jagirdar. When visiting her land, she was probably accompanied by a retinue of attendants (the surest mark of power in Mughal Hindustan). And she may have appeared atop a horse. Jean-Baptiste Gentil's stirring vision of Juliana as a Christian virago—an Indian Joan of Arc riding majestically into battle alongside Bahadur Shah—may be mere fancy. But it also may be loosely grounded in the spectacle of a female jagirdar visiting her property on horseback, clad in high-end sarapa or jama.

The villages Juliana was awarded have long been absorbed into the urban sprawl of southeast Delhi. Since Independence, their remains have been built over by swanky colonies as well as the poorer Okhla District. The area is a mess of gleaming new developments and crumbling old buildings whose original occupants have long been lost to memory. But the names of some of these villages remain, and in ways that indirectly remember Juliana. Sarai Jullena is now a swarming complex of shops near Bharti Nagar and the upmarket New Friends Colony; it hints at the Persian pronunciation of her Portuguese name. Masihgarh—meaning Christ Citadel—is named for a church in Okhla, built in 1918 on the foundation of the much earlier church that was probably built at Juliana's command.

Most intriguing is a still-extant village in Jamia Nagar, next to Jamia Millia Islamia University, called Jogabai. Like Sarai Jullena and Masihgarh, Jogabai is part of the original grant to Juliana Dias da Costa. It is a mixed neighbourhood, populated by equal numbers of Muslims and Hindus. Many in the village are poor: a considerable portion of its population live in unauthorized settlements built on soil adjacent to the Yamuna River, where they drape their newly-washed saris and fabrics and lay out well-shaped cowpats for use as heating fuel. Unlike the better-known neighbouring colony of Batla House, which has suffered aggravated communitarian tension in recent years, Jogabai is a model not just of communal peace but also of how to cross borders of identity. The village's Muslims celebrate Diwali, and the Hindus mark Eid. If this tradition of cross-communal celebration pays oblique homage to a firangi woman who crossed many borders in her own life, the name of the village subtly memorializes her too. During the eighteenth and nineteenth centuries, 'Juliana' seems to have morphed in the local village dialect into 'Joga'. What remained constant about Juliana in the village's name, however, was her title: after all, Bibi Juliana Dias da Costa was the 'bai' of Jogabai. This honorific recognizes her rank as a senior lady in the Mughal harem, which presumed of her certain types of bodily comportment, whether in her formal libas-i-darbari or in other activities.

'Jogabai' also chimes with the name of Jodha Bai. In that echo of an echo, we might recognize again how Mughal women's history is scattered in the susurrations of stories. These stories, like a Cubist painting, refract single figures into confusing multiplicities. The fictional Juliana Bourbon subdivides into two historical women. But even the real-life Julianas subdivide further in the stories told about them. Jean-Baptiste Gentil, Juliana Dias da Costa's grand-nephew-in-law, claims that Bahadur Shah created an official senior post in the harem known as the 'Juliana'. Upon Juliana Dias da Costa's death, Gentil maintains, the title was passed on to a succession of five of her grand-nieces. Gentil's unsubstantiated claim, perhaps typical of family attempts to boost their status, makes 'Juliana' a portable name whose many bearers add considerably to the store of Julianas we have met in this chapter. This surreal multiplication might seem to underscore Salman Rushdie's point about the elusiveness of Mughal-era women amid the swirl of stories about them. Yet the names of these storied women still yield revealing historical information about life in the imperial harem. Jogabai, Jodha Bai and Bibi Juliana Bourbon may all be distorted names dreamed up by later generations of tale tellers. But the titles embedded in their names—Bai, Bibi—point to very real social relations that imprinted in diverse ways on the bodies of women, firangi as much as Mughal. These social relations were most apparent in the khil'at rituals that hierarchically bonded Mughal women to each other. After all, as we have already seen, biography is what's in a firangi's Indian name. And in the Mughal harem, one's Indian name also mandated certain forms of re-clothing. Juliana Dias da Costa's biography can be read not just in the 'bai' of Jogabai. It can be read also in her libas-i-darbari and the larger social fabric into which it was stitched.

Because in Mughal Hindustan, clothes made the woman. Or rather, they made the firangi woman become Indian.

ON SWERVING

Living in India demands that the body as much as the mind become adept in the art of swerving.

Swerving is endemic throughout the subcontinent. Locals as well as visitors complain about drivers' lack of what they call 'lane discipline'—the tendency, even when there are clearly demarcated lanes, to lurch willy-nilly between them. But lane indiscipline is of a piece with Indians' pervasive tendency to refuse the constraint of one track, physically and verbally. Indians are, by habit as much as inclination, swervers.

This is particularly so in Delhi. The ubiquity of swerving was brought home to me when I first visited the city. Often I would eavesdrop on conversations that, like a Delhi car repeatedly weaving in and out of supposedly discrete lanes, lurched from English to Hindi to Punjabi and back again. I had studied shuddh Hindi before moving to Delhi, but that pure tongue bore scant resemblance to any language I heard spoken here. The problem with what I'd learned is that it stayed too confined to one Sanskritized lane. My better education by far has been courtesy of Bollywood and its music, whose language is a mongrel blend of Hindi, Urdu, English, Punjabi, and other tongues. Listening to my car radio, weaving between lanes of road and language, I have learned the demented lyrics for a song from the film Dev D, *'Emosunal Atyachar' (Emotional Tyranny), which hurtle between Bhojpuri Hindi and English: 'Bol bol why did you ditch me?/ Zindagi bhi lele yaar kill me!' And I have picked up choice Hinglish expressions such as 'B. T. mat de, yaar'—don't give me a B. T., or Bad Trip.*

Swerving between languages occurs not just at the level of thought or word choice. It is also an embodied phenomenon, as I learned early in my life. My Warsaw-born, Jerusalem-raised mother, though fluent in English, would shift between several languages, often in the space of a single sentence. She would intersperse her remarks with snippets of Hebrew (l'briyut, literally 'to health', when I sneezed; laila tov, or 'good night', when I went to bed). As the Hebrew tripped off her tongue, she would hold her head and move her eyebrows differently from how she did in English. And she would always count in Polish (jeden, dwa, trzy, cztery, pięć), touching her fingers in a way that she wouldn't in English. When she changed languages, therefore, her body would change too—the shape of her lips and mouth as she produced sounds different from those of English, her expressions and gestures as she swerved into Hebrew and Polish.

The art of verbal swerving represents for me an exhilarating form of code-switching, a freedom to cross borders of imagination as well as language. It has impressed on me how there is always more than one choice for expressing a thought, and that a thought can subtly change, and grow, by moving into other languages. But this freedom paradoxically entails an element of submission. It means abiding by theatrical scripts not of one's own making—scripts that are of the body as much as the tongue. Swerving into a new language obliges you not only to observe its rules of grammar and syntax but also to perform the body languages that come with it: stylized facial expressions, postures, movements of the hands, and so on.

As I haltingly acquired Hinglish, with its khichdi of diverse tongues, I was struck by how my own movements between languages prompted my body to conform to multiple scripts. Without realizing it, I had started waggling my head when conversing with people. And in my car, when encountering Delhi's bad drivers, I began raising my hand in the city's universal back-handed, splay-fingered 'Tu kyaa kar raha hai, you bloody sala?' gesture, accompanied by an appropriate expression of deeply aggrieved hurt. I had, in short, become a pukka Delhi driver-cum-swerver.

The art of swerving has given me a point of entry into the biographies of two firangis who assumed itinerant lives in Mughal India and the Deccan. Each lurched from location to location, making public orations in Persian, Arabic, Hindavi and other languages to gain food, money and shelter. Their speeches and poems underline their unusual abilities in becoming Indian. To communicate effectively, each man acquired polyglot expressive skills: he learned how to move not just between diverse local tongues but also local codes of gesture and dress. It is no coincidence that, to keep their bellies full, the two migrants took on the body languages of spiritual communities distinguished by highly theatrical rituals of begging—the fakirs of Ajmer, the yogis and qalandars of North India and the Deccan.

The Indian art of swerving is, ultimately, an embodied one, contorting and re-contorting the body in order to sustain it.

10 | THOMAS CORYATE,
THE FAKIR OF AJMER

It is a muggy day in the Rajasthan monsoon season of 1616. A beggar presents himself before the jharoka or (public window) of the Akbari Qila in Ajmer. Sitting in the window is the Mughal emperor Jahangir, who has based himself in Ajmer since 1613 in order to subdue Amar Singh, the rebel Rajput chief of Mewar. Despite his campaign, Jahangir still makes time for his customary daily darbar or audience with the public. The beggar below him cuts a striking figure. A very short man with a tiny torso, an abnormally large head, and a face darkened by long exposure to the sun, he is decked in shabby Central Asian clothing. The beggar looks up to Jahangir seated in the jharoka and proceeds to deliver a long and somewhat rambling speech in Persian. But he speaks with flair, projecting his words in a forceful voice despite his small chest, and accompanying his speech with animated gestures. Jahangir listens to the beggar amusedly if distractedly; once the speech is over, he throws down a small bag of silver coins worth around 100 rupees. It's not as large a sum as what Jahangir gives some of his more distinguished supplicants. Yet it's clearly a windfall for the beggar, who describes himself in his speech as a fakir dervish. The phrase normally refers to an itinerant Muslim Sufi who begs for alms. Remarkably, however, this fakir is a Christian firangi from England.

A fakir is not just an itinerant religious beggar. He is also a performer. He has to resort to certain formulas of supplication in his speech and gesture—acknowledging his potential benefactor's god, scraping the ground, touching his lips to request alms, etc. The word comes from the Arabic 'faqr', meaning poverty. Yet for modern English speakers, fakir has also come to acquire an echo of its unintended English homonym, 'faker'. Early twentieth-century English photographs of 'Indian fakirs' present them sitting on beds of nails and walking through fire—circus-style stunts that involve an element of theatrical performance. The 'fakirs' in these photos are not Sufis, of course, but Hindu sanyasis or holy men, whose ascetic rituals are more dramatic than those of fakir dervishes. But any performance that seeks to obtain something from its audience— alms, food, awestruck submission—is easily associated with charlatanism, as if acting were simply a synonym for deception and fakery. And in India, beggars are all too often dismissed as theatrical fakers. Yet if a fakir performs a type of theatre, he doesn't do so to deceive. Instead, he performs to put food in his belly, using his body—particularly his mouth and hands—as a highly stylized medium of expression. As a result, the biography of a fakir is not just a collection of events organized in chronological sequence. It is also a tale of bodily need, training and transformation.

In Mughal Hindustan, a fakir couldn't train his body in comfortable circumstances, at least not in the way that a Dhrupad singer or a Kathak dancer was able to train her body in the imperial zenana. The theatre of begging always took place in a setting of poverty. No matter how wealthy the background of the fakir, he had to cultivate his skill on the streets, often having eaten little, with very few clothes on his back, and in the hot sun. The religious beggar's theatre, moreover, was not a high performance art like Dhrupad and Kathak which, for all their expressive capabilities, require rigorous training according to sets of clearly specified rules. The Mughal fakir may have abided by certain scripts—spoken formulas and gestures of supplication—but he also had to keep adapting to new locations, new audiences, and new mediums of expression. After all, the fakir had to be able to move between the many tongues of the Mughal Empire—Persian, Turkic, Arabic, local vernaculars—depending on who he was speaking to. He had, in short, to be good at swerving.

What could compel a firangi to become a fakir? And what in particular could compel an Englishman to become a beggar in the galis of Ajmer? Wasn't it a form of deception or imposture? One immediate answer is that the Englishman's transformation was motivated by genuine economic and physical need. But there is another factor, one which at first might seem incommensurate with a grinding poverty that offers few choices. The English firangi who became a fakir was motivated by love. He was motivated by a love of public theatre, a love of languages, a love of attention and, as we will see, a more objectless love—a restless desire to keep moving across space, cultures, and styles of bodily expression. In combination, these loves drove the firangi fakir to a life of near-starvation, in which he subsisted on the most meagre of diets. This is the story of Thomas Coryate. It is also the story of khichdi, that humble combination of rice and daal that is a powerful metaphor for any mixture.

◆

Thomas Coryate was known to his London friends and detractors alike as 'Odd Tom'. As this might suggest, he was something of an eccentric. Coryate cheerfully embraced his nickname: born in approximately 1577 and raised in the small Somerset village of Odcombe in west England, he admitted that he embodied the 'odd' of his village's name. Yet he was the scion of a family that embodied middle-class normality. His father, George, was the local church rector, a solid Protestant reputed for his public orations; his godfather Thomas Phillips, for whom he was named, was a respected Somerset landowner. We know little about Coryate's mother, though Tom was emotionally close to her. He was to write several letters to 'his loving Mother' from India.

Coryate's eccentricity may have had much to do with his unusual physique. He was dwarfish, and his face—with bulbous eyes and a ruddy complexion—attracted sometimes derisive attention. Early on, perhaps to flee the taunts of local villagers, he became an inveterate walker, exploring the terrain of rural west England's hills and dales as well as the road to London. Despite his short stature, he was dubbed by a friend 'the long strider'. The English playwright Ben Jonson, whom Coryate counted among his friends, described him as 'an Engine, wholly consisting of extremes, a Head, Fingers and Toes'. Coryate was to put those engine-like toes—and his head and fingers—to good use in a lifetime of perambulation.

Coryate received his school education at Winchester College, the alma mater of that other English firangi, Thomas Stephens. Clearly there was something in the air at Winchester. Stephens's poetry master Christopher Johnson was long gone by the time Coryate reached the school in the late 1580s. But young Tom, like his older namesake, received a thorough training in classical rhetoric, which included the arts of oratory. These demanded the cultivation of not just speaking skills but also forms of gesture. Classical Greek treatises on rhetoric emphasized that hands are as eloquent as tongues, and should be used accordingly. Following these treatises' example, English actors and orators alike resorted to highly stylized hand movements and facial expressions to communicate passion: beating the hand on the heart to express sorrow, raising the arms to express supplication. At Winchester, Coryate seems to have excelled in Greek and Latin. Both languages were associated with the arts of rhetoric; classroom instruction in Latin, for example, saw students perform passages from writers such as Horace and Ovid, and these performances included elaborate gestures according to the codes of classical oratory. It was probably at Winchester that Coryate first turned his oddities of appearance and voice to theatrical account, developing a reputation as a skilled if eccentric orator.

Unlike Stephens, Coryate completed his university studies. In 1596, he was admitted as 'a commoner' to Gloucester Hall, Oxford University. Coryate spent three years there; apparently he attained a measure of competence in logic, but he seems to have excelled in 'humane learning'—history, philosophy and literature—as well as classical Greek. At Gloucester Hall, Coryate also developed an interest in theatre. Plays were often performed at Oxford. Some of the best playwrights of the Jacobean stage—including Thomas Middleton and John Ford—were at Oxford at the same time as Coryate, though they attended different colleges. Odd Tom may not have performed in university plays. But he almost certainly further honed his skill in oratory while at Gloucester Hall. His father, a church rector, had been reputed for his speeches; the son followed in his father's footsteps with histrionic flair. As Jonson observed of him, 'He is always Tongue-Major of the Company.'

Upon graduating, Coryate probably moved back to Odcombe. But by 1603, perhaps through some of his old Oxford contacts, he had secured a plum job in London. King James of Scotland had just come to the throne; his son Prince Henry, who seems to have developed a fondness for Odd Tom, hired him as a de facto court jester. Coryate's job at court was to chatter away, coining new fantastical words in his endless orations. One of his neologisms was 'hyperaspist'—derived from the Greek 'hyper' (above) and 'aspis' (shield)—to refer to a patron or protector; this may have been what Coryate called Prince Henry. At court, he got used to making speeches that straddled the grey areas between deferential and madcap, between ripe praise of royalty and implied praise of himself. Odd Tom seems to have been appreciated as a pleasing enough oddity, though some people's patience clearly palled in the presence of such a bizarre, self-regarding chatterbox. Many years later, King James remembered Coryate with some disdain as 'that fool'.

Coryate cultivated his histrionic skills also with a group of writers and wits that met on the first Friday of every month at London's Mermaid Tavern in Cheapside. The group's name, the Sireniacs, was a pun on Siren (often confused with Mermaid) and Cyrenaic, an old Greek movement committed to the pursuit of pleasure. The Sireniacs included many notable literary figures, including the playwright Ben Jonson and the poet John Donne. William Shakespeare is rumoured to have been an occasional member too. With them, Coryate honed his reputation as a non-stop talker but also, more specifically, as someone who loved moving between different languages in his never-ending orations. One of his fellow Sireniacs observed that 'With Latin he doth rule the roast,/ And spouteth Greek in every coast.'

John Donne, parodying Coryate's style, wrote lines of verse that hurtle at neck-breaking pace between Latin, Spanish, Italian, French and English:

Quot, dos haec, LINGUISTS perfetti, Disticha fairont,
Tot cuerdos STATES-MEN, hic livre fara tuus.
Es sat a MY l'honneur ester hic inteso: Car I LEAVE
L'honra, de personne nester creduto, tibi.

Donne pokes fun here at the gobbledygook Coryate was given to spouting. To the extent that the lines are translatable, they say something like 'As these two verses, perfect linguists, will make all the sensible statesmen, this book will make yours; it is enough for my honour to be understood this way, for I leave the honour of someone never to be believed to you.' Donne's nonsense lines hint that Coryate is a show-off and windbag whose claims are not be credited. Yet they acknowledge Odd Tom's curiosity, at least at the level of language, about other cultures. They also communicate the heady thrill of Coryate's flair in swerving between different tongues during his bizarre speeches.

Coryate's style as a speech-maker may also have been honed by his exposure, whether in London or earlier, to a play by Christopher Marlowe. While working at the court of Prince Henry, Coryate probably saw a production of Marlowe's *Tamburlaine*—arguably the biggest blockbuster of the London commercial stage in the late sixteenth century, and frequently performed for decades after that. Marlowe's title character is a rendering of the fourteenth-century Turkic warrior-king Timur-i-Lang (Timur the Lame), who briefly ruled much of Central Asia, including Persia, Turkey, and Mesopotamia. Timur is usually supposed to have conquered Hindustan in 1398 and become its 'emperor', though he only ever briefly crossed the Indus and, in a short but bloody campaign, took possession of what is now Punjab in Pakistan and the territories surrounding Delhi. Marlowe's play makes passing reference to India. But what might have stuck with Coryate was the memory of Tamburlaine as a global traveller: over the course of the play, he moves from the Asian steppes to Persia, Syria, Egypt and Baghdad, and refers to Europe, Africa, and even the Americas. Coryate may have found Tamburlaine's oratory equally memorable. In the play's opening lines, Marlowe promises to dazzle the audience's ears with 'high astounding terms'. The actor who played Tamburlaine through the 1590s, Edward Alleyn, delivered on Marlowe's promise: he made the character a byword for extraordinary speech-making and gesture. Tamburlaine's distinctive sounds and body-languages must have grabbed Coryate's attention. On both scores—as global traveller and as innovative theatrical orator—Coryate was soon to follow Tamburlaine's example.

◆

In 1607, Coryate made an extraordinary decision. Having already cultivated a taste for long-distance walking in his youth, he left the English royal court in London to tour Europe on foot. This decision may not seem remarkable to us now in a time when travel is commonplace and the English Grand Tour of the continent a seemingly timeless institution. But in the early seventeenth century, Coryate's course of action was singular. Very few people left the country other than in straitened circumstances—escaping poverty or religious persecution—or for reasons of business or state. England was at odds with the Catholic countries; the linguistic challenges were immense; and the threat of being accosted by robbers or felled by diseases was high enough to dissuade most people with curiosity about other cultures.

Coryate's journey, which lasted a little more than five months, took him on foot through France, Switzerland, Italy, Germany and Holland. We do not know exactly how and why he made the decision to leave Prince Henry's service. Perhaps he sensed his time at court was up. Or perhaps he was looking for an opportunity to pursue his curiosity in ways that might earn him both fame and money. It is clear that, from the outset, he intended to convert his experiences into a published travelogue: he took copious notes about all the places he visited. But this was to be no straightforward ethnographic report. Coryate's inspiration was primarily theatrical: in 1600, the well-known actor-clown Will Kemp—a member of Shakespeare's company—had undertaken an extended morris dance from London to Norwich, performed over nine days in front of cheering crowds. (In a prefatory poem to Coryate's account of his European tour, a poet says of him, 'Kemp yet doth live'.) In other words, if Coryate sought to write a record of foreign cultures, it was not as a silent or invisible ethnographer. He instead intended to be a leading actor in the spectacles he described—every bit as much an exotic curio as continental Europe's people, buildings, and landscapes.

This is made abundantly clear by the frontispiece to *Coryate's Crudities*, Odd Tom's account of his travels. The frontispiece presents a collection of images of foreign countries. But what is most striking about these is not their exotic characters, landscapes or buildings but Coryate's body. It's prominently displayed in a sequence of theatrical scenes—transported by ship and palanquin across the English channel and the Swiss alps; chased by a Venetian Jew brandishing a knife; riding a gondola, drenched by rain and pelted with fruit thrown by an angry courtesan; even vomited on by a figure representing Germany (or so a caption tells us). Odd Tom's body is not just the object of spectacle: it is repeatedly exposed to, and potentially transformed by, foreign elements.

First published in 1611, the *Crudities* went into several editions and made Coryate a celebrity. Coryate's theatrical flair is one reason why the book became so popular. His book captures, with particular vividness, not just the experience of travelling abroad. It also comes across as a dazzling performance piece. Some have described Coryate as the first modern tourist. But if he is a sightseer, his stories are not so much accounts of other lands as they are show-and-tells about himself in strange settings, designed to win the approval of both friends and a larger audience. In this regard, the *Crudities* reads less as a tourist's narrative and more like a modern Facebook page: the book is full of self-important status updates, shout-outs to tagged friends, and selfies of Coryate in exotic locations. I keep looking for a non-existent 'like' button beneath each illustration of Coryate standing atop a giant beer vat in Heidelberg or being harangued by Jews or prostitutes in Venice. We even have a list of his 'friends' at the book's beginning—fifty-seven poets who have written commendatory verses for the *Crudities*. And these 'friends', like their modern social media counterparts, often adopt a tone of quip-rich irony as they comment on Coryate's various posts, praising and poking fun at him in the same breath. The *Crudities* depend on the same blurred lines between inclusiveness and one-upmanship, witty self-promotion and wry self-deprecation, social networking and unalloyed narcissism that distinguish Facebook.

Coryate's report of his experiences in Europe blurs lines in another way. He does not see his body as unchanging, but in dynamic conversation with its environments: in other words, his body changes as its physical and cultural locations change. It's striking how much Coryate willingly submits to the possibility of bodily alteration throughout his narrative. We can get a sense of this from the extended gastronomic metaphor of the *Crudities'* title. The full title—typical of Coryate's madcap way of speaking—is '*Coryate's Crudities Hastily Gobbled up in Five Months Travels in France, Savoy, Italy, Rhetia Commonly Called the Orison's Country, Helvetia Alias Switzerland, Some Parts of High Germany and the Netherlands, Newly Digested in the Hungry Air of Odcombe in the County of Somerset, and Now Dispersed to the Nourishment of the Travelling Members of this Kingdom*'. As this indicates, Coryate didn't simply see foreign cultures. He took elements of them into his body—or, in his words, 'gobbled' them up—hoping that his readers would find the flavours of his foreign experience similarly appetizing.

It is no accident that Coryate was most likely responsible for introducing to England the fork, which he had encountered in Venice. For this, he won the additional nickname 'Furcifer', or bearer of the fork. His experiments with cutlery typify how his response to foreign cultures was that of a highly embodied actor, training his body how to work with unfamiliar stage properties. In other words, his goal was never simply to describe foreign cultures. His goal rather was self-transformation by extending and altering his body in concert with foreign people and objects. Over and over again he sought to get outside himself, or attempted to make his body do things that it didn't or couldn't do previously. Hearing the Italianate Latin spoken by the residents of Bergamo, for example, he resolved 'to abandon my old English pronunciation' and emulate their example. This meant studying hard to change the motor habits of his tongue, lips, and facial muscles. His tour of Europe, then, was not a luxurious tourist holiday. It was, rather, travail, the French word for 'work' that is also the original meaning of 'travel'. Coryate not only laboured to walk from place to place; he also worked on his body to transform it according to the customs of each place he visited. He performed the work, in other words, of a committed method actor.

Following the publication of the *Crudities* in 1611, Coryate cooled his toes for a year in Odcombe. During this time he seems to have met a Lady Hartford in Somerset and developed something of a passion for her. Dom Moraes, the co-author of a biography of Odd Tom, speculates that Coryate had a one-off sexual encounter with her, and his unrequited love was one of the reasons for his decision to leave England again. But I suspect a rather different love motivated him: a love of celebrity, alloyed with a genuine love of language and strange cultures. How to follow up on—or even top—his continental tour? First he donated the shoes he wore during his walk through Europe to the Odcombe church, where they were publically displayed until the early eighteenth century. (The shoes were stolen in the early 1700s, after which they were replaced by a stone facsimile pair that are still hanging on the church wall.) Then, in the autumn of 1612, he delivered an oration at Odcombe Cross. In it, he announced his plan to travel for no less than ten years. His destination? In a theatrical flourish, he planned to walk in the footsteps of Marlowe's Tamburlaine through Asia. He may not have known it at the time, but his epic walk would take him to the court of a direct descendant of Tamburlaine, the great Mughal emperor, Jahangir.

◆

'All the world's a stage', writes Shakespeare. The phrase has become such a cliché that we can easily lose sight of its peculiar ethnographic resonance at a time when 'all the world' was opening up in unprecedented ways to English travellers. What does it mean to think about the world as a stage? The question has at least two possible answers. The first is that all the cultures of the world can be viewed as strange theatrical spectacles. This was the assumption of the earliest English ethnographers. The ethnographer watched people of foreign cultures act out strange scenes; he kept himself mostly invisible in his descriptions, assuming a separation from the exotic scenes he described in much the same way that spectators in a darkened auditorium are divided from what is enacted on stage. This mindset added to the authority of the ethnographer: he possessed the power to make sense of what he saw, to map it and to know it—indeed, to know it better than the actors in the spectacle do. All the world's a stage, watched carefully by an English spectator, and all its cultures merely players on it.

The second answer is rather different. It doesn't allow for that safe distance between spectator and spectacle. Instead, it believes that '*all* the world's a stage', and everyone is an actor, even those who believe themselves to be just spectators. The tension between this mindset and the previous one is particularly apparent in two rather different English encounters with the Mughal court of Jahangir. These encounters involved not just two very different understandings of theatre, but also two very different understandings of Tamburlaine. They additionally brought together two different Thomases whose lives were to be dramatically intertwined between 1615 and 1617—Odd Tom Coryate of Odcombe, and Sir Thomas Roe, King James I's ambassador to the court of Jahangir from 1615 to 1619.

Thomas Roe arrived in India in 1615. He came as King James's personally appointed representative to try and secure special trading privileges from Jahangir for the East India Company. We who are used to the East India Company as a byword for supreme British colonial power in India can easily forget that, in its earliest decades, the Company was a poor and not particularly sound venture. Uncertain as to whether the Company had a future in India, James withheld full funding for Roe's mission, which forced the ambassador to live in humbling—and, to his mind, humiliating—conditions. In Ajmer, his quarters were a small mud house. He also repeatedly fell sick; after arriving in India, he was flat on his back for two months, and he was dogged by bouts of ill health throughout his time there. Unsurprisingly, much of Roe's journal reads like an extended self-pity party.

Yet one wouldn't know of his body's difficulties from his description of his first meeting with Jahangir. Roe is a character in his own story, but he is simultaneously absent from it, because his narrative focuses on the strange, theatrical bodies of Indians—especially Jahangir's—while leaving his own just out of view:

> *January 10.*—I went to Court at 4 in the evening to the *Darbar*, which is the Place where the Mogul sits out daily, to entertain strangers, to receive petitions and presents, to give Commands, to see, and to be seen. ...He comes every Morning to a window called the *Jarruco* [jharokha, or interview window] looking into a plain before his gate, and shows himself to the Common People. ...The king sits in a little Gallery overhead; Ambassadors, the great men and strangers of quality within the inmost rail under him, raised from the ground, Covered with Canopies of velvet and silk, under foot laid with good Carpets; the Meaner men representing gentry within the first rail, the people without in a base Court, but so that all may see the king. This sitting out hath so much affinity with a Theatre—the manner of the king in his gallery; the great men lifted on stage as actors; the vulgar below gazing on—that an easy description will inform of the place and fashion.

For Roe, all of Mughal India's a stage. And he is its invisible spectator. Note what he does here: even as he describes the theatrical power of

Jahangir's body—a body whose power is understood in terms of how it is positioned above other bodies within the spectacle—Roe grants himself a rival power as ethnographer by removing his own, persistently unwell, body from the scene he describes.

The analogy between the Mughal court and the theatre is one that Roe repeatedly drew. He described his audience with Jahangir in more or less identical terms in a letter to Lord Carew, written from Ajmer on January 17: 'I found him in a Court, set above like a King in a Play and all his Nobles and myself below on a stage covered with carpets—a just Theatre; with no great state, but the Canopies over his head, and two standing on the heads of two wooden Elephants, to beat away flies.' As this makes clear, Roe used metaphors of theatre not just to produce ethnographic knowledge of India. He also used them to underscore his conviction that what he saw in India was somehow fraudulent or deceptive. Mughal power, in his view, was a dubious form of theatrical imposture.

We can see this tendency everywhere in his journal. Granted an audience with Jahangir's son Pervez in Berhampur in late 1615, en route to Ajmer, Roe complained that 'the place was Covered overhead with a Rich Canopy, and underneath all Carpets. To describe it rightly it was like a great stage, and the Prince sat above as the Mock kings doth there'. The analogy between royal court and theatrical stage here pivots on that word 'Mock'. For Roe, 'Mock kings' were both theatrical counterfeits of kings *and* real kings who make a mockery of their status by surrounding themselves with mere stage properties—canopies, carpets. Both senses of the 'Mock' king are key to understanding Roe's descriptions of the Mughal court. Perhaps the most glaring instance is his extended discussion of Jahangir's darbar in October 1616 with the Persian ambassador. As the subtitle of this section of the journal makes clear, Roe was both fascinated and troubled by Jahangir's 'Super-exceeding Pomp'. The entire scene played out for Roe as a theatrical nightmare: the Persian ambassador greeted Jahangir with so many garish gifts that 'he appeared, rather a Jester or Juggler, then a person of gravity, running up and down and acting all his words like a Mimic Player'.

So long as this nightmare only involved foreign actors, Roe's descriptions could remain prudishly ethnographical: all of Mughal India's a stage, and he is simply its appalled spectator. But sometimes the Mughal theatre threatened to include Roe and his otherwise invisible body. One such instance was his receipt in November of 1616 of a gift from Jahangir's favourite son, Prince Khurram:

> By and by came out a Cloth of gold Cloak of his own, once or twice worn, which he Caused to be put on my back, and I made a reverence very unwillingly. When his Ancestor Tamburlaine was represented at the Theatre the Garment would well have become the Actor; but it is here reputed the highest of favour to give a garment worn by the Prince, or, being New, once laid on his shoulder.

Roe here describes—and misrecognizes—the ritual of khil'at, the gift of clothes as tokens of imperial favour. As we saw in the previous two chapters, the ritual performed an important political function by producing bonds of reciprocity and obligation. But Roe understands it only as the theatrical performance of a 'Mock king'. His reference to Tamburlaine—simultaneously Khurram's historical ancestor and Christopher Marlowe's stage character—works to make the Mughals creatures of the theatre. Khurram's gold cloak is, for Roe, a gaudy garment more suited to the playhouse than an imperial court; as such, it is a particularly unwelcome addition to the now visible back of an English ambassador who saw his clothes not as theatrical costumes but, rather, as irrevocable signs of his God-given national identity. Edward Terry, Roe's chaplain, noted that 'For my Lord Ambassador and his Company, we all kept to our English habits, made as light and cool as possibly we could have them; his waiters in Red Taffeta cloaks, guarded with green Taffeta, which they always wore when they went abroad with him; myself in a long black Cassock'. Not the best attire for the hot Ajmer sun, perhaps, but certainly powerful markers of Englishness for Roe and his men. This is why Roe spurned not just the theatrical vestments of Mughal self-display but any demand that he himself wear them. His response to Khurram's gift betrays a horror that, placed on his back, Mughal cloth might change him by turning him into an ethnically cross-dressed stage-Tamburlaine.

Imagine Roe's horror, then, when another ethnically cross-dressed English body—a body possessed, moreover, of a very different disposition to the theatrical Tamburlaine—walked on stage. Enter (again) Thomas Coryate.

◆

Coryate set sail for Constantinople in October 1612. We don't know if

India was part of his original travel itinerary. En route to Constantinople, he visited the ruins of Troy; here he engaged in some characteristic theatrics by persuading a travelling companion to dub him, with his sword, as a Knight of Troy, much to the horror of some local onlookers who feared he was about to be decapitated. It's easy to imagine Coryate supplementing his Trojan role-play with long orations inspired by Homer's *Iliad*. After reaching Constantinople in April, he stayed there until the New Year, after which he proceeded via Damascus to Jerusalem: there, like many Christian pilgrims of the time, he got his wrists tattooed with crosses. Then in the summer of 1614 he headed to Aleppo, where he waited four months for a caravan bound for Persia along the Silk Route. Disaster befell him in eastern Turkey: a soldier robbed him of nearly all his money. Yet somehow he kept trudging towards his destination, one foot at a time.

Coryate was now terribly poor. But he was also thrifty, and managed to live by depending largely on the kindness of strangers. He tarried for two months in Isfahan in Persia, before resuming his journey on foot, via the Silk Route through Kandahar and Multan, to Lahore, which he reached in early 1615. At the desert threshold between Persia and the Mughal Empire, Coryate had encountered another travelling Englishman—Sir Robert Shirley, an English ambassador to the Persian Shah. Shirley was returning from his trip to Mughal Hindustan, where he had met Augustin Hiriart Hunarmand and been gifted an elephant by the Frenchman. And, much to Coryate's excitement, Shirley was carrying with him a copy of the *Crudities*. Ever hungry for affirmation, Odd Tom felt validated by Shirley, who also gave him forty shillings. Coryate needed the money even more than he needed the ego-boost. He was about to embark on one of the most difficult phases of his perambulations.

Coryate had begun to fantasize about an audience with Jahangir. His mad dream of meeting the Great Mughal was probably pricked in part by Robert Shirley's travel tales, not to mention his elephant. Perhaps Coryate hoped that, with the reputation he had gained in Prince Henry's court as a speech-maker, he might win favour by speaking to Jahangir in similar fashion. Another factor motivated him: as he was to admit later, he hoped that Jahangir might give him a promise of protection for his proposed journey to Samarkand to visit Tamburlaine's tomb. After leaving Lahore, Coryate made his way on Akbar's tree-lined highway to Delhi and then Agra, guiding himself by the pink kos minars—milestone towers—that are still standing in many places. Once in Agra, he found out that Jahangir was now based in Ajmer. He then turned tail and headed west, again following the kos minars across the parched terrain of Rajasthan. He reached Ajmer in July 1615, just as the first monsoon rains were lowering the temperature and raising the humidity.

The Ajmer of 1615 was, in certain respects, not very different from the Ajmer of today. It is a small city; surrounded by the Aravalli Mountains, its environs are greener and cooler than the arid brown plains of Rajasthan. Jahangir claimed that Ajmer's 'cold season is very equable, and the hot season is milder than in Agra'. The main landmark is the Ana Sagar, a man-made lake built by one of the Chauhan rajas in the twelfth century. Jahangir enjoyed the cool lake breeze from the Daulat Bagh, a garden he built on the Ana Sagar's shore; the baradari or pavilions added to the garden by Shah Jahan still offer splendid views. Ajmer itself, however, is not a particularly beautiful city, and in this too it has not changed much since Coryate's time. Now as then, the Dargah Sharif, the tomb of the Sufi saint Moinuddin Chishti (an ancestor of the Chishti buried in Fatehpur Sikri who predicted the birth of Jahangir), is at the centre of a maze of narrow galis congested with pilgrims, shops, and tongas. Thomas Roe called Ajmer 'the dullest, basest place that ever I saw'. But to the impoverished, foot-weary Coryate, Ajmer was a welcome haven. He stayed for fourteen months.

During Coryate's time in Ajmer, he was repeatedly dependent on the kindness of others. The money he had received from Shirley must have run out fairly quickly. So it is likely he needed to find alms and free food. In a letter to a friend in England, he wrote that he would never forget Jahangir's act of generosity in feeding 5,000 poor people khichdi from an 'immense brass pot' at the Dargah Sharif. The passionate enthusiasm with which Coryate describes Jahangir's charity makes it likely that he himself was one of its recipients. And khichdi—that simple, inexpensive concoction of daal and rice—was doubtless one of Coryate's staple fares during his time in Ajmer, both inside and outside the Dargah Sharif. The interior of the dargah is still as it was described by a visiting English merchant, William Finch, in around 1610: 'you pass through three fair courts...paved all with black and white marble', before arriving at the sepulchre, whose 'door is large and inlaid with mother-of-pearl'. Jahangir's immense brass pot, or degh, was in the first court. Every year during the Urs Mela, an annual feast that commemorates the death of Moinuddin Chishti, a rich devotee still sponsors the preparation of khichdi for 5,000 poor pilgrims at the Dargah Sharif. Following in Coryate's footsteps 400 years later, I passed the huge Urs Mela degh—a nineteenth-century replacement for Jahangir's original—just past the dargah's entrance.

The approach to the Dargah Sharif is also much as it would have been in Coryate's time: to reach the entrance, one has to run a gauntlet of fakirs, or religious beggars. These beggars are sometimes cripples; many are barely clad. They prostrate themselves before the dargah, but also before the pilgrims who walk up the main gali to the dargah's entrance. Their counterparts 400 years ago must have looked not that dissimilar. In need of money and food, Coryate almost certainly begged alongside them. He no doubt acquired from them some of the skills he needed to be an effective beggar, including formulas and gestures of supplication. Coryate certainly observed their habits keenly, noting for example that they begged Christian alms-givers in the name of 'Bibi Maria' and not of 'Hazrat Isa' (the Persian name for Jesus), which led him to suspect that the Jesuits 'have preached more Mary than Jesus'. But he must also have observed and copied small details of gesture that won money from alms-givers, such as the performance of salaams and namastes.

One skill that most of the seventeenth-century fakirs of Ajmer probably possessed, and which their modern counterparts do not always have, is a basic fluency in several Asian languages. Coryate worked hard on emulating this skill. He had already learned some Persian during his time in Isfahan and his long trek across the Silk Route. But he also made a point of formally studying Turkish and Arabic while in Ajmer, and he picked up the local Rajasthani dialect as well. (Edward Terry tells a story of how Coryate so out-talked a feisty washing-woman in her own language that 'she had not one word more to speak'.) Coryate needed all four languages to be able to communicate with the multicultural population of Ajmer, including its Mughal rulers. Yet he didn't simply learn new ways of communicating. Coryate would have probably relied on old English aptitudes as well. He doubtless made use of his talent for oratory, including stylized hand gestures and facial expressions, as a foundation for his begging performances. In other words, like so many firangis who train their body to master Indian physical habits, his body had almost certainly become a palimpsest—a mixture, or khichdi, of skills, gestures and linguistic abilities from England and the subcontinent. Ultimately it was Coryate's skill in linguistic swerving that most benefited him.

Some scholars have scoffed at firangi claims of fluency in Indian languages, pointing to Mughal records that bemoan in particular the incompetence of certain Europeans who claimed to have mastered Persian. Coryate doubtless attempted, as he had with the Bergamo dialect of Italian, to emulate the accents of the locals in their vernaculars. But his Somerset accent must have stubbornly stuck with him as he attempted to mouth Persian and Hindustani. He may have struggled with the body language required of him too. Modern Farsi is a highly gestural language: a hand under the chin is a sign of being fed up, covering one's eye with four fingers signifies 'you're welcome'. Mughal speakers of Persian also used their hands to express ideas and emotions. The Urdu performance art of dastangoi or storytelling employs an elaborate series of hand gestures that derive from Persian forms of public speaking: pointing, slashing the air, the respectful adaab that precedes the recitation of a she'r or line of poetry. Coryate must have observed such gestures in the performance of public petitioners at Jahangir's darbars. It's likely that he grafted some of them to the ensemble of oratorical gestures he had learned at Winchester and Gloucester Hall. In other words, Coryate's Persian was probably impure both in its sounds and its gestures, employing a mix of aptitudes that included elements of Elizabethan England, classical Greece and Rome, and Mughal Ajmer.

But perhaps Coryate's impure Persian was less rare or ridiculous a phenomenon than we might think. Because Persian had been imposed by Akbar as the official court language in order to provide a neutral lingua franca for his multicultural and multilingual court, it would have been spoken in a variety of accents, and in a variety of different forms with loan words and gestures from the courtiers' other mother tongues— Arabic, Turkic, Hindustani. In this, spoken Mughal Persian was no doubt like spoken modern Hindi, whose pronunciation and vocabulary vary greatly depending on one's other native tongues. It is not one uniform language but rather an assortment of khichdis that collate, to varying degrees, Sanskrit, Braj Bhasha, Persian, Urdu, English, and local dialects. Early Mughal Persian was likewise a multi-accented language diversely flavoured by different regional tongues and gestures.

◆

Coryate's circumstances changed when Sir Thomas Roe reached Ajmer in late 1615. The English fakir, no doubt looking to augment his standard of living, made sure to butter up someone he regarded as a potential patron. He met Roe and his party at the outskirts of Ajmer, greeting them, of course, with a theatrical oration. 'His exercise here or recreation', Roe observed tartly of Coryate in his journal, 'is making or repeating orations, especially of my Lady Hartford'. But the ambassador for the most part put up with Odd Tom, giving him shelter in his mud house and enjoying his madcap chatter as a diversion from his annoyances with India. It was probably from the relative comfort of Roe's house that Coryate wrote some of the surviving five letters back home to England that make up the bulk of what we know about his time in Ajmer.

Coryate clearly wrote these letters with an eye to enhancing his celebrity in England. Their language typifies the colourful bombast and whimsy of his orations. Again he shows a fondness for coining new words: he describes himself, for instance, not as a 'peripatetic' (which derives from the Greek peripatein, to walk around) but as a 'propatetic…that is, a walker forward on foot'. And again he employs a ripe rhetorical style, one clearly designed to play to a gallery of English readers familiar with the nonsense-spouting voice of the *Crudities*. In a letter addressed to the 'Right Worshipful Fraternity of Sireniacal Gentleman'—his old associates at the Mermaid Tavern—he thanks them for a gift they gave him just before his departure 'for the security of my future peregrination, concinnated by the pleasant wit of that inimitable artisan of sweet elegancy, the moiety of my heart.' What?

Such outlandish utterances were exactly what readers had come to expect of Coryate. And his publisher back in England sought to capitalize on what readers knew of Odd Tom. The title page to one of his published letters, 'Travailer for the English Wits and the Good of This Kingdom' (1616), mines the Coryate 'brand' made famous by the *Crudities*, resorting to the same theatrical display of his body that had characterized his European travelogue. Here the publisher responds to Coryate's express desire 'to have my picture expressed in my next book sitting upon an elephant'. Odd Tom sits imperially atop the animal, clutching his book and attired in English clothes. The image of the traveller on the title page duplicates Coryate's likeness from another woodcut in the *Crudities*, which depicts him—again in English garb— atop the Great Tun of Heidelberg, an enormous beer vat. The doubling of the image helps create the illusion of an unchanging English body, one that masters foreign cultures by sitting or standing atop their most distinctive objects.

But this illusion is belied by Coryate's letters. For there was little that was obviously English about Odd Tom or his body by the time he reached India. Robert Shirley may have recognized him in the deserts of eastern Persia as the renowned English travel writer. But when Coryate met Sir Thomas Roe just outside of Ajmer, he was—unlike Roe—wearing Asian clothes and he was speaking Persian. He had also been eating little. In other words, through both choice and circumstance, Coryate's body had been radically transformed by his journey across Asia. He himself insisted, as if to underscore the 'Travailer' of the title to his published letter, on the travail that his journey had demanded of him, distinguishing its fruits from other forms of knowledge purchased 'without labour or travel'. His was an embodied knowledge, he argued, derived from 'continual...practice'—that is, from the repetitions of bodily training, a transformative knowledge not unlike the muscle memory on which both the athlete and the actor depend. It was this 'continual practice' that allowed Coryate to speak to those he met without the mediation of a translator. He had also continued his earlier practice, noted by John Donne, of swerving boisterously between languages; as he entered Hindustan, he addressed people in a mixture of Persian, Arabic and, of all things, Italian. He was possessed of a committedly xenophiliac tongue and body.

Coryate's xenophilia did not extend to religion, however. While passing through Multan in Punjab, he delivered an oration to a Muslim who had accused him of being a giaour or infidel. Coryate, hot under the collar, denounced the prophet and Islam in general, claiming that the only true musulman (or one who submits to God) is a Christian, and that the Muslim was the true giaour. Coryate may have been saved from a sticky outcome because he delivered his oration in Italian; apparently the Muslim had been a galley slave in a Florentine ship, though one suspects that the preening Coryate spoke in this tongue largely so he could boast of his linguistic mastery to friends in England. But this was not the only anti-Islamic oration Coryate gave. According to Edward Terry, he also used his command of local languages to denounce a mu'ezzin in Agra. Apparently Coryate did so from the top of a building, on the opposite side of the town square from the mu'ezzin. In response to the latter's utterance of the Arabic Kalimah Tayyibah—lā ilāha illā-llāh, Muḥammadun rasūlu-llāh (there is no God but God, and Mohammed is the messenger of God)—Coryate supposedly intoned: lā ilāha illā-llāh, Hazrat Isa Ibn Allah (there is no God but God, and Jesus Christ is the son of God). This potentially inflammatory oration was disregarded by the people in the square below because they believed the English fakir to be mad, although Terry, with some justification, attributed Coryate's indifferent reception also to the deep tolerance of Mughal culture.

What to make of Coryate's two Islamophobic orations? They replicated his attempt some years earlier to persuade a Venetian rabbi, in Latin, to give up his Jewish beliefs and embrace Christ or face eternal damnation. The common theme here, beyond Coryate's seeming Christian zealotry, is his self-regarding pleasure in out-arguing a non-Christian in a foreign language (Italian, Hindustani vernacular, Latin). There is something of Little Jack Horner about this: Coryate crows 'what a good boy am I', and he does so less because of his Christian virtue and more because of his command of languages and rhetoric. What is particularly interesting about Coryate's pair of orations in Mughal Hindustan is how each adopts the words and rituals of his particular adversary. In the earlier oration from Multan, Coryate reversed the valences of musulman and giaour. In the later one from Agra, he adopted the formulas of the mu'ezzin in the public space—formulas of devotion, sung cadences, even gestures. In neither case was Coryate's theatre a synonym for deception or imposture: indeed, he clearly saw himself as locked in a struggle for the truth. But that struggle also meant his taking on the bodily skills of the other, of making his theatrical performance a deliberate khichdi of English and Indian aptitudes. This khichdi is apparent in what was perhaps Odd Tom's most startling oration in Hindustan.

◆

Coryate's linguistic skill gave him access to Jahangir of a kind that was denied to the exclusively anglophone Roe. This access underlines too how he had trained his body to become a histrionic, expressive medium legible to its Mughal audience. Dressed in the clothes of an Indian beggar, Coryate delivered a lengthy oration in Persian to Jahangir at Ajmer's Akbari Qila. Coryate transcribed the oration in one of his letters, supplementing it with a translation. It is a remarkable document. His Persian is somewhat garbled; but the opening words of Coryate's oration employ a stylized mode of address suited to his royal audience:

> Hazaret Aallum pennah salamet, fooker Daruces ve tehaungeshta hastam kemia emadam az wellagets door, ganne az mulk Inglizan:

ke kassanaion petheen mushacas cardand ke wellagets, mazcoor der akers magrub bood, kemader hamma iezzaerts dunmast.

Coryate translates these lines as follows:

> 'Lord protector of the world, all hail! I am a poor traveller and world-seer, who am come here from a far country, namely England, which ancient historians thought to have been situated in the farthest bounds of the West, and which is the queen of all the islands of the world.'

Which version of Coryate is speaking here? It's hard to imagine that Jahangir saw Coryate as anything other than a bizarre specimen from a small, distant country—and that Coryate, despite speaking in Persian, came across primarily as a mad Englishman. His Persian, at least as written here, is riddled with mistakes. Some of these may be chalked up to the incomprehension of the English typesetter. But others are clear evidence of Coryate's odd pronunciation and loopy grammar. As historian Sanjay Subrahmanyam has rightly pointed out, foreign attempts at speaking Persian were often received with derision by their Mughal audiences, and Coryate's oration may have been no exception. Everything about the speech—its strange sounds, its wonky syntax, its patriotic content—seems to point back to its speaker's Englishness. And Coryate was doubtless consciously attempting to draw here on his past experience in England as an antic orator in Prince Henry's court.

Yet Coryate's translation of his speech finesses how, in Persian, he had begun to characterize himself as Indian and in ways that took on the body languages of India. His term for himself is 'fooker Daruces', or fakir dervish, a wandering Sufi ascetic who begs for alms. Coryate's makeover as a Sufi fakir is all the more remarkable given his readiness elsewhere to inveigh against what he regarded as the heresies of Islam. This makeover was arguably an imposture for the sake of making money. But Coryate's self-identification as a fakir in his oration to Jahangir was more than an instance of self-serving fakery. It also gives some indication of how he had transformed his body during his time in Ajmer, following the model of the many poor fakirs outside the Dargah Sharif. Coryate, in other words, had learned not only the Persian spoken by the Mughals, he had also acquired the theatrical bodily practices—of scant clothing, respectful prostration, and pleading for alms—that he needed to master in order to be visible to Jahangir as a worthy supplicant. And he may have supplemented these gestures too with some of the body language of Persian orators and dastangos or storytellers. After all, his long speech was not just an oration: it was also a story about himself, about his travels and his travails. Sitting at his jharoka at the Akbari Qila, Jahangir was sufficiently impressed by the English fakir's oration that (according to Edward Terry) he immediately made him a gift of 100 silver rupees—a not insubstantial sum at the time, especially for a man who had lived on tuppence a day throughout his long Asian odyssey.

But Roe was not so pleased by the oration. Coryate complained that Roe 'nibbled at me', fearing that his performance 'might redound to the discredit of our nation, for one of our country to present himself in that poor and beggarly manner before the king, to crave money from him by flattery'. Roe doubtless feared that Coryate's bravura turn as a beggar had damaged the reputation of the English, not least by exposing Roe's own precarious standing as King James's unremunerated (and therefore financially struggling) ambassador. But one might also sense another element in Roe's response to the sight of an Englishman becoming Indian. Unlike Roe, who had quivered at the thought of wearing Khurram's culturally contaminating costumes, Coryate had consented to be transformed by Indian objects. And Roe's animus may have been provoked also by what he perceived to be a theatricality that paid homage to, rather than scorned, Marlowe's stage-Tamburlaine.

In his journal, Roe observes that Coryate's desire was to visit 'Samarkand in Tartarya, to kiss Tamburlaine's tomb'. One can hear a note of Protestant derision in Roe's language, which translates Coryate's desire into an act of religious and theatrical idolatry. Not surprisingly, Coryate describes the desire somewhat differently in his Persian oration to Jahangir, referring to Tamburlaine by his Mughal honorific, Sahib-i-Qirani or Lord of Conjunctions, which he renders as 'Saheb crawn' and, in his translation, as 'Lord of the Corners':

I have a great desire to see the blessed tomb of the Lord of the Corners for this cause: for that, when I was in Constantinople, I saw a notable old building in a pleasant garden near the said city, where the Christian emperor, Emanuel, made a sumptuous great banquet to the Lord of the Corners, after he had taken Sultan Bajazeth in a great battle that was fought near the city of Brusa, where the Lord of the Corners bound Sultan Bajazeth in golden fetters, and put him in a cage of iron.

Coryate here is referring to the historical Tamburlaine. But his imagination is clearly inspired by the theatrical one. The historical Timur took the Ottoman Sultan Beyezid captive; yet Coryate's story of Bajazeth's enslavement inside an iron cage is a later Arabic embellishment that would most likely have been unknown to Jahangir. It is also one of the most memorable scenes in Marlowe's play. So why was Coryate so curious to see the tomb of the stage-Tamburlaine's historical counterpart? Coryate evidently saw Tamburlaine not as a 'Mock king', as Roe did, but rather as a legitimate object of fascination. Is it too much to speculate that Coryate identified with Marlowe's Tamburlaine—less Tamburlaine the warrior and imperial conqueror of Asia, perhaps, than Tamburlaine the highly histrionic shape-shifter of humble provincial origins who got to perambulate around Asia delivering mighty lines?

This suggests again how much Coryate's improvisational performance as a fakir dervish drew on English as much as Indian forms of theatre. And this theatrical khichdi challenged the authentic English ethnicity in which Roe was so invested. If Roe's journal asserts a clear-cut difference between theatrically visible Mughal and largely invisible English ethnographer, Coryate was the fly in Roe's ointment. Not only did Coryate publicly flaunt his body in the Mughal court; he also made it over as a transnational body. Coryate himself insisted as much with his hyperbolic sign-off as 'the Hierosolymitan-Syrian-Mesopotamian-Armenian-Median-Parthian-Persian-Indian Legstretcher of Odcomb in Somerset'. On the one hand, this multi-hyphenated nickname might suggest a Tamburlaine-like accumulation of territories, reminiscent of the accumulation of stamps in a passport. On the other hand, it also suggests how Coryate's travel entailed opening up to numerous elements of the Asia he walked through and lived in—its terrain, its food, its clothes, its languages—and how he allowed them to fundamentally change him and his body.

If all Mughal Hindustan was a stage for Coryate, then, it wasn't simply an ethnographic spectacle to be watched and ridiculed as it was for Thomas Roe. His extraordinary histrionics in Ajmer suggest a conscious embrace of what Roe deplored. Coryate indeed believed that all the world's a stage. But to function in it and to profit from it, he enthusiastically leapt onto that stage and submitted to what Roe regarded as its contagious touch. Unlike Roe, the English fakir of Ajmer welcomed the theatricality of the Mughal court.

Coryate's contagious theatricality may strike us as liberating. It certainly allowed this poor firangi migrant to survive in Mughal Hindustan: his willingness to wear local clothes, speak local languages, and assume local gestures for his performances as a fakir in the galis of Ajmer and outside the Akbari Qila won him money, food, and even some friends. (He was a guest in Sambhar, for instance, of Mirza Zul-Qarnain, Bibi Juliana Firangi's son.) But India's contagious touch also proved unhealthy for Coryate: some time in 1617, an Indian virus or bacteria got inside him and sickened him terribly.

Roe was ill for most of his time in India. Coryate, by contrast, had arrived in good health (he boasted that 'I do enjoy at this time as pancratical and athletical a health as ever I did in my life'), and he stayed that way for a long time. Perhaps their relative healths had something to do with the route each took to Ajmer. Roe's passage to India was by sea, which exposed him to few people and therefore to few diseases: he was poorly prepared to deal with all the viral artillery India flung at him. Coryate arrived via the overland Silk Route, which meant he had repeated contact en route with foreign peoples, foods, and diseases—and probably acquired some immunity as a result. The sad irony is that Roe feared contamination, was persistently sick, yet somehow survived, while Coryate embraced foreign bodies, remained healthy, yet was suddenly struck down with a deadly disease. Sickness in India was and is inevitable, as it is anywhere. Yet as we'll see, his disease didn't need to have been mortal for him. So what was the tipping point that ultimately killed this firangi fakir who had shown such improvisational flair in keeping his belly fed and his body healthy?

We know precious little about the last act of Coryate's theatrical life. He kept copious records of his travels in Asia. But most of these have now disappeared, as he stored his papers at places he stayed at along the way: Roe quipped that he had written enough to keep England's stationers busy for years. Only a handful of the letters Coryate sent back to England have survived. The last of these is a note he wrote to his mother from Agra in October 1616. In it, he said he wouldn't write to her for another two years, partly because he was planning to be on the move again. We know he reached Surat, on foot, December 1617. What Coryate was doing in the intervening fourteen months is largely shrouded in mystery. From Agra he had tracked north to Delhi where, in Feroz Shah Kotla, he saw one of the Mauryan Emperor Ashoka's famous pillars, an experience that he later reported to Roe's pastor Edward Terry. He then seems to have gone up to the Himalayan foothills, to Hardwar in what is now Uttarakhand, to see the tributary of the Ganges River. After a long gap, he resurfaced in the fort city of Mandu, Madhya Pradesh, in November 1617.

Sir Thomas Roe and his pastor Edward Terry were also in Mandu at this time. They came in the retinue of Jahangir, who was using the city as a base for his skirmishes with the Deccan sultanate rulers, including Malik Ambar. Coryate was by this stage very ill. His affliction was probably dysentery, the bug of many a traveller to this day, probably contracted from contaminated water. Terry seems to have afforded Coryate some comfort in Mandu, looking after him in his quarters. He wrote extensive notes about Odd Tom during this time, which he later included in his published account of his travels in India. Terry praises him while recording many of his exploits, but he also notes his peccadillos and vulnerabilities: apparently Coryate was deeply hurt when he met an Englishman in Mandu who, having recently worked for King James, reported that the king had referred to Coryate as 'that fool' and expressed surprise that he was still living. Terry also notes how ill Odd Tom was: in one alarming incident after his arrival in Mandu, Coryate fainted in his arms. According to Terry, Coryate confided a fear that he would not survive to see England again. The fear proved prescient.

Coryate had fewer dealings with Roe in Mandu than he had in Ajmer. Roe took thirty-five rupees from Coryate, on the understanding that he could draw the same amount from the treasury of the English factory in Surat. Coryate had relied on Roe's charity often during his two years in Agra and Ajmer, despite the latter's occasional annoyances with the English fakir. I presume the indigent Coryate had stalked Roe all the way to Mandu in the hope of getting more money from him; the bill of exchange he received from Roe suggests that the ambassador was less inclined to be charitable. (Perhaps he was still carping over the 100 rupees Coryate had 'begged' from Jahangir.) The bill also makes clear that Coryate had Surat on his mind as his next destination. On the one hand this is a little surprising, as his express aim in coming to Asia—as Roe had observed, and as Coryate had admitted in his oration—was to visit Samarkand so he could see Tamburlaine's tomb. Surat was a stepping stone not to Samarkand but back to England. On the other hand, you never know when nostalgia can strike the most hardened traveller. By the end of 1617, perhaps, the ever-curious Coryate—who had opened himself up to the cultures, languages, and foods of India like few other visitors—had finally had enough and just wanted to go back to his mother's home.

Roe was to return to England in 1619. He had extracted a farman from Jahangir that granted the English trading privileges in Hindustan and laid the foundation for centuries of empire. After returning to England, Roe served as an ambassador to the Ottoman Empire, brokered peace between Sweden and Poland, and sponsored an expedition to the Arctic. In other words, he was one of the earliest architects of English global power. Coryate, however, represented something quite different. When he said goodbye to Roe in Mandu, he was also parting ways irrevocably with the trajectory of English colonial history.

Desperately ill, Coryate staggered off from Mandu to Surat. It is not a short walk: the approximately 400 kilometres between the two cities covers rocky north Deccan terrain and Gujarat marshlands that would test even a fit person like Malik Ambar. It was also teeming with bandits. It is hard to imagine how an underfed foreigner, tottering with hunger and fever and having to pause often to relieve himself, could have survived the journey. Yet somehow Coryate made it. On a cool winter evening in December of 1617, he was greeted by the rowdy men of the English East India Company factory in Surat. They demanded that their newly arrived countryman join them in a night devoted to the drinking of sack, a cheap fortified wine resembling sherry and much favoured by the English. Although Coryate was terribly unwell and not much of a tippler even at the best of times, he obliged them with a heavy night's carousing. By the next morning he was dead.

In other words, it wasn't Coryate's Indian dysentery that killed him; it was the English Company's alcohol. It is tragically ironic that, having opened up his body to so many Indian elements, both sustaining and sickening, Coryate was arguably killed instead by his reacquaintance with an English substance to which his body had become unaccustomed in Asia. Indian mixtures had always agreed with him more. That deadly night in Surat, the English fakir of Ajmer would have been much better served with a bowl of khichdi.

11 | SA'ID SARMAD KASHANI, THE YOGI-QALANDAR OF HYDERABAD AND DELHI

Visitors to Delhi's Jama Masjid, the subcontinent's largest mosque, must first pass at its entry the dargah of Hazrat Sarmad Shaheed, a much venerated saint who died in Delhi in 1660. One couldn't find a more typical north Indian shrine. Despite its sacredness, it is not a quiet place. The dargah abuts a chai shack, a biryani stall, and an open-air clinic next to the crowded Meena Bazaar. Hordes of shoppers and animals—stray dogs and goats—throng the space immediately outside it. The shrine too is usually teeming with people. Many of them leave flowers on Sarmad's tomb; their petals only add to the bright colours of the dargah. It is also the resting place of another seventeenth-century Indian Sufi saint, Hazrat Hare Bhare Shah, whose name means 'evergreen king': his side of the dargah is painted in a rich emerald hue, and pilgrims tie green threads to the jaali over his tomb. Sarmad's side is a deep blood-red, the colour of martyrdom, to commemorate his execution by the Mughal emperor Aurangzeb. Here pilgrims tie crimson-coloured threads, and they slip coins into a padlocked crimson box inscribed with the slogan 'PLEAS GIV GIFT FOR HAZRAT IN THIS BOX'. In a uniquely north Indian way, Sarmad's tomb is both a sacred and a profane site. The dargah is colourful but it is also dirty, crowded with people seeking favours from the saint for this and that; it smells of gutkha and sweat as much as it does of flowers and perfume.

Yet this Indian saint was born an Armenian Jew, possibly to parents of European origin, in a Persian city. His religious affiliation reflects this transnational heritage. A committed scholar of the Hebrew Torah, his spiritual path also meandered between Islam and Hinduism. In India he was regarded as both a qalandar, a spiritually elevated Sufi infused with a deep, intoxicating love of God, and a yogi, an ascetic who had reached an elevated state of awareness and renounced all worldly attachments. Sarmad's religious identity has been commandeered by the official Sunni Islam of the Jama Masjid, by a modern Hindu sect known as the Rama Soami Satsang, and by a handful of scholars who are convinced that he remained fully immersed in mystic Judaism all his life. Attempts to nail Sarmad to one religious tradition, however, must contend with his own self-characterization as 'a follower of the Furqan, a priest, a monk, a Jewish rabbi, an infidel, and a Muslim'.

Sarmad's border-crossing identities might seem exemplary of the golden age of Mughal syncretism. This age is commonly supposed to have enjoyed its last gasp under Shah Jahan's son Dara Shikoh, whom Sarmad served as a spiritual advisor. But Sarmad's multiple identities are a far cry from the state-mandated syncretism we have seen in Mughal painting, architecture, jewellery, music and dance. Sarmad typifies a more grass-roots cosmopolitanism, one that we might characterize as the syncretism of the Silk Route and its Indian offshoots. This cosmopolitanism needed no Akbar to dream it into existence. Instead it emerged from a culture of trade, one very different from that of European colonialism. The latter sought to accumulate Indian wealth in ways that demanded European state control. By contrast, the Silk Route trading culture was stateless: it was grounded in face-to-face negotiation and exchange between people of different ethnicities, speaking different tongues. As we will see, this was very much the milieu in which Sarmad operated—even as a saint supposedly divorced from the vanities of the material world.

The Silk Route trading culture definitively shaped Sarmad's unusually syncretic spiritualism. His movement into India, however, was driven by a more individual factor: his sexuality. Sarmad's border-crossings took place on the Central Asian highways of the Silk Route and its Indian byways. But the fuel in his tank was a high-octane love—a love that had both a spiritual and an erotic dimension. Once he reached the subcontinent, all his movements were inspired by his love for another man in whom he saw khuda or God. And these movements prompted him, in theatrical fashion, to change the way in which he used his body. In the manner of an Indian holy man, Sarmad gave up wearing clothes and grew his hair and fingernails. This decision won him deep veneration throughout the subcontinent, from Thatta and Lahore to Hyderabad and Delhi. But it also led ultimately to his death.

So who exactly was this firangi who wandered naked across India?

◆

We know very little about the first forty years of Hazrat Sarmad Shaheed's life. It is only after his arrival in the subcontinent that he enters the historical record. And even the various references to him from this time are full of partisan, often conflicting information about his past. Most of what we know comes from Mughal sources written after his death: these are torn between wide-eyed hagiography and politically motivated opprobrium. The two Europeans who wrote about him during his lifetime are just as one-eyed, dismissing Sarmad as an atheist (which he wasn't) and a charlatan (which is a matter of debate).

Most Mughal commentaries on Sarmad's life, worshipful as well as critical, claim that he was born a Jew of Armenian origin in about 1590. A handful of others assert that he was born a Christian. A poet in Aurangzeb's court, Sher Khan Lodi, says that Sarmad's parents came from 'Faranghistan', i.e. Christian Europe. The confusion may be due to the fact that Armenia, because of its majority Christian population, was regarded in Mughal India as a firangi nation. But a small community of Jews had lived in Armenia for centuries. Some were of Assyrian origin, others of European Ashkenazi ancestry. Possibly Sarmad's parents were the latter. If Sarmad had an Armenian or a Hebrew name, we don't know what it was: Mughal writers usually call him Mohammed Sa'id Sarmad Kashani. This name suggests two things. First, at some point he had converted to Islam, taking the name of the Prophet as well as the names Sa'id, Arabic for 'happy', and Sarmad, Arabic for 'everlasting'. And second, Sarmad had lived in Kashan, a town in central Persia near Isfahan. He may have been born there; the Ottoman and Safavid wars of the sixteenth century had displaced many Armenians to Persian cities. But it is also possible that Kashan was simply one of the many cities Sarmad called home during a lifetime of wandering. After spending a few years in Lahore much later in his life, he came to be addressed in some Mughal records as Sa'id Sarmad Lahori.

With its mild climate and many orchards, Kashan was a favourite holiday location for the Safavid emperors. Shah Abbas had built there a large pleasure garden that he intended to be a vision of paradise. But Kashan was also a notable centre of commerce, well-known for its carpets, textiles, and silks as well as its precious stone emporiums. Like other cities of central Asia such as Bukhara and Isfahan, it had attracted a large community of Jewish merchants. The community numbered into the thousands well into the twentieth century. Indeed, the Jews of Kashan were so rooted in the town that they developed their own distinctive dialect of Persian. At the time of Sarmad's birth, they prospered not just financially but also socially: Shah Abbas's personal physician was a Kashani Jew named Mollah Masih. And the community was large and wealthy enough to build thirteen synagogues. Perhaps it was in one of these that the young Sarmad studied Hebrew and the Torah and acquired, by his own admission, the status of a rabbi. Despite the religious freedom the Kashani Jews enjoyed, however, there was also an undercurrent of intolerance towards them: during periods of economic crisis, businesses in Kashan run by Jews—coffee-houses, fur-trading outlets, brothels—were closed down as 'pollutants'. For seven years in the mid 1600s, Kashan's Jews were even made to convert to Islam. Sarmad had left Kashan by this point, but the periodic outbursts of anti-Jewish sentiment may have played a part in his conversion and migration.

Whether Sarmad came to Islam voluntarily or through coercion, he seems to have continued to work in the trade of many Armenian Jews—as a merchant, specializing by some accounts in precious stones and ceramics. And the Islam to which he converted was most likely of a rather unorthodox stripe, one that could have appealed to a Jewish scholar whose conventional training in Torah was accompanied by an abiding interest in philosophy and mysticism. According to one record, Sarmad was a follower of Sadruddin Muhammad ibn Shirazi, better known as Mulla Sadra, the leading Iranian philosopher of the early seventeenth century. Sadra's teaching synthesized esoteric Shi'i theology with classical Greek philosophy and Sufi metaphysics. It also engaged elements of mystical Christian and Jewish thought, particularly on the cultivation of the soul's potential. If Mulla Sadra's philosophy was the young Sarmad's spiritual compass, it would have introduced him to an Islam that was committedly cosmopolitan and syncretic.

Sarmad also became highly literate in Persian poetry: he was a self-professed devotee of the *Rubaiyat* of Omar Khayyam. The son of a tent-maker—which is the meaning of the name 'Khayyam'—Omar was born in Persia in the eleventh century. He was a brilliant mathematician, writing a book on algebra, and he dabbled in astronomy. But it as a poet that Omar Khayyam is best known. In his *Rubaiyat*, the plural form of the Arabic ruba'i, a type of rhymed quatrain of verse, he combined elements of Sufi and Platonic philosophy. Khayyam's poems are brilliant exercises in spiritual contemplation. But, like Mulla Sadra's philosophy, they are also evidence of the extraordinarily cosmopolitan culture of medieval Persia. This cosmopolitanism owed as much to the mingling of Persian, Arabic, Greek and Jewish ideas as to the exchange of commodities along the trading artery of the Silk Route. The route also contributed to the spread of the ghazal, the tightly structured, rhymed love poetry that expressed the exquisite pain of loss and separation. Transmitted partly by wandering Sufis and partly by travelling merchants across Central and South Asia, the ghazal's distinctive preoccupation with separation resonated in particular for people who had left their homes. This was the culture into which Sarmad was initiated as both trader and scholar.

Sarmad's business took him, in approximately 1632, to Thatta, near the Indus River in what is now the Pakistani province of Sindh. We have already encountered Thatta: it was some fifteen years later the home of Gilbert Harrison, the renegade English East India Company factory worker. The river-city was at that point part of the Mughal Empire. It was also a Sufi cultural centre: its bakhshi or official scribe in the early 1630s, Mohammed Beg, was a reputed Sufi poet, and ghazal recitals were common there among not just its Muslim but also its Hindu inhabitants. It was here, one night, that Sarmad attended a mushaira and heard the performance of a ghazal by a young teenaged boy named Abhai Chand, a Hindu of the vaishya caste. Although the account of the evening is now swathed in many layers of myth, it was clearly one of those events that changed everything for both men.

This is how legend reports the evening and its aftermath. Abhai Chand sang a ghazal in a beautiful, clear voice; and Sarmad, enraptured by what he heard and saw, fell head over heels in love with the boy. Abhai Chand at first rebuffed Sarmad's advances. But the Kashani businessman was an effective negotiator and evidently knew how to strike a deal. He worked on Abhai Chand's parents, who were initially horrified by Sarmad's interest in their son. The father hid the boy and alerted the authorities. Sarmad responded by taking off all his clothes and sitting completely naked at the parents' doorstep for several days and nights. Astonishingly, this seems to have convinced Abhai Chand's parents that Sarmad's love was pure. They concluded that he would be a good mentor to their son and permitted Sarmad to take him away, on the condition that he had him properly educated.

The experience was to prove transformative for both Sarmad and Abhai Chand. In Sarmad's company the boy adopted the life of a mendicant beggar. Sarmad too was never the same. From the time he undressed outside Abhai Chand's house, he refused to wear clothes; he also allowed his hair and fingernails to grow. What might these changes tell us about Sarmad and Abhai Chand's love, their religious convictions, and the cultures of northern India?

◆

For most westerners, the story of how Abhai Chand's parents were persuaded to give up their son to Sarmad begs two questions. What would possess them to believe that a nude stranger-cum-stalker at their

JONATHAN GIL HARRIS

doorstep was a more worthy partner for their child than a clothed one? And why would they consent to a seemingly erotic relation between their son and a much older man? The story of Sarmad's stripping outside Abhai Chand's house in Thatta might not be historically true—it smacks of myth-making. But a successful myth presumes a set of values shared by its believers. And in the case of Sarmad's story, these values are grounded in the distinctive syncretic religious culture of seventeenth-century Sindh and, indeed, Mughal Hindustan and the Deccan. Although this syncretism was connected—via the ghazal sung by Abhai Chand—to the Silk Route cultures of West and Central Asia, it also took a local subcontinental form. Sarmad's theatrical display of his naked body and his refusal to cut his hair and fingernails were distinctively Indian forms of bodily transformation.

Why would Abhai Chand's parents regard Sarmad's nakedness as praiseworthy rather than creepy? Most likely because they were accustomed to a subcontinental tradition in which holy men shun clothing. The figure of the holy yogi, attaining enlightenment by refusal of all material possessions—including clothes—is a set piece of various Hindu and Buddhist traditions. Nakedness is simultaneously *both* a symbol *and* a physical realization of the yogi's rejection of worldly vanities. A text of Tibetan Buddhism, for instance, teaches that rigpa—the equivalent of the Hindu vidya, or the meditative knowledge that acknowledges the emptiness of self and other—'is like your naked body, and dualistic mind is like clothing. Throw away all clothing and remain naked. ...Without imagining, without thinking of anything, awareness is primordially empty and rootlessness. Whoever sees this is a true yogi.' This passage exemplifies the way in which nakedness was both a symbol and a committed way of life for certain Buddhists.

Many Hindu holy men too would wander naked through the subcontinent. Naked yogis still can be seen in many parts of the country, especially in the vicinity of Varanasi and the Ganga. They include ascetic mendicant beggars from the Bairagi communities throughout India and the Gosain community from Gorakhpur, Uttar Pradesh. The Bairagi mendicants worship Vishnu; carrying a bairaga or crutch-like stick, they often wear little more than a dot on the forehead and a strip of a loin-cloth, though many rub their bodies with the ashes of cow dung. The Gosain mendicants are devotees of Shiva, who was supposed to have appeared on earth as a naked beggar of ashy complexion. To honour the god, they too rub their naked bodies with the ashes of cow dung;

they also grow their hair into matted dreadlocks and don't cut their fingernails. Sarmad seems to have adopted the bodily practices of these Hindu mendicants, as did Abhai Chand. In the words of one Mughal commentator, Abhai Chand 'khakastar nahin shuda' (took to sitting on the ashes).

In his negotiations with Abhai Chand's parents, Sarmad took on the trappings of Hindu yogi behaviour in a way that lent legitimacy to his love. His nakedness was legible to them not as an erotic provocation but as an embrace of spiritual purity. This embrace was at odds with orthodox Muslim behaviour: as one Mughal record puts it, 'Abhai's lover has withdrawn himself from every worldly object, wealth and riches. He has dropped even his clothes and ignoring the shariat, he has begun to live in the nude.' But I doubt Abhai Chand's parents responded just as devout Hindus of the vaishya caste to Sarmad's canny self-identification as a yogi. To accept the love of an older man for their young son, it is almost certain that they understood Sarmad's self-presentation also from the perspective of a Sufi tradition that was widespread in Sindh, northern India, and the Deccan.

There are many instances of same-sex love between men in Hindu mythology, literature and culture: Vishnu assumes the form of a woman, Mohini, and is impregnated by Shiva; Krishna and Arjuna enjoy a special intimacy in the Mahabharata and various other related Puranas; in southern legends, Vishnu and Shiva's son Ayyappa is inseparable from a Muslim pirate named Vavar. The guru-disciple relation could also acquire an erotic dimension: the sixteenth-century Oriya poet-mystic Jagannath Das fell in love with his teacher, Sri Chaitanya, who saw Jagannath as a manifestation of Radha and himself as an incarnation of Krishna. But the love in which an older man cherishes the beauty of male youth as a manifestation of the divine is a hallmark of Sufi religious and erotic traditions. Although Sarmad's nakedness was unorthodox for a Muslim, the love that inspired him to shed his clothes conformed much more to Sufi than to Hindu same-sex traditions.

Arabic and Persian poetry has had a long-standing homoerotic dimension. The eighth-century Baghdadi poet Abu Nuwas, for example, wrote explicit panegyrics about the beauty of boys. In the Sufi ghazals of medieval Persia and India, same-sex attraction was transformed into a vehicle of religious love: the beloved was synonymous with God, and separation from him was synonymous with separation from the divine—even though that separation was in and of itself a spur to religious devotion. So the thirteenth-century poet and mystic Amir Khusro mourned his teacher Nizamuddin Chishti's death in language that was both erotic and religious: 'Looking at the empty bed, I weep day and night/ Every moment I yearn for my beloved, cannot find a moment's peace.' Indian Sufi tales also spoke of the love of an older man for a beautiful younger boy in a way that grafted the spiritualism of Khusro to the eroticism of Abu Nuwas, building on the Greek Platonic understanding of earthly beauty as a manifestation of divinity. We have already encountered the story of Mahmud, the tenth-century sultan of Ghazni, and his erotic captivation by his slave-boy Ayaz. Mahmud was represented as an exemplary Muslim ruler, and his love for Ayaz a salutary recognition of divine beauty. The story of Mahmud and Ayaz was popular in Sindh, which was part of Mahmud's historical territory. It is likely that the story was known to Abhai Chand's parents.

They would have been familiar too with the figure of the Sufi qalandar. The qalandar, like the yogi, is a wandering ascetic who has reached a superior spiritual state. However this state prompts the qalandar not to nakedness but rather to wearing a coarse woollen cloth known as a suf. The state is distinguished too by the qalandar's ecstatic love, expressed in whirling dances and in music, particularly qawwali songs. It is also repeatedly expressed in poetry and lyric form through metaphors of intoxication by wine: to feel ecstasy, to be in the presence of the divine, is akin to an experience of drunkenness. This gives some indication of how, for the qalandar, the spiritual is less a retreat from the body than an embrace of its ecstatic experiences as portals to divinity. And that is why the experience of erotic attraction could so easily be incorporated into the language of spiritual longing and striving. It also means that Sufi poetry keeps blurring the line between the holy and the profane, as if they were not opposites but simply part of the same revolving turnstile. This is a feature too of the love Sarmad described in his poems for Abhai Chand. As one of his couplets has it, 'I do not know whether under the heaven my God is Abhai Chand, or someone else'. It is little wonder that, to those who wished to clearly separate the material and the spiritual, Sarmad's spiritualism and its mixture of the sacred and the profane was heretical.

But Sarmad's self-presentation as an Indian holy man not only mixed the sacred and the profane. As this brief summary has made clear, it also mixed the Hindu and the Sufi. Indeed, Sarmad pointedly combined yogi and qalandar traditions in a Persian verse he wrote many years later. In this quatrain, Sarmad recalls the experience of falling in love with Abhai Chand:

A luscious beauty has vanquished me
His eyes with their two goblets have robbed me of myself
He fell in my arms and I am in his quest
An extraordinary robber has stripped me naked.

Here we can see Sarmad code-switching—swerving between naked yogi and intoxicated qalandar. This matches the linguistic switches he must have performed in Thatta, where he probably had to move between Persian and Sindhi. And subsequently, in his education of Abhai Chand, he must have moved between Hebrew, Persian and other Indian dialects. Indeed, their next few destinations would have required the yogi–qalandar Muslim Jew and his Hindu Sufi beloved to keep swerving over many borders of language, religion, and culture.

◆

The couple led a migratory life. Over the next twenty-eight years, Sarmad and Abhai Chand changed their location several times. It is notable that, on each occasion, they chose to move to a city rather than a rural setting. It seems likely that Sarmad spent some time living as an ascetic in a forest; but for all their renunciation of material possessions and their embrace of mendicant bodily techniques from more rural Indian settings, he and Abhai Chand repeatedly gravitated to urban spaces. These were trading spaces in which different cultures, religions, and languages met and mingled. In other words, even if Sarmad abandoned the merchant career that took him to Thatta, he remained for the rest of his life very much a man of the mercantile culture that had produced him—inhabiting the border-zones that brought people from different backgrounds face to face with each other. And the two lovers themselves physically embodied the border-zones they inhabited, in ways that illuminate the urban cosmopolitanism of the subcontinent as much as that of Persia and the Silk Route.

Sarmad and Abhai Chand left Thatta in 1634 and went to Lahore, which was then still the official capital of the empire. During their time there, the royal Mughal historian Mu'tamad Khan—author of the latter parts of the *Tuzuk-i-Jahangiri*—met Sarmad in a garden. Mu'tamad Khan praised the relationship between Sarmad and Abhai Chand, and especially the effect of the older man on his younger charge: 'As the love of Sarmad was pure and chaste, it produced a miraculous effect on the boy who cut off his connection with his parents and joined Sarmad.' He was not entirely impressed by Sarmad himself, observing that 'he spoke too much'. The 'pure and chaste' man's physical appearance also seems to have given him pause: Mu'tamad Khan found Sarmad sitting 'naked, covered with thick, crisped hair all over the body and long nails in his fingers'. But Mu'tamad Khan was impressed that 'he spoke correct Persian and was a poet'. As this suggests, he regarded Sarmad the naked yogi as something of a low-brow theatrical spectacle and Sarmad the shayar (or Persian poet) as a man of considerable cultural refinement.

Mu'tamad Khan—a man of Persian letters—attempted to separate these two versions of Sarmad. But they were clearly interrelated, facets of his ongoing commitment to drawing points of connection across borders of religion, culture and language. While in Lahore, Sarmad seems to have made Abhai Chand submit to a course of rigorous instruction in diverse languages and comparative religion. Sarmad imparted to Abhai Chand his training in Hebrew and Torah—as a rabbinical student in Kashan, he probably had committed most of the latter to memory. Sarmad also trained his student, who would doubtless have been a native Sindhi speaker, in classical Persian. The boy from Thatta acquired some skill in the latter: he himself became a shayar. Indeed, a couplet sometimes thought to be by Sarmad has also been attributed to Abhai Chand. It is a self-description that reveals a committed rootlessness, one appropriate to both men's religious training and their peregrinations in space and thought:

I follow the Koran as much as I follow Torah and Talmud
But I am neither a Jew nor a Christian nor a Muslim.

Indeed, Abhai Chand went on to become a translator of some note: he is cited in the *Dabistan-i Mazahib* or School of Religions, a work of comparative religion from the middle of the seventeenth century, for his rendition of the Hebrew Torah into Persian. (It is in the *Dabistan* that the above couplet appears.)

Sometime in the late 1630s or 1640s, Sarmad and Abhai Chand moved south to the Deccan sultanate of Golconda. Here they lived in the new city of Hyderabad. It had been built in 1591 at the request of Mohammad Quli Qutb Shah, the sultan of Golconda, by his chief minister, Mir Mohammad Momin. The city was designed by architects from Persia; at its centre was the Charminar, an impressive four-towered building from whose sides four long, straight boulevards led in the four directions of the sultanate. The architects also filled the city with green gardens designed to replicate heaven on earth. Indeed, the sultan's palace included a fountain intersected by four channels—a re-creation of the Garden of Eden. But Mohammad Quli named the city not for Paradise but for his favourite wife, a Hindu village girl named Bhagmati who received the title Hyder Mahal—Lion Palace.

Hyderabad quickly became a major political, economic and cultural force. The Golconda Sultanate, already rich because of its diamond mines, greatly increased its wealth through the conquest of much of the old Vijayanagar Empire in what is now Karnataka, all the way to Chennai. Even as it expanded, Golconda was a tribute kingdom within the Mughal Empire; in 1636, the teenaged Sultan Abdullah Qutb Shah had signed a deed of submission to Shah Jahan, and Aurangzeb was appointed viceroy of the Deccan. Despite this, the culture of Hyderabad remained strongly non-Mughal. Thanks to its design and the dominance of the Shi'i sect, it felt much more like a Persian city. And it was Persian in a way that a Silk Route trader would have recognized: open to and respectful of other cultural traditions. Kathak dance was practiced in Hyderabad, but the Qutb Shahis also lent support to local village dance forms such as Kuchipudi. The court sponsored mushairas of Persian poetry, but Telugu lyric also prospered. Vestiges of Golconda's cosmopolitan culture remain in modern Hyderabad where signs are written in four languages—Telugu, Urdu, Hindi and English.

Adding to Hyderabad's cosmopolitanism was a huge influx of traders from all over the world. The French traveller Jean de Thévenot, who visited Hyderabad in 1666, wrote that 'there are many Franks in the kingdom'. By this he meant firangi merchants from diverse nations: Portugal, Holland, and England as well as France. Sarmad and Abhai Chand lived in Hyderabad about the same time as one such French merchant, Jean-Baptiste Tavernier, who visited Golconda repeatedly from the 1630s to the 1660s in search of valuable stones from its famed diamond mines. Tavernier loved Hyderabad. He marvelled at the Charminar as well as Hyderabad's wide boulevards and bridges. He also noted, without any hint of moral condemnation, that the city boasted an unusually high number of 'public women'—20,000 by his reckoning. And he was impressed by how they plied their trade in concert with toddy-retailers, who got potential customers in the mood for love.

What prompted Sarmad and Abhai Chand to move to Hyderabad? The city's reputation for 'great liberty'—a liberty that could be embraced by not just public women but also a naked yogi–cum–qalandar and his male lover—may have been one factor. Hyderabad's cosmopolitanism may have been another. This extended not just to the city's trading cultures but also to its scholarly community. It was in Hyderabad that Abhai Chand and Sarmad seem to have begun their contribution to the *Dabistan-i-Mazahib*, the comparative study of South Asian religions. The book was composed by its anonymous author in about 1655; with remarkable tolerance, it describes Persian religions (including Zoroastrianism), Hinduism, Jainism, early Sikhism, Tibetan Buddhism, Judaism, Christianity, Islam, Hellenistic pantheism, Sufism, and Akbar's Din-i-Ilahi. The book's section on Judaism contains a few poems by Sarmad, portions of Abhai Chand's Persian translation of the Torah, and a brief biography of Sarmad. That these contributions were written while the couple was living in Hyderabad is underscored by a quatrain penned by Sarmad in praise of Shaikh Muhammad Khan, Abdullah Qutb Shahi's chief minister. The section on Judaism also notes Sarmad's prescient predictions about the Shaikh's imminent death and a Golconda functionary's promotion to a position in the Mughal Empire. All this suggests that Sarmad had earned a reputation in Hyderabad as a seer, one that had afforded him access to Golconda's corridors of power. Whether the reputation had been acquired in Lahore and prompted an invitation to Golconda, or whether it had been acquired in Hyderabad over a period of years, we cannot be sure.

It is clear from the *Dabistan* that, by the 1650s, Sarmad had also acquired a considerable reputation as a poet. While in Hyderabad, he seems to have honed his skill in writing Persian rubaiyat in the manner of Omar Khayyam. Many of these quatrains were destroyed during Sarmad's own lifetime, much to his chagrin. However, more than 300 still survive. Most are still in print to this day, diversely collated in various editions. They are read largely as inspirational poems full of Sufi or yogic wisdom. But they also offer remarkable insights into the bodily experiences of a migrant merchant to the subcontinent. In short, they not only hint at the extent to which Sarmad had fully embraced the physical as well as spiritual habits of an Indian yogi-qalandar by the time he left Hyderabad. They also underscore how, despite his Indian makeover, he retained the disposition of a Silk Route merchant.

◆

Sarmad's rubaiyat are a challenge to any reader. It is difficult to pin down exactly what or whom they refer to. And their meaning is persistently slippery: Sarmad deliberately uses open-ended, cryptic language. It is no surprise that the four English translations I have consulted vary wildly in their renderings of the rubaiyat. The interpretative challenges Sarmad's quatrains pose are, however, typical of Sufi poetry. Often the quatrains are quasi-musical variations on a general theme rather than singular descriptions of unique individuals or events. Like a jazz musician, Sarmad will work on a motif over and over again, stretching it this way and that to give it full suppleness and suggestiveness. Meanings appear not instantly, but over the course of reading the rubaiyat. Still, through the seductive mist of generalities flicker the shadows of some very distinctive biographical experiences.

Some of these experiences seem directly to involve Abhai Chand. In one ruba'i, Sarmad writes:

> The curly hair of my Beloved enchants me;
> I did not plan it; it was my good fortune.
> I am imprisoned in the whirlpool of curly hair;
> I am in fetters because of my own evil mind.

Here we seem to glimpse the particularity of the Beloved's curly hair. Yet this vivid image, which may evoke Abhai Chand's own ringlets, also blurs into the general: curly hair is a common sign of beauty and divinity. The Buddha, for example, is often described as having curly hair. This quatrain also turns on a more general paradox typical of Sufi poetry. For all that the Beloved 'enchants' Sarmad, and that his enchantment is an unplanned 'good fortune', the delight the poet takes in his Beloved is also an imprisonment that bespeaks an 'evil mind'. Liberation and bondage, sacred and profane, particular and general blur into each other. The embrace of paradox is a hallmark of Sufism, in which the seeming differences of the world are illusions that veil a divine oneness.

Paradox is at the heart of another quatrain that seems to glance at Abhai Chand:

> O Sarmad! Thou hast worked havoc in attacking
> Organized religion. Thou hast sacrificed
> Thy religion for a Man whose eyes are red with intoxication.
> All thy wealth hast thou thrown at the feet of the Master, who is
> an idol-worshipper.

Here Sarmad seems to lament his love for a red-eyed 'Man' who has dragged him from the respectability of organized religion. Presumably this organized religion is Islam; the offending 'Man', who has taken all of Sarmad's wealth, is an 'idol-worshipper' or Hindu. Yet the paradox here is that this lamentable fall can also be read as a spiritual ascension. The quatrain hints at Sufism's debt to Platonic philosophy, which sees material beauty as a manifestation of a higher divinity. Here the particular 'Man' for whom Sarmad has given up his wealth, religion and respectability is 'the Master'. This Master is both an earthly teacher and a divinity incarnated in human form. And if his eyes are 'red with intoxication', it is because of a state that can be interpreted simultaneously as the profligate stupor of a drunk and the divine ecstasy of the enlightened Sufi.

This paradoxical coupling of the profane and the sacred is arguably the dominant theme of Sarmad's rubaiyat. A first reading might lead one to conclude that Sarmad was a committed tippler. Every second quatrain mentions wine and its effects: he exhorts his readers to drink 'big draughts of wine', he vows he will never set foot 'out of the Wine-shop', he insists that 'The Cup and the Wine-flask reveal Reality and the treasures of Knowledge'. Sarmad's valorization of wine is not surprising, perhaps, for a man who grew up only a few hundred kilometres from Shiraz. The city's wine—Shirazi sharaab—was much coveted by Mughal and Deccan aristocrats from Lahore to Hyderabad. But as always in Sarmad's poetry, the profane is a portal to the sacred. Wine is for him, as it is for many Sufi poets, both a physical substance and a metaphor for the medium of divine inspiration. Indeed, at times he draws a sharp distinction between divine and worldly wine. The former is a means to spiritual advancement—'with Wine Divine my heart is set ablaze'. The latter, however, 'gives no real intoxication, only terrible reactions'. As the primary source of Sarmad's intoxication, the beloved Abhai Chand straddles the disdained worldly wine and the longed for Wine Divine that 'will make you long to meet the Beloved'—i.e. the divinity manifested in the beloved's material form.

Everywhere in his rubaiyat Sarmad paradoxically disdains the things of the material world yet praises them as gateways to the divine. And it is here that we see not only his yogi-qalandar disposition but also his mercantile sensibility. He repeatedly denounces the pursuit of material wealth: 'The bird that leaves the sky and eats the grains/ Gets caught in the wily trapper's net', which he glosses as 'Wealth brings not happiness, but many troubles, and possibly a transitory joy'. Yet trade converts commodities into new possibilities, a suggestive metaphor for the translation of worldly possessions into divinity. Like the good merchant he was before his transformation in Thatta, Sarmad understands the value of shrewd capital investment and management:

> Neither fancies nor pleasures here are permanent.
> All thy life wert thou in search of the perishable,
> Now only a few breaths are left, thy only capital.
> My friend, waste them not; thou has not as yet made any gain.

In mercantile fashion, Sarmad sees the material things of this world—here, the breath—as 'capital' that can produce spiritual profit. Sarmad the thrifty merchant here blurs into Sarmad the shrewd seeker of spiritual gain. His worldly love for Abhai Chand is another instance of capital investment that yields the dividend of divinity:

> I am a hundred times thankful that my Friend is pleased;
> Ever so gracious is He, He showers Nectar on me every moment,
> Have I lost anything by loving Him?
> The bargain of love I have made is gain everlasting.

Later on, reworking this theme, he notes that 'The bargain's done, but of the profit I am unaware,/ For love counts not the cost nor the profit'. Sarmad qualifies here the profit-motive that lurks in many of his mercantile references. Yet this still shows how ideas of bargain and profit are ubiquitous throughout Sarmad's rubaiyat. Even when at his most didactic about his spiritual aims, he resorts to the language of the merchant: 'Seekest thou peace and riches in both worlds?/ His contemplation is the quickest way to Wealth/ …Seclusion is a pearl of greatest price, it gives thee peace and bliss;/ And in seclusion thou wilt find Secret Treasure'. Thatta and Hyderabad could take the merchant out of Kashan. But they couldn't take the merchant out of the Kashani.

Sarmad's mercantile sensibility was hardly an incongruous relic of his previous life. It was, rather, the enabling ground of his pluralistic yogi-qalandar disposition. It was also familiar to Abhai Chand, the scion of a vaishya trading family. We should remember that the mercantile world of Sarmad and Abhai Chand was very different from the commerce of today. In the commercial hubs of Kashan and Thatta, the two men were initiated into a culture that depended not on fixed prices but rather negotiation and barter, not on one-time anonymous sales but rather enduring reciprocal bonds, not on one language of trade but rather a Babel of tongues that needed to be accommodated. And this culture would have found a lively counterpart in the Deccan trading cosmopolis of Hyderabad. To insist on one's own unique way of doing business—as colonialism and modern capitalism tends to—was to commit violence against the plurality of interests and needs that the merchant must acknowledge. Perhaps this helps explain Sarmad's enduring mistrust of organized religion. In commercial terms, it is a closed shop whose traders will not do business with others. If the Silk Route was a cosmopolitan culture premised on accommodating differences then so too was Sarmad's spiritual sensibility. As he says to his beloved: 'Thou art a merchant of Love, not a peddler of piety.'

And that is why Sarmad speaks against piety in all its institutionalized Indian forms. He criticizes both Hindu holy men ('O sadhu, this robe of thine covers the sacred thread;/ 'Tis a deception involving struggle unending') and Muslim imams ('O Mullah, throw this long woollen robe/ From off thy shoulders, and free thyself from the anxious burden of faith and piety'). He inveighs against those who 'search for happiness… in temples, mosques and churches' and insists that 'I care not for the rosary or the sacred thread… Nor do I wear this long woollen robe.' Yet he can also identify with Mohammed and his experience of the shab-kadar or night of enlightenment ('He who was an Emperor of Persia and Arabia,/ Has in his grace given me a glimpse of His beauty') *and* with the Tantric insistence that the body is one with the universe ('Thy heart is like an ocean… If thou could'st dive there wouldst thou dive into the seven heavens,/ Through the ocean of thy body'). Which is to say: he mixes and matches from various religious traditions. In one memorable quatrain, Sarmad talks about how he 'came to Islam and got away from Judaism', but then 'became a disciple of Ram and Lakshman'. Two different translations of Sarmad's rubaiyat published through the auspices of the Radha Soami Satsang—a monotheistic sect of Hinduism that emphasises meditation and attention to inner sounds and lights—place this quatrain at the end of the quatrain sequence, as if it represented a final Hindu apotheosis for Sarmad. Yet this reading is something of a mystification. Throughout his time in India, Sarmad kept moving between elements of Islam, Hinduism, and other religions, never settling with finality on one.

This movement was of a piece with Sarmad's nakedness. We in a racial age are inclined to locate the 'truth' of a body in its skin colour. The thought of a naked firangi in India is startling not just because of the image of nudity. It is also because his nudity would seem to broadcast his foreignness at the level of his flesh. Yet his nakedness didn't advertise an identity—quite the opposite. In the age of khil'at, group identity was arguably grounded far less in skin colour than in clothes: wearing a thread, or a rosary, or a woollen mantle signified allegiance to one particular religious truth and identity. Sarmad refuses any such allegiance when he writes that 'Sometimes I am pious; at others I am a master drunkard./ Like a tree, at times I am green with leaves;/ But in autumn I shed them all and stand naked'. This refusal of a steady state was, in its own way, an embrace of syncretism, of the possibility of constant movement between identities. It was this committed syncretism, so allied to the Silk Route trader's refusal of any one singular way of fixing value, that attracted Dara Shikoh's attention in Delhi.

◆

In about 1656, Sarmad and Abhai Chand moved from Hyderabad to Delhi. Or, more accurately, they moved to Shahjahanabad, the new city built by Shah Jahan next to the Yamuna River, where he transferred his capital from Lahore in 1638. It was dominated by two new landmarks: the huge Qila-i-Mubarak or Blessed Fort, later known as the Lal Qila or Red Fort, and the Jama Masjid or World-Reflecting Mosque, freshly completed in 1656.

To the south of the Red Fort, near Shahjahanabad's Kashmiri Gate, Shah Jahan's favourite son Dara Shikoh had a small palace next to the river. It still exists, although in radically different form, as the Delhi Department of Archaeology. Dara's small palace was substantially remodelled by the British Resident, Sir David Ochterlony, in the early nineteenth century. But in Dara's time it served as the venue for a remarkable Indian experiment in comparative religion. He had constructed the palace as his personal library, which was devoted in large part to inter-faith dialogue. It was here that Dara wrote a number of works that attempted to reconcile mystical Islam with the tenets of Hinduism, ranging from the philosophy of the Upanishads to Tantric mysticism. It was here too that he hosted many evening discussions—on the model of his great-grandfather Akbar's inter-faith conversations in the Ibadat Khana of Fatehpur Sikri—between people of different religions, especially Sufi qalandars and Tantric yogis. These discussions included many of the leading Muslim and Hindu mystics of the time: Shah Muhibulla, Shah Dilruba, Jagannath Mishra, Baba Lal Das Bairagi. But Dara's principal teacher and interlocutor was the Sufi master Mian Mir, who had laid the cornerstone of the Sikh Golden Temple in Amritsar.

Sarmad's fame as a mystic luminary had preceded him in Delhi, and he was already something of a celebrity by the time he arrived. It is quite possible that he came to Delhi at the invitation of Dara Shikoh. The two became close associates and even friends. It is easy to see why: the royal scion of Akbar and his state-mandated syncretism found a ready interlocutor in the naked exemplar of Sindhi and Hyderabadi cosmopolitanism. In a letter to Sarmad, Dara addresses him as 'my master and preceptor'. And Sarmad enthusiastically responded in kind, predicting that of all Shah Jahan's sons Dara would attain to the greatest success. For Niccolò Manucci, who was living in Delhi at the time, Dara and Sarmad's affinity was rooted in what he regarded as their atheism. He noted of the Mughal prince that 'Dara had no religion. When with the Muslims, he admired the tenets of Mohammed; when with the Jews, he praised Judaism; and when with the Hindus, he upheld Hinduism. That is why Aurangzeb dubbed him an infidel.' And Manucci faulted Dara for consorting with 'a Hebrew called Cermad—an atheist much liked by him'.

Manucci's ire was provoked most by Sarmad's nudity. He complains that the yogi-qalandar was 'always naked, except when he appeared in the presence of the prince—when he contented himself with a piece of cloth at his waist', and that he 'was an object of contempt and curiosity'. Another firangi resident in Delhi at the time, the French physician François Bernier, likewise wrote that 'I was for a long time disgusted with a celebrated Fakir, named Sarmet, who walked in the streets of Delhi as naked as he came to the world'. The two Christians' response to Sarmad's nakedness was not unlike that of Shahjahanabad's strictest Muslims. Sarmad's nudity disgusted not just Manucci and Bernier but also pious members of Dara's family. Shah Jahan asked Sarmad to wear a mantle; Dara's brother and deadly adversary, Aurangzeb, was to take even more pointed exception to Sarmad's refusal to wear clothes, especially following the execution of Dara in 1659.

Indeed, an intricate web of myth has been woven around the stand-off between Aurangzeb and Sarmad, with the latter's nudity as the primary point of contention. In these stories, Sarmad's nakedness is associated with magical powers. One story has it that Abhai Chand was taken off to be flogged by Aurangzeb's court officials, on account of his sinful relationship with Sarmad. Afterwards, Sarmad was summoned and informed that he too would be flogged if he remained close to Abhai

Chand. Sarmad replied: 'What do you think you have done? You go by appearances and reality eludes you. You did not flog Abhai Chand but you flogged me.' Then he turned his naked back to the officials, who saw that it was covered with the scars of his lover's lashing.

Another story has it that Sarmad was sitting naked in the Jama Masjid when the newly crowned Aurangzeb visited the mosque. Upon seeing the naked holy man, Aurangzeb said, 'People passing by your side see you naked and have their wazu [washing of arms before prayers] polluted.' And so Aurangzeb asked him to cover himself with a blanket lying next to him. Sarmad asked Aurangzeb to hand it to him; upon lifting the blanket, the Mughal emperor was shocked to see the bloody decapitated heads of his brothers, all of whom he had executed. As Aurangzeb recoiled from the sight, Sarmad asked him: 'now tell me whether I should cover your sins with my clothes or my own body. All the clothes I had are needed to cover your sins; I am necessarily left nude.'

As we have seen, Sarmad presented his nakedness as a refusal not just of worldly vanities but also of supposedly singular religious identities. But these two stories show how his nakedness was easily turned into a symbol that served more political ends. In both stories, nudity became a sign that Sarmad, unlike the Machiavellian emperor, had nothing to hide: his body was an open book that disclosed the crimes of Aurangzeb and his court. After Aurangzeb won the battles of succession and killed his brothers, he is supposed to have reminded Sarmad of the latter's now questionable prediction that Dara would be the most successful of Shah Jahan's sons. Sarmad is said to have replied that his prediction had in fact come true: in heaven, Dara would forever be held in higher esteem than Aurangzeb. And after his execution, popular legend has it that Sarmad picked up his severed head and ran in a rage up the steps of the Jama Masjid, vowing to end Aurangzeb's bloody rule. But then he heard a voice from Hare Bhare's tomb at the foot of the steps, and he went back down to the tomb to rest there in peace.

Sarmad's nakedness is also a central feature of stories about his execution. It's probable that he was executed largely for his association with Dara. But Mughal and foreign reporters alike—including Sher Khan Lodi and François Bernier—insist that it was Sarmad's refusal to wear clothes that led to his death. The story goes that, refusing Aurangzeb and the court officials' demands that he repudiate his nakedness, Sarmad was asked to recite the Kalima. Like Thomas Coryate, he is supposed to have satirized it: told to repeat the Kalima's affirmation of faith—there is no God but God, and Mohammed is his messenger—Sarmad reportedly was moved to say only that 'there is no God'. In another version of this story, he says only that 'there is no God but God', omitting only the statement about Mohammed. For some, this is supposed to confirm his rejection of Islam and embrace of Hinduism. Both versions of the Kalima story try to find a cryptic revelation of Sarmad's true religious identity at his moment of death, embracing the honesty of nakedness and refusing the will of the emperor. So too do a variety of reports of his uttering a poetic couplet as the blade fell on his neck. The couplet varies greatly from reporter to reporter. One claims he welcomed the executioner with his sword as if he were the divine Beloved, resigning himself to his decapitation as an act of God; a second says he made a joke about having his head severed by a 'flirt' who cut the matter 'short' and spared him a 'headache'. Each supposedly offer a revelation of the 'true' Sarmad—a spiritual seeker till the end, a wise fool in the face of death.

A third couplet attributed to Sarmad at his scene of execution is no less myth-making, but it is interesting because, even as it focuses on his nakedness, it pointedly refuses the revelatory impulse of the other stories. In this couplet, Sarmad supposedly said: 'It's wrong to ascribe any miracle to the naked Sarmad,/ The only revelation he has made is the revelation of his private parts.' Here Sarmad's nakedness is not a sign of anything, let alone a symbol of honesty or religious enlightenment: it is simply a state of undress that discloses the stubborn physicality of his body. We too might do well to think of his body independent of the twin mystifications of myth and morality. What is clear is that, at the time of his execution, Sarmad's was a very different body from the one that had turned the pages of the Torah at a synagogue in Kashan, or carried expensive ceramics for sale in Thatta. It had become an expressive medium according to Indian cultural conventions, allowing itself to be read simultaneously as the body of a holy yogi and an intoxicated qalandar. In other words, Sarmad's body in India swerved between different Indian identities and forms of self-presentation, just as his mouth swerved between different Indian tongues. And this swerving served him well in Sindh, Punjab, the Deccan and Delhi, nourishing his heart and stomach alike.

Because the Indian art of swerving is, ultimately, an embodied one, contorting and re-contorting the body in order to sustain it.

ON WEATHERING

When I was a small child, my father used to amuse me with an old rhyme: 'Whether the weather be fine, whether the weather be not; whether the weather be cold, whether the weather be hot; we'll weather the weather, whatever the weather, whether we like it or not.' This tongue-twister underlines how complex a word 'weather' is. It is both a noun—a meteorological state external to us—and a verb—something that we do. 'To weather' means to survive a crisis, as in weathering a storm. But 'to weather the weather' isn't simply to be battered by the weather. It is also to work with it; as the phrase indicates, we can imitate the weather and become one with it.

And that is why weathering the weather of the subcontinent is a special instance of becoming Indian.

In India, the weather is notoriously extreme. To cope, locals have devised all manner of inventive solutions. The jaalis of northern India mitigate the heat and humidity; the steep sloping red-tiled melkkoora of Kerala divert the torrential monsoon rains; the coarse wool pherans and kangris of Kashmir keep at bay the winter chill. The extreme Indian weather also forces alterations of one's body clock. In summer I get up earlier, go to bed later, and nap during the afternoon to take advantage of the cooler parts of the day. In winter, my daily pattern is altogether different. I sleep in, go to bed early, but soak up as much sun and Vitamin D as possible by sitting outside at midday. In other words, my body has acquired different senses of time, both diurnal and seasonal, in India. Perhaps it's no coincidence that, in French, the words for weather and time are the same (temps). To weather the Indian weather, you have to be in time with its demands. Otherwise you risk an untimely demise.

In Chennai's Fort St George, the old centre of English Madras, stands St Mary's Church; it is full of the tombstones of British Raj-era colonists who died early deaths. Many of these deaths are weather-related. One memorable inscription records the demise of a poor soul due to a 'coup de soleil' (blow of the sun), a wonderfully daft euphemism for heatstroke. His affliction is not surprising given that the colonists were accustomed to wearing thick English cloth in the noonday sun. Succumbing to a coup de soleil is a telling failure to adapt to the local environment: this colonist was weathered by the weather, but he spectacularly failed to weather it. And that is because he imagined his body should be the same—or should be clad in the same outfit—wherever in the world it might find itself.

I shouldn't laugh, though. A day after I smirked about the coup de soleil victim buried inside St Mary's Church, I took a trip from Chennai to the temple complex of Mahabalipuram some 50 kilometres south on the Coromandel Coast. That night I was felled by a severe case of heatstroke. It had been an unusually hot and humid day; although I thought I had been replenishing my fluids sufficiently, I'd made the mistake of drinking Limca. Its aerated water was the worst thing I could have drunk as I clambered around the temples in the hot, sticky midday sun. Totally dehydrated by evening, I collapsed on the beach at Fisherman's Cove. For two days I was nauseous and barely conscious. After that, Electral became my new best friend. But my coup de soleil was one of the most important lessons I have learned: the Indian weather must be respected.

Weathering the Indian weather in both senses—not just getting battered by it, but also finding ways of coping with it—is a challenge that most firangi migrants have faced. This challenge is especially apparent in the biographies of two unusual characters, enterprising, if somewhat reckless, self-made men who were exposed to the elements more than some of the other firangis in this book. Their biographies trace an interesting paradox. On the one hand, both men by and large operated outside the bounds of the state, whether Indian or colonial European; in the latter part of their careers, they served themselves rather than others. Yet despite this self-reliant statelessness, they were completely in thrall to the state of the weather. In other words, both men were fugitives from justice who (partially) refused the laws of humans yet abided by the laws of the climate. Each man's body was transformed by the extreme conditions to which he was exposed. And he didn't submit passively. He also adapted to the weather—the torrential monsoons of the northern Bay of Bengal, the heat and humidity of Tamil Nadu—in ways that allowed him to survive and, indeed, prosper.

We weather the weather, whatever the weather. Even though it might also mean that our weathered and weathering bodies change so much that we are unable to go back to the place we once called home. Because home is now India, whether we like it or not.

This chapter tells the story of a singular and unscrupulous rogue who lived in Bengal during the early seventeenth century: the former salt trader, later self-appointed harmaadi raja (Bengali for 'pirate king'), Sebastião Gonçalves Tibau. But Tibau's story is less about an individual than about an unusual migrant community that, over time, became desi even as it continued to be regarded as firangi. And that transformation is ultimately a story of adaptation to the torrential rain and monsoon-fed waterscapes of Bengal.

In modern Chittagong, on the north bank of the Karnaphuli River, is a district called Patharghata. If you walk from west to east along Chittagong's riverfront, you come to the Sadarghat, which is now less a ritual bathing place than a shabby dock. It is crowded with cargo ships and small fishing boats unloading their produce to workers who scurry, bulging bags on head and shoulders, across the stony silt of the riverbank. Turning left into Sadarghat Road, you enter the Patharghata enclave through a market lane now called Kazi Nazrul Islam Road. The enclave has some industries—sawmills, a kiln—but it also boasts a fine Portuguese church built in the seventeenth century, a reminder that Patharghata was once the Christian quarter of the city. Among the church's modern-day parishioners are Catholics with names like D'Souza and Pereira. Despite their Portuguese names, they look entirely Bangladeshi. Some of them live in the Patharghata enclave; one or two live in the more ramshackle area immediately to the south, adjoining the river, where they run small fishing boats. Patharghata may be poor, but the neighbourhood is spic and span—at least until one is assailed by the smell of raw prawns at its fish market, the Feringhee Bazaar.

As its name suggests, Feringhee Bazaar was built to serve foreign migrants. These foreigners' descendants became Bengali by language, culture and complexion. Yet despite their cultural and physical assimilation they have continued for the longest time to be regarded as foreign: as recently as the late twentieth century, they were still called 'feringhees'. The Chittagong Feringhee community has shrunk radically since independence in 1947, and even more since the birth of Bangladesh in 1971. Many have emigrated to Australia and Canada. Others have married local Bengali Muslims or converted and taken on new names.

Yet beneath the Bangladeshi Muslim veneer of Patharghata lurks some unexpected history. Indeed, Kazi Nazul Islam Road—named for one of the great revolutionary poets of Bengal—was once called Feringhee Bazaar Road, and it is still unofficially referred to by that name. Like water from a delta tributary emptying into the Bay of Bengal, the Feringhees have over time merged with the common ocean of Bangladeshi identity.

The analogy is only fitting, as the Bengali Feringhees' more than 400-year-old history is one of weathering the waterways of the region. They have long laboured as fishermen and sailors. Water is their element—a legacy, perhaps, of their seafaring Portuguese ancestors, but more tellingly a sign of centuries of intimate contact with not just Bengal's delta rivers but also its monsoon rains and tropical cyclones. Long before the Feringhees settled into the more law-abiding trades of fishing and piloting small boats, their ancestors plied the waterways of the region as freebooters and pirates. They were not part of the Estado da Índia but outlaws and renegades. In a sodden terrain that kept changing under the pressure of heavy precipitation, the early Feringhee outlaws too had to keep changing—not just their sailing routes or their pirate hideout locations in a delta region where the map needed to be redrawn after each monsoon season, but also their strategies for coping with the local conditions. Some of these strategies can strike us now as ruthless. But they were part of a culture of rapid-response adaptation, attuned to the rhythms of the area's extreme weather.

Sebastião Gonçalves Tibau stands out in this early history of Feringhee adaptation to the Bengali weather and waterscape. He was not the first Portuguese in the area—far from it. But his biography is striking inasmuch as it cannot be readily assimilated with the colonialist Portuguese presence in India. It tells us much about the adaptive prowess of the Feringhee pirates in the east of the subcontinent. Just as importantly, his brief but eventful life helped shape the unusual culture, politics, and history of the region, at the point of contact between Bengali, Burmese, Mughal and Portuguese factions. This is the story of a man who lived in a multi-cultural delta as criss-crossed by changing tributaries as the physical delta on which his story unfolds.

◆

Tibau was born in a tiny village near Lisbon, probably in the early 1580s. A seventeenth-century Portuguese historian, Manuel de Faria e Sousa, names this village Santo Antonio del Torzal (Saint Antony of the Twine);

there is no other record of it, and it may be the same as Santo Antonio da Charneca (Saint Antony of the Heath), a fishing village immediately to the south of the Rio Tejo, facing across the river from Lisbon. We know nothing of Tibau's life in Portugal. If he did indeed grow up in Santo Antonio da Charneca, he may have been born into a family of fishermen. It's quite likely that he knew from an early age how to sail a boat. In 1605, he joined the crew of a Portuguese warship and was dispatched to India. We don't know whether this was by choice or by coercion. Tibau was probably, like most Portuguese naval recruits, of low social station. Perhaps he sailed to India hoping for a better life and a share of wealth. But he may have also been press-ganged from the ranks of those in prison, like many of the humble sailors who served on the India-bound Portuguese ships.

Tibau almost certainly made his first Indian landfall at Goa. But he didn't stay there or in any of Portugal's relatively prosperous colonies on the west coast of India. Instead he gravitated, for unknown reasons, to the northern end of the Bay of Bengal. For a Portuguese wayfarer, life in the Bay was a very different proposition from settling in the more established west coast cities of Diu, Goa and Cochin. It was different even from life in the southeastern Coromandel Coast factory towns of Masulipatão in Andhra Pradesh (now known as Machilipatnam, occupied by the Portuguese from 1598 to 1610) and São Tomé de Meliapor in Tamil Nadu (now known as Santhome, occupied by the Portuguese from 1523 to 1749). Each of these colonies was a gateway to the Portuguese trade with Southeast Asia and the Spice Islands. The northern end of the Bay, by contrast, was its own unique zone, both commercially and environmentally. Because of seasonal monsoons and cyclones, sailing here tended to be coastal rather than oceanic. The harsh weather meant trade was largely confined to the stretch between Bengal and Burma. The enormous deltas of the Bay were also the hubs of a river-oriented trading economy. This necessitated careful cultivation of relations with culturally diverse Bengali and Burmese trading partners inland. Finally, the northern end of the Bay is one of the wettest parts of the world. The Bengal delta keeps changing its contours: torrential rain, the resulting pressure on the rivers, and the build-up and dispersal of silt are forever erasing and recreating bodies of solid land. Settlements in this part of the world are always provisional.

The area was not just geologically but also politically unstable. Upriver, Bengal had been ruled in the fifteenth and sixteenth centuries by a series of Abyssinian, Arab, and Afghan sultans; by the late sixteenth century, it had been conquered by the Mughals. The downriver area next to the Bay, however, was variously ruled by independent, so-called delta rajas who carved out fiefdoms on small islands. These rajas came variously from Bengal, the kingdom of Tripura, and the Magh kingdom of Arakan, now part of Myanmar. Some of them were Muslim; some Hindu; some Buddhist. Although the Mughals nominally ruled the delta by the turn of the seventeenth century, its ever-changing terrain still remained contested by would-be rajas from a variety of backgrounds.

The Portuguese arrived in this rain-swept land in the 1520s. They added to its already diverse ethnic mix; they also added to its political tensions. After setting up a factory in Chittagong (or what they called Porto Grande de Bengal) in 1528, they also imposed a new system whereby any ship in the area had to purchase from the Portuguese a naval trading license called a cartaz or face destruction. The cartaz system was intended to enrich the coffers of the Estado da Índia and the Portuguese crown. But in practice it licensed unregulated piracy, allowing rogue ships under the control of individual Portuguese captains to help themselves to plunder. This greatly transformed the political ecosystem of the region. The imposition of the cartaz broke the earlier Bengali monopoly on trade; in the process, it lent a fillip to previously suppressed Arakan commercial interests, creating competition between Bengali and Arakan goods even as it lowered prices to Portuguese trading advantage. Throughout the sixteenth century, the Arakans grew in wealth and power and, as a result, became more actively engaged in a struggle for trading supremacy in the area.

The Portuguese who lived in the Bay of Bengal were a wild bunch. They functioned largely as stateless freebooters and pirates out of a number of river settlements in the region, all of which remained outside the control of the Estado da Índia. Hooghly, about 40 kilometres north of what is now Kolkata on the Hooghly River, was founded by the Portuguese captain Pedro Tavares in 1580 after Akbar gave him permission to build a city anywhere in Bengal. The settlement paid tribute not to the Estado da Índia but to the Mughal Empire. Hooghly boasted a convent and a beautiful basilica, but it quickly became a nest of pirate raiders and slave-traders. The same applied to other Bay of Bengal river-port towns where the Portuguese settled—Pipli in what is now West Bengal, Chittagong and Dianga in what is now Bangladesh, and Balasore in what is now northern Orissa. The Portuguese communities that took shape in these settlements were different from those of Goa, Diu or Cochin, not just in their professions but also in their culture and complexion. Just as the delta kept erasing the solid lines of the map, so did the Bay of Bengal settlements blur the boundaries between different peoples. There were numerous tensions between them; but there was considerable sexual as well as commercial and linguistic traffic too. Large numbers of mixed-blood offspring were to be found in the Bay of Bengal trading towns.

Chittagong was typical in this respect. In the early seventeenth century, when Tibau would have first berthed there, its inhabitants were Bengali, Arab, Mughal, Arakan, and Portuguese. The modern-day dialect of Chittagong, Chatgaiyan Buli, is technically a version of Bengali; but it is unintelligible to a Bengali-speaking resident of Kolkata or Dhaka. Chatgaiyan Buli contains an unusually large number of loan words from Arabic, Assamese, Burmese, Persian, Turkish and Portuguese. The Portuguese loan words are particularly revealing, indicating the kinds of social interactions that took place between Portuguese and Chittagong locals. In particular, Chatgaiyan words associated with sailing are often of Portuguese origin: the word for mast—mastul—derives from the Portuguese mastio; the word for caulking—kaalapaati—derives from the Portuguese calafaté. And the word for pirate—harmaadi—seems to derive from the Portuguese armada or warship. Another Bengali term for pirate, bombete, derives from the Portuguese bombardeiro or bombardier.

Chittagong had already had a long history of trans-cultural piracy. The city kept switching between Bengali and Arakan rule throughout the sixteenth century, though in practice Chittagong remained a lawless frontier zone. This encouraged the formation of multicultural enterprises unaffiliated with any state. Before the arrival of the Portuguese, corsairs of many nations—Arakans, Bengalis, Tripuris, Malabaris, Arabs, and even a few Europeans—served as fellows in Chittagong-based crews. (Chittagong's multicultural pirate culture is colourfully painted by Rimi B. Chatterjee in her historical novel, *The City of Love*.) Into this culture came the Portuguese after 1528, first as state-backed antagonists and later as fellow freebooters. Some of the latter started off as merchant adventurers, though the distinction between 'legitimate' adventurer and 'illegitimate' pirate was a blurry one at best.

Most of the Portuguese in Chittagong based themselves in the enclave of Dianga—the area south of the river now known as Bandar (port) and sometimes called Feringhee Bandar. In early 1607, Dianga became embroiled in a conflict involving the Portuguese adventurer and mercenary, Filipe de Brito e Nicote. Although his father was French—he was the brother of Jean Nicot, who introduced tobacco to Europe—de Brito was born and raised in Lisbon. He had come to India as a cabin boy on board a Portuguese ship in the 1570s. But he soon found service as a mercenary with the Magh prince Min Razagyi, who in 1592 became king of Arakan. De Brito did well enough under Min Razagyi's patronage that he was awarded the governorship of the Arakan province of Syriam in the Irrawaddy delta region of southern Burma, or what the Portuguese called Pegu. There, supported by a retinue of Portuguese and Eurasian mercenaries, he built a more or less autonomous fiefdom for himself bankrolled by trade in salt. As his power grew in the early years of the seventeenth century, he began to eye Dianga as a possible addition to his salt-trading empire.

De Brito's interest in Dianga was motivated by a desire to acquire a trading port in Bengal. This was for reasons of weather as much as commerce and politics. During the rains of September and October, the prevailing wind blows from west to east; salt-trading ships can travel across the Bay of Bengal in that direction, discharging their cargo and harbouring in the Arakan ports until the monsoons abate, after which they can sail back safely to Bengal and pick up salt there during the dry seasons. Not surprisingly, de Brito's Arakan masters—already unnerved by his autonomy in Syriam—regarded his interest in Dianga as hostile, as they were the supposed rulers of the larger Chittagong area. They were upset too that, to further his aims of Bengali expansion, he had also sought official recognition by the Portuguese state. De Brito had visited Goa in 1603, and managed sufficiently to impress Aires de Saldanha, the then viceroy, that he was awarded the titles 'Commander of Syriam' and 'King of Pegu' and given Saldanha's niece as a bride. He was also given nominal authority over Bengal; in return, he was expected to bring the renegade Portuguese there back into the fold of the Estado da Índia. Even as he brokered an understanding with Saldanha, de Brito continued to cultivate his local connections: he married his son Simon to the daughter of the king of Martaban, a vassal kingdom next to Syriam. The net result was a political deal that required all non-Portuguese ships passing through the Irrawaddy delta region to weigh anchor at de Brito's custom house in Syriam—a major source of revenue for him. This angered his Burmese masters even more. In 1605, the Arakans joined forces with the Toungoo army of upper Burma to retake Syriam from de Brito. They failed. Two years later, in 1607, a decidedly cocky de Brito sent an embassy to Dianga to negotiate the possibility of its joining the Estado da Índia.

At that time, some records tell us, Sebastião Gonçalves Tibau was living in Dianga, where he made his living as a salt-trader. During his two years in the Bay, he had done well enough to buy his own boat, in which he transported cargo from the Bengal delta for sale in de Brito's Syriam entrepôt. The Arakans had annexed Chittagong in the 1590s; they regarded the Portuguese enclave in Dianga as a major irritant to their supremacy in the region because it had become a semi-independent slave port where Magh captives were sold. While de Brito's embassy negotiated, the Arakans attacked Dianga, seeking to wipe out the Portuguese. They were by and large successful: six hundred firangi merchants, pirates, slave-traders, and their families as well as most of de Brito's embassy were massacred. De Brito himself, who had stayed in Syriam, survived the attack. But it was to be the beginning of the end for him. The rising Toungoo power of the Burmese north—also intimately familiar with the horrors of the Portuguese traders—made a second attempt to invade Syriam in 1613. This time, de Brito was captured and his head impaled on a spike; his son Simon—the husband of the local Martaban princess—was also put to death. And thus began a long period of unalloyed Burmese hostility to foreign migrants and merchants.

Tibau too survived the 1607 Arakan massacre in Dianga, although in more spectacular fashion than the wily de Brito. He had arrived in Dianga from the Meghna River with his salt-boat on a trading expedition just days before the Arakan force pounced. But luck smiled at him. He managed to escape with about 400 others in a fugitive flotilla consisting of nine fishing boats and small commercial vessels like his own; they fled to Bhola, a large island in the mouth of the Ganges delta. Now outlaws, Tibau and his fellow fugitives were forced to pursue piracy. Initially they operated upstream from Bhola. Two years later, however, they relocated to Sandwip, a 50-kilometre-long island at the sea lip of the delta next to Chittagong through which the Padma, Meghna and Brahmaputra rivers empty into the Bay of Bengal. One of the escapees, a man named Estêvão Palmeiro, was elected by the pirates as their leader but he refused the post. Tibau, evidently a popular figure, was then asked to lead the group, which by 1609 consisted of 1,000 Portuguese and 2,000 Bengalis and Burmese. He eagerly accepted. His first act as leader was to declare himself 'king' of Sandwip. Tibau was now a firangi delta raja ruling over a motley transnational crew.

◆

Sandwip would have already been well known to Tibau from his salt-trading expeditions. And there he would have encountered people from diverse ethnic and religious backgrounds. Because of its strategic location in the Bay of Bengal and, more particularly, its rich salt deposits, many different regional powers had competed to wrest control of it. Indeed, the saga of competition for Sandwip in the late sixteenth and early seventeenth centuries reads something like an installment of *Game of Thrones*. It is hard to think of any other location in India that changed hands as often among as many different rulers of different ethnicities.

The Venetian traveller Cesare Federici spent forty days on Sandwip in 1565, when it was ruled by a Muslim governor, possibly from the northeastern state of Tripura. In 1586, Ralph Fitch passed by it en route to the Burmese kingdom of Pegu; by then Sandwip had become a Mughal possession following their conquest of Bengal in the 1570s. The Mughals built a fort on Sandwip. But a delta raja named Kedar Rai, from the tiny Bengali principality of Sripur, seized control of the island in the 1590s. At this time, the Portuguese took the fort of Chittagong from the Arakanese, and also claimed Sandwip. But Kedar Rai hung on with the help of a renegade Portuguese mercenary named Domingo Carvalho. In 1602, Carvalho fought off the Mughals and assumed full control of Sandwip. But his rule was brief; the local islanders rebelled against him, and he was forced to seek support from other Portuguese sailors. Manuel de Matos, who led the Portuguese enclave at Dianga, captained an expedition of 400 men in support of Carvalho. The two men then split Sandwip between them. Kedar Rai sought the support of the Arakan king, Min Razagyi, to flush out his former Portuguese employee and de Matos; but Kedar Rai and the Arakan force were vanquished by Carvalho. The Arakans made another failed attempt to wrest the island from Carvalho in 1603. Sensing that he was in a tight spot, Carvalho petitioned the Goan viceroy to make Sandwip an official possession of the Estado da Índia. He and de Matos were proclaimed by the Portuguese king as Fidalgos da Casa Real (Nobles of the Royal House); but the proclamation arrived only after Pratapaditya, the Hindu raja of Jessore, attacked Carvalho's stronghold and had him beheaded. De Matos promptly turned tail, leaving the island in the hands of a lieutenant named Petro Gomes; then Gomes too fled, handing control to an Afghan officer, Fateh Khan. De Matos was among those killed in 1607 when the Arakans invaded Dianga. Upon receiving the news of the massacre, Fateh Khan promptly proclaimed himself 'Lord of Sandwip, Shedder of Christian Blood, and Destroyer of the Portuguese Nation'. But within two years, Tibau had unseated Fateh Khan and taken control of Sandwip. He was to remain in power for eight years—an exceptionally long spell in comparison to his immediate predecessors.

Sandwip is typical of the delta islands of Bengal. Often flooded by the sea and then baked by the sun in the dry months, it annually produces huge dry saline deposits. These deposits—visible on the island's shores and in rice paddies during the dry season—are easily extractable. In Tibau's time, about 300 ships a year could be loaded with Sandwip salt. Filipe de Brito e Nicote, thanks to a concession from the Arakans, controlled the industry on the island in the early 1600s; he continued to do so even after the island had been seized by Portuguese freebooters such as Domingo Carvalho and Manuel de Matos. It is likely that Tibau was one of de Brito's agents from 1605 to 1607. Before Tibau took control of the island in 1609, he must have docked there often.

Salt has always been a prized commodity in the Bay of Bengal. It is one of the reasons Sandwip was such fiercely contested terrain. Regarded as auspicious by the area's Hindus, Buddhists, and Muslims, salt is used in rituals from house-warmings to weddings. It has also acquired enormous symbolic value throughout the subcontinent. In the Upanishads, Uddalaka Aruni instructs his son Shvetaketu to take some salt, store it in water, and bring it back to him the next day; the salt dissolves without a visible trace, but when Uddalaka asks his son to drink the water, it tastes salty. This is a metaphor for the presence of atman throughout the body: it cannot be seen, but it is pervasive, and what you are in essence. And salt is also freighted with significance as a means of social bonding. Aristotle says that people cannot know each other until they have eaten salt together. A version of this proverb had currency in Mughal Hindustan too: Dara Shikoh told his foreign servants that, despite their different religions and languages, they were bonded to him and each other as 'eaters of his salt'. But salt has always been far more than simply a ritual accessory or a symbol. In a land of tropical heat, it is a universal staple, needed to replace body salts lost through sweating. It is needed also to cure food, especially meat, and prevent it from rotting due to the heat and humidity. As Gandhi observed during his salt satyagraha of 1930: 'next to air and water, salt is perhaps the greatest necessity of life'. In this respect at least, salty Sandwip is a veritable land of plenty.

Yet Sandwip is not just a salty land. It is also one of the most fertile locations in Bengal, thanks to its sustained rainy season. The southwest monsoons drench the island from July to September; during this time, the prevailing winds pick up moisture from the Bay of Bengal and rainstorms flood Sandwip. In July and August, up to 300 millimetres of rain falls per month. But even outside the rainy season, Sandwip's direct exposure to the Bay keeps it wet. In May, low pressure over the Bay draws wind from the northwest, producing often devastating cyclones and tropical storms that again dump up to 300 millimetres of rain at a time. As recently as 1991, a horrendous hurricane with winds of 225 kilometres per hour destroyed nearly 80 per cent of Sandwip's houses and killed 40,000 people.

The rains of the Bay of Bengal have a ferocity that shocked European travellers. The Venetian traveller Cesare Federici, sailing in the Bay in 1569, describes a 'Touffon or cruel storm' that endured 'for three days and three nights', during which time the ship was so filled with water that all sixty men on board 'did nothing but cast the Sea into the Sea'. The Portuguese missionary Sebastião Manrique travelled to Orissa and the Bay of Bengal in 1640, where he too experienced a violent shipwreck in a violent monsoon cyclone; he describes the loss of a ship amidst a 'fierce storm of rain, thunder and lightning' whose force was so strong that, even with all the anchors cast, the ship was driven on to some rocks and broken 'into a thousand pieces'. It wasn't just in the Bay itself that the violence of the rain was felt. François Bernier, who journeyed by river boat through the Sundarbans delta of western Bengal in the 1660s, describes being caught in a storm 'so violent' that his boat cable snapped from the tree to which it had been fastened. He survived by hugging the branch of a tree, which he clutched tightly for two hours; during this time, the tempest rain 'fell as if poured into the boat from buckets, and the lightning and thunder were so vivid and loud, and so near our heads, that we despaired of surviving this horrible night'. This was just the climax of what was evidently a water-logged journey that drenched his clothes and destroyed his food store. Bernier says that he arrived in Hooghly four days later, his 'trunk' and all his 'wearing-apparel' wet; the rain had also left 'the poultry dead, the fish spoilt, and the whole of my biscuits soaked'.

This decimating rain is what Tibau was up against on Sandwip. Yet unlike Federici, Manrique or Bernier, he had to adapt to the rain in order to make the island his home. Taking out Fateh Khan, the 'Shedder of Christian Blood and Destroyer of the Portuguese Nation', was a small challenge compared to that of coping with the torrential downpours of the monsoon season. Wood and even brick houses don't last long in such weather. Even when they do, they need constant repair. Mould forms in minutes. Roofs frequently spring leaks or are destroyed altogether. The land on which houses stand easily erode. And one needs constantly to attend to one's ships, recaulking them, repairing their wind-ripped sails, and making sure they are harboured at the right times of the year. As raja of Sandwip, Tibau may have lived in the solid fort built by the Mughals. But he would have had to be constantly rebuilding his community's houses, ships, and docks.

And that's only when he was physically able to do so. As Bernier's experience in the Sundarbans makes clear, the rainy season of Bengal can decimate food supplies—either destroying crops in the ground or drenching preserved and cured foods and rotting them. No matter how fertile Sandwip might be, the food Tibau ate must often have been of compromised quality. Even when the food didn't make him sick, the local insects almost certainly did. Bengali mosquitoes would have bitten and taken many gulps of Tibau's blood, potentially infecting him with diseases like malaria and dengue. And despite Sandwip's abundant water—so different from arid environments like Malik Ambar's Deccan or Mandu Firangi's Fatehpur Sikri—Tibau would have to contend with contaminated supplies that could have given him diseases such as dysentery. Doubtless he adapted, sleeping under nets and boiling his drinking water; he also probably acquired over time a body whose immune system could withstand the challenges of mosquito bites and brackish water.

Tibau would have had to adapt in other ways as well. When they arrived, the Portuguese migrants to Sandwip may have still been wearing European clothes—breeches, boots, jackets—though many of them had probably started wearing more traditional Indian attire while they were living in Dianga, including flowing robes and churidars. Indeed, reports from this time suggest that the Portuguese in the Bay of Bengal were given to wearing 'Muhammadan' clothes. But after exposure to Sandwip's heavy rain, Tibau may have donned the wet-weather friendly lungi—a far better option for dealing with the damp undergrowth through which he would have to walk, and easily folded up to air soaked legs. He may also have worn a pagri or turban to keep his head dry. Both items are still worn by Sandwip islanders to this day.

Tibau presumably had to adapt too in terms of his sailing skills. Initially, he and his men seem to have operated out of small vessels—fishing and salt-trading boats—best suited for the delta region's rivers. But as time wore on, and the Sandwip pirates' power expanded, they seized control of larger ships, including galliasses—merchant galley ships rowed by oarsmen, but also carrying many sails. Their most distinctive feature is a row of heavy guns on their top-decks, which makes them particularly dangerous fighting machines. The galliasses were also better adapted to sea travel and would have allowed the pirates to venture further into the Bay of Bengal. Sailing a galliass in a Bengali monsoon, however, is a very tough proposition. It requires artful manoeuvring, as well as a set of rapid responses to sudden storms. Captaining a pirate galliass, Tibau must have been repeatedly drenched in heavy Bengali rain; he must also have become intimately familiar with the rain's different forms and what each of these meant for his sailing options.

But perhaps the biggest challenge the rain poses in Sandwip is to the land itself. Sandwip keeps changing size. The 2011 Bangladesh census lists the area of the island as 245 square kilometres—about 50 kilometres long and 5 kilometres wide. Yet its size fluctuates greatly from year to year. In 1981 it was 762 square kilometres; in 1951, 432 square kilometres; in 1921, 327 square kilometres; in 1891, 1,084 square kilometres. Although there are numerous villages on Sandwip—currently it has a population of some 350,000 people spread over sixty or so villages—these massive fluctuations in the island's size and contours mean its residents have to keep relocating. In 1565, Cesare Federici found Sandwip to be much larger than it is now: 1,629 square kilometres, or some seven times as big as its current landmass. We don't know if it continued to be this big during Tibau's rule. Rainstorms and the force of monsoon-swollen rivers flowing into the island must have washed away parts of Sandwip every year, but also created new arable and saline silt areas. Tibau and his men would have had to change not only their bodily habits but also their sense of home, shifting their houses and boats to new locations not ravaged by that season's rain.

The silt that washed up from the Brahmaputra and Ganga was good alluvial soil. To this day Sandwip is extraordinarily good for agriculture. Rice paddies do very well here, as do numerous other vegetable crops:

sugarcane, brinjal, cauliflower, radish. Fruit trees are abundant in Sandwip too: mangoes are common, as are guavas, water melons, and jackfruit. And there are plenty of fish in the rivers. Tibau may have spent a lot of his time wet and sick. But when his food hadn't been spoiled by the rain, he probably ate well—good Bengali khana consisting of fish, rice and sabzi. Not Paradise. But not far from it either. Call it a Sodden Eden.

◆

What kind of society did Tibau build in his Sodden Eden?

In William Shakespeare's *The Tempest*, written during the years Tibau was living on Sandwip, several Europeans are shipwrecked in a storm on a strange island. Two of them debate the virtues of the island. Although they are Italians, they have Portuguese-sounding names: Sebastian and Gonzalo. Sebastian is a reckless scoundrel who compulsively stirs up trouble and is willing to betray and even murder his brother the king; he laments what he perceives to be the barrenness of the island, saying that 'there's none, or little' means to live on it. Gonzalo is a utopian dreamer who fantasizes that the island will be a fertile new world; he proposes a back-to-nature social experiment that he believes will revive the Golden Age. The two characters' different attitudes to the island are mirrored by their different attitudes to non-Europeans. Sebastian is enraged that a European princess would choose to marry an African (the occasion for the sea voyage that has taken him and the others out of Europe); Gonzalo is fascinated by the native islanders and sees them as potential partners in his utopia.

Shakespeare wasn't writing about Sandwip when he imagined the location of *The Tempest*. But the similarities between the two isles are striking nonetheless. Sebastian's and Gonzalo's different perspectives on Shakespeare's imaginary island are historically mirrored in conflicting accounts of the origin of Sandwip's name. The nihilistic Sebastian, who dismisses the island as a barren wasteland with only 'an eye of green' in it, finds a counterpart in those who believed the name 'Sandwip' was a local bastardization of the English 'Sandheap'—a pile of useless sand and salt. By contrast, the utopian Gonzalo, who dreams of the island's Golden-Age 'foison' (Shakespeare's word for fecundity), is a first cousin of those who argued that 'Sandwip' derives from Sona Dweep, meaning Golden Island. Shakespeare's Sebastian and Gonzalo uncannily merge in the names as well as the character of Sebastião Gonçalves Tibau, who was both a violent outlaw and a utopian dreamer.

Tibau's violent outlaw side is more evident. Like Shakespeare's Sebastian, he betrayed a king who trusted him. Much of his piracy consisted of attacking Arakan merchant vessels in the Bay of Bengal and selling the booty at various ports in the Hindu-ruled delta kingdom of Jessore in what is now southwestern Bangladesh. Jessore, having ceded from the Mughal Empire, was keen to cultivate alliances with other non-Muslim powers in the region. Tibau entered into a trading arrangement with Pratapaditya, the Hindu raja of Jessore. The arrangement gave Pratapaditya half of Tibau's revenue in exchange for right of sale in Jessore port towns. However, Tibau soon reneged on the arrangement and attacked Pratapaditya, capturing the island of Bhola—the largest in the delta—to the west of Sandwip. With control over the two islands, Tibau now had considerable power over Bay of Bengal traders' access to upriver delta market towns. Tibau's treachery against Pratapaditya also upset the delicate political calculus of the region. Jessore had signed an opportunistic treaty with the Estado da Índia, according to which the kingdom's ports were available to the Portuguese, on condition that the Jessore fleet could trade with Goa, and the Portuguese give up on trade with Arakan-ruled areas. Tibau's aggression against his former ally in Jessore led him, like de Brito, to appeal to Goa, asking for official Portuguese support for his kingdom. But this time the Estado da Índia spurned Tibau, refusing to do business with a man they regarded as a common thief.

Sebastian-like, Tibau sought even to murder a local prince to whom he supposedly owed loyalty. This is apparent from the chilling tale of his unlikely and ill-fated friendship with Anaporam, a Magh prince and brother of Min Razagyi, the Arakan king. Even as Tibau's pirates preyed on merchant ships along the Arakan coast, he cultivated alliances with certain Arakan powers. In about 1609, Anaporam, then the governor of Chittagong, fell out with his brother Min Razagyi and sought refuge with Tibau in Sandwip. Tibau welcomed him and his daughter with open arms. Anaporam then accompanied his new Portuguese friend on a raid of the Arakan coast to retrieve family treasure; upon their triumphant return, however, Anaporam suddenly died. Reports indicate that Tibau had had Anaporam poisoned. Not coincidentally, he got to pocket all the Arakan treasure.

Despite Anaporam's defection to and murder by Tibau, his brother Min Razagyi himself entered into a nervous alliance with Tibau in 1610. The alliance was prompted by Mughal attempts to seize the Arakan port-town of Noakhali at the mouth of the Ganges. Min Razagyi sent a flotilla to fight alongside the Sandwip harmaadis against the Mughals. True to form, the slippery Tibau promptly broke the alliance and seized Min Razagyi's ships during a council with their captains. Tibau then used these seized ships to attack the royal Arakan city of Mrauk-U as well as Chittagong, destroying trading vessels in both. His intention was to blockade the Arakan coastline and force merchant ships in the Bay to do business with Sandwip alone. The blockade, not surprisingly, provoked the Arakan kingdom to violent retaliation—sometimes in league with other foreign powers. In 1615, a joint Arakan-Dutch fleet attempted unsuccessfully to force Tibau out of Sandwip.

It is hard to imagine that such an unscrupulous double-dealer could also be a Gonzalo-style utopian. But Tibau arguably engaged in a social experiment on Sandwip. This experiment may have been far removed from Gonzalo's golden age dream of returning to nature in *The Tempest*. Yet it too can be seen as a dream of a radically new world. Although Tibau occasionally tried to enlist Goa's aid in his skirmishes with the Arakan kingdom, he was a very different ruler from Filipe de Brito e Nicote. De Brito never gave up on the dream of reintegrating the Bay of Bengal Portuguese into the Estado da Índia. By contrast, Tibau throughout his eight-year rule of Sandwip operated outside the control of the Portuguese colonial state. And in this stateless space, he imagined a society very different in at least two ways from what he had known in Portugal.

First, Tibau's Sandwip society was an experiment in democracy. He had been elected leader of the pirate community by his fellows; one presumes that, for 3,000 men to remain loyal to him in often miserable physical conditions, the community also observed other democratic principles. Although no charter survives (and presumably one was never written), the pirates of Sandwip probably divided up the spoils of their raids equally. This would have helped foster among them a collective sense of commitment to a terribly dangerous enterprise. At most, the senior officers—those like Tibau who had proven themselves as the most courageous and valiant fighters—might have had a greater share in the spoils. But because Tibau was an elected leader, he was also presumably capable of being recalled if he abused his office. The irony, of course, is that this experiment in island democracy was headed by a self-proclaimed 'king'. This is yet another way in which Tibau resembles Shakespeare's Gonzalo, who dreams of a classless island society with 'no sovereignty', yet—as Sebastian interjects—'he would be King on't'.

Second, Tibau's Sandwip society was committedly multicultural. And this multiculturalism was as responsible as were the monsoons for the transformation of Portuguese firangis into Bengali Feringhees. The 400 men who accompanied Tibau from Dianga may have included mostly Portuguese sailor-traders and would-be pirates. But as we have seen, by the time Tibau arrived in Sandwip he commanded a crew that consisted of 1,000 Portuguese and 2,000 Bengali and Burmese men. To become a community capable of producing new generations as opposed to simply remaining a renegade stateless army, the fugitives had to find wives. Most of them had offspring with non-Portuguese women—including local Sandwip Bengalis, as well as women from Chittagong, Dianga, and Burma. These women would have played a significant role in helping the Portuguese pirates adapt to the new water-logged environment of the island. The children they bore would have also learned local mother tongues: Bengali, Chatgaiya Buli, and Arakanese.

Tibau played a leading role in implementing this multicultural society. Sometime around 1609, in the course of variously plotting alliances with and scheming attacks against the Arakan kingdom, he married Anaporam's newly baptized daughter, Min Razagyi's niece. It was almost certainly not a love marriage but rather a union of political convenience. And it is quite possible that Tibau treated his royal Arakan wife badly, especially after murdering her brother. We don't know if she was his only wife, and how long she survived with him on Sandwip. But it is quite likely that she bore him a son. By 1640, when Sebastian Manrique was in the Bay of Bengal, we hear of another Sebastião Gonçalves Tibau—identified in some reports as the elder Tibau's son. Interestingly, the son is part of a community that other travellers no longer called Portuguese but 'Arakaner'. This suggests that, despite his Portuguese name, Tibau the younger probably looked like, and identified with, his mother's people. Tibau the elder's marriage was in some ways typical of the Portuguese in the Bay of Bengal: we have already seen how Filipe de Brito e Nicote's son was married to a Burmese princess. But whereas de Brito always looked to retain his ties to a central Portuguese state, Tibau's marriage seems to have been part of a deliberate policy of becoming local.

Tibau's kingship came to an end in 1617, when Min Khamaung, the successor to Min Razagyi, finally conquered Sandwip. Tibau's power had been diminishing since November of 1615. In that month, despite commanding a flotilla of fifty vessels, he lost a river battle against the Arakans, who were supported by some Dutch ships. After this, a considerably weakened Tibau retreated to Sandwip, where he awaited his by-now inevitable defeat at the hands of the Arakans. We don't know what happened to Tibau after he was unseated. Because he was married to the first cousin of Min Khamaung, he may have had his life spared; Tibau and his Magh wife's son certainly survived, as Manrique's meeting with him several decades later makes clear. Some accounts suggest that Tibau was allowed to escape from Sandwip. But at this point, he vanishes from the historical record as abruptly as a monsoon cloud that has discharged its rain. Whatever became of him, it was a sudden and humbling end to the reign of a firangi delta raja who had risen from his humble origins to become the most powerful political force in the Bay of Bengal for close to a decade.

Yet even if he was wiped out politically, Tibau left a significant legacy culturally. Absorbed into the territory of their former enemies, Tibau's community pledged loyalty to the Arakan kingdom. But they continued to function as pirates under the loose patronage of Min Khamaung and the myd-za or Arakan governor of Chittagong. Giving half their booty to their Arakan masters, they conducted raids in lower Bengal; Sandwip became the hub of an Arakan slave trade that ultimately developed links to Goa, Southeast Asia, and then Africa and America. The pirates were also forced to keep their wives and children in Arakan territory, which helped further assimilate them into the local culture. For the next few decades, they acquired a horrific reputation as 'the Arakaners'. François Bernier damned them as 'outlaws and ruffians' comprised of Portuguese and 'a great number of their Mestices', i.e. their mixed-blood offspring. The English merchant sailor Thomas Bowrey, writing of the Bengal delta region in the late seventeenth century, said that the natives dread to 'dwell there, being timorous of the Arakaners with their jalias, who many times have come through the rivers and carried away captive many poor families'. Bowrey's reference to the 'jalia' is interesting: this is the local Bengali word for a Portuguese galliass. Here we can see how the 'Arakaners' had become culturally and ethnically hybrid: Portuguese by name, Arakan by communal identification, Bengali by language.

The Mughals saw the Arakaner pirates as a major threat to their rule in Bengal. This was largely because of the booming slave trade in Hooghly, dependent on captives supplied by the Arakaners. The trade had prompted the town's leaders to stop paying tribute to the Mughal Empire; in response, Shah Jahan ordered the city to be blockaded in the early 1630s. The siege and eventual invasion resulted in mass killings of Portuguese settlers, and the enslavement and deportation of many others—including, it would seem, Bibi Juliana Dias da Costa's then very young father, Agostinho. He does not seem to have been the son of an Arakaner pirate or slave trader. But given the ethnic mix of the area, it is not inconceivable that Agostinho da Costa's mother—Juliana's grandmother—may have been Arakan or Bengali.

The Arakaner pirates proved just as disloyal to the Arakan kingdom as had Tibau. They provided mercenary aid in 1665 to Shaista Khan, the Mughal subedar of Bengal, in the conquest of Chittagong from the Arakans. Shaista Khan had long wished to flush the pirates out of the delta region; in a stroke of tactical genius, he realized that the best way to achieve his goal was not to fight the pirates but join with them. Interestingly, Shaista Khan was assisted in his Chittagong operation by a third Sebastião Gonçalves Tibau who seems to have been a grand-nephew of the first. Who was Tibau III ethnically, and what languages did he speak? As his alliance with Shaista Khan suggests, he was certainly not an Arakan loyalist or a fifth columnist for the Estado da Índia. He was, rather, a creature of the fickle Bay of Bengal, embracing and emulating the rapid changes of the region. Weathering the Bay's weather, political as much as meteorological, is crucial to survival there. And it was the third Tibau's unlikely alliance with the Mughals that saved the pirates from almost certain devastation and led to their relocation from Sandwip to land upstream of Chittagong. In honour of the new residents, their new home was called Feringhee Bazaar. The modern D'Souzas and Pereiras who live there are the descendants of Sebastião Gonçalves Tibau's Sandwip community.

◆

There is in fact some confusion about the Feringhee Bazaar to which the Arakaner pirates were relocated after joining forces with Shaista Khan. Bernier tells us that the Mughal subedar gave them a land grant in Dhaka. And there is indeed a Firingi Bazaar in Dhaka, immediately south of the Buriganga River, which probably became home to some of the pirates. But over time, a larger and more vibrant community developed around the Feringhee Bazar of Chittagong, especially in Patharghata. Part of the reason is that Shaista Khan had employed the Sandwip pirates as mercenaries in his successful invasion of Chittagong; doubtless many of them stayed in the city after its capture. There was no small incentive to do so. Even after the Mughal invasion, Chittagong was to remain Bengal's most multicultural melting pot of regional ethnicities and religions—a more comfortable home for the mixed-blood Arakaner pirates. And just as importantly, a community that had by now spent three generations alternating between a rain-drenched delta island and the wet decks of pirate ships had little affinity with the inland terrain of Dhaka. Chittagong's river and sea location was a better fit for them, dispositionally and professionally.

The Chittagong descendants of the relocated pirates of Sandwip remained creatures of the water. Over time, the Feringhees, as they were soon called, became a Chittagong sailing community. The Mughals carefully cultivated them as a mercenary force to protect the frontier city from Arakan incursions. Theirs was a force that operated on river and sea rather than on land. Members of the community were known as kulah-posh, literally wearers of hats—in their case, caps with ears. These were badges of their seafaring life, which demanded headgear to protect exposed heads and ears from the sun, the wind and the rain. Ironically, when the Arakans attempted to take Chittagong again in 1786, the invading force consisted of Burmese-based kulah-posh Feringhees. In this borderland zone, the hybrid Feringhees were able to identify with both the Bengalis and the Burmese.

Over time, the Chittagong Feringhee water-mercenaries retreated into less socially prominent positions as merchant ship captains, fishermen and sail-makers. But they also assumed the status of a distinctive community. An article published in the 1871 edition of the *Calcutta Review* offers an ethnographic sketch of the Chittagong Feringhees: it typifies the then-rampant British colonialist condescension towards 'native' peoples. The anonymous author laments the Feringhee's mixed blood. They had evidently retained their ancestors' commitment to crossing borders in their sexual choices: the author claims that 'a large number of the Feringhees maintain connections with Magh and Muhammadan women'. The Feringhees also retained their ancestors' Christianity. Yet the author sees this as a compromised faith, complaining that 'from long intercourse with the natives the standard has become somewhat debased'. For the author, this debasement is evident in the Feringhee's unnaturally dark physique. He mutters that most of the 'race' has 'Magh and Muhammadan blood flowing through their veins'; this is why 'in appearance the Feringhee is darker than the Hindustani, his complexion having a brownish tint'. The author's colonialist horror of racial 'darkness' translates into stern judgement about the Feringhee's ability to do productive labour: 'the men are short, thin, flat-chested and generally ill-made…their industry cannot be depended on'. The Feringhee, in other words, was by now a world apart from the 'pure' European.

The author was just as appalled by the evident hybridity of Feringhee culture. Despite their observance of old Portuguese Christian rituals such as dressing up in bright clothes for Easter and Christmas (which the author denounces as a 'hideous effect'), the Feringhees had also absorbed both Hindu and Muslim traditions. Their local system of governance, for example, seems to have been modelled on the ancient north Indian institution of a five-strong elected assembly of communal elders: the author notes that 'cases of scandal' in the Feringhee community are resolved by a panchayat. It is quite possible that the pirate democracy of Tibau's Sandwip found a congenial counterpart in this Indian tradition of local rule. And the Feringhee's post-childbirth rituals, the author insists, are the same as those observed as among Bengali 'Muhammadans': every gap in the new mother's room is sealed and a fire is lit next to her bed, after which she is 'plied with hot masalas' to make her sweat.

It is this cultural mixing that made the Feringhees such recognizable denizens of the northern Bay of Bengal. In a monsoon-sodden zone where distinct boundaries of culture as much as geography are forever hard to maintain, the Feringhees literally embodied the fluid terrain in which they lived. They remained open to crossing borders, not only in their boats but also in their cultural affiliations and their family bonds. And this openness is part of the reason why they managed to survive as a distinct group for so many centuries. In 1859, a British census of Chittagong put the number of Feringhees in the city at 1,025. It was a small yet evidently robust community.

An old Bengali proverb says: 'sravaner puro bhadrer'—grow as much as possible in the rainy season. And the Feringhees, like the surprisingly abundant crops of Sandwip, flourished in the monsoon-swollen waterscapes of the Bay. Yet they were also damaged by them. As early as the mid nineteenth century, Chittagong's Feringhee population was diminishing rapidly, in no small part because of the Bay of Bengal's stormy climate. The anonymous author of the *Calcutta Review* article notes that, in the 1866 census, the Chittagong Feringhees numbered 865—a drop of more than 15 per cent in just seven years. How could the population shrink at such speed? The author explains the shrinking Feringhee population with the racist condescension that typifies nineteenth-century colonialist ethnography. For him, the Feringhees were a backward people on their way out: as only befitted a dying race, their women had become prone—or so he claimed—to barrenness. But in a throwaway remark, he also notes a more likely cause for the drop in population: the Chittagong Feringhee fishermen and sailors are unusually susceptible to 'losses by ship-wreck'.

In this one remark is hidden the tragedy of not just a people but also an entire region traumatized by increasingly severe monsoon seasons. Between 1737 and 2006, the Bay was ravaged by no less than 636 tropical cyclones—an average of two a year. The Great Calcutta Cyclone of 1864 had been almost unprecedented in its ferocity: 50,000 people lost their lives in the city alone, and the entire northern Bay of Bengal, including Chittagong, was devastated by flooding caused by 40-foot-high waves. Few Feringhee sailors caught in that cyclone can have been spared. Climate change has only increased the cyclones' frequency and force in recent decades, as the recent disaster in Sandwip makes so horrifyingly clear. Through several centuries of artful adaptation, the Feringhee descendants of Sebastião Gonçalves Tibau had prospered in the Bay of Bengal's monsoon-drenched environment. As another Bengali saying goes, 'samudre petichhi shajya, shsishire ke bhay'—I have made the sea my bed, why fear the dewdrop? A dewdrop on land was no challenge to the Feringhees. But they couldn't hope to assimilate to a mountainous sea-swell or tsunami. Nor could any other Bengali.

13 | NICCOLÒ MANUCCI,
THE SIDDHA VAIDYA OF MADRAS

I end by returning to the migrant with whom I began: Niccolò Manucci, the teenaged victim of the two firangi bandits, Thomas Roch and Raben Simitt. It is the summer of 1686, thirty long years after that hot day at the Hodal Sarai in Haryana. Manucci, now middle-aged, is sweltering through another sultry Indian day. But he is suffering the heat in a very different location and in very different circumstances.

Manucci has journeyed to Pondicherry to meet his good friend François Martin, the founder and governor of the French colony. The two men know each other from Surat: they briefly spent some time there together a few years earlier. The heat wafts in from the parched south Indian hinterland. Colliding with the sea-haze of the Bay of Bengal, it acquires a humidity that hangs over Martin's house like a tropical airborne swamp, leaving both men drenched in sweat. Manucci and Martin like to get together to discuss the past—their adventures in India, their memories of Venice and Paris. But now Manucci wants to share with Martin his plans for the future. After thirty years of drifting through India, Manucci is fed up: he wants to go back home to Europe. Much to Manucci's surprise, however, Martin strongly advises his friend against returning. Indeed, he questions whether Europe can be home anymore: Martin thinks Manucci has become so acclimatized to India's spicy food and hot weather that he will struggle to cope with Europe's blander cuisine and its cooler climes. Instead, Martin advises Manucci, he should settle permanently in India and find himself a wife. Manucci is persuaded: within months he is married, and he will spend the rest of his life in southern India. It will be a very long life too. He will die in Madras in 1720, aged 82.

What to make of Manucci's encounter in Pondicherry with Martin? It was to prove every bit as formative on his subsequent life as his earlier meeting with the bandits had been, but in a rather different way. Manucci's tangle with Roch and Simitt led him to spend three decades of service, on and off, under Mughal masters. By contrast, his conversation with Martin ushered in three more decades as a masterless resident of the Coromandel Coast in Tamil Nadu. By 1686, the coast was dotted with trading towns controlled by the Portuguese (São Tomé de Meliapor), the English (Madras), the French (Pondicherry), the Dutch

(Pulicat and Nagapatnam), and even the Danish (Tranquebar). Manucci's encounter with Martin, in other words, played out on a stage-set of early European colonialism. This encounter, like Manucci's earlier one with Roch and Simitt, also took place against a backdrop of intense heat. But if the summer furnace of Haryana disabled Manucci, making him vulnerable to the depredations of firangi bandits, his meeting with Martin in the Pondicherry humidity provided him with an unequivocal acknowledgement of how his body had adapted to the subcontinent's tropical climate. Manucci had, in short, weathered the Indian weather. And this not only allowed him to live a long and (mostly) healthy life in the European settlements of the Coromandel Coast, it also contributed significantly to his choice of career as a siddha vaidya, a practitioner of a specifically south Indian tradition of homeopathic medicine.

As this might suggest, Manucci embodied a striking contradiction. For the last thirty-four years of his life, he chose the company of Europeans over that of Indians. Yet his body chose the company of India over that of Europe. And his profession demanded that he acquaint himself with local forms of knowledge that derived from first-hand experience of south India's immense heat. The sultry weather of Madras is as physically demanding as the monsoon climate of the Bay of Bengal. A nineteenth-century medical guide for English colonists by the deputy coroner of Madras, Dr R. S. Mair, singled out the town as one of the unhealthiest places in the subcontinent. This was because of its 'hot season', which predisposed Europeans to attacks of 'fever, dysentery, diarrhea, cholera, or heat apoplexy'. Yet Manucci kept these illnesses mostly at bay by consuming local foods and medicines. In sum, Manucci may have been provincial in his choice of company, but his body was committedly cosmopolitan.

So who was Manucci in this early period of European settlement before the high tide of the British supremacy in India? Was he a model multiculturalist or an arrogant white communalist? The historian Sanjay Subrahmanyam has cautioned against naïve celebration of border-crossing figures such as Manucci. In our age when divisions between religious and ethnic communities can seem intractable, we can too hastily idealize the lives of those migrants who unexpectedly moved across boundaries of language and culture: it's tempting to assume that they represent inspirational alternatives to the communal hatreds of the present. As Subrahmanyam rightly points out, Manucci's life in India—especially his professed preference for European over Indian company—is an instructive case study in how border-crossing can foster intolerances as much as erode them.

Subrahmanyam doesn't consider Manucci's biography in the sense I have developed throughout this book. But Manucci's embodied experiences of India's heat, its hot foods, and its medicines arguably complicate any attempt to position him firmly on one side of the communalist-cosmopolitan divide. At the dawn of British supremacy in the subcontinent, what can Niccolò Manucci's body tell us about the tension between remaining insistently European and becoming Indian?

•

Much of what we know about Niccolò Manucci comes from one source: the *Storia do Mogor*, his eccentric five-volume history of the Mughals from Timur to Aurangzeb. Manucci claims that he had access to official Mughal records as he composed his history; but the five volumes—written in a mix of Italian, Portuguese and French dusted with Persian—also include many racy details about his own life. There is, however, one major problem with the *Storia*. It is riddled with historical inaccuracies. Reconstructing the basic details of Manucci's life-story requires cautious cross-checking of the *Storia*'s claims against other, frustratingly sparse Venetian, Portuguese, English, and Mughal records. We need to take many of Manucci's assertions about not just Indian history but also his own life with a grain of salt. Even his story of the encounter with Roch and Simitt at the Hodal Sarai raises questions.

We know that Manucci was born on 19 April 1638, in Venice. His parents, Pasqualino and Rosa, were very poor; one record states that his father was employed as a road-sweeper. Others indicate that Manucci had a brother named Andrea, three other younger brothers, and one sister, Pierina, who was born after he left for India. We don't know how much if any education the Manucci children received. Andrea was certainly literate, as some of his correspondence survives; so was Niccolò, though it is quite possible that he learned to read and write only after leaving Europe. Manucci's larger family was not quite as impoverished. According to the Venetian poet Apostolo Zeno, who wrote an unpublished one-paragraph biography of Manucci in the early years of the eighteenth century, Niccolò had an uncle who was a trader based in the Venetian outpost of Corfu. It may have been partly because of this uncle that Manucci began dreaming of a life elsewhere, beyond his parents' straitened circumstances in Venice. But to live in Venice was already to dream about other parts of the world. It was one of the most cosmopolitan port-cities of Europe, attracting traders from many countries who brought with them tales of Africa and the Orient. Even a poor child such as Niccolò may have heard such tales and travelled, in imagination, to other lands.

In the mid seventeenth century, Venice was still one of the chief superpowers of the Mediterranean. The city had long considered itself the Christian bulwark against westward Ottoman expansion; it had significant colonies in the borderland regions of Dalmatia, Crete, and Cyprus, and the victory of its naval force over the Ottomans at the Battle of Lepanto in 1560 was widely touted throughout Europe as a triumph for Christendom. Yet for all Venice's religious and political enmity with the Ottomans, the city's trade interests were very much directed towards the Levant and the Muslim territories beyond it. Venice had a long-standing presence in the major Ottoman trading depot of Aleppo, the gateway to the lucrative silk and spice trades of the east. Indeed, many Venetians had found their way to India, from Marco Polo in the thirteenth century to Cesare Federici in the sixteenth. They came not as conquerors or colonists, however, but as merchants and travellers. As a result, they weren't representatives of larger state entities the way the early Portuguese and English travellers to India were. The Venetians tended to be individual drifters propelled along the maritime trade routes. And as non-aligned travellers, they were often better positioned than officials of the Estado da Índia and the English East India Company to cross borders of culture and language.

This would seem to be especially true of Manucci. Even before he reached India, he was already something of a stateless shape-shifter. In November 1651, at the age of 13, young Niccolò decided to run away from his family and city. According to Apostolo Zeno, Niccolò had travelled to Corfu to visit his uncle; from Corfu, he stowed away aboard an English ship bound for Aleppo. Manucci claims that he was discovered by Lord Bellomont, an English Catholic lord sailing on the ship, who took a shine to him and employed him as a page. The teenaged Venetian and his English master then travelled together overland through Turkey and Armenia to Persia, where they tarried for several years. Here Manucci learned Persian and took to wearing Asian clothes. He and Lord Bellomont met Shah Abbas in the hope of gaining the latter's support for the exiled King Charles II of England; but little was forthcoming, so they eventually sailed on, via Hormuz, to Surat. By the time they made landfall on 12 January 1656, the now 17-year-old Manucci was already a seasoned veteran of movement across borders of geography, culture and language.

As documented in his *Storia do Mogor*, Manucci's adolescent saga reads a little like a romance fiction. It may indeed be one: some scholars have speculated that little or none of it is true. The historical Lord Bellomont, Henry Bard, had lost an arm in battle—a serious disability that Manucci, perhaps surprisingly, never mentions. And this omission casts some doubt over his claim to have arrived in India with Bellomont or, for that matter, his report on the encounter, in the days after Bellomont's sudden death in June 1656, with Roch and Simitt at the Hodal Sarai. Nevertheless, we know from East India Company records that the two English bandits were real. It is highly likely that Manucci did indeed meet them that day in Haryana, though perhaps some of the details of the encounter were not quite as he described them. Given that he wrote his report some forty years later, his actual memory of the encounter with Roch and Simitt had probably been superseded by a much repeated—and probably embellished—narrative version of it. As Manucci himself admits in the *Storia*, he was a born raconteur; and like most raconteurs he seems to have had a bent for masala, narrative condiments added to a supposedly true story.

After reaching Delhi, Manucci spent sixty-four years acclimatizing to India in an astonishing variety of locations. Indeed, his life comes across as a colourful quilt stitched out of the stories of all the other firangis we've met so far. Like Garcia da Orta, Manucci practiced as a doctor and met several undercover Jewish physicians. He may not have been a priest like Thomas Stephens, but he did meet Jesuits who had adopted the languages, clothes and customs of Brahmins. He wasn't a mamluk like Malik Ayaz or Malik Ambar, but he served as an artilleryman in an Indian army and visited both Gujarat and the Deccan highlands. Like Chinali and Dillanai, he was involved in naval military operations on India's west coast. Like Mandu Firangi he worked with local artists in producing paintings that crossed the divide between the Indian and the European. Like Hunarmand he took a keen interest in jewels and married an Indian-born woman. Like Juliana Firangi, he often received gifts of khil'at from Mughal and other Indian masters. He claims to have had special access to the royal harem and may have even met Juliana Dias da Costa; he almost certainly met her father. Like Thomas Coryate, he knew abject poverty yet became relatively fluent in court Persian. He may not have wandered naked through India with a male lover, but he seems to have known—and disliked—Sai'd Sarmad and, like him, spent time in Hyderabad and Delhi. And like Sebastião Gonçalves Tibau, he sailed through the river deltas of Bengal.

As this suggests, Manucci's life in India was rich in experience. Yet it is poor in verifiable detail. It is hard to sift the hard truth from the morass of embellished stories that make up the *Storia do Mogor*. If we read the more autobiographical sections of the *Storia* against Mughal, East India Company, and Venetian records, however, we can provisionally reconstruct the basic sequence of Manucci's sixty-four years in India following his meeting with Roch and Simitt. It unfolds something like this.

Days after the incident at Hodal in 1656, Manucci reached Delhi. There he quickly found service with Shah Jahan's son Dara Shikoh, joining his European artillery division. The division was a force to be reckoned with: by Manucci's estimate, it numbered 'over two hundred'. In May of 1658, he fought in the decisive battle against Aurangzeb, which Dara comprehensively lost. Manucci offers a dramatic and quite credible first-hand account of the conflict in the *Storia do Mogor*. In the wake of the battle, Manucci says he followed Dara to Lahore, disguised (not for the last time) as a holy mendicant; then, with a handful of firangi soldiers and some Mughal loyalists, he retreated deeper into Punjab, holing up in the fort at Bhakkar. Following Dara Shikoh's capture and execution, Manucci claims to have been offered service by Aurangzeb in the latter's artillery regiment. But he declined the invitation to serve the new emperor, telling him that he intended to return home to Europe. At this point, though, he had no intention of leaving India. He jumped at an opportunity to travel by river to Allahabad and Patna, after which he journeyed on by river-boat through Bengal. Facing various difficulties there, he returned to Delhi. Here he found service with the Rajput king and Mughal lord Mirza Raja Jai Singh, whom he served as captain of his artillery until 1666.

After ten years in Mughal service, Manucci decided he had to live among Christians. So he packed up and relocated to Goa. But after a year of bad health, he determined instead to make his living as a physician and moved again to Lahore. There he acquired a reputation as an effective blood-letter. He came to the attention of the wife of Aurangzeb's son, Shah Alam, who wanted to retain his services as a court doctor. But once again, Manucci balked at living among the

Mughals and returned, in 1677, to Goa. His second spell there was no more successful than the first. This time he lost much of his wealth and, according to one report, an illegitimate son in a shipwreck. He then re-joined the retinue of Shah Alam, who by this time was governor of the Deccan in Golconda. This period of service did not last long; Manucci went for a third time to Goa in 1682, where he positioned himself a negotiator between the Mughals and the Estado da Índia. Initially he did well, and was even admitted to the order of Santiago as a knight. Two years later, however, he found himself at odds with the Portuguese authorities. He defected again to the Mughals, who by this time also had little tolerance for him. Manucci then fled to Hyderabad; Shah Alam attempted to have him arrested. Disguised again as a priest,` he escaped to Madras in the mid 1680s. Soon afterwards he had his fateful discussion with François Martin. For the rest of his life, Manucci was to be a masterless man.

Heeding Martin's advice to find a wife, Manucci married Elizabeth Hartley Clarke in Madras on 28 October 1686. Elizabeth was the Indian-born widow of one of the first English settlers in Madras, Thomas Clarke. Her father was also English, but her Portuguese-named mother may have been partly Indian. Niccolò and Elizabeth's marriage seems to have been a happy one: he speaks with considerable emotion about her in the *Storia*. Manucci's first decade in Madras clearly agreed with him. Through his wife, Manucci inherited Clarke's house and garden on Broadway in Madras. He was asked to serve as an envoy between the English and the Mughals, who had, by this time, forgiven him for escaping Shah Alam's service. He made some extra pocket money through business ventures in the Bay of Bengal. And he also successfully resumed his practice as a physician. Indeed, he turned enough of a profit that he was able to buy a country bungalow retreat on St Thomas Mount, a hill some 3 miles from Madras.

But Manucci also tasted hardship in the south of India. His only child with Elizabeth, an unnamed son, died in infancy. And in the 1690s, he began to develop serious problems with his eyesight that he claimed left him close to blind. With the help of a scribe, he started writing his memoirs. Manucci sent the first three volumes back to Europe, where they were bowdlerized by a Jesuit priest, François Catrou, who published them under his own name. As a result Manucci developed an abiding hatred of the Jesuits. Much worse was to come. His wife died in Madras on 15 December 1706; utterly heartbroken, Manucci sold his St Thomas Mount house and relocated to Pondicherry. No sooner had he arrived than his old friend François Martin died. At much the same time his brother Andrea's son, also named Niccolò, seems to have perished at sea after voyaging to India to join his uncle. Old, alone, and embittered, Manucci continued writing his memoirs, devoting much of them to tediously lengthy Capuchin arguments against the errors and evils of Jesuit theology. In late 1719, he wrote his last will and testament, and he most likely died the following summer.

In his long life as artilleryman, physician, envoy, merchant trader, and historical chronicle writer, Manucci repeatedly crossed boundaries of geography, language and culture. The *Storia do Mogor* documents his travels across the entire Indian subcontinent—from Kashmir in the north to the Karnatik kingdom in the south, from Goa in the west to Bengal in the east. It also swerves—Coryate-style—between multiple tongues. Manucci uses French, Italian, Portuguese and sometimes Persian throughout the volumes: he claims that he had to alternate between the first three because, with his dimming eyesight, he required the help of firangi scribes who didn't speak his mother tongue. The genre of the *Storia* is just as hybrid as its language. It is written partly in the chronicle style employed by Mughal historians such as Abu'l Fazl, the author of the *A'in-i-Akbari*. But Manucci's history of the Mughals is punctuated by autobiographical details that seem to owe something to the European genre of romance—a genre that records the travels and travails of hapless questers who bounce from misfortune to misfortune but somehow prevail.

Manucci also commissioned local artists to produce a series of paintings for his *Storia*. These paintings are as hybrid as the *Storia*'s language and genre. They depict the historical Mughal kings, but they also contribute to the *Storia*'s flavour of European romance by representing scenes from Manucci's travels. One of the paintings presents Manucci as an Indian-style hakeem: taking the pulse of a dark bearded man, he is shown as a pasty and slightly paunchy firangi dressed in qaba, sash and turban. As Manucci himself points out, he deliberately made his Indian dress an exercise in cross-cultural fusion: he fastened his qaba on the right side 'in the fashion of Mohammedans', but he shaved his beard and wore only 'moustaches like the Rajputs'. As a result, Indians asked him if he was 'a Mohammedan Christian or a Hindu Christian'.

All this would suggest that Manucci, like Sai'd Sarmad, was an admirable exponent of code-switching, even a spokesperson for cross-cultural respect. Repeatedly he was called upon to work as an envoy, a go-between with no state affiliation who could move easily across borders of language and culture. He also describes himself as 'carried away by curiosity', keen to see as much as he could of different peoples and places. Yet his status as a curious go-between did not always translate into an ethos of tolerance. For all that Manucci managed to stay a citizen of the world rather than of one state, whether Portuguese or Mughal, his *Storia do Mogor* keeps returning to one particular leitmotif. Indians, he says, are uncultured barbarians and pathological liars who are not to be trusted.

◆

Perhaps the most frequently used word throughout the *Storia do Mogor* is 'friend'. In virtually every Indian city and town Manucci finds himself, he encounters a dear 'friend' or 'friends'. They give him shelter and food; they assist him in sticky situations; they fight alongside him; they respect his skills as a physician; they instruct him in the customs and languages of India. Manucci, in short, gets by with more than a little help from his 'friends'. But who were these friends? By and large, they were not Indians.

To be fair, Manucci numbered a few powerful Mughals among his friends. Da'ud Khan, an officer who had loyally served Dara and joined Manucci in the party that retreated to Lahore, was one such; several decades later, Manucci was to meet Da'ud Khan again in Madras, and he described their reunion as full of 'tenderness and friendliness'. Shah Alam too is referred to as a 'friend', as are two Mughal court eunuchs. But these are rare exceptions. For the most part, Manucci uses the term to refer to Europeans. Early in the *Storia*, he even glosses his use of the word 'friends' as meaning the 'artillerymen in Prince Dara's service'. And as the *Storia* unfolds, the word 'friend' is applied to many other Europeans. These include 'some English and Dutch friends' in Patna; a Portuguese doctor in Delhi, João de Souza; an Englishman in Golconda, Thomas Gudlet; a possible Spaniard, Francisco Guety; and François Martin in Pondicherry. Manucci also refers to an Armenian 'friend' in Patna, Khwaja Safar.

As this suggests, Manucci's multinational sphere of 'friends' was confined primarily to Christians. It's revealing that, in the midst of Manucci's march from the fortress of Bhakkar to Lahore, he refers to 'we Europeans'. The phrase is poised here at the cusp between religious and racial solidarities. Something similar can be glimpsed when he talks about how India is not good for 'we Europeans'. 'I assure the reader', Manucci observes, 'that few Europeans could live there with the advantages and honours I was able to achieve'. And this, Manucci maintains, is not just because India is bad for Europeans' physical health; it is also due to the 'absence of Catholic observances'. Admittedly, 'we Europeans' is for Manucci a somewhat vexed and fractured group. The *Storia* makes clear that he in fact sees Europeans as divided between good friends and perfidious traitors. His Catholic solidarities are compromised by his conviction that the Portuguese are never to be trusted: he provides long catalogues of their deceptions. As we have seen, he similarly regarded Jesuits as arch-deceivers. And although he came to India as a devoted servant of the Catholic Lord Bellomont, Manucci's regard for Bellomont's country-people survived the jump across the bitter English sectarian divide. In the section of the *Storia* set in Madras, he repeatedly talks of the colonial town's Protestant English governors—especially Thomas Pitt—with respect and admiration. At the top of his of hierarchy of preferred European company, however, were the French, thanks in no small part to his deep friendship with François Martin and the comfort Manucci felt in Pondicherry.

Manucci's network of 'friends' presumed a world of non-Christian enemies. And the native inhabitants of Mughal Hindustan fell squarely into this category. According to Manucci, Hindustan has 'nothing that can delight or win people from Europe, or make them desire to live there'. And that, Manucci argues, is because one has to live in a state of constant suspicion 'since no one ever says a word that can be relied on'. He complains, repeatedly, that he is not happy living with 'Mohammedans', whom he regards as inveterate liars. It's quite possible that sentiments like these are occasioned by what he presumed to be his readership—Christians in Europe. But it is clear that the *Storia do Mogor*, written more than a decade after Manucci moved to Madras, reflects habits of thought developed in a cultural milieu very different from that of Mughal Hindustan. Madras was the first of the presidency cities that would become the linchpins of Britain's Indian empire. Although the still tiny settlement at this time witnessed considerably more cultural mixing and intermarriage than it was to do in the age of the British Raj proper, Madras already abided by divisions based on religion and ethnicity. Manucci's house on Broadway was at the dividing point between the 'white' English settlement of Fort St George, organized around the church of St Mary, and the neighbouring Black Town, as it was known—the area where Indian textile workers employed by the East India Company lived. In this segregated settlement, the tensions between being a firangi who has become Indian and being a colonial European began forcefully to assert themselves.

If Manucci regards 'Mohammedans' with mistrust, he is even more openly contemptuous of Hindus. This is particularly clear from the series of paintings he commissioned for his *Storia*. He accompanies these with notes that make clear his disdain for what he regards as the idolatrous practices of Hinduism. We have already seen in a previous chapter how Manucci had met Sai'd Sarmad and abhorred his nakedness. Interestingly, one of the 'Hindu' pictures of the *Storia* depicts a yogi much like Sarmad, with matted hair, long fingernails, and no garments other than a loin-cloth added by the artist at Manucci's insistence. He comments acerbically on the yogi's refusal of clothes as 'indecent and dishonest'. Other pictures of scenes from Hindu worship and mythology are even more damning of what Manucci describes as 'the Idolaters'.

Perhaps the most vehement anti-Hindu passage in the *Storia* concerns an incident in the south of India in the late 1690s, after Manucci had moved to Madras. He was due to meet his old friend Da'ud Khan to negotiate on behalf of the Madras authorities with the Mughals. Aurangzeb had dispatched Da'ud Khan as his regional subedar to pressure the European factory towns into containing the ongoing problem of piracy in the Bay of Bengal; if they did not comply, Aurangzeb had warned that they would be expelled from the subcontinent. In his account of the meeting, Manucci persuaded Da'ud Khan that the English had nothing to do with the pirates, and that to expel them would not only provoke drastic retaliation but also deprive Madras's Black Town Indians of employment opportunities. But Manucci claims that his negotiations almost came to naught because of an incident involving a Black Town Indian in the negotiating team. The Indian in question was a 'Brahmin clerk' named Ramappa. Although Ramappa accompanied Manucci to Dau'd Khan's camp, he excused himself from meeting with the Mughal subedar, insisting that he wanted instead 'to bathe his body according to their custom, which is to bathe every day'. Ramappa's aim in avoiding the meeting, Manucci says, was to withhold from Da'ud Khan the gift of money they had brought from Madras for the Mughal treasury. Manucci overruled him, and Ramappa was publicly reprimanded before Da'ud Khan while Manucci was showered with gifts.

In Manucci's words, this is what then ensued:

The Brahmin was jealous beyond measure of all the honours received by me from Da'ud Khan, from the chief minister, and all the other officers of the army, a feeling intensified by seeing himself despised and hated.

For this reason he designed covertly to make me lose the esteem and reputation that I had among the Mohammedans, and the property I held within the English jurisdiction... But the most intimate friends of the man knew that all he said was false, and all his inventions diabolic.

After this, Manucci tells us, the 'diabolic' Ramappa tried to frame him. The clerk told him that Da'ud Khan wanted Manucci to hand over the gift-money to the servant of Ramappa's Brahmin friend, Langkaran. The plan was that the Brahmins would pocket the money between them, while Manucci would be fingered for its disappearance. Manucci, smelling a rat, gave the money directly to Da'ud Khan's treasurer. When Manucci confronted Ramappa about what had happened, 'he began to make excuse, just as is their habit; for it may be truly said that these people are very much like crocodiles, whose skin changes at their will and pleasure'. Manucci's report uses the standard tactic of high colonial ethnography: a single anecdote becomes illustrative of an entire religious community and 'their' habits.

One might also see in Manucci's bitter characterization of 'these people' as changeable 'crocodiles' a certain amount of bad faith and projection. If there is any consistent thread throughout his time in the Mughal Empire, it is his recourse to deception: he tells many tall tales, deliberately manipulates the people he meets, and repeatedly disguises himself to his advantage. But what is perhaps most striking about his slurs against Hindus and Hinduism is that they mask something else about his activity in Madras: his Hindu-themed choice of profession. In addition to serving as an envoy and negotiator, he practiced as a physician conversant with an antique form of Indian medicine. Not only did this entail knowledge of Hindu traditions of botany and chemistry, it also meant opening up his body to the effects of the local climate and local substances in order to weather the distinctive challenges of the intense Indian heat. But Manucci had been doing this for decades before he settled in Madras.

Long before Manucci reached India, he was intimately acquainted with the physical challenges of Asian climates. Indeed, the early pages of his *Storia do Mogor* are not just ethnographic reports about strange customs from Muslim lands. His own body, constantly encountering and transformed by the new environments of Turkey and Persia, becomes one of his narrative's principal focuses. Chief among these new sensations is the immense heat of Asia, so different from what he had been used to in mild and often chilly Venice. During the day in Turkey, he says, 'you are much troubled with the heat of the sun'. Although he claims that Persia's 'frosts and snows' make its climate more like that of England, he notes of Bandar Abbas, the chief Persian sea-port, that 'the climate… is most noxious by reason of the salt ridges, and of certain hot winds'. He notes too that this climate has long-term effects on the bodies of local residents, many of whom have 'defective sight and teeth'.

For Manucci, the sultry Turkish and Persian climates demanded that he adapt his body in a variety of ways. His body-clock changed: he altered his sleeping habits, getting up early in the mornings to load camels and horses for travel while the temperature was still cool, and staying up late to take advantage of the cooler midnight hours in the company of hookahs and tale-tellers. He also changed what he wore: he says that, upon crossing into Persia, 'we were forced to have new clothes', partly to prepare for their meeting with the Shah but also to adapt to the demands of the weather. He doubtless donned flowing shalvar pants—identical to the Indian salwar—and a qaba, or long cloak. Manucci was to wear the qaba for the rest of his life. The garment is tightly fitted around the torso, but it is loose enough in its skirt region to allow freedom of movement. It is also lined; in the dry heat of Persia, it helps trap moisture and prevent dehydration. While in Persia, he seems to have worn a turban too, to protect his head from the sun.

Most of all, though, Manucci changed his diet in Persia. The early pages of the Storia Do Mogor are a foodie's dream: Manucci documents at length his pleasurable gastronomic experiences, including his first tastes of various types of pulao rice flavoured, he says, with 'cloves, cinnamon, mace, pimento, cardamoms, ginger, saffron, raisins, and almonds, to which is added the flesh of sheep, or fowl, or goats, and the whole dressed with plenty of butter'. And he offers equally mouth-watering descriptions of his experiments with Persian fresh and dried fruit, including kishmish.

He had no choice but to sample the exotic foods and cuisines of Persia, of course; he wasn't going to find traditional Venetian fare such as seafood, polenta, or bigoli pasta in the dry Persian hinterland. But Manucci's attention to new foods was motivated by more than simple curiosity. Like most Europeans, he had grown up with an understanding of health that demanded careful calibration of diet with the features of the environment. A hot climate, the classical Roman physician Galen wrote, could produce in the body an excess of the bodily fluid or 'humour' called 'choler' or yellow bile. This humour was believed to provoke irritable and angry moods: indeed, the modern terminology of a 'hot temper' is related to Galen's medical system, in which a hot climate inevitably produces a hot body and personality alike. Diet played an important part in this system as a corrective to the excesses of the environment. In hot weather, one was meant to eat naturally cool foods, to balance the body's mix of humours.

We can see something of this Galenic world-view in Manucci's remarks about the inhabitants of Hormuz. He claims that they manage the heat badly because they love to eat dates, a fruit that was traditionally regarded by Galen and his disciples as full of heat. Yet he also quickly found that the heat of certain Persian foods had a pleasantly cooling effect on him, no doubt because they allowed him to sweat and therefore lower his body temperature. The wonderful pulao he describes, for instance, 'is cooked with many spices': it contains hot pimento, or red chilli peppers, as well as mild saffron. Galen's understanding of diet is allopathic: it presumes that heat should be treated with its cool opposite. By contrast, the cuisines that Manucci encountered in Persia introduced him to the possibility of a homeopathic diet—of treating like with like, or heat with heat.

Manucci's homeopathic awareness grew with his experiences of Indian foodstuffs. Upon reaching Surat, he had his first experience of paan, a stimulating, psychoactive preparation of betel leaf combined with areca nut and slaked lime. He lists its effects at considerable length in the *Storia do Mogor*, describing an occasion when paan was administered to him by a woman in Surat. The scene reads a little like Irving Walsh's descriptions of Scottish hard drug-users in his cult novel *Trainspotting*:

> ...my head swam to such an extent that I feared I was dying. It
> caused me to fall down, I lost my colour, and endured agonies,
> but she poured into my mouth a little salt, and brought me to

my senses. The lady assured me that everyone who ate it for the first time felt the same effects... It happens with the eaters of betel, as to those accustomed to take tobacco, that they are unable to refrain from taking it many times a day. Thus the women of India, whose principal business it is to tell stories and eat betel, are unable to remain many minutes without having it in their mouths.

Manucci's seemingly debilitating experience at first leads him to pronounce paan an addiction suitable only for 'the women of India', who have nothing better to do with their time than gossip and remain idle. Yet this early negative experience seems not to have dissuaded him from picking up the habit himself. And that was because of its properties in managing the Indian heat. Garcia da Orta, who refused to take paan, pronounced both the betel and the slaked lime paste used in paan to be warm. It is the betel and lime, along with the bitter katha paste often used to bind the ingredients, which induce a light sweat in the paan-taker. The paan's heat, in other words, helps one endure the hot weather.

A similarly homeopathic logic lurks in Manucci's other favoured antidote to India's torrid climate. The antidote is mentioned also by François Bernier: water mixed with saltpetre or gunpowder. Saltpetre was thought of as a 'hot' substance because, when combusted, it generates even more heat. But it has marvellously cooling effects when dissolved in water. Manucci affirms that Lord Bellomont, who had suffered from 'the great heat that has to be endured in that country', found that water mixed with gunpowder allowed him to 'experience great relief and coolness'. For Manucci, then, weathering the hot weather of India meant opening up to explosively hot foodstuffs. He abided by a version of the old adage that if you can't stand the heat, you should get out of the kitchen. More precisely, he believed that you need to savour the hottest foods of the Indian kitchen—chilli, paan, gunpowder—to stand the heat of the Indian climate.

How to reconcile the Indian dietary habits that Manucci acquired with his express disdain for Indians and Indian cultures? The two positions are not quite as opposed as one would think. Manucci repeatedly represents Indians as being ignorant of local resources that would best help them in dealing with the heat: they simply do not know which local foods are appropriate for which season. He notes how Aurangzeb mistakenly hankered for cool watermelons 'owing to the great heat he was in'; rather than helping him, however, the water-melons induced 'a paralysis of the tongue, so that he very nearly lost his power of speech entirely'. This is of a piece with the ill preparations Indians generally make for dealing with the heat. In war, for instance, Manucci claims that 'heat and thirst' killed more of Dara's men than Aurangzeb's troops did. And he claims that the Hindu raja of Pent's otherwise healthy son refused Manucci's advice about how best to cope with the heat, as a result of which he was killed by 'the great heat of the sun, which inflamed his blood'. In his account, then, Manucci weathers the Indian weather better than the Indians themselves do.

Manucci harps on this position throughout the *Storia do Mogor*. He repeatedly presents Indians as the witless victims of heat, and not just in their bad dietary choices. The Mughals, he says, do not know how to service old buildings damaged by the heat and humidity: he notes how the hilltop fortress at Narwar is crumbling because of 'the inclemency of the weather' and 'the negligence of the Mughal king'. He smirks at Dara Shikoh's fondness for paper as a writing surface even though, as any user of Indian historical archives knows, paper quickly acquires mould in hot humid weather: Manucci informs Dara that 'it was the usage for European kings, when forwarding letters to far-off kingdoms, to have the more important matters written on vellum skin, in order that they might be better protected against the inclemencies of the weather and of the journey than they would be if they were on paper'. Not just Indian buildings and paper but also Indian bodies are deformed by the heat. Manucci even believed that the heat made female Indian bodies prematurely fertile at the age of nine.

Indians are, in Manucci's account, incapable of weathering the hot weather. Yet he repeatedly learned from them how to do so. He carefully observed the effects of Indian foodstuffs on his body; he also paid close heed to Indian customs of clothing and sleeping. In the process, he slowly but surely trained his body to adjust to the extreme heat. At times he comes close to acknowledging his debt to local customs of weather-management. 'In India, where the climate is so hot,' he observes, 'even the nobles are forced to go about with a simple qaba, and nothing more; and they sleep uncovered in the dew, or on the damp ground upon a simple mat.' These are habits that Manucci himself doubtless emulated—habits that, like the taking of paan, he couldn't entirely dismiss as the customs of weak non-Christians. And it is his close attention to the effects of heat and how to deal with them that led Manucci to the practice of medicine in India.

◆

During his first stint in Goa in the 1660s, Manucci fell repeatedly sick. He blamed his poor health on the local climate: he thought its heat and humidity were terrible for young people of robust constitution. But his experience of illness seems to have heightened his already keen interest in how to manage physical health in relation to one's environment. Perhaps it's no coincidence that it was here in Goa that the ailing Manucci resolved, despite his complete lack of formal training, to follow through on his long-standing ambition to become a doctor. Interestingly, he was to acquire his skills not from European doctors in Portuguese colonial Goa, but from local experts in Indian territories—Mughal Hindustan, the Golconda Sultanate, and southern India.

Manucci's medical career was a long one, spanning five decades. But it is often dismissed by his biographers as an extended exercise in charlatanism and quackery. In this regard, at least, Manucci was his own worst enemy. He himself admits in the *Storia* that he often barely knew what he was doing. One memorable episode about his medical practice comes across as pure theatre. When Manucci was still barely out of his teens, and living in Delhi, he was suddenly and surprisingly summoned to the house of an Uzbek envoy from Balkh in what is now Afghanistan. The summons came because a relation of the envoy had fallen sick and the envoy, believing all firangis to be physicians, assumed Manucci was one. Rather than disabuse the envoy of his fanciful notion, Manucci played the part with gusto. He rushed to the patient's bedside. 'To induce him to believe that I was a great physician', Manucci writes, 'I asked the patient's age, and then for a time I assumed a pensive attitude, as if I were seeking for the cause of the illness'. Warming to his role, Manucci continued to play-act. 'As is the fashion with doctors', Manucci writes, 'I said some words making the attack to be very grave'. His Uzbek audience was impressed: 'all of them were in a state of admiration, saying among themselves that I was a great physician, and that the Franks had received from heaven the gift of being accomplished doctors'.

Some ten years later, Manucci began to practice as a 'real' doctor in Lahore. He claims that, by this stage, he had actually begun to study the principles of medicine: he was occasionally aided by tips from travelling firangi physicians on how to let blood, perform enemas, and cure fistulas, though he was just as if not more indebted to the knowledge of local hakeems. But he concedes in the *Storia* that his practice still consisted largely of theatrical performance. In Lahore he traded on the Indians' widespread belief that firangis are the best doctors and his evident gift of the gab. Having ordered his servants to 'inform everyone that I was a firangi doctor', would-be patients came to talk with him; 'in return', he says, 'I had no want of words, God having given me a sufficiently mercurial temperament'. As a result, word got out in Lahore that 'a Frank doctor had arrived, a man of fine manners, eloquent speech, and great experience'. Manucci was thrilled by his new reputation, but the fact that it was based on little more than theatrical flair caused him considerable anxiety: 'my heart beat fast', he confesses, 'for then I had had no experience'. It is perhaps no surprise that, when talking about his work as a doctor in Lahore, he often speaks about himself in the third person—as if his new career was simply a theatrical role. He likes referring to himself, as the Mughals did, as 'Hakim Niccolao, the Frank'. And he presents this third-person character as a daring charlatan: 'but now came the moment', he writes dramatically about having to improvise medical treatments he knew nothing of, 'when our Nicolao Manuchy found himself in a difficulty'.

There were many such difficulties. Some Europeans, and many more Indians, believed that Manucci resorted to highly dodgy practices. In Lahore, he was accused of letting Indians' blood for private cannibalistic purposes. Even more sensationally, the supposed Vampire of Venice was accused of using human body fat as an ingredient in his ointments. The Mughal governor of Lahore had arrested the fearsome bandit giant Thika Arain, scourge of Punjab, and had him and his equally enormous lieutenant paraded through the streets of the city in between four elephants. Because Thika Arain was the brother-in-law of the qazi of Lahore, the parade drew a huge number of onlookers. Among them was Manucci. Perhaps, on seeing Thika Arain and his lieutenant, Manucci remembered his encounter with the two English bandits more than a decade earlier. But what he seems primarily to have seen in the two hulks was a good source of premium fat. He wrote to the governor, requesting—and receiving—permission to tap their bodies after their execution. Their beheaded corpses were privately delivered to Manucci, and he and his helpers managed to extract from them no less than 500 ounces of purified fat, which he incorporated into unguents for medicinal use. Thika's brother-in-law, the qazi, got wind of what Manucci had done and started proceedings against him. When these failed, he personally visited Manucci and tried to trap him into confessing that he had used the fat for oral medicines—which would amount to cannibalism. Manucci claimed that he used the fat only on the skin. Then the qazi asked for medicine for a cough; Manucci suggested that he imbibe 'human myrrh', a term for 'mummy' or burned human flesh. The qazi replied that he had already done so. Manucci then triumphantly pointed out to the qazi that human myrrh is, in fact, made of human flesh, and therefore he should not be so upset about fat used in oral medicine.

For a modern reader, Manucci's exchange with the qazi might reinforce the suspicion that the firangi doctor was nothing but a quack. And it is certainly the case that Manucci often used substances that had little or no medicinal value. Human fat and myrrh would seem to rank among these. Yet there was in fact a long-standing and highly respectable medical tradition in both Europe and the Arab world of prescribing medicines derived from human bodies. Old European medical recipes often included pinguedo hominis, or human fat; the sixteenth-century German doctor Johann Agricola described at length how to retrieve it from bodies. (For all we know, Manucci followed Agricola's protocols when lipo-suctioning the bodies of Thika Arain and his lieutenant.) And both Arab and European physicians valued the medicinal properties of 'mumia' or mummy, the charred residue of human corpses. It seems highly distasteful to us now, but perversely Manucci's suggestion that the qazi of Lahore take human fat to treat his cold may have been one of his more conventional medical recommendations in his long and often unscrupulous career in India.

Yet to see Manucci simply as a quack is problematic. He may not have had the book learning of a Garcia da Orta or even a Juliana Dias da Costa; he was certainly not acquainted as Orta was with Avicenna or Juliana Dias da Costa with Indo-Persian medicine, nor did he have any deep understanding of Galen—and, as we have seen, he departed from Galenic tradition. But Manucci did acquire a certain skill through careful empirical observation. 'Experience is my great teacher', he writes. Manucci certainly started out as a charlatan, but he was a quick learner; his knowledge and reputation grew in Lahore, where he practiced as a physician from 1670 to 1678, partly because he enjoyed an enviable success rate in his treatments. And this success had much to do with his heightened sensitivity to the effects of the environment, particularly the climate, on health. Some of his supposedly 'quack' remedies emerged from his understanding of the climate. Take blood-letting, for example:

for us it is a barbarous practice, a byword for the ignorant practices of a pre-scientific age. But in a hot climate, blood-letting can mitigate the effects of fever by reducing blood pressure. Manucci clearly saw for himself how the practice could help patients afflicted by the heat.

But it was on matters of diet that Manucci most learned from his experiences. As we have seen, he had personally experienced the homeopathic benefits of hot substances in mitigating the heat. However, his dietary remedies emerged not from any systematic theory of homeopathy, or any other medical theory; in the *Storia*, he simply recommends those Indian foodstuffs that, in his experience, have had the best medicinal effects. And Manucci's faith in what works, rather than in this or that theory of medicine, can make him seem by turns a good folk healer and an unabashed quack. He swears, like any Jewish mother, by chicken soup; he also insists on the proven medicinal power of the bezoar stone, an ulcerated carbuncle extracted from the intestines of goats. Such endorsements, no matter how bizarre, are usually accompanied by an anecdote about how the miracle foodstuff in question has restored their eaters to a state of good health. Indeed, Manucci repeatedly observes what foods do to his own body and those of others, whether human or animal. For example, he tells the tale of how, while travelling in the Deccan, his horse had accidentally devoured a nutmeg; the next day, writes Manucci, 'I noticed that he was much more lively in his gait.' Testing his observation, Manucci continued to feed his horse a nutmeg each day, as a result of which 'he became every more ready and clever.'

Manucci, in other words, was a student not of medical books but of medical biography. Which is to say: he was unusually attuned to the ways in which his own body and those of others interacted with, and were imprinted by, their local environments. Manucci's personal embodied experiences in India—whether of the hot climate or of ingesting local substances in order to weather it—arguably provided the foundation for his later practice as a physician in Madras. And there he worked not just as any physician, but more specifically as a medical practitioner conversant with a local south Indian tradition.

◆

The best view of Madras, now Chennai, is from the top of St Thomas Mount, near the airport. An effigy of a smiling Pope John Paul II stands by the rails at the summit; behind him, you can see the megacity sprawling all the way to the horizon. The hill's name in Tamil, Parangi

Malai, means Firangi Mountain. It allegedly commemorates the apostle St Thomas, who is said to have evangelized on the Malabar and Coromandel coasts from 52 CE before being martyred twenty years later on the hilltop. Several churches in St Thomas's name have been built on its summit; the present structure dates back to 1523. But Parangi Malai was also the home of another firangi some 1,640 years after the saint was martyred—Niccolò Manucci.

By the late 1600s, the name of Parangi Malai may have paid homage less to Jesus's travelling apostle than to the growing number of Englishmen who lived on the hill. It had become something of a fashion for East India Company officials to build country bungalows on its slopes. This was in large part to escape the intense heat of Madras. When the local Vijayanagar chief Damarla Venkatadri Nayaka granted the town of Madrasapatnam to the Company in 1639, it was hardly a favourable acquisition: although the Cooum and Egmore rivers flowing on either side of the town promised a haven of sorts to the Company's merchant ships, it was located on a mostly barren sandbar that radiated the sun's heat through the day. The earliest English houses in Madras, as it came to be called, were probably ill-fitted for the weather; if they were the simple four-walled bungalows favoured by the Company, they would have been heat-traps for much of the day, absorbing the hot air rising off Madras's baking sand. By contrast, the slopes of St Thomas Mount were not only cooler; they also offered soil rather than sand in which to grow flowers and herbs.

Manucci and his wife Elizabeth were among the first firangis to join the exodus from the White Town to St Thomas Mount. Manucci acquired a garden property there in the 1690s; we do not have a sense of his new house's design, but it was sufficiently large and comfortable that he was able to host eminent guests there, including Da'ud Khan. Perhaps Manucci incorporated elements of Mughal design—jaalis, terraces—into his new house in order to weather the hot weather of the south. But it was outdoors at Parangi Malai that Manucci was most exposed to the local environment. The hill's rich alluvial soil allowed Manucci to grow the flowers and herbs he used in his medical practice. He doubtless grew some medicinal plants also in the garden of the house on Broadway that he had inherited through his wife: that property had become sufficiently well-known that, in his map of Madras from 1711, Thomas Pitt referred to it as 'Manoucha's Garden'. But Manucci's St Thomas Mount garden would have afforded him many more opportunities to grow the plants he needed for his medical practice. One of the two surviving pictures of Manucci is a Mughal-style miniature portrait; wearing Indian garb, he twirls a flower. In his case, however, the flower may be less the traditional Mughal sign of aesthetic refinement than evidence of the kind of material he worked with as a physician in Parangi Malai, using materials plucked from his garden.

Manucci didn't practice simply as a herbalist. Europeans and Indians alike valued his medical skills in potions and cordials made from minerals. Especially in demand was his efficacious concoction, 'the Manooch's Stone', made of a local mineral substance called lingam. The term derives from the Sanskrit word for 'mark' or 'sign'; it is most often associated with the shivalingam, a phallic symbol representing the male creative power of Shiva. But no, Manucci's lingam was not what one might think it to be. Despite his prior experiments in hacking medicinal substances out of men's bodies, no precious parts of male anatomy—human or divine—were used in the manufacture of Manucci's lingam. His lingam was, rather, cinnabar, known to Western chemists as mercuric sulphide.

The substance was a staple of the siddha vaidyas, Indian doctors skilled in an antique form of Tamil medicine close to Ayurveda and Unani. Siddha medicine is thousands of years old; ancient palm-leaf manuscripts claim that its principles were first formulated by Lord Shiva to his wife Parvathi, but it seems to have been devised by spiritual adepts named siddhars, a term derived from the Sanskrit siddhi, meaning 'perfection' or 'attainment'. Siddhars traditionally employed frequently elaborate combinations of thavaram (herbal), thadhu (mineral), and jangamam (animal) drugs—some of their medicines involve more than 250 ingredients—to treat disruptions of the body's health. In siddha medicine, disease is understood not to be an infectious condition but rather a state of disequilibrium. This state is largely internal, occurring when the body's basic elements are out of balance. But it is also understood holistically in relation to the external environment, inasmuch as the body's health is potentially disrupted by external elements such as climate and foodstuffs. Siddha drugs, including lingam, work by restoring balance to the body in relation to its environment. As a result, both the maintenance of health and the curing of disease demand careful attention to what one eats.

We don't know how Manucci chanced upon the medicinal properties of lingam, such as they are. The substance has few proven health benefits: indeed, the mercury in it has decidedly toxic effects—including blindness—when consumed even in minor quantities. It's possible that the failing eyesight of which Manucci complained in the 1690s was less the product of Madras's glaring sun and heat than of mercury poisoning induced by his contact with lingam. Yet the substance was believed to have beneficial effects on those suffering from impotence. It is likely that, as with the earlier remedies he had employed in Mughal Hindustan, Manucci used lingam simply because he believed it to work; it's hard to imagine him becoming a zealous convert to a whole theoretical system such as siddha, let alone becoming a Shiva devotee. And we have little evidence of him working with other siddha medicines. Nevertheless much of siddha philosophy—particularly its emphasis on the intimate relation between the body and its food and climate—would have resonated with Manucci's experiences in India. Although the traditional Galenic medicine of Europe also emphasized the relations between health, diet and climate, siddha philosophy does so in slightly different ways. It doesn't believe simply that, as in Galenic tradition, a new climate disrupts the body's constitution and potentially makes it fall sick. For siddhars, a new climate also transforms the body irrevocably, making it belong in unexpected ways to its new location. Manucci's decision to heed François Martin's advice not to risk his life by returning to the cooler climes of Europe illustrates the siddhar philosophy, as does his conviction that eating certain Indian foods contributed to his physical health as much as his gastronomic pleasure.

By prescribing lingam in the heat of Madras, Manucci arguably resorted to a homeopathic treatment reminiscent of his dietary regime of hot foods. Like the phallic linga and the god Shiva with whom it is associated, lingam is supposed to be infused with the element of fire. Indian medical manuals warn that an excess of lingam can aggravate the pitta humour (or bile) and cause sluggishness, and should not be used in cases of fever. Manucci seems to have been unaware of this caveat; for all we know, he was unaware too of lingam's heat. But his lingam-filled 'Manooch's Stone' was touted as a miracle remedy for all sorts of heat-related ailments in Madras.

Searching for traces of Manucci more than three decades in or near Madras is a near-impossible task. The town in which he lived is enormously different from the Chennai of today. The one was a tiny European outpost ethnically segregated from the community of Indian workers who sustained it. The other is a sprawling, traffic-clogged megacity of nine million that constantly and insatiably swallows up its past—including the historical remnants of the neighbouring Portuguese colony, now remembered only in the name of the Chennai suburb Santhome and its church. The cannons that Manucci describes seeing at Madras's Fort St George survive; but his two houses and gardens are long gone, their foundations destroyed or buried deep beneath the rickety buildings of Broadway near China Bazaar Road and the army barracks near St Thomas Mount. What remains, though, is the local medical culture absorbed by Manucci. Siddha medical practice is still very much alive in the city. In Chennai's leafy suburb of Anna Nagar, one can find the Siddha Central Medical Research Institute. Its dispensary features powders and potions that would have been familiar to Manucci, including ground lingam. Many Tamil patients still avail themselves of lingam in the treatment of disorders from impotence to chronic arthritis.

How can we reconcile Manucci's Hinduphobia with his embrace of siddha medicine? The truth is that we can't. And that is because he was simultaneously a committed European (referred to in East India Company records as 'Signor Manuch') and an assimilated Indian (the 'Hakim Niccolao' of Mughal fame). Here he might remind us of another Venetian traveller, albeit a fictional one: Othello. At the end of Shakespeare's tragedy, Othello tells of meeting a Turk in Aleppo who has bad-mouthed the Venetian state; recalling how he killed this 'circumcised dog', Othello demonstrates what he did by stabbing himself. Othello acts here as both loyal Venetian and renegade Asian: his identity is not single but double. Manucci's identity was similarly bifurcated.

Manucci late in life cultivated a mad desire to return 'home' to England. In 1716, the Madras Council wrote to him that 'when Senr. Manuch desires to come to England', the authorities 'will let him'. Yet the occasion never arose, because Manucci continued to feel most comfortable in the heat of Tamil Nadu. We can glimpse something of Manucci's self-division in one passage from the *Storia*. In it, he mourns the fact that although he has 'acquired several secrets' from his time in India, he has 'no heir to whom to bequeath these treasures that preserve our bodily health'. In this context, 'our bodily health' seems to refer specifically to the health of European bodies. Such a view was aided and abetted in early colonial Madras, where Manucci consorted with Europeans and could marry the daughter of an Englishman. But the fact is that his knowledge of 'our bodily health'—a patrimony he wished to pass on to future generations of Europeans—was a product of

Indian customs and Indian climate, as too was the body whose health was preserved by that knowledge. Even as Manucci narrated himself at the dawn of the British Raj as a European through and through, his transformed body told an entirely different story, a firangi story of becoming Indian.

Othello's and Manucci's double identities have another point of commonality. It is not as if Othello's self-identification as a Turk radically undermines his Venetian identity. On the contrary, it is that identity's very foundation. Othello's suicide underscores how his being Venetian demands of him a simultaneous identification with the evil Turk in order to demonstrate European might and supremacy over its enemies. Similarly, Manucci's Indianized body allowed him to be 'European' in segregated Madras. How? Manucci needed to adapt to the Indian weather to survive as someone who could complain to other Europeans about the duplicity and ignorance of Hindus and Mohammedans. His biography is undoubtedly much the same as those of many British colonists of this time, whose bodies inevitably changed in response to Indian climates, terrains, clothes, foods, and medicines. With Manucci's life-story, it is hard not to see a decisive transition from the startling biographies of pre-Raj firangi migration to the more familiar histories of British colonialism. After Manucci's move to Madras, becoming Indian began to serve very different ends from what it had for previous firangi migrants: British colonial settlers' bodies collectively adapted to Indian environments in order to conquer, divide and rule their new home away from home.

But there, in that word 'home', is the rub. Manucci weathered the weather, whatever the weather, of India. Yet his weathered and weathering body changed so much that he was unable to go back to the place he once called home. Because home was now India, whether he liked it or not.

ON BEING INTERRUPTED

In India, I am always interrupted.

For someone brought up in an Anglo-Saxon culture that respects the right of (certain) people to finish expressing a thought without interruption, the rhythms of Indian conversation can seem non-dialogic and even downright rude. Exchanges between Indian friends often involve finishing others' sentences, cutting them off, or abruptly changing the topic at hand. If Anglo-Saxon decorum imagines conversation as a polite game of gentleman's lawn tennis with two people taking turns to lob a theme to and fro ('your shot, partner!'), Indian conversation feels more like a rough-and-tumble game of hockey with many clubs swinging—or, perhaps more accurately, a game of hockey with many balls being simultaneously whacked.

I'll never forget a conversation I was part of while travelling many years ago. My partner, her parents, and her aunt were driving with me through Coimbatore. I had been trying to talk about something or other. But I was interrupted simultaneously by everyone in the car: my partner spoke about the itinerary for the day, her father muttered about the dining options, her mother absent-mindedly read out street signs, and her aunt updated us on the local family gossip. All through this, our driver tunelessly sang Tamil film songs along with the car radio. Everyone was interrupting everyone else. I felt distressed, frustrated and passed over. Yet slowly it dawned on me that what I was listening to were not five simultaneous monologues. Somehow the conversation flowed organically, with each of the passengers—except for fussy me—cheerfully submitting both to the certainty of interruption and to the necessity of listening to several channels at once. After all, in a country with a population of 1.2 billion where it is hard to escape being in a crowd, interruption on multiple frequencies is only inevitable.

If there is one skill I have had to pick up while living in India, it is the art of handling interruption. I have spoken about this challenge with some of my Western friends. One of them quips that, in India, he has learned 'how to be interrupted in five languages'. But interruption isn't just a conversational phenomenon. It's far more pervasive. Lives in India are interrupted by flash floods and power outages, by drought and hunger, by farmer suicide and mass migration to cities, by sexual violence and honour killings. In a culture addicted to the cell phone, lives are additionally interrupted by calls and SMSes. Thanks to the machinations of politicians, humdrum daily routines are interrupted by sudden edicts and flare-ups of communal tension. The Indian past has been interrupted by colonialism, just as the Indian present is interrupted by global capitalism and the forces of 'development'.

Perhaps it's no coincidence that, in India's national sport, interruption is a given: a cricket game can be interrupted because of bad light, rain, or (more disturbingly) rioting crowds. To play cricket well means, among other things, learning how to cope with such interruptions—which usually entails carrying on somehow, but in a different mode and on different terms from what one may have been used to previously.

Handling interruption entails above all a change of mindset. One has to give up on the sanctity of one's customary individual trajectory—whether in thought, space, or time—and embrace the possibility of both pleasant and unpleasant surprise. One has to accept that the immediate environment—whether social, cultural, or physical—might in an instant become something completely different. This also means accepting that one's body should be versatile enough to respond and adapt to unanticipated possibilities. My favourite Hindi word, jugaad—perhaps best translated as 'makeshift fix'—captures something of the improvisational flair that is required to cope with India's thousand and one varieties of interruption.

In many ways, this has been a book all about interruption and the diverse forms of jugaad that interruption can inspire. The first firangis whose stories I have told here all had to deal with interruption in a myriad of ways. Their lives in their native countries were interrupted; the bodily habits into which they had been socialized were interrupted; their ways of thinking about themselves and the world were interrupted. And in turn, the first firangis interrupted, and continue to interrupt, what it means to be Indian. But that doesn't make them in any way unique. No one single trajectory of Indianness—whether religious, cultural or linguistic—can go uninterrupted for long. At risk of making a sweeping generalization, one might even say that the 'authentically Indian' can never be identified with a singular trajectory but, rather, has always been a series of interruptions and creative responses to those interruptions.

Because, ultimately, what it means to be authentically Indian is—

14 | HOW TO BE AUTHENTICALLY INDIAN

Since my first visit to India in 2001, I've been fascinated by the word 'firangi'. A variant form will be familiar to aficionados of *Hobson-Jobson* and British Raj literature, in which 'feringhee' is a common Indian term of abuse for white colonists; another form will ring bells for fans of *Star Trek*, in which the 'Ferengi' are a race of unscrupulous intergalactic traders. The term's most common English translation, 'foreigner', doesn't do justice to its subtle shades of meaning. Firangi is a broad synonym for the Hindi videshi (alien) and pardesi (outsider). But these two Hindi words are also a world away, quite literally, from 'firangi', a Mughal-era Persian loan word from the Arabic farenji, meaning 'Frank' or Frenchman, but applied broadly to Christians. Franks, after all, dominated the ranks of the first waves of the Crusaders.

Garcia da Orta insisted that the word 'firangi' should be understood as referring exclusively to European Christians, on the basis that north African Coptic Christians were distinguished from farenji Christians living in Cairo. Yet the term's multiple, shifting Indian usages from the sixteenth century to the present tell a much more complicated story. First employed by the Mughals as a blanket term for any Christian, 'firangi' has been subsequently applied to white Europeans, brown Armenians, 'black' mixed-blood Portuguese Indians, Muslim Africans, and now foreigners resident in India. In sum, its referent is far from self-evident. 'Firangi' doesn't so much describe a specific ethnic or religious identity as it troubles the very idea of identity itself. To the extent that it does point to any specific identity, it is an identity at odds with itself: a migrant to India who has become Indian, even as—or because—s/he continues to be marked as foreign.

From 'feringhee' to 'ferengi', and through all its other shifts in usage, firangi has by and large retained its derogatory implications. This is not surprising for a term that was long used in colonial India as a synonym for syphilis as well as for the British. Perversely, however, it has also been repeatedly employed as an affectionate name for Indians, especially in lower-caste and rural circles. One of the leaders of the Quit India movement in Bengal was a Dalit from Darjeeling named Munshi Firangi. And British Raj court records from the mid twentieth century list dakaits from Bihar and Uttar Pradesh named Firangi Rai and Firangi Singh. Likewise, one of the gangsters in *Omkara*, the 2006 Uttar

Pradesh-located Hindi film adaptation of *Othello*, is named Kesu Firangi.

In its contemporary rural underworld usage, the name 'Firangi' possesses a hint of outlaw glamour. This may derive in part from a buried memory of those sixteenth-century military regiments in the Deccan sultanates known as the firangiyan, foreign soldiers who had gained a double-edged reputation as lethal experts in artillery and as low-life drunks. Perhaps a similar buried memory lurks also in the Urdu tradition of dastangoi, a form of story-telling popular in north India until the late nineteenth century and derived from Persian narratives of the life of Amir Hamza. In one dastangoi cycle, Hamza's chief trickster Amar Ayyar joins forces with another trickster from Firangistan named Barq Firangi, leader of a platoon whose members speak English. This Barq Firangi is not a British invader, or even a closet imperialist, but a mischievous, shape-shifting ally of the Urdu-speaking characters. He even disguises himself as a female seductress to slay the evil sorcerer Azlam.

From underworld criminal culture to popular story-telling tradition, then, the word 'firangi' connotes foreignness in potentially positive ways. And as a proper noun, it paradoxically signals one's place—liminal or criminal though it may be—within a specifically Indian community, and in a way that pardesi or videshi does not. In addition to Indian bandits named Firangi and the firangiyan regiments loyal to the Deccan sultanates, we find several foreigners entering into service with an Indian master and being given the new name Firangi Khan. As we saw in Chapter 1, this was the desi name of the sixteenth-century renegade Sancho Pires. And as we saw in Chapter 5, another person to receive the name was João de Santiago, an African Muslim enslaved and forcibly converted to Christianity as a youth before being taken to Goa by his Portuguese owner in the 1530s. After his master's death, Santiago fled Goa, reverted to Islam, and found service with the Sultan of Gujarat, who renamed him Firangi Khan.

In other words, the proper noun 'Firangi' could name a local partisan as much as a foreign enemy. Who knows which, if any, Indian names were bestowed on Manucci's English adversaries Thomas Roch and Raben Simitt after they found employment with Shah Jahan. But they were doubtless addressed as 'firangi!' by their Indian masters and fellows—an epithet, I am arguing, that would have served *both* to highlight their foreign origin *and* to integrate them into the culture of the Mughal military.

The elasticity of 'firangi' in the sixteenth and seventeenth centuries has led me to use the word throughout this book in capacious, counter-intuitive ways that may raise some eyebrows, at least among those habituated to the 'feringhee' as a white invader. I have included among the first firangis not only European Christian migrants but also others with whom we might not readily associate the term: a warrior sailor of Chinese or Malayan origin, a slave-turned-urban planner from Ethiopia, a wandering Armenian Jew from Persia. Which is to say: this book trades on the fact that the word 'firangi' possessed—and still possesses—an imprecision that neither the English 'foreigner' nor the Hindi pardesi or videshi can quite communicate. Yet this imprecision is precisely what I love about the word. 'Firangi' can never mean simply British or Christian or white non-Indian (although it is still often used that way) and it can never be simply derogatory (although it is, again, still often used to that effect). In its history of diverse usages, 'firangi' evokes less a fixed identity of the kind presumed by our modern racial or ethnic categories than complex processes of migration, transformation and self-division—processes that have produced foreigners who are not foreign and Indians who are not Indian. Videshi and pardesi are home-grown terms derived from Sanskrit. By contrast, the word firangi is like what it describes throughout this book: a migrant to India that has somehow become Indian yet continues to be marked as alien.

My former Hindi teacher in Washington DC favours a chaste Sanskritised language purged of all supposedly alien interlopers. So she grimaces whenever she hears the word firangi. 'Yeh shabd kyaa hai?' ('What is this word?'), she asks. 'Hindi nahin hai. Sahi shabd "videshi" hai.' ('It isn't Hindi. The correct word is "videshi".') As this might suggest, she considers 'firangi' an impure term, a linguistic foreign body that has illegitimately become Indian. Yet Indian it undeniably is. Even today, as I flick through the pages of *Filmfare*, I see a photo of the Bollywood actress Nargis Fakhri accompanied by the caption 'true firangi charm'. The mixed-language caption underlines how this foreign word that has become Indian is the perfect term for foreigners who have become Indian. Fakhri, of course, was born in America of mixed Pakistani and Czech heritage.

The idea that something or someone foreign can become Indian raises the question: what does it mean to be authentically Indian? For my teacher, the answer to that question is a loaded one. I suspect she objects to the word 'firangi' less because of its derogatory associations than because it came to India with the Mughals. In her view, the more

Hindi can be made to approximate the Sanskrit of pre-Muslim India, the more authentic it will be. Yet this conflation of the authentically Indian with a supposedly original Indian culture (and, by implication, with Hinduism) disavows the extent to which the subcontinent has always been a land of migrants. In the words of former Indian Supreme Court judge Markandey Katju, 'India is a country of mostly immigrants who came to the country over the past 10,000 years.' Katju presumably has in mind the many waves of migration to the subcontinent through its northwest, which has added Turkic, Mongolian, Afghan, Greek, Persian, Arab, Armenian, and Jewish DNA to India's exceptionally diverse genetic mix. As a result of migrations through the northeast, Chinese, Tibetan, Thai, and Burmese genes have also mingled with the local pool. And countless waves of maritime migration have brought peoples from all over the world—Yemeni, Syrian, African, Australoid, European—to the subcontinent. All Indians, even Hindus like my teacher who insist on the purity of their Indianness, even tribal peoples who have made their homes in the forests of Chattisgarh or the hills of Arunachal Pradesh for millennia, ultimately have some foreign ancestry.

In the face of such diversity, however, what can it mean to be 'authentically Indian' other than to be a migrant to India or the descendant of one? How, as a consequence, might the history of firangis such as Roch and Simitt shed unexpected light on what it means to be 'authentically Indian'? How might it allow us to recognize that the human history of the subcontinent—despite the weight of tradition, despite the vituperations of Hindutva, despite the rigidities of varna—is less one of pure origins than of multiple migrations, mixings, and adaptations? What if the 'authentically Indian' were to name not a pure but an impure condition? Indeed, what does it even mean to be 'authentically Indian' when the very word 'India' is itself a firangi invention, derived from the Greek name for a river in what is now Pakistan—the Indus (Sindhu in Sanskrit)?

Many poor firangis such as Roch and Simitt passed as Indian, at least to outsiders. To do so, they needed to master local languages, wear local clothes, and learn local customs; they needed too to be absorbed into local social structures—political, professional, religious, familial—which bonded them closely to Indian masters, co-workers, friends, and lovers. But what made these firangis most 'authentically Indian,' at least in the somewhat ironic sense I'm using the phrase here, was not their assimilation into indigenous cultures. They were not authentically

Indian because they wrote verse Puranas in the Marathi ovi style, or had studied the philosophy and practice of Tamil siddha medicine, or waggled their heads and ate with their hands. Many of them did, but that is not the point. What I've tried to recover in this book is not a purely indigenous 'Indian-ness' that the first firangis acquired as if it were simply one exotic commodity in the global supermarket of local cultures. Rather, the first firangis were most authentically Indian when what they created in India was simultaneously local *and* foreign. Becoming Indian, in the various cases I have examined, was—and still is—intimately connected to a process of Indian-Becoming. Which is to say: the 'Indian' is always becoming something new, and is constantly being renegotiated and transformed in a multitude of ways, because of unexpected conversations between local traditions and foreign elements.

As its very etymological history suggests, 'India' has never been a pure entity. Nor have Indians ever had a purely local origin. India and Indians are, linguistically and culturally as much as genetically, the outcomes of multiple border-crossings. So much of what we regard as authentically Indian has been, and continues to be, born of transnational migrations and mixings: for instance, a beloved Marathi and Konkani epic poem written by an Englishman and embraced by twentieth-century Indian freedom fighters; a legendary Mughal throne incorporating Basque artisanal techniques that has become an enduring synonym for Indian power; the rubaiyat of a Jewish Armenian Sufi-cum-Yogi still revered by present-day Indian Muslims and Hindus. In all these cases, the 'authentically Indian' is the handiwork of firangis who crossed borders and became something other than what they were. And in the process of becoming Indian, they also helped make India something other than what it was.

JONATHAN GIL HARRIS

ACKNOWLEDGEMENTS

More than any other book I have written, this feels like the product of collective enterprise—or rather, of several collective enterprises. The book had its origin in two very different venues in two different continents: a graduate course I taught at George Washington University in 2008 called 'Becoming Indian', and a series of articles I wrote for the *Hindustan Times* in 2011. I thank my graduate students for pushing me to embrace my rather bizarre seminar theme as a workable book project, and to Poonam Saxena at the *Hindustan Times* for cajoling me into writing it up for a popular audience—some of whom have given me invaluable feedback and helped make this book what it is.

My editor at Aleph Book Company, the incomparable David Davidar, recognized that the half-academic, half-populist genesis of this book was not a liability but an asset. It is because of him that I wrote a more experimentally autobiographical book than I would otherwise have dared. And Pujitha Krishnan, my astute copy-editor, has made my prose better than it would have otherwise been.

I am deeply grateful to the many friends and strangers in India and Pakistan who have showered me with advice, food and astonishing hospitality, including a nameless man who gave me the tastiest banana I have ever eaten after I was pickpocketed in Ajmer. Nadhra Khan, Anjum Altaf and Furrukh Khan were ideal hosts in Lahore; Nadhra made it possible for me to enter the startling underground apartments of the Lahore Fort. Fr. Pratap Nayak gave me access to the materials housed in the library of the Thomas Stephens Konknni Kendr in Bardez, Goa. Fr. Dennis Fernandes, at the Rachol Seminary, led me on an unforgettable tour of the premises. In Delhi, Sanghamitra Mishra and Rahul Govind helped me track down some rare information about Mandu Firangi. For stories about Bengal, colonial and pre-colonial, I am indebted to Subha Mukherjee and Supriya Chaudhuri. Nandini Das knows far more about Thomas Roe than I do, and I have learned much from her. Mahmood Farooqui, Danish Husain and Anusha Rizvi told me tales about Barq Firangi, Sa'id Sarmad Kashani and Juliana Dias da Costa. Nabina Das has regaled me with stories about Bengali pirates and Thomas Coryate. Roopanjali Roy introduced me to the mystery of Garcia da Orta and Goa's undercover Jews. Yaaminey Mubayi gave me a crash-course in Malik Ambar's ceramic pipe technology. Antony Arul Valan first alerted me to the life and works of Veeramamunivar/Costanzo Giuseppe Beschi, and the importance of the European Jesuits like Pâtri Guru/Thomas Stephens who 'acculturated' to Indian languages and cultures. Conversations with Rita Kothari have helped me better understand Gujarat and linguistic swerving. Thanks too to Jyotirmoy Talukdar for being an early champion of the book and writing about it in Assamese as well as English long before its publication. Marzook Bafakhy, Samay U. Chowdhury, Jasmine Luthra, Ulises Mejias, and P. S. Sudheer all chipped in with invaluable photographs when I needed them. Vibha Kamat, who read my early piece in the *Hindustan Times* about Thomas Stephens, helped me with my translations of the *Kristapurana*, as did Suresh Walawalikar. And I am deeply grateful to the intellectual generosity of William Dalrymple, who provided me with considerable support and invaluable archival materials at critical junctures during this long march.

Ashoka University and the Young India Fellowship have gifted me a stimulating workplace and students beyond compare. It was after first presenting a talk on Odd Tom Coryate and Becoming Indian to the Young India Fellows in 2011 that I realized this was more than just a wild idea and could be massaged into a book. The Young India Fellowship also provided me with four research assistants—Mrudula NS, Sanchit Sharma, Ankita Shirodariya, and Antony Arul Valan—who helped make some of the characters in this book come alive for me in a way that they might not have otherwise.

As one of the Montaignean interludes in this book makes clear, I owe a special debt to my running group. Their camaraderie as well as the many miles we have run together over the roads, parks and hills of Delhi are among the chief reasons why India has come to feel like home. I am happy to name them here: Rajat Chauhan, Harsh Dhillon, Percy Fernandez, Dave Hogg, Zubin Irani, Akshay Jaitly, Dev Khare, Adarsh Kumar, Ritin Rai, Himmat Rana, Nivi Samanta, Rajat Sethi, Sher Verick, and Simon Wright. I owe an ongoing and unpayable debt to my parents, Stella Niederhoffer Freud Harris and Norman Harris. They have watched their son leave home and play transnational hopscotch, just as they once did themselves. It's been wrenching for all of us to live so far away from each other. But my migrant story, despite its local habitation and name, is a version of theirs. I am also grateful to Mohan Chandar Menon and Indira Menon for giving me a home away from home in Delhi. Familial support has also come from Miriam Harris, Kalyani Menon and Kevin Schjerning. And I happily dedicate this book to my nephews Nikhil Armaan and Rohan Jannek, who are only half-Indian but tell me they want to be fully Indian like me.

Last, and certainly not least, I must thank Madhavi for her patience when I needed to buckle down and finish my manuscript. She has been this book's biggest champion throughout, from inception to completion, and I couldn't have done it without her.

NOTES

There are many sources I have drawn from to write this book, but three demand to be singled out as particular influences and even catalysts. William Dalrymple's *White Mughals: Love and Betrayal in Eighteenth-Century India* (New Delhi: Viking Penguin, 2002) first prompted me to think about the pre-colonial history of firangi crossovers who became Indian. Sanjay Subrahmanyam's *Three Ways to Be Alien: Travails & Encounters in the Early Modern World* (Waltham, MA: Brandeis University Press, 2011), like his earlier work on Vasco da Gama, showed me that biography needn't be just about individuals but can also think across borders of nationality to retrieve otherwise forgotten global networks of cultural movement and exchange. Likewise, Amitav Ghosh's sublime travel history of medieval Indian Ocean migration between North Africa and the Malabar Coast, *In an Antique Land: History in the Guise of a Traveller's Tale* (London: Granta, 1992), has greatly shaped my thinking about not just the subcontinent's pasts but also how these refuse seemingly timeless schisms in the present. Ghosh has taught me too how the writing of history can be all the more effective when it doesn't efface the historian's own biography.

I am equally influenced by one of the most important intellectual movements to have emerged from India in recent decades—the school known as Subaltern Studies, associated with the scholarship of Ranajit Guha, Partha Chatterjee, Dipesh Chakrabarty and others. Subaltern Studies builds on the Italian political philosopher and activist Antonio Gramsci's concept of the subaltern to refer to the oppressed and the poor classes; in doing so, the school seeks to tell history from below, from the perspective of non-elite groups largely effaced by the official record. Although the school follows Gramsci in understanding the subaltern to be a global category, its leading scholars' emphasis on South Asian peasants and tribal peoples has contributed to the term becoming in some Western circles a synonym for non-elite Indians. Yet we can equally tease out a subaltern history of firangis—including even those firangis who served powerful masters—that doesn't quite align with the imperialist and colonialist trajectories of official history.

Studies of these earliest firangis aren't plentiful. But I follow in the enabling footsteps of the British Raj-era historian William Foster, whose *Early Travels in India, 1583-1619* (London: Humphrey Milford/Oxford University Press, 1921) has been my constant companion for the past five years. I also stand on the shoulders of the historian Michael H. Fisher, whose *Beyond the Three Seas: Travellers' Tales of Mughal India* (New Delhi: Random House India, 2007) first introduced me to Niccolò Manucci. And I must note too Sudhir Kakar's historical novel *The Crimson Throne* (New Delhi: Viking Penguin 2010), which offers a modern psychologically-tinged perspective on what it meant for a firangi to cross over in the time of the Mughals.

1. BECOMING INDIAN

My account of Niccolò Manucci's meeting with Thomas Roch and Raben Simitt is drawn from William Irvine's imperfect translation of Manucci's *Storia do Mogor—Mogul India, or Storia do Mogor*, 4 vols. (London, 1907-8); an abridged version was produced by Margaret Irvine, *A Pepys of Mogul India 1653-1708* (New York: E. P. Dutton and Company, 1913), and I refer to the account that appears there, pp. 37-41. Thomas Roch is mentioned in East India Company records from May 25 1655 as an employee who has received a gratuity of 4 shillings; see Ethel Bruce Sainsbury (ed.), *A Calendar of the Court Minutes Etc. of the East India Company 1655-1659* (Oxford: Clarendon Press, 1916), p. 66.

My information about Sancho Pires comes from Maria Augusta Lima Cruz, 'Exiles and Renegades in Early 16th-Century Portuguese India', in Anthony R. Disney (ed.), *Historiography of Europeans in Africa and Asia, 1450-1800* (Farnham, Surrey: Ashgate, 1995), pp. 235-48, esp. p. 247. For more details about Fernão Rodrigues Caldeira, see Dejanirah Silva Couto, 'Some Observations on Portuguese Renegades in Asia in the Sixteenth Century', in Antony R. Disney and Emily Booth (eds.), *Vasco da Gama and the Linking of Europe and Asia* (Oxford: Oxford University Press), pp. 178-201, esp. p. 187. William Dalrymple discusses the case of Joshua Blackwell and other renegade English mercenaries in *White Mughals*, pp. 24ff. The strange case of Gilbert Harrison reveals itself in a letter written by the East India Company factor Henry Garry, portions of which are reproduced in William Foster, *The English Factories in India 1618-69*, vol. 8, 1646-50 (Oxford: Clarendon Press, 1906), p. 151.

François Bernier's life in India is documented in his *Voyages de F. Bernier (angevin) contenant la description des Etats du Grand Mogol, de l'Indoustan, du royaume de Kachemire*, first published in 1699. Bernier's work was translated into English in the early nineteenth century by Irving Brock as *Travels in the Mogul Empire by François Bernier* (London: Archibald Constable, 1891); his accounts of his health travails in Delhi, his illness in Punjab, and his recovery in Kashmir, are on pp. 350-423.

2. GARCIA DA ORTA

Garcia da Orta's recollection of smelling the cargo of cloves off the shore of Kerala can be found in his *Colloquies* (cited in the notes for Chapter 1), p. 220;

Shakespeare also dreams of the 'spiced Indian air' in *A Midsummer Night's Dream*, 2.1.124. My many references to Shakespeare throughout this book are based on the *Norton Shakespeare*, (eds.) Stephen J. Greenblatt, Walter Cohen, Jean E. Howard and Katharine Eisaman Maus (New York: Norton, 1997).

Most of the details in my account of Orta's life come from C. R. Boxer's invaluable study, *Two Pioneers of Tropical Medicine: Garcia d'Orta and Nicolás Monardes* (London: Welcome Institute, 1963). Boxer builds on the invaluable scholarship of Augusto da Silva Carvalho in his study 'Garcia d'Orta', *Revista da Universidade de Coimbra* 12 (*1934*): 61–246; Carvalho combed the Portuguese Inquisition records and found in them numerous important details of Orta's life, including his name, the fact that he was married, his sister Catarina's trial, and the names of their relatives. My references to Inquisition records are through Carvalho via Boxer. Boxer's and Carvalho's biographies of Orta correct the previous patriotic Portuguese accounts of his life, such as Francisco Manuel de Melo Conde de Ficalho's *Garcia da Ortae O Sue Tempo* (Lisbon: Imprensa Nacionale, 1886) and José Gerson da Cunha's *Origin of Bombay: Illustrated with Coins, Inscriptions and Maps* (Bombay: Society's Library, 1900), pp. 99–112.

The reference to Luís Vaz de Camões's poetry is to Landeg White's edition of the *Lusiads* (Oxford: Oxford University Press, 2001), Book 12, Canto 132; details about Camões's life are found in the introduction. Clements Markham reproduces Camões's poem for Orta in the introduction to the *Colloquies*, p. x. Orta's comments about Indian smells are on p. 45; about mangoes, on pp. 284–8. The Colaba mango tree that, like Orta's, fruited twice a year is referred to by Gerson da Cunha in *The Origin of Bombay*, p. 109. My information about Ahmadnagar and Burhan Nizam Shah derives in part from Radhey Shyam, *The Kingdom of Ahmadnagar* (Delhi: Motilal Barnasidass, 1966). Orta's remarks about the nizam's Arabic medical knowledge are on p. 306 of the *Colloquies*. On Dr Gabriel Boughton, see Jaswant Lal Mehta, *Advanced Study in the History of Modern India 1707-1813* (New Delhi: New Dawn Press, 2002), p. 337; on Dr D'Estremon, see O. P. Jaggi, *Medicine in India: Modern Period* (Oxford: Oxford University Press, 2000), p. 220; on Dr Poterliet, see Dr A. Lakshmanaswami Mudaliar, 'A History of Medical Relief in Madras', in Dewan Bahadur S. Runganadhan (ed.), *Madras Tercentenary Commemoration Volume* (Madras: Madras Tercentenary Celebration Committee, 1939), pp. 51–9.

Orta's support for Arabic over European medicine is repeatedly affirmed throughout the *Colloquies*, most strongly on p. 436. On the closeness of Jewish and Arabic cultures in Al-Andalus, see Gil Anidjar, *'Our Place in Al-Andalus': Kabbalah, Philosophy, Literature in Arab Jewish Letters* (Stanford, California: Stanford University Press, 2002); and Esperanza Alfonso, *Islamic Culture through Jewish*

Eyes: Al-Andalus from the Tenth to the Twelfth Century (London and New York: Routledge, 2008). On the multicultural medical world of pre-expulsion Spain, see Chris Lowney, *A Vanished World: Muslims, Christians and Jews in Medieval Spain* (Oxford: Oxford University Press, 2005); he discusses the pre-eminence of Avicenna in late medieval Iberian medicine on pp. 150-53. The best survey of Avicenna's life and works is Lenn E. Goodman, *Avicenna* (Ithaca, New York: Cornell University Press, 2005).

My account of the terrible chapter of history spanned by the Goa Inquisition derives partly from Anant Priolkar, *The Goa Inquisition, Being a Quatercentenary Commemoration Study of the Inquisition in India* (Bombay: University of Bombay Press, 1961); it is supplemented by the overview of Sanjay Subrahmanyam, *The Portuguese Empire in Asia, 1500-1700: A Political and Economic History* (Harlow, Essex: Longman, 1993), pp. 80-85. Subrahmanyam states that it is uncertain whether Orta met his fellow New Christian Sancho Pires in Ahmadnagar, but Orta insists in the *Colloquies* (p. 414) that he knew him. Orta's references to Dominican friars are on p. 406; to the conversion of Tamil fishermen on p. 297; to Gujarati Parsis on pp. 445-6; to Hindus eating milk with fish on p. 290; to the loss of Jewish and Arabic medicine from Spain on p. 4; to his abilities in Arabic on pp. 4, 258, and 358; to Isaac of Cairo on pp. 276 and 351; and to the story of Abraham on p. 406.

3. THOMAS STEPHENS/PÂTRI GURU

'Father Stephens' is briefly referred to by Ralph Fitch in his improbably long-titled report of his travels, 'The voyage of M. Ralph Fitch marchant of London by the way of Tripolis in Syria, to Ormus, and so to Goa in the East India, to Cambaia, and all the kingdome of Zelabdim Echebar the great Mogor, to the mighty river Ganges, and downe to Bengala, to Bacola, and Chonderi, to Pegu, to Imahay in the kingdome of Siam, and backe to Pegu, and from thence to Malacca, Zeilan, Cochin, and all the coast of the East India: begunne in the yeere of our Lorde 1583, and ended 1591, wherein the strange rites, maners, and customes of those people, and the exceeding rich trade and commodities of those countries are faithfully set downe and diligently described, by the aforesaid M. Ralph Fitch.' The report is included in Richard Hakluyt, *Principal Navigations, Voyages, Traffiques and Discoveries of the English Nation*, Volume 5 (Cambridge: Cambridge University Press, 1904), pp. 465-504. Shakespeare seems to remember details of Fitch's eastward journey, or at least of the name of his ship and landing point, in *Macbeth*, 1.3.6. John Eldred's letter about Fitch and company's 'long and cruel imprisonment' is reproduced in J. Courtenay Locke (ed.), *The First Englishmen In India* (London: George Routledge and Sons, 1930), p. 59; Fitch's letter, with its reference to Stephens, is in the same volume, p. 89, as is van Linschoten's report, pp. 89-99.

Biographical information about Stephens derives from the following sources: Joseph L. Saldanha's introduction to *The Christian Puranna of Father Thomas Stephens of the Society of Jesus* (Mangalore: Simon Alvares, 1907); Georg Schurhammer, 'Thomas Stephens 1549-1619', The Month 13 (1953): 197-210; Brijraj Singh, 'The First Englishman in India: Thomas Stephens (1547-1619)', Journal of South Asian Literature 30 (1995): 146-61; and James Southwood, 'Thomas Stephens, S. J., The First Englishman in India', Bulletin of the School of Oriental Studies 3 (1924): 231-40. On the history of Winchester College, see Roger Custance (ed.), *Winchester College: Sixth Centenary Essays* (Oxford: Oxford University Press, 1981); for information about Stephens' master Christopher Johnson, see Ian Green, *Humanism and Protestantism in Early Modern English Education* (Farnham, Surrey: Ashgate, 2009), p. 234. Stephens's time with Thomas Pounde, and his later praise of him, is related in some detail in Schurhammer's article (see above).

Stephens's letter to his father is reproduced in Saldanha (see above), pp. xxvi-xxx. Sebastian Manrique's and Pietro della Valle's experiences of Indian heat—so similar to Stephens's—are chronicled, respectively, in Michael H. Fisher (ed.), *Beyond the Three Seas: Travellers' Tales of Mughal India* (New Delhi: Random House India, 2007), p. 103, and E. Grey (ed.), *The Travels of Pietro della Valle in India: From the Old English Translation of 1664, by G. Havers*, 2 vols. (London: Hakluyt Society, 1892), I. p. 172. Stephens's Latin letter to his brother Richard is also reproduced in Saldanha, pp. xxx-xiv.

For rather different discussions of pre-Portuguese and early colonial Goa, see Teotonio R. de Souza (ed.), *Goa through the Ages, II: An Economic History* (Delhi: Concept Publishing, 1990), Donald F. Lach, *Asia in the Making of Europe, Volume 1: The Century of Discovery* (Chicago: University of Chicago Press, 1965), pp. 381-91, and Sanjay Subrahmanyam, *The Portuguese Empire in Asia 1500-1700* (cited above in notes to Chapter 2). Georg Schurhammer offers an extensive if somewhat reverential biography of Francis Xavier in India in *Francis Xavier His Life, His Times: India, 1541-44* (Chicago: Loyola Press, 1982).

Stephens's attempts at inculturation in Rachol were part of a larger global Jesuit strategy that is widely discussed by scholars of ethnography and theology. The best analysis of Jesuit attempts at inculturation in India, including those by Henrique Henriques, Roberto de Nobili and Giuseppe Beschi or Veeramamunivar, is Ines G. Županov, *Missionary Tropics: The Catholic Frontier in India (16th and 17th Centuries)* (Ann Arbor, Michigan: University of Michigan Press, 2005). Original editions of the *Kristapurana* do not survive, so I have worked with Joseph L. Saldana's 1907 Marathi edition (cited above). All English translations are mine, with considerable help from Vibha Kamat and Suresh Walawalikar. The cited passages are from p. 6 (Auasuari 1, ovis 123-24), p. 179 (Auasuari 33, ovi 16), and p. 42 (Auasuari 7, ovi 77). The anecdote about freedom fighters reciting Stephens's praise of Marathi comes to me from Vibha Kamat. Stephens's debts to Dnyaneshwar and Eknath are discussed by Hans Staffner, 'Fr. Stephens' *Christa Puranna* (Reflections on the Coming Devanagari edition), *The Examiner*, Bombay 107:14 (1956), 177-8; and Claude Silva, 'Thomas Stephens, S. J.', *The Examiner*, Bombay, 107:27 (1956), 341-2. George Herbert's remarks about the 'Indian nut' appear in his poem 'Providence', from *The Temple* (first published in 1633); I have used C. A. Patrides's Everyman edition of *The English Poems of George Herbert* (London: J. M. Dent and Sons, 1974), p. 132.

The story about Ramani comes from Subha Mukherjee; the story about the posting of Stephens's stanzas about Marathi in the Saraswat Brahman Samaj's Library in Margão during the Quit India movement comes from Vibha Kamat.

4. MALIK AYAZ, CHINALI, DILLANAI

In retelling the tale of Mahmud of Ghazni and Ayaz, I cite Balaji Sadasivan, *The Dancing Girl: A History of Early India* (Singapore: ISEAS Publishing, 2011), p. 121. My account of the erotic dimension of slavery in Sufism is indebted to Ruth Vanita and Saleem Kidwai, *Same-Sex Love in India: Readings from Literature and History* (New York: Palgrave Macmillan, 2001); and Kama Maureemootoo, 'The Nation as Mimicry: The (Mis)Reading of Colonial Masculinities in India', in Rohit K. Dasgupta and K. Moti Gokulsing (eds.), *Masculinity and its Challenges in India: Essays on Changing Perceptions* (Jefferson, North Carolina: McFarland and Company, 2014), pp. 106-25.

My historical overview of slavery has been significantly shaped by the incomparable work of Indrani Chatterjee and Richard M. Eaton. Their edited collection, *Slavery and South Asian History* (Bloomington, Indiana: Indiana University Press, 2006), offers an extraordinarily nuanced account of the diverse historical forms of slavery in the subcontinent and the ways in which these deviate from the better-known plantation model of the Atlantic slave trade. For more information about the mamluks of the Delhi sultanate, see Peter Jackson, *The Delhi Sultanate: A Political and Military History* (Cambridge: Cambridge University Press, 1999). For Sultan Ghori's remark about his mamluk 'sons', see Stanley Lane-Poole, *History of India, Volume III: Medieval Indian from the Mohammedan Conquest to Akbar the Great* (New York: Cosimo, 2009).

My biography of Malik Ayaz draws on the following sources: M. N. Pearson, 'Merchants and States', in James D. Tracy (ed.), *Merchant Empires: State Power and World Trade, 1350-1750* (Cambridge: Cambridge University Press, 1991), pp. 41-116; Muzaffar Alam and Sanjay Subrahmanyam, *Writing the Mughal World: Studies on Culture and Politics* (New York: Columbia University Press, 2011), esp. pp. 39-42; Khuzippalli Skaria Mathew, *The Portuguese and the Sultanate of Gujarat* (Delhi: Mittal Publications, 1986), esp. pp. 24-40; the latter also contains important documents about Malik Ayaz's battles with the Rajputs. My thinking about the mechanics of defending Diu, and the engineering feats of Malik Ayaz, has been influenced by M. S. Naravane, *The Maritime and Coastal Forts of India* (New Delhi: APH Publishing, 1998). Jenkinson's account of Russian slaves in Central Asia can be found in E. Delmar Morgan and C. H. Coote (eds.), *Early Voyages to Russia and Persia by Anthony Jenkinson and Other Englishmen* (New York: Burt Franklin, 1886), p. 89. The Portuguese viceroy's retort to Malik Ayaz is quoted in Duarte Barbosa, *The Book of Duarte Barbosa: An Account of the Countries Bordering on the Indian Ocean and their Inhabitants*, ed. Mansel Longworth Dames (London: Halkluyt Society, 2010), II. p. 130.

My account of Chinali's life draws on two principal sources: Diogo Do Couto, *Da Asia de Diogo de Couto, Decada Setima* (Lisbon, 1616) and François Pyrard, *The Voyage of François Pyrard of Laval to the East Indies, the Maldives, the Moluccas and Brazil*, Issue 80, Volume 2, Part 2 (London: Hakluyt Society, 1890). It has been supplemented by details from C. R. Boxer, *Fidalgos in the Far East: Fact and Fancy in the History of Macao* (London: Oxford University Press, 1968), pp. 225-6, and Rajaram Narayan Saletore, *Indian Pirates from the Earliest Times to the Present Day* (Delhi: Concept Publishing, 1978), pp. 132-50. The quote about the Kunhali's affection for Chinali comes from Pyrard, p. 523. On the history of the Kunhali Marakkars, see K. K. N. Kurup, *India's Naval Traditions: The Role of Kunhali Marakkars* (New Delhi: Northern Book Centre, 1997). On the fusta, see K. M. Mathew, *History of the Portuguese Navigation in India, 1497-1600* (Delhi: Mittal Publications), pp. 283-5.

The Chola kaikkolars are discussed in Daud Ali, 'War, Servitude, and the Imperial Household: A Study of Palace Women in the Chola Empire,' in Chatterjee and Eaton (cited above), pp. 44-62. On slavery in Vijayanagar, see T. V. Mahalingam, *Administration and Social Life under Vijayanagar, Vol 2: Social Life* (Madras: University of Madras Press, 1975), pp. 10-11. For Portuguese descriptions of Vijayangar and its slave-soldiers, see Domingo Paes and Fernão Nunes, *A Forgotten Empire: Vijayanagar, A Contribution to the History of India, 'Chronica Dos Reis de Bisnaga'* (Fairford, Gloucester: Echo Library, 2006). My account of the life of Dillanai, a.k.a. Eustachius de Lannoy, draws on Mark de Lannoy, 'European Soldiers in the Service of Travancore in the Eighteenth Century,' in J. Everaert and J. Parmentier (eds), *Shipping, Factories and Colonization* (Brussels: Koninklijke

Academie voor Overzeese Wetenschappen en Wetenschappelijk, 1996), pp. 430-7, and P. C. Alexander, *The Dutch in Malabar* (Madras: Annamalai University, 1946), pp. 50-87.

5. MALIK AMBAR

On the politics of Ahmadnagar at the beginning of the seventeenth century, see Radhey Shyam, *The Kingdom of Ahmadnagar* (cited above in the notes for Chapter 2). I draw here on the account of the battle given in the *Tuzuk-i-Jahangiri or Memoirs of Jahangir*, trans. Alexander Rogers and ed. Henry Beveridge (Delhi: Low Price Publications, 1989), pp. 206-8; the reference to the *chihla u jamjama* comes on p. 207. I am using the translation of Mu'tamad Khan's eulogy for Malik Ambar that appears in Aditya Vardhan's article 'Malik Ambar Was One of the Greatest Personalities of His Times in Medieval India', archived at http://www.preservearticles.com/2011102916022/malik-ambar-was-one-of-the-greatest-personalities-of-his-times-in-medieval-india.html (accessed 16th August, 2014).

Abraham Verghese refers to his experience of being called a ferengi in *My Own Country: A Doctor's Story of a Town and its People in the Age of AIDS* (New York: Vintage, 1994), p. 233. The history of that other African firangi, 'Frangi Khan,' is related by R. S. Whiteway in *The Rise of Portuguese Power in India, 1497-1550* (see also citation above in notes to Chapter 1).

My account of Malik Ambar's biography owes much to two works by Richard Eaton: his short chapter on 'The Rise and Fall of Miltary Slavery in the Deccan', in Chatterjee and Eaton (eds.), *Slavery and South Asian History* (cited in the notes for Chapter 4), pp. 115-35, and his longer chapter on Malik Ambar in *A Social History of the Deccan, 1300-1761: Eight Indian Lives* (Cambridge: Cambridge University Press, 2005), pp. 105-28. It is to Eaton I owe the attribution of Malik Ambar's place of birth in the south, rather than Harar. I have drawn also on Shanti Sadiq Ali, *The African Dispersal in the Deccan: From Medieval to Modern Times* (New Delhi: Orient Longman, 1995), especially pp. 57-108; and Edward J. Rapson, Wolsely Haig, and Richard Burn, *The Cambridge History of India, Volume 1* (Cambridge: Cambridge University Press, 1956), pp. 260-64.

Pieter Van den Broecke's comments about Chapu are to be found in his travelogue, *Pieter Van den Broecke in Azie*, 2 vols., ed. W. Coolhaas (The Hague, 1882), I. p. 146; I am using the English translation of the passage that appears on p. 185 of E. J. van Donzel, 'Primary and Secondary Sources for Ethiopian Historiography: The Case of the Slave Trade', in C. Lepage (ed.), *Études Éthiopiennes, Actes de la Dixieme Conference International des Études Éthiopiennes*

(Paris: Societé Francaise de Études Éthiopiennes), I. 183-8. On the ensete and the Ethiopian climate, see Fran Osseo-Asare, *Food Culture in Sub-Saharan Africa* (Westport, Connecticut: Greenwood Press, 2005), p. 101. On medieval Baghdad and its water-supply system, see Donald Hill, *A History of Engineering in Classical and Medieval Times* (Abingdon, Oxfordshire: Routledge, 1996), pp. 23-4.

To recover the Maratha-centric cultural dimension of Malik Ambar's life in India, I have supplemented my main historical sources with H. S. Bhatia (ed.), *Mahrattas, Sikhs, and Sultans of Southern India: Their Fight against Foreign Power* (New Delhi: Elegant Printers, 2001). Shivaji's support for 'Frankish padres' is mentioned by Bernier in his *Travels in the Mogul Empire* (cited above), p. 188.

On the construction of the Neher-e-Ambari, see Dulari Qureshi, *Tourism Potential in Aurangabad: With Ajanta Ellora and Daulatabad* (New Delhi: Bharatiya Kala Prakashan, 1999). I am also greatly indebted to Yaamini Mubayi for sharing with me invaluable details of her research into the water systems of Aurangabad and its vicinity. The reference to bi-jagiri in the *Tuzuk-i-Jahangiri* (cited above) is on p. 207.

6. MANDU FIRANGI

Bichitr's extraordinary painting of Jahangir favouring the Sufi Sheikh over King James has been the subject of much academic discussion in the West—not surprisingly, perhaps, because of its European themes. See, for example, Richmond Barbour, *Before Orientalism: London's Theatre of the East, 1576-1626* (Cambridge: Cambridge University Press, 2003), p. 172; Milo Cleveland Beach, *Mughal and Rajput Painting: The New Cambridge History of India* (Cambridge: Cambridge University Press, 1992), pp. 100-4; Richard Ettinghausen, 'The Emperor's Choice', *De Artibus Opuscula* 40 (1961): 341-63; David Smith, *Hinduism and Modernity* (Oxford: Blackwell, 2003), p. 57.

The jeweller William Leeds's employment in India—and the favour shown to him by Akbar—is related by Ralph Fitch in his travelogue (cited above in the notes to Chapter 3), pp. 174-5. For a useful discussion of Leeds and company's mission to India, see Kenneth R. Andrews, *Trade, Plunder and Settlement: Maritime Enterprise and the Genesis of the British Empire* (Cambridge: Cambridge University Press, 1984), pp. 93-7. My discussion of the design details of Fatehpur Sikri draws in part on E. B. Havell, *A Handbook to Agra and the Taj, Sikandra, Fatehpur-Sikri and the Neighbourhood* (London: Longmans, Green and Co., 1912), pp. 107-132. The English translation of Abu'l Fazl's remarks about Akbar and his love of painting is provided by H. Blochmann in *The A'in-i Akbari of Abu-l-Fazl*, 2 vols. (Calcutta: Asiatic Society, 1927), I. p. 34. For a general survey of the culture of Akbar's painters, see J. P. Losty and Malini Roy, *Mughal India;*

Art, Culture and Empire (London: British Library, 2012), pp. 26-79.

Akbar's remarks about painting and God are also in the *A'in-i Akbari*, I. p. 34. Many of the paintings of the Razmnama have been made available in Asok Kumar Das, *Paintings of the Razmnama: The Book of War* (Ahmedabad: Mapin Publishing, 2005). The Ramayana manuscript is housed in the Maharaja Sawai Man Singh Museum in Jaipur, along with two folios ascribing the paintings (Folio No. Ag 1904 and Folio No. Ag 1896). For a discussion of the anonymous Portuguese painter who came with a Jesuit mission to the Mughal court in Lahore in 1595, see Gauvin Alexander Bailey, *The Jesuits and the Grand Mogul: Renaissance Art at the Imperial Court of India, 1580-1630* (Washington, DC: Smithsonian, 1998). The distinctive art of Mandu (the place rather than the person) is discussed by Milo Cleveland Beach in *Mughal and Rajput Painting* (cited above), pp. 9-14. On the artisanal skills and instruments used by Mughal painters, see Rosemary Crill and Kapil Jariwala (eds.), *The Indian Portrait 1560-1860* (Ahmedabad: Mapin Publishing, 2010), pp. 170-2.

My discussion of the two paintings attributed to Mandu Firangi/Mandu (Folio No. Ag 1914 and Folio No. Ag 1922) draws heavily on the astute analysis of Nuzhat Kazmi, 'Mandu Firangi—A Case Study of an Akbari Painter', *Indian History Congress Proceedings* (1986): 441-5. Given the daunting inaccessibility of the paintings in their current storage space, I have relied entirely on Kazmi's description of the paintings as well as the photographic reproductions in Kazmi's article. But I have also tried to introduce some new interpretations, especially on the divisions of painterly labour and the larger cultural politics of a firangi painter's contribution to a Mughal art project. On the use of peori or cow urine to produce yellow pigments for paint, see Gregory Minnissale, *Images of Thought: Visuality in Islamic India 1550-1750* (Newcastle-upon-Tyne: Cambridge Scholars Press, 1999), p. 95.

7. AUGUSTIN HIRIART HUNARMAND

Perhaps the most astute discussion of the Taj Mahal and its pietra dura details is Giles Tillotson, *Taj Mahal* (London: Profile Books, 2008); see especially pp. 75-7 and 89-91. William Henry Sleeman proposed that the Taj Mahal was entirely the design of 'Austin of Bordeaux' in his memoir *Rambles and Recollections of an Indian Official*, 2 vols. (London: J. Hatchard and Son, 1844), I. p. 385. He also attributes the Agra and Delhi palaces to Austin.

My discussion of Mughal jewellery derives from the following sources: William C. Brice, *An Historical Atlas of Islam* (Leiden: Brill, 1981), pp. 257-9; Marilyn Jenkins and Manuel Keene, *Islamic Jewelry in the Metropolitan Museum of Art* (New York: Metropolitan Museum of Art, 1982), pp. 103-8; Annemarie

Schimmel, *The Empire of the Great Mughals: History, Art and Culture*, trans. Corinne Attwood (London: Reaktion, 2004); and Oppi Untracht, *Traditional Indian Jewelry* (New York: Harry N. Abrams, 1997). My description of the jewellery of Agra draws again on E. B. Havell, *Agra* (cited in the notes to the previous chapter). Ralph Fitch's remarks about the jewels of Agra are in his travelogue (cited in the notes to Chapter 3), p. 161. The figure of 60,520,521 rupees is given by Joannes de Laet in his 'Description of India and Fragment of Indian History', a Dutch text translated into English by J. S. Hoyland and S. N. Banerjee as *The Empire of the Great Mogol* (Bombay: D. P. Taraporevala and Sons, 1928); see p. 108. William Finch's account of his experience of visiting Agra can be found in William Foster, *Early Travels to India* (cited above in my opening note), p. 146. Jean-Baptiste Tavernier describes his experience of the Mughal jewels in his *Travels in India between Years 1640-1676*, trans. Valentine Ball, 2 vols. (New Delhi: Asian Educational Services, 2007), pp. 314-19. My account of Mildenhall's meeting with Akbar derives from a letter he wrote to England in 1606, included in Foster's *Early Travels to India* (cited above); see in particular p. 55.

My account of Augustin Hiriart's life in Bordeaux draws on his own words as recorded in his letters from India, printed in E. D. McLagan, 'Four Letters by Austin of Bordeaux', *Journal of the Punjab Historical Society* 4 (1916): 3-17. For more on Basque traditions of jewellery, see Gloria Totoricagüena, *Basque Diaspora: Migration and Traditional Identity* (Reno, Nevada: University of Nevada Centre for Basque Studies), pp. 456-7. Hiriart's remarks about Monsieur Castaniac are in the 'Four Letters', p. 7; his letter to the Baron du Tour is on p. 9. My discussion of the London counterfeit jewel scandal builds on Hazel Forsythe's illuminating account in *London's Lost Jewels: The Cheapside Hoard* (London: Philip Wilson, 2013), pp. 68-76. Hiriart's letter to Cecil survives in an undated holograph from the *Calendar of the Cecil Papers in Hatfield House*, vol. 16 (1604); Forsythe quotes from it on p. 68. Hiriart's remark about all his fellow French travellers dying is in the 'Four Letters', p. 7.

Robert Shirley's elephant is documented in William Foster (ed.), *Letters to the East India Company, Vol II: 1613-15* (London: Sampson Low, 1897), p. 141. Hiriart's reference to the elephant is in the 'Four Letters', p. 7; his remark about his wife on p. 11; to his sons on pp. 7 and 11. The letter by Alvarez to Hiriart is excerpted in *Topoi Orient-Occident* 7 (1997): 710. Hiriart's allusion to the death of one or more of his children is in the 'Four Letters', p. 17. The grave inscription commemorating Hiriart's daughter Jane was noted by the Reverend H. Hosten a century ago, and is recorded in McLagan's introduction to the 'Four Letters', p. 2. The references to 'Hunarmand' in the *Tuzuk-i-Jahangiri* (cited in the notes to Chapter 5) are in Vol. II, p. 80. He glosses the meaning of his Persian name in the 'Four Letters' on p. 7; the reference to him by the German traveller, Heinrich von Poser, is quoted in McLagan's introduction, p. 1; Hiriart's references to Jahangir's balas rubies are on p. 7. The *Tuzuk-i-Jahangiri*'s description of the Navroz celebrations is in Vol. II, p. 80. Hiriart's 1625 description of his throne design is in the 'Four Letters', p. 13; Jahangir's praise of the throne is in the *Tuzuk-i-Jahangiri*, p. 80. Hiriart's account of his rewards and his attempts to re-gift some of them is in the 'Four Letters', p. 7; his description of his military fighting machine is on p. 13. Von Poser's account of his visit with Jahangir in Lahore is excerpted in William Foster, 'Austin of Bordeaux', *Journal of the Asiatic Society of Great Britain and Ireland* October 1910), 1343-5. Hiriart describes his elephant-corralling machine in the 'Four Letters', p. 13; his disparaging remarks about Shah Jahan are on pp. 15 and 17. Bernier's description of the Peacock Throne, and possible reference to Hiriart, is in his *Travels in the Mogul Empire* (cited in the notes to Chapter 1), p. 269. For Manrique's claims about Veroneo, see Donald Lach and Edwin J. Van Kley, *Asia in the Making of Europe: A Century of Advance, Volume 3* (Chicago: Chicago University Press, 1993), p. 689.

8. BIBI JULIANA FIRANGI

The reference to Abdus Samad's painting of Jodha Bai is in Salman Rushdie, *The Enchantress of Florence* (London: Random House, 2008), p. 27. Gulbadan Banu Begum's memoirs, the *Avhal-i Humayun Badshah* ('Circumstances of Emperor Humayun'), were translated—rather awkwardly—into English by Annette Beveridge as *Humayun-Nama: The History of Humayun* (London: Royal Asiatic Society, 1902). For a useful discussion of Gulbadan's writing and life, see Jyotsna G. Singh, 'Boundary Crossings in the Islamic World: Princess Gulbadan as Traveler, Biographer, and Witness to History, 1523-1603,' *Early Modern Women: An Interdisciplinary Journal* 7 (2012): 231-40.

My understanding of the Mughal harem is deeply indebted to the ground-breaking study of Ruby Lal, *Domesticity and Power in the Early Mughal World* (Cambridge: Cambridge University Press, 2005). I have also drawn on Faraz Anjum, 'Strangers' Gaze: Mughal Harem and European Travellers of the Seventeenth Century', *Pakistan Vision* 12 (2011): 70- 113, and Soma Mukherjee, *Royal Mughal Ladies and Their Contributions* (New Delhi: Gyan Publishing, 2001). Finch's claims about the harem are in R. Nath, *India as Seen by William Finch* (Jaipur: The Historical Documentation Programme, 1990), p. 57. Coryate's remarks about the harem are in William Foster, *Early Travels in India* (cited in the notes at the beginning), p. 247. Catrou's remarks are in the anonymously translated *History of the Mogul Dynasty from its Foundation by Tamerlane in the Year*

1399 to the Accession of Aurengzebe in the Year 1657 (London: J. M. Richardson, 1826), p. 287. Manucci's account of his visit to the harem is in the *Storia do Mogor* (cited in the notes to Chapter 1), p. 203. Bernier's account is in his *Travels in the Mogul Empire* (cited in the notes to Chapter 1), p. 267. Abu'l Fazl's description of the harem is in the *Ain-i-Akbari* (cited in the notes to Chapter 6), II. Pp. 45-7. My account of Dhrupad's fusion of cultural forms draws on Bonnie C. Wade's *Imaging Sound: An Ethnomusicological Study of Music, Art and Culture in Mughal India* (Chicago: University of Chicago Press, 1998). For more on the cultural fusions of Kathak, see Reginald Massey, *India's Kathak Dance, Past, Present and Future* (New Delhi: Abhinav Publications, 1999). On ankh-michauli and pachisi in Fatehpur Sikri, see E.B. Havell, *Agra* (cited above in the notes to Chapter 6), pp. 114-16. The best discussion of khil'at is Stewart Gordon, *Robes of Honour: Khilat in Pre-Colonial and Colonial India* (Oxford: Oxford University Press, 2003). My discussion of foreigners in the harem and rituals of renaming draws from Ruby Lal and Soma Mukherjee's books (cited above), but also from Gavin G. R. Hambly's article on female urdubegis, "Armed Women Retainers in the Zenanas of Indo-Muslim Rulers: The Case of Bibi Fatima',' in Hambly (ed.), *Women in the Medieval Islamic World* (New York: St Martin's Press, 1998), pp. 429-67.

The fanciful legend of Bibi Juliana Bourbon is told by Mesrovb Jacob Seth, *Armenians in India: From the Earliest Times to the Present* (New Delhi: Asian Educational Services, 2005), pp. 92-5. The 22 March 2013 *Times of India* article about the supposed Bhopali scion of the Bourbons is archived at http://timesofindia.indiatimes.com/city/bhopal/France-for-better-ties-with-MP/articleshow/19119705.cms (accessed 17th August, 2014). The French novel about Jean-Philippe Bourbon de Navarre is Michel de Grèce, *Le Rajah Bourbon* (Paris: Jean-Claude Lattès, 2007).

Sikander Zul-Qarnain is referred to in the *Tuzuk-i-Jahangiri* (cited above in the notes to Chapter 5) on p. 194, as is his grandfather Abdul Hai. Abu'l Fazl's reference to the latter in the *Ain-i-Akbari* (cited above in the notes to Chapter 6) explicitly identifies him as "Abdul Hai Ferenghi"; I. p. 373, n. 1. Corsi's letter, in which he names Abdul Hai's daughter as Juliana, is reproduced in Seth, *Armenians in India* (cited above), pp. 35-47. My information about the Armenian migration to India, and the names of Juliana's sons and grandsons, also comes from Seth.

For information on Mughal and medieval Indian writing practices and accessories, see Anna Jackson and Amir Jaffer (eds.), *Maharaja: The Splendour of India's Royal Courts* (London: Victoria and Albert Museum, 2009). For more on Armenian Christianity, its history, and its rituals, see Vrej Nersessian, *Treasures from the Ark: 1700 Years of Armenian Christian Art* (Los Angeles: John Paul Getty Museum, 2001), and Ken Parry (ed.), *The Blackwell Companion to Eastern Christianity* (Oxford: Blackwell, 2007), pp. 23-46. On Mughal women's clothing, see Annemarie Schimmel, *The Empire of the Great Mughals* (cited above in notes to Chapter 6), pp. 169-71; and Jill Condra (ed.), *The Greenwood Encyclopedia of Clothing through World History Volume II, 1501-1800* (Westport, Connecticut: Greenwood, 2008), pp. 207-20.

9. JULIANA DIAS DA COSTA

My thoughts on the re-clothing of Mughal women are very much indebted to the work of Ann Rosalind Jones and Peter Stallybrass. See their *Renaissance Clothing and the Materials of Memory* (Cambridge: Cambridge University Press, 2000), in which they think through clothing as an act of fashioning, both in the sense of high "fashion" and as a fashioning, or making, of identity.

My account of the life of Juliana Dias da Costa would not have been possible without the extraordinary scholarship of Taymiya R. Zaman. In her essay "Visions of Juliana: A Portuguese Woman at the Court of the Mughals", *Journal of World History* 23 (2013): 761-91, Zaman collates an astonishingly multilingual array of stories and archival sources relevant to Juliana Dias da Costa's life, many of them previously unknown. I have drawn extensively on these in stitching together my version of her tale here. Dias Da Costa's letter to the Portuguese king, written in Persian and translated into Portuguese, is reprinted in J. Ismael Gracias, *Uma Dona Portuguese na Corte da Grao-Mogol, O Oriente Portuguez* 15 (1918): 113-20, esp. p. 119. Ippolito Desideri's Latin account of Dias da Costa is translated into English as *An Account of Tibet: The Travels of Ippolito Desideri of Pistoia, S.J., 1712-1727*, ed. Filippo de Filippi (London: G. Routledge, 1932); see p. 65. Francois Valentijn accompanies his description of Juliana with an illustration of her in his Dutch travelogue, *Oud en nieue Oost-Indien* (Amsterdam, 1724-6), p. 297. Jean-Baptiste Gentil's short description of Dias da Costa appears in his French memoirs, *Memoires sur L'Hindoustan* (Paris: Didot, 1822), pp. 367-74. On the D'Eremaos, see Zaman, pp. 783-91; the quote from the *Tarikh-i-Muhammadi* is also from Zaman, p, 783.

Antony Botelho's remarks about Agostinho Dias da Costa are cited in an article by the Reverend H. Hosten, S. J, "The Family of Juliana Dias da Costa (1658-1732)", *The Journal of the Punjab Historical Society* 7 (1918): 39-49, esp. 39. Manucci's reference to Agostinho is in *Storia do Mogor* (cited above in the notes to Chapter 1), p. 91. On the women of Aurangzeb's court, see Soma Mukherjee, *Royal Mughal Ladies and their Contributions* (cited above in the notes to Chapter 8), p. 155-7. On Nur al-Din Shirazi and his work in the Mughal court, see Fabrizio Speziale, "The Encounter of Medical Traditions in Nur al-Din Muhammad Shirazi's Treatise Dedicated to Prince Dara Shukoh", *eJournal of Indian Medicine, University of Groningen* 3 (2010).

Manucci's encounter with the cross-dressed girl in Shah Alam's court is described in *Storia do Mogor* (cited above in the notes to Chapter 1), pp. 374-5. Zaman discusses the "Habits of Christ" presented to Dias da Costa's supposed male relatives on pp. 769-70. Gaston Bruit's extraordinary *Avhal-i Bibi Juliana* survives in manuscript form in the British Library (British Library MS Add. 14,374); Zaman's synopsis of the manuscript, from which I have drawn (including the quote about her "price of purchase", p. 777), extends pp. 775-780. It includes the details about Juliana's iffat and taqwa cited earlier in the chapter. The most useful details in the *Avhal-i Bibi Juliana* about Dias da Costa's daily life in the court, including her praying, cooking, and clothing habits, are on fol. 13 and 14. My information about Jogabai and Juliana's other village grants comes partly from Zaman, esp. p. 785, but is also supplemented by R. V. Smith's article, "Was It Juliana or Joga?", from *The Hindu*, September 23, 2013; archived at http://www.thehindu.com/todays-paper/tp-features/tp-metroplus/was-it-juliana-or-joga/article5157822.ece (accessed August 18th, 2014).

10. THOMAS CORYATE

My tale of "Odd Tom" Coryate draws on some very good extant biographical writing about him. Chief amongst these is Dom Moraes and Sarayu Srivatsa, *The Long Strider: How Thomas Coryate Walked from England to India in the Year 1613* (Delhi: Penguin India, 2003) and R. E. Pritchard, *Odd Tom Coryate: The English Marco Polo* (Stroud: Sutton Publishing, 2004). I have also made use of Edward Terry's memoirs of Coryate in his *A Voyage to East-India* (London, 1655), excerpted in William Foster, *Early Travels in India* (cited above), pp. 282-7. But Coryate's best biographer is, arguably, the relentlessly self-publicizing Coryate himself, including *Coryat's Crudities Hastily Gobbled up in Five Months Travels in France, Savoy, Italy, Rhetia Commonly Called the Orison's Country, Helvetia Alias Switzerland, Some Parts of High Germany and the Netherlands, Newly Digested in the Hungry Air of Odcombe in the County of Somerset, and Now Dispersed to the Nourishment of the Travelling Members of this Kingdom*, 2 vols. (London, 1611) and Coryate's letters from India in William Foster, *Early Travels in India* (cited above in the opening notes), pp. 234-82. Ben Jonson's characterization of Coryate as an "Engine" is in Vol. 1, p. 15; as "Tongue-Major" is in Vol. 1, p. 17. On the relations between rhetoric and gesture as taught in the sixteenth-century English school classroom, see Neil Rhodes, *The Power of Eloquence and English Renaissance Literature* (New York: St. Martin's Press, 1992). King James's remark is reported by Terry (cited above), p. 286. Coryate's "Hyperaspist" coinage is to be found Vol. 1, pp. 20 and 23 of the *Crudities*; the fellow Sireniac's remark about his fondness for Latin and Greek is on p. 24; Donne's parody of Coryate is on p. 38. Christopher Marlowe's reference to "high astounding terms" is in the Prologue to *Tamburlaine*, ed. J. S. Cunningham and Eithne Henderson (Manchester: Manchester University Press, 1998), line 5.

The prefatory poem that refers to Will Kemp is in Vol 1, p. 33 of *The Crudities*; Coryate's nickname of "Furcifer" is in Vol 1, p. 236. The reference to abandoning his old style of "English pronunciation" is in Vol 2, p. 60. The text of Coryate's oration at Odcombe Cross is not available, unfortunately, but he clearly indicated his attention of going beyond Europe and on to Asia.

"All the world's a stage" is, of course, from Shakespeare's *As You Like It*, 2.7.9. Thomas Roe's comments about his first meeting with Jahangir and his *darbar* are in *The Embassy of Sir Thomas Roe to the Court of the Great Mogul, 1615-19*, ed. William Foster, 2 vols. (London: Hakluyt Society, 1894), I. pp. 106, 108; about Jahangir's theatre of elephants, I. p. 112n.; about his meeting with Pervez, I. p. 91; about his meeting with the Persian ambassador, II. pp. 299–300; about Khurram's khil'at gift, II. p. 334. Terry's remark about Roe and company's English dress is from *A Voyage to East-India* (cited above), p. 205.

Roe's complaint about Ajmer is from *The Embassy of Sir Thomas Roe*, I. p. 170. Coryate's description of the immense brass pot and its khichdi is in Foster, *Early Travels*, p. 280; Finch's description of the dargah's three courts is also in Foster, p. 171; Coryate's observation about the Christian figures invoked by Ajmer beggars is in Foster, p. 276; Terry's anecdote about Coryate's out-talking a local washerwoman in her own language is in Foster, p. 284. Sanjay Subrahmanyam has rightly questioned European travellers' self-congratulatory remarks about their abilities in Persian. But we can think about fluency in the language as not just a linguistic but also an embodied skill, one that entails a command of specific gestures such as those enumerated in the My Persian Corner blog, http://mypersiancorner.blogspot.in/2014/02/gestures-and-body-language-in-iran.html (accessed August 18, 2014).

Roe's disparaging remarks about Coryate's many orations are in *The Embassy of Sir Thomas Roe*, I. p. 104. Coryate's coinage of the word "propatetic" is found in Foster, *Early Travels*, p. 244; his letter to the Sireniacs, p. 256; his desire to sit on top of an elephant, p. 247; his comments about his "continual practice', p. 274; Terry's account of his travesty of the kalimah, in Terry (cited above), pp. 270-1; his account of his oration to the Muslim in Multan, in Foster, pp. 271-5.

Coryate's oration to Jahangir is presented in 'Persian' and English translation in Foster, pp. 263-5; Terry's estimate of how much Jahangir gave Coryate is on

p. 284; Coryate's remarks about Roe's response, p. 266; Roe's remarks about Coryate and Tamburlaine, *Embassy of Sir Thomas Roe*, I. p, 104; Coryate's remarks in Persian about Bajazeth in Foster, p. 264; in English, p. 265; his multinational sign-off, p. 258; Coryate's remarks about his health, p. 249. The best account of Coryate's stay in Mandu is Charles Nicholl, 'Field of Bones', *London Review of Books* 21 (1999): 3-7. My account of Coryate's last day is based on Terry's and Foster, p. 287, but also builds on Dom Moraes's *The Long Strider* (cited above), pp. 336-8.

11. SA'ID SARMAD KASHANI

Because of Sa'id Sarmad's veneration by diverse if sometimes mutually fractious religious communities, there have been many spiritually partisan accounts of his life and philosophy, each usually accompanied by a translation of his *Rubaiyat* that makes a strong case for his being a true practitioner of one particular spiritual path rather than others. I have consulted several of these in writing this chapter, including I. A. Ezekiel, *Sarmad: Jewish Saint of India* (New Delhi: Radha Soami Satsang Bas, 1966); M. G. Gupta, *Sarmad the Saint: Life and Works* (Agra: M. G. Publishing, 1991); Syeda Saidain Hameed, *The Rubaiyat of Sarmad* (New Delhi: Indian Council for Cultural Relations, 1991); and Chhaganlal Lala (ed.), *The Rubaiyat of Sarmad*, trans. Bankey Behari (Delhi: B. R. Publishing, 1998). I have also consulted two excellent but somewhat divergent academic essays about Sarmad: Nathan Katz, 'The Identity of a Mystic: The Case of Sa'id Sarmad, a Jewish-Yogi-Sufi Courtier of the Mughals', *Numen* 47 (2000): 142-60; and Natalia Prigarina, 'Sarmad: Life and Death of a Sufi', *Shraq: Islamic Philosophy Yearbook* 3 (2012): 314-29. My account of seventeenth-century Kashan and its Jews derives in large part from Mehrdad Amanat, *Jewish Identities in Iran: Resistance and Conversion to Islam and the Baha'i* (London: I. B. Tauris, 2011). For a useful introduction to Mulla Sadra's philosophy, see Mohammed Rustom, *The Triumph of Mercy: Philosophy and Scripture in Mulla Sadra* (Albany, New York: State University of New York Press, 2012).

The quote explaining the Tibetan Buddhist understanding of rigpa is from Tulku Urgen Rinpoche, *As It Is, Volume 2* (Hong Kong: Rangjung Yeshe Publications, 2000), p. 68. The Mughal commentary on Saramd's nudity and refusal of shariya is cited in Masood Ali Khan and S. Ram, *Encyclopedia of Sufism* (Delhi: Anmol Publications, 2003), p. 5. My discussion of male homoerotic love in Hindu and Sufi tradition— including the tale of Ayyappa, the legend of Chaitanya and Jagannath Das, and the lament of Khusrao for Nizamuddin Chishti—draws on Ruth Vanita and Saleem Kidwai, *Same-Sex Love in India* (cited above in notes to Chapter 4). All quotes from Sarmad's *Rubaiyat* are taken from the translation that I. A. Ezekiel includes in his *Sarmad* (cited above); I have resorted to this translation not because it is beautiful or melodious, but because it offers the best attempt to capture Sarmad's arresting metaphorical themes.

Mu'tamad Khan's description of Sarmad in Lahore is taken from his *Iqbal Nama-i-Jahangri*, and is quoted in M. G. Gupta (cited above), p. 4. Gupta attributes the *Dabistan*'s couplet about being 'neither a Jew nor a Christian nor a Muslim' to Abhai Chand, p. 8. My description of the early years of Hyderabad, where the *Dabistan* seems to have been written, draws on Narendra Luther, *Hyderabad: A Biography* (Oxford: Oxford University Press, 2006); Thevenot is quoted by Luther on p. 51; Tavernier on p. 48.

The rubaiyat of Sarmad are numbered differently in different editions. Here I use Ezekiel's numbering, as well as referring to specific pages. 'The curly hair of my Beloved enchants me' is rubai 189, pp. 342-3; 'O Sarmad! Thou hast worked havoc in attacking' is rubai 314, p. 378; 'Neither fancies nor pleasures here are permanent' is rubai 43, p. 305; 'I am a hundred times thankful that my Friend is pleased' is rubai 50, p. 307; 'Seekest thou His Grace, Mercy and Bliss' and 'Seclusion is a pearl of greatest price, it gives thee peace and bliss' are rubaiyat 81 and 82, p. 315.

The passages from Manucci are not in the truncated edition of the *Storia do Mogor* that I have used throughout this book, but from the longer five-volume edition in Portuguese, Italian and French. They are translated and quoted by M. G. Gupta (cited above) on p. 15. On Sarmad, Manucci is for once in accord with his rival Bernier, whose disparaging comment about Sarmad is in the *Travels* (cited above in the opening notes), p. 317. For the discussions of the miracles and legends associated with Sarmad, I have drawn in part on Sadia Delhvi, *The Sufi Courtyard: Dargahs of Delhi* (New Delhi: Harper Collins, 2012). Gupta relates the miracle that supposedly accompanied Abhai Chand's flogging, p. 41; the miracle that accompanied Sarmad's meeting with Aurangzeb at the Jama Masjid, p. 40; his travesty of the *Kalima*, p. 48. Sarmad's couplet about his private parts is quoted in Natalia Prigarina, 'Sarmad: Life and Death of a Sufi' (cited above), p. 332.

12. SEBASTIÃO GONÇALVES TIBAU

It is particularly difficult to reconstruct the details of Tibau's life, not least because he figures in very few seventeenth-century Indian or Portuguese archives. The basic outlines derive in large part from the brief biographical account written by Manuel de Faria e Sousa in his *Asia Portuguesa* (Lisbon, 1666), translated by Captain John Stevens as *The Portugues Asia: Or, The History of the Discovery and Conquest of India by the Portugues* (London, 1695). Faria e Sousa's account is excerpted also in *Henry Beveridge, The District of Bakarganj: Its History and Statistics* (London: Trubner and Co, 1876), pp. 37–8. This simple foundation has been made to support some more detailed accounts of Tibau's life, supplemented by research into the historical and cultural contexts of early seventeenth-century Bay of Bengal. These accounts include the fascinating but somewhat speculative section on 'Continuation of the Transactions of the Portuguese in India, from 1597 to 1612', in Robert Kerr (ed.), *A General History and Collection of Voyages and Travels*, Vol. 6 (Edinburgh: George Ramsay and Company, 1812), pp. 475–97. Perhaps the most useful contextualization of Tibau in the Bay of Bengal is Rila Mukherjee, 'The Struggle for the Bay: The Life and Times of Sandwip, An Almost Unknown Portuguese Port in the Bay of Bengal in the Sixteenth and Seventeenth Centuries', *Historia* 9 (2008): 67–88. For a useful contextualization of Tibau within the Arakan-Portuguese-Bengali nexus, see Michael W. Charney, 'Min Razagyi, and the Portuguese: The Relationship between the Growth of Arakanese Power and Portuguese Mercenaries on the Fringe of Mainland Southeast Asia 1517–1617', SOAS Bulletin of Burma Research 3 (2005): 976–89. For an account of Tibau within the context of Bengali Portuguese piracy, see Rajaram Narayan Saletore, Indian Pirates (cited above in the notes to Chapter 4), pp. 65–8. I have drawn on all these works in putting together my own account of Tibau's life.

For a useful discussion of Hooghly and its capture by the Mughals within the larger context of the Portuguese presence in Bengal, see Sanjay Subrahmanyam, *The Portuguese Empire in Asia* (cited above in notes to Chapter 2), pp. 165–9. For more on the Chatgaiyan Buli dialect, see Srijaul Islam (ed.), *Banglapedia: National Encyclopedia of Bangladesh* (Dhaka: Asiatic Society of Bangladesh, 2003), p. 491. Rimi B. Chatterji's novel, *The City of Love* (Delhi: Penguin, 2007), colourfully captures the cultural diversity of pre-Mughal Chittagong and Bengali pirate culture. On the life of *Filipe de Brito e Nicote*, see Wil O. Dijk, *Seventeenth-Century Burma and the Dutch East India Company 1634–80* (Singapore: Singapore University Press, 2006), pp. 10–12, and Donald F. Lach and Edwin J. Van Kley, *Asia in the Making of Europe*, Volume 3 (cited above in notes to Chapter 7), pp. 1124–30.

My information about Sandwip's physical features is in large part derived from the Bangladesh Ethnography Online Database entry for Sandwip Island, http://www.ebbd.info/sandwip-island.html (accessed 22nd August, 2014). My information about its history draws on Mukherjee, 'The Struggle for the Bay' (cited above). The Upanishads' tale of Uddalaka Aruni instructing his son Shvetaketu to take some salt is discussed in Michael Brannigan, *Striking a Balance: A Primer in Traditional Asian Values* (Plymouth: Lexington Books, 2006), pp. 4-5. Dara's remark about 'eaters of his salt' is reported by Manucci in his *Storia do Mogor* (cited above in notes to Chapter 1), p. 77. Gandhi's remark about salt appeared in an article he wrote for the magazine *Young India* 12 (1930): p. 68. Federici's and Manrique's comments about Bengal storms are quoted in Mukherjee, 'The Struggle for the Bay' (cited above). Bernier's account of his experience in Bengal is in *Travels in the Mogul Empire* (cited above in the notes to Chapter 1), pp. 445-6.

The exchange between Sebastian and Gonzalo in *The Tempest* takes place in Act 2, Scene 1, lines 1-170. For a discussion of Jessore and Tibau's alliance with then treachery against Pratapaditya, see Jos. J. L. Gommans, *Mughal Warfare: Indian Frontiers and Highroads to Empire, 1500-1700* (London: Routledge, 2002), pp. 170-1. On Tibau and Burmese royal politics, including the episode with Anaporam, see Michael W. Charney, 'Min Razagyi, and the Portuguese' (cited above). On Manrique and Tibau, see Mukherjee, 'The Struggle for the Bay'. Bernier's comments on the mixed-blood pirates of Bengal are in his Travels in the *Mogul Empire* (cited above in notes to Chapter 1), p. 439. Thomas Bowrey's reference to the jalia (or 'Gylyars') is in Thomas Bowrey, *A Geographical Account of Countries Round the Bay of Bengal, 1669-79* (New Delhi: Asian Educational Services, 1993), p. 212. On Shaista Khan, his invasion of Chittagong, and the third Tibau, see Abdul Karim, *The History of Bengal: The Reigns of Shah Jahan and Aurangzib* (Rajshahi: Institute of Bangladesh Studies, 1995), p. 559-61.

On the 'Ferenghi Bazar' of Chittagong and the history of the pirates' descendants there, see the anonymous yet enormously informative article, 'The Feringhees of Chittagong', *Calcutta Review* 105 (1871): 57-89; I have drawn on this extensively. The two Bengali proverbs I quote are from Sudeshna Basaka, *A Cultural History of Bengali Proverbs* (New Delhi: Ananda Publishers, 2007), pp. 24, 63.

13. NICCOLÒ MANUCCI

I have derived many details in my account of Manucci's life—such as his fateful meeting with Martin in Pondicherry—from his *Storia do Mogor*, using primarily the abridged version by Margaret Irvine (cited above in the notes to Chapter 1); Manucci describes their interaction, and Martin's advice, on p. 196. But there are numerous other details in other archives, many of which are discussed by Sanjay Subrahmanyam in his excellent chapter on Manucci (or Manuzzi, as he prefers to spell it), 'Unmasking the Mughals,' in *Three Ways to Be Alien: Travails & Encounters in the Early Modern World* (cited above in the opening notes), pp. 133-72; it is here that he argues against more utopian readings of border-crossing figures such as Manucci. R. S. Mair's remarks about

Madras's climate and its effects on the health are in an appendix to Edmund C. P. Hull, *The European in India, Or Anglo-Indian's Vade-Mecum: A Handbook of Useful and Practical Information for Those Proceeding to Or Residing in the East Indies* (New Delhi: Asian Educational Services, 2004), p. 225.

Early details of Manucci's life—including his birth date, his relations, and the date of his departure for Asia—have been uncovered by the Venetian historian Piero Falchetta, 'Per la biografia di Niccolò Manuzzi (con postilla casanoviana),' *Quaderni Veneti* 3 (1986): 85–111. Subrahmanyam builds on Falchetta in 'Unmasking the Mughals' (see above), pp. 140–1. Questions about the reliability of the *Storia do Mogor* have been raised by, among others, G. S. L. Devra, 'Manucci's Comments on Indian Social Customs and Traditions: A Critical Study', in Ugo Marazzi (ed.), *La conoscenza dell'Asia e dell'Africa in Italia*, vol. 1 (Naples: Istituto Universitario Orientale, 1984), pp. 351–71. Manucci's account of his artillery is in Margaret Irvine's abridged version of the *Storia do Mogor* (cited above in notes to Chapter 1), p. 52; the account of the battle with Aurangzeb, pp. 55–69; his description of his 'Indian' clothes and moustachios, p. 126; his self-characterization as 'carried away by curiosity', p. 45.

Manucci describes his reunion with Da'ud Khan on p. 236; identifies his 'friends' with 'European artillerymen', p. 51; refers to his 'English and Dutch friends', p. 124, to João de Souza, p. 100, to Thomas Gudlet, p. 191, to Francisco Guety, p. 193, to Khwaja Safar, pp. 115–16. Manucci's reference to 'we Europeans' appears on p. 92; his remarks about the absence of 'Catholic observances', p. 199; his complaints about India and the unreliability of its inhabitants, p. 198. The paintings that Manucci commissioned of Hindu rituals and people are discussed by Subrahmanyam, 'Unmasking the Mughals' (cited above), pp. 163–8. His discussion of the episode involving Ramappa is on pp. 236–48 of the *Storia do Mogor*; the passage I have quoted is on p. 243, and his comparison of Hindus to crocodiles is on p. 245.

Manucci's remarks about the Turkish and Persians climates are on pp. 4, 14, and 28; about new clothes, p. 8; about pulao, p. 11; about paan, p. 30; about Lord Bellomont benefiting from saltpetre dissolved in water, p. 36; about Aurangzeb and water melons, p. 49; about Dara's men dying of heat, p. 68; the Raja of Pent's son, p. 130; about Narwar and the heat, p. 35; about vellum skin, p. 48; about sleeping habits in hot climates, p. 209.

Manucci's account of the episode in which he treated the Uzbek envoy is on pp. 99–102; of how he started as a doctor in Lahore, p. 142; of how he named himself in the third person, pp. 148 and 143; of the incident with Thika Arain, pp. 152–5. The accusation against Manucci of cannibalism is discussed by Musharraf Ali Farooqi in his article 'Mughal Shughal: Niccolao Manucci and the Cannibal Qazi of Lahore', in Dawn.com, 29 September 2013: http://www. dawn.com/news/1046247 (accessed 22nd August, 2014). Manucci's remarks in *Storia do Mogor* about experience being his teacher are on p. 197; about his horse eating nutmegs, p. 140. Thomas Pitt's map of Madras is discussed by Carl H. Nightingale, *Segregation: A Global History of Divided Cities* (Chicago: University of Chicago Press, 2012), pp. 47-9.

For a discussion of Siddha medicine, see O. P. Jaggi, *Healing Systems: Alternatives and Choices* (New Delhi: Orient Paperbacks, 1992), pp. 60-4. Manucci's medical practice, and his time in the south, is discussed by Rao Bahadur K.V. Rangaswami Iyangar in his article 'Manucci in Madras', in Dewan Bahadur S. Runganadhan (ed.), *The Madras Tercentenary Commemoration Volume* (cited above in notes to Chapter 2), pp. 147-51. Shakespeare refers to the 'circumcised dog' in *Othello*, 5.2.356. Manucci refers in *Storia do Mogor* to 'our bodily health' on p. 198.

14. HOW TO BE AUTHENTICALLY INDIAN

Garcia da Orta's meditations on the meanings of firangi (or, as he renders it, 'frangue') are to be found in his *Coloquios dos simples e drogas he cousas medicinias da India*, first published in 1561; an English translation can be found in Clements Markham's *Colloquies on the Simples and Drugs of India* (London: Henry Sotheran, 1893), pp. 253-4. On Munshi Firangi, see *Dalits, Assertion for Identity: Proceedings of the National Seminar of Dalit Postgraduate Studies and Research Students* (Delhi: Indian Social Institute, 1999), p. 110. On the dacoits named 'Firangi', see *Organizer* 25 (1972): 7. I encountered the bizarre legend of Barq Firangi in a dastangoi performance at the India Habitat Centre in Delhi in 2012 by Mahmood Farooqui and Danish Husain. The history of the African firangi, 'Frangi Khan', is related by R. S. Whiteway in *The Rise of Portuguese Power in India, 1497-1550* (Delhi: Asian Educational Services, 1989), p. 235..

Marjandey Katju's remarks were made in his address, 'What is India?', the 8th Nehru Memorial Lecture delivered on 14 November 2011.

INDEX

Acquaviva, Rodolfo, 121
African-American slaves, 109
African military slaves, 90, 97–98
African Vijayanagar soldiers, 90
Agricola, Johann, 273
Ahmad, Malik, 32
Ain-i-Akbari, 122, 124
Ajmer, 200
Akbar, emperor, 5, 118–119, 122–123, 134
Alam, Shah, 176, 178
al-Baghdadi, Mir Qasim, 102, 104
Albuquerque, Afonso de, 49
Alfaz-al-Adwiya, 176
al-Ghawri, Al-Ashraf Qansuh, 82
Al-Ghazni, Amam ibn Ibrahim, 101
Alleyn, Edward, 192
Almeida, Francisco de, 83
Amal-i-Bhagwan, 128
Ambar, Malik, 19, 94, 259
  border-crossing life of, 97
  childhood experiences at Kembata, 100
  in Chingiz Khan's service, 102–104
  command of bargi-giri, 96–97, 106, 108–110, 113–114
  in Deccan, 102–104
  identity of, 97–98
  reformation of Ahmadnagar revenue system, 106
  return to Ahmadnagar, 104–105
  slave life, 102–103
  urban planning, designing the city of Khadki, 105
  vanishing act, 96
  water-supply design, 111–113
Andalusian Arabic culture, 43
Arain, Thika, 272
Arakaner pirates, 250–251
Arakan kingdom, 247–249
Arakan slave trade, 250
Aurangabad, 106
Aurangzeb, emperor, 6, 10, 229
Austin of Bordeaux, 131–132
Averroës, 35
Avhal-i-Bibi-Juliana, 179
Avhal-i Humayun Badshah, 150

Avicenna, 43
Avicenna's medical theories, 33–34
Ayaz, Malik, 17, 19, 91, 259
  alliance with al-Ghawri, 82
  alliance with Zamorin of Calicut, 83–84
  archery skills, 80
  combat with Portuguese, 82–83
  defence of Gujarat coast, 82
  governorship of Diu, 81–82
  in Gujarat, 80–81
  innovative safeguards in Diu, 82
  master-slave relation with Mahmud, 73
  origin, 79
  political survival skills, 83–84
  privileges and status, 79–80
  transnational affinities, 82
Aybak, Qutubuddin, 76

Bahmani Deccan sultanates, 5–6
Bai, Jodha, 150, 158, 184
Bai, Nawab (Rahmat-un-Nisa), 176
Bai, Uma, 108
Banu, Begum Gulbadan, 150, 156
Barid, Qasim, 76
Battle of Plassey, 5
Beg, Mohammed, 216
Begarha, Sultan Mahmud, 81
Begum, Jahanara, 155
Bellomont, Lord, 2
Bernardo, 58
Bernier, François, 10, 18, 153, 243, 250, 268
  and Aurangzeb's illness, 10
  on Delhi's environment, 10
  European racial identity, 12
  on heat of Punjab, 11
  theory of race, 10
Beschi, Costanzo Giuseppe, 60
Bhosale, Chhatrapati Shivaji, 94
Bibi, Fatima, 157
Bibi, Karima, 104
Bichitr, 118–119, 123, 132
Bijapuri Jews, 39
biography (ies), 13–14
  of migrants, 15

Eknath, 63
Eldred, John, 48
English ethnographers, 195
English Levant Company, 48, 120
English migrants, early, 7
erotic attraction, 219
escudo coin, 24
Estado da Índia, 6, 13, 17, 25–26, 31,
    33, 49, 68, 83, 172, 175, 235, 237,
    239–241, 247–248, 251, 258, 261
Estêvão, Tomás, 59, 61, 65
Ethiopian orthodox Christians, 98
Eucharists, 47
European Ashkenazi ancestry, 214
Euskal arrosarioa, 137

Fakhri, Nargis, 284
fakirs, 187–188
  of Ajmer, 201
Fatehpuri Mahal, 158
Fatehpur Sikri, 120–122, 129, 154, 161,
    164, 244
  Buland Darwaza, 121
  Diwan-i-Am, 122
  Diwan-i-Khas, 122
  Jama Masjid, 121
  Mahal-i-Khas, 122
Fazl, Abu'l, 122, 124, 161
Federici, Cesare, 241, 243, 245
Feringhee Bazaar, 234
Finch, William, 135, 152–153, 200
Firangi, Abdul Hai, 162, 164
Firangi, Barq, 283
Firangi, Bibi Juliana, 18, 132
Firangi, Mandu, 19, 124–126, 259
  Akbar's service, 129
  Miskin's collaboration with, 128
  place of origin, 125
  Ramayana illustrations, 127
Firangi, Munshi, 282
firangi warriors
  social mobility of, 78
firangiyan, 6
Fitch, Ralph, 48, 119–120, 132, 134,
    241
Ford, John, 190
foreign migrants to India
  becoming Indian, 4
  economic refugees, 4
  as indentured servants, 4

as mercenaries, 3
in multicultural spaces, 16
as slaves, 4
women living in Mughal harems, 18
Fort St George, 264

Gama, Vasco da, 5, 27, 77
Gentil, Jean-Baptiste, 173, 183
global economic power, 5
Goa, Jewish influence, 38–40
Goan Inquisition, 40
Golconda, 222
Gomes, Lenore, 36–37
Gonzalo, 246
Gosain community from Gorakhpur, 217
Gujarati, Kesav, 125
Gujarati, Meghav, 125
guru-disciple relation, 218

habshis, 106–107
Hamza, Amir, 283
Harrison, Gilbert, 7–8
Henriquez, Henrique, 59–60
Hindu same-sex traditions, 218
Hindustani musical identity, 154–155
Hiriart, Augustin, 19, 137, 199
  in Agra, 140
  counterfeiting skills, 143
  as Ingenieur des Grossen Mogouls,
    142
  innovative military contraption,
    144–145
  in Jahangir's service, 140, 142
  jewellery business, 137
  Peacock Throne, 145
  wife, 140–141
Hunarmand. see Hiriart, Augustin
Hyderabad, 222, 261

Iberian Jewish culture, 43
Ibrahim, Siddi, 109
Indian diaspora populations, 97
Indian-ness, 286
Isabella of Aragon, 37
Iskandrus, Mirza, 163

Jagannath, 218
Jahan, Noor, 158, 167–168
Jahangir, emperor, 95, 118–119, 131–
    132, 145, 187

Silk Route, 5, 134
Silk Route trading culture, 213
Silk Street of Calicut, 84
Sireniacs, 190–191
Slavic slaves, 79
Sleeman, Sir William Henry, 131, 145
Sousa, Martim Afonso de, 22–23, 25, 32, 38–39
Stephens, Thomas, 19, 47
  as an English Jesuit, 50
  biography, 51
  bodily habits, 63–64
  and Brahmin–Jesuit tension, 57–58
  on 'calpataru,' or kalpataru tree, 64–65
  on coconut, 56, 64–68
  education, 51
  on Eknath's distinctive style, 63
  Fitch's reference, 50
  in Goa, 56
  on Goa's bacteria or viruses, 55–56
  as Jesuit missionary, 53–54
  Johnson's classes and its influence, 51–52
  knowledge of Konkani customs and tongues, 58–59
  Kristapurana (Story of Christ), 59–63, 67, 112
  letters to mother, 54
  letter to Richard, 51, 55
  linguistic structure of local languages, knowledge of, 61–62
  parents, 51
  Pounde's influence, 52–53
  religious convictions, 51
  revival of Marathi literature, 62–63
  on toddy, 65
Story, James, 48, 123–124, 126
Sufism, 15, 73, 155, 218-219, 224
Sultan, Muhammad, 176
Sultan, Tipu, 92

Syrian Christian community of southwest India, 91

Taj Mahal, 131
Tavernier, Jean-Baptiste, 135, 222
Tibau, Sebastião Gonçalves, 19, 234
  adaptation to the Bengali weather and waterscape, 235
  in Dianga, 239–240
  on hybridity of Feringhee culture, 253
  life at Bay of Bengal, 236–238
  life in Portugal, 235–236
  in Sandwip, 241, 244–245
  on Sandwip society, 248–253
  treachery against Pratapaditya, 247
  violent outlaw side, 247–248
Tuzuk-i-Jahangiri, 161, 220

Varma, Maharaja Marthanda, 91
Verghese, Abraham, 97
Veroneo, Girolamo, 146

White Mughals (Dalrymple), 4–5
white racial supremacy, 8–9
women in the zenana, 151–152, 154
  under Akbar, 154, 166
  under Aurangzeb, 175
  medical work in, 178
  physical pastimes, 156
  physical space of the royal zenana, 166
  recreational pastimes, 154
  slave-girl culture, 157

Xavier, St Francis, 40–41, 47, 56, 58

Yitzhak, Avraham ben, 34

Zamorin of Calicut, 83–84, 88
Zeb-un-Nisa, 176
Zul-Qarnain, Mirza Sikander, 163